Codes of Modernity

CODES OF MODERNITY

Chinese Scripts in the Global Information Age

ULUĞ KUZUOĞLU

COLUMBIA UNIVERSITY PRESS *NEW YORK*

Columbia University Press
Publishers Since 1893
New York   Chichester, West Sussex
cup.columbia.edu
Copyright © 2024 Columbia University Press
All rights reserved

Library of Congress Cataloging-in-Publication Data
Names: Kuzuoglu, Ulug, author.
Title: Codes of modernity : Chinese scripts in the global information age / Ulug Kuzuoglu.
Description: New York : Columbia University Press, [2023] | Includes bibliographical references and index.
Identifiers: LCCN 2023009616 (print) | LCCN 2023009617 (ebook) | ISBN 9780231209380 (hardback) | ISBN 9780231209397 (trade paperback) | ISBN 9780231557917 (ebook)
Subjects: LCSH: Chinese language—Reform—History—20th century. | Chinese language—Writing—History—20th century. | Chinese language—Political aspects.
Classification: LCC PL1175 .K89 2023 (print) | LCC PL1175 (ebook) | DDC 495.11/1—dc23/eng/20230525
LC record available at https://lccn.loc.gov/2023009616
LC ebook record available at https://lccn.loc.gov/2023009617

Cover design: Milenda Nan Ok Lee
Cover image: Chen Qiu 陳虬, *Xinzi ouwen qiyin duo* 新字甌文七音鐸 (Beijing: Wenzi gaige chubanshe, 1958 [1903])

Contents

Acknowledgments   vii

Introduction   1

ONE   Alphabetic Labor Time: Scripts, Wires, and Brains in the Late Qing   24

TWO   The National Phonetic Alphabet: Scripts and the Birth of Language Politics   57

THREE   Basic Chinese: Cognitive Management and Mass Literacy   89

FOUR   Simplification of Chinese Characters: Mining, Counting, Seeing   117

FIVE   The New Dunganese Alphabet: Latinization Across Eurasia   153

SIX   The Chinese Latin Alphabet: A Revolutionary Script   186

SEVEN   The Empire of Pinyin   213

CONTENTS

Epilogue: A New Age of Codes   238

Notes   243

Bibliography   273

Index   295

Acknowledgments

WHENEVER MY FRIENDS and colleagues ask me how I decided to write a book on Chinese script reforms, I go back to my days as a student at Boğaziçi University. About fifteen years ago, when I graduated college with a degree in sociology, I wanted to do nothing but travel to China. Options, however, were limited. Boğaziçi, my alma mater, had almost no connections with China, and I barely spoke any Chinese. I instead arranged a meeting with Selçuk Esenbel, the professor of Japanese history at Boğaziçi, and told her that I wanted to enroll in the MA program in history and write a thesis on Sino-Ottoman relations—a topic that I thought would take me to China at some point. At the time, I had no desire to become a historian and I still don't know why the History Department decided that someone with no formal training in Ottoman history and no Chinese-language skills would be a good fit for such a topic, but to my surprise, I was admitted. Without the support of my mentors at Boğaziçi, I would have never even embarked on this journey. Selçuk Esenbel, Meltem Toksöz, and İsenbike Togan have a special place in the making of this book.

I'd like to think that the seeds of this book were planted somewhere around then. With an ambition that far exceeded my skills, I was learning Mandarin in the morning and studying Ottoman Turkish at night, while keeping up with the pace of graduate-level reading. I was trying to memorize not only Chinese characters, but also Arabic letters to read my native tongue as it was written before the Turkish Alphabet Revolution in 1928,

ACKNOWLEDGMENTS

when the Turkish Republic officially changed its alphabet from Arabic to Latin. If readers would like to empathize with my frustration and fascination with learning Ottoman Turkish, they may try to write English in an alphabet they never studied. Why, I would ask myself, would anyone try to change their own script and cut ties with their own history? Back then, I thought Turkey was unique in performing such a bizarre act. Only later, in graduate school, did I realize that script reforms and alphabet revolutions were truly a global phenomenon, stretching from China to Europe. Sometime around the turn of the twentieth century, it seemed, the entire world lost its mind. Today, after more than a decade of research, I think I finally know why.

I had no plans to study the global history of Chinese script reforms when I entered graduate school in the United States. Turning my immature fascination into a manageable research topic, and finally into a book, took place in conversation with mentors, colleagues, and friends at Columbia University. My advisor Madeleine Zelin's skepticism about my half-baked ideas made me reflect deeply on what I wanted to accomplish. Eugenia Lean taught me how to enjoy historical detective work and ground my abstract ideas in actual sources, and Lydia Liu's thoughts about translingual practices and the cybernetic unconscious have always been my sources of intellectual inspiration.

The path to finishing this book was long, and I owe a great debt to those who guided me at different points. The support of Dorothy Ko, Elizabeth Blackmar, Deborah Coen, Zvi Ben-Dor Benite, Jing Tsu, Janet Chen, Meng Yuan-yuan, David Branner, Mark Mazower, Manan Ahmed, Seth Schwartz, Tarik Amar, Richard Bulliet, Marwa Elshakry, and Michael Gordin meant the world to me. Rebecca Karl provided invaluable feedback as I was revising the manuscript. One person who will not be able to read this book is Adam McKeown, who deserves a special note, for I began thinking about global history as method with him. I only wish that I could take him out for some Ethiopian food and talk about Cambodian dogs, psychedelic drugs, global warming, or about anything and everything that matters to human life. His memory lives on.

Those who are the closest are the most difficult to place in this long list. Without Anatoly Detwyler, I would have never thought about information history and the informational turn in the humanities. As a friend, a colleague, and a brother, his intellectual impact on this book has been

ACKNOWLEDGMENTS

profound. And so has Adrien Zakar's. Over the years that we shared the same apartment in NYC and built our own Soviet Kitchen, his energy, curiosity, and sensitivity made me not only a more creative thinker, but also a better person. And just a couple of blocks from our apartment, I met Elizabeth Reynolds in the early years of graduate school. Who would have thought that I would marry her in Central Park, move with her to St. Louis, and write the final pages of this book with her by my side? I do not think I ever deserved the patience, love, generosity, and kindness that she so effortlessly gave to me. She stood by me through my hardest times, laughed at my worst jokes, and read and edited every single sentence in this book more than once.

I wish I could have the space to talk about each person who walked me through the past decade, some with the help of copious whiskey and tobacco, and others with friendly warmth and camaraderie: Rahul Sarwate, John T. Chen, Shehab Ismail, Clay Eaton, Myra Sun, Tyler Walker, Sayantani Mukherjee, Matthew Felt, Colin Jones, Arunabh Ghosh, Chloe Estep, Chris Peacock, Joshua Schlachet, Tania Bhattacharyya, Bradley Gorski, David Brophy, Chris Chang, Chien Wen Kung, Selda Altan, Fırat Kurt, Berfe Gündüz, Joshua Batts, Dongxin Zou, Sean O'Neill, Hannah Elmer, Jack Neubauer, Nataly Shahaf, Ye Yuan, Zach Berge-Becker, Owen Miller, Kumhee Cho, Tristan Revells, Yanjie Huang, Tristan Brown, Kyoungjin Bae, Benjamin Kindler, Harlan Chambers, Selim Karlıtekin, Roy Bar Sadeh, Yurou Zhong, Gina Anne Tam, Jeffrey Weng, Seung Hyun Cho, Giulia Carbone, Victor Seow.

Research for this book took place before the COVID-19 pandemic, when I thought I had to travel to all seven continents plus the moon. I would like to especially thank the archivists in the First and Second Historical Archives, Shanghai Municipal Archives, Academia Sinica, Academia Historica, and KMT Party Archives. Some of the archives in the PRC that mysteriously shut their doors just when I arrived are also much appreciated, for, unbeknownst to them, they channeled my energies toward finding sources outside of China. That is how I ended up enjoying the libraries and archives in St. Petersburg and Moscow, where Liudmila Novikova helped me immensely in my research.

In China, I would have accomplished very little without the help of Zhang Baichun, Liu Daxian, Cai Shuji, Niu Dayong, Ye Fang, and Liu Shigu, who generously shared with me their expertise on how to navigate the Chinese archives and bureaucracy. Throughout my travels, Margherita Trento was my pen friend in an age when letters are fast becoming a subject of historical inquiry. But no matter where I went, I somehow always ended up in Istanbul, where my *khankha* Ümit Fırat Açıkgöz treated me to the best of *meyhanes*. And running into old friends on the streets, in the archives, or on bicycles in the middle of mountains energized my mind—Yavuz Sezer, Ceren Abi, Oya Arıkan, Buket Köse, Onat Kıcalı, Akın Öztürk, Atilla Çıdam. My friends @ HuntorCafe know who they are and how much I owe them.

My travels and research were funded by a number of grants and institutions: TUBITAK Fellowship for Doctoral Studies, Columbia University Richard Hofstadter Fellowship, Weatherhead East Asian Institute, Henry Luce Foundation/ACLS Predissertation Travel Grant, Social Science Research Council, Chinese Government Scholarship for Visiting Scholars, the Center for Chinese Studies in Taiwan, Heyman Center Fellowship, Harriman Institute, and Mellon/ACLS Dissertation Completion Fellowship.

After receiving my PhD, I was lucky to be surrounded by supportive colleagues first in the Department of East Asian Languages and Cultures at Columbia, and then in the History Department at Washington University in St. Louis. I would especially like to thank Shang Wei, Haruo Shirane, Tomi Suzuki, Gray Tuttle, David Lurie, Ying Qian, Takuya Tsunoda, Paul Kreitman, John Phan, and of course Laura Schlein in EALAC. At Washington University in St. Louis, I was welcomed by colleagues who made me feel safe even during the pandemic: Sowande' Mustakeem, Douglas Flowe, Lori Watt, Peter Kastor, Nancy Reynolds, Christina Ramos, Diana Montaño, Corinna Treitel, Kristina Kleutghen, Zhao Ma, Letty Chen, Shefali Chandra, Andrea Friedman, Daniel Bornstein, H. H. Kang, Jianqing Chen, Chang Xu, Xin Yu, Ruochen Chen, Chenxi Luo, and Kejian Shi.

Some chapters of this book were previously published in academic journals. An extended version of the second chapter's first section appeared as "Capital, Letter, Empire: Romanization in Late Qing China" in *Twentieth-Century China* 46, no. 3 (2021). An earlier version of the third chapter was published as "Basic Chinese: Cognitive Management, Communication Engineering, and Mass Literacy in China" in *Modern Chinese Literature and Culture* 34, no. 1 (2022). And a condensed version of chapters five and six came out in *Journal of Asian Studies* 81, no. 1 (2022) under the title "The Chinese Latin Alphabet: A Revolutionary Script in the Global Information Age."

There were multiple times during the past several years when I wanted to throw in the towel. But every time the thought crossed my mind, I found the strength I needed in my family—in my mom's resilience, my dad's

ACKNOWLEDGMENTS

romanticism, my brother's idiosyncrasy, my sisters' courage, my aunt's quilt, my uncle's library, my grandfather's garden, my Nana's pastries, and my grandmother's clarity. Some of them had to bid farewell before they could see me put an end to this work, but it comforts me to know that they will always live in the pages to follow, for it is to them that I dedicate this book.

Codes of Modernity

Introduction

IN 1896, Shen Xue 沈學, a young medical student in Shanghai, penned a treatise on the need to phoneticize the Chinese writing system called *Primordial Sounds for a Prosperous Age* (*Shengshi yuanyin* 盛世元音).[1] Chinese characters, claimed Shen, slowed down the flow of information in the Qing Empire (1637–1912). They blocked the telegraphic wires, clogged the arteries of the brain, and prevented the advancement of scientific knowledge. The only solution to the empire's pending doom, he contended, was a phonetic script that could facilitate communication and increase knowledge production. Before inventing his own script, Shen compared a variety of phonetic scripts in terms of their speed and efficiency in promoting literacy and their adaptability to Morse code. But Shen's concern was not only with reading and writing and dots and dashes. He suggested that a phonetic script also had a transcendental neurophysiological power. It could unite the outside world with the brain, because nouns, adjectives, and verbs, respectively, triggered the three cerebral parts—pons Varolii (*zhongnao* 中腦, "middle brain"), cerebrum (*danao* 大腦, "big brain"), and cerebellum (*xiaonao* 小腦, "small brain"). The shorter the distance between speech and writing, argued Shen, the faster the union was between humans, machines, the universe, and the self.

Shen Xue's engagement with the human brain and communications technologies may seem idiosyncratic, but he was only one among many reformers in the late Qing who were deeply troubled by the Chinese script.

INTRODUCTION

From the 1890s to the fall of the empire in 1912, dozens of reformers called for a phonetic script, and the following decades witnessed hundreds of more reformers and revolutionaries pledging to change the Chinese characters. Each proposed script was different. Among the more famous ones was the National Phonetic Alphabet (*Guoyin zimu* 國音字母 or *Zhuyin zimu* 注音字母), first promulgated in 1918 by the central government and later renamed Phonetic Symbols (*Zhuyin fuhao* 注音符號) in 1930. Known as *bopomofo*, it is still the most commonly used input method for Taiwanese computer technologies. Another script was the Chinese Latin Alphabet, also known as Sin Wenz, which was invented by Russian and Chinese revolutionaries in the Soviet Union to replace Chinese characters with latinized letters in the early 1930s. Some of the proposed scripts were not at all phonetic. Especially in the 1920s and 1930s, there was a large movement to simplify the Chinese characters that was spearheaded by Chinese psychologists in the United States as well as liberal reformers and left-wing writers in Shanghai. The movement threatened the "native culture" of China so acutely that the ruling Nationalist Party (Guomindang, GMD) decided to ban it in 1936.

There were other proposals as well. There was, for example, the reformed Arabic script of the Chinese Muslims in Central Asia, whose significance for Chinese script reforms is largely forgotten in scholarship. Then there were scripts invented by prominent linguists, such as Yuen Ren Chao's (Zhao Yuanren 趙元任, 1892–1982) Gwoyeu Romatzyh. And of course, there was Pinyin, devised in 1958 by Zhou Youguang 周有光 (1906–2017), which eventually became the international standard for transcribing Chinese characters into the Latin alphabet. But the history of script reforms did not stop even then, as Pinyin took an unexpected life of its own in the multiethnic frontiers of the People's Republic of China in the 1960s and the 1970s and replaced some of the centuries-old ethnic minority scripts. It was only in 1986 that the State Council of the People's Republic of China (PRC) officially put an end to script reforms, as it announced that Pinyin would not replace Chinese characters. Almost a hundred years of reforms finally came to an end.

From Shen Xue's treatise to the State Council's final announcement, the variety of Chinese scripts manifested a century of uncertainty and a profound sense of alienation from a millennia-old writing system. This book is an attempt to understand the historical emergence of this alienation within a global framework and carve out a space for studying the history of scripts as distinct from languages. In doing so, I aim to revise the predominant narratives about Chinese script reforms. If we put aside Shen Xue's treatise and other early works on script reforms, it would be tempting to explain this alienation, as many historians have, as an outcome of national language reforms. In fact, the most extensively researched and lucidly written book on Chinese script reforms did not even contain the word "script" in its title. Published in 1950, John DeFrancis's *Nationalism and Language Reform in China* chronicled the development of Chinese script reforms as they intersected with language reforms from the late Qing to the establishment of the PRC. His concern with "language reform" was certainly warranted. When DeFrancis was writing in the 1940s, the definition of a "Chinese" national language was far from certain. Mandarin was designated as the national language in the 1920s and 1930s by the ruling GMD, but the place of other "Chinese" languages, such as Cantonese, in the new linguistic order was unclear at best. The language politics of the era were intimately tied to script reforms as well, and DeFrancis was the first Western scholar to capture the relationship between the two in vivid detail. Yet, in doing so, he implicitly demarcated a clear hierarchy between language reforms and script reforms. The former was of vital political importance; the latter was just a technical instrument that facilitated it.

DeFrancis was not alone in prioritizing language politics over script politics. He was drawing from leading Chinese language reformers who were politically invested in conceptualizing scripts as representative technologies. Li Jinxi 黎錦熙 (1890–1978), whose *A Brief History of the National Language Movement* (*Gwoyeu yunndonq shyy gang* [*Guoyu yundong shigang*] 國語運動史綱, 1934) deeply informed DeFrancis, was a May Fourth radical and an ardent supporter of alphabetizing Chinese in the 1920s. Like the majority of May Fourth iconoclasts, Li blamed the Chinese characters for cultural backwardness, as the complexity of their physical composition posed a seemingly insurmountable problem for literacy. More importantly, Chinese characters were not conducive to creating a "national language" because they lacked precision in phonetic values, causing a variety of different pronunciations for each character. If only China had a unified national language, then its alphabetic script would naturally facilitate literacy and aid modern scientific progress. National language was again the end; script was just the means to achieve it.

The subsequent scholarship on Chinese script reforms internalized the secondary place that early twentieth-century Chinese reformers had ascribed to scripts. On the one hand, this resulted in outstanding works that explored a variety of topics ranging from the *baihua* movement to the intricacies of language politics and the troubled place of dialects in Chinese linguistic modernization.[2] On the other hand, the unintended consequence of this scholarship has been to reproduce the language-centered framework concocted by Chinese reformers themselves. Recently, there have been attempts to go beyond this framework. Scholars such as Yurou Zhong, for example, stepped away from language reforms and observed that the main culprit behind script reforms in China and elsewhere was a "phonocentric" epistemology that prioritized speech over writing and aimed to close the gap between the two.[3] Following a Derridean line of thought, she argued that the epistemic violence of phonocentrism, not the desire for a national language, turned the Chinese script into an inadequate technology in need of reform. And yet, while Zhong's work was among the first to draw scholarly attention to linguistic epistemology at large, her positioning of phonocentrism as the driving force behind script reforms ironically perpetuated the language-centered framework that has been dominating the scholarship for the past century. And in doing so, it continued to leave fundamental questions unanswered: How, for instance, should we explain phonocentrism's historical emergence in the first place? Why was the phonocentric paradigm able to establish itself with such unprecedented force in modern China? Is it possible to write a history of scripts outside of the phonocentric paradigm, i.e., without prioritizing language? Or, to put it differently, do scripts have an ontology of their own, separate from language?

The link between language and script is undeniable, but conflating the two is problematic and confusing, for the concerns of script reformers went far beyond languages. The late-Qing reformer Shen Xue's 1896 treatise on script, brain, and telegraphy indicated a different problem that he was trying to come to terms with. During the initial years of script reform, Shen was part of a group of reformers who scrutinized the impact of communications technologies and biotechnologies on the Chinese society at large and searched for new ways of reform that would redefine the Chinese bodies and minds. They were less concerned with speech and language, and more with the materiality of scripts themselves. Scripts, for them, were critical technologies in constructing a new economy of communication and knowledge for China.

INTRODUCTION

Tan Sitong 譚嗣同 (1865–1898), for example, another radical late-Qing thinker and proponent of script reform, brought together translated Western works on the brain and the telegraph to conjure a new philosophy of communication. Similar to nineteenth-century Euro-American philosophers who used electric telegraphy as a metaphor for the nervous system, Tan argued that the brain was at the center of an electrified bodily cognition. The outside world was connected to the brain through the brain-*qi* tendons (*naoqijin* 腦氣筋), i.e., nerves, and all sensory input was traveling to the brain in the form of "messages" or "information" (*xin* 信). Electrified information, according to him, animated cerebral life and connected people to the world and each other—it stood at the core of communication and interconnectivity (*tong* 通). What set him apart from Western thinkers was that Tan located the highest form of Buddhist consciousness, the eighth consciousness (*ālaya*), in the brain as well and envisioned the electrification of the brain and the higher input of sensory information as a gateway into enlightenment.[4] His highly influential book, *An Exposition of Ren* (*Renxue* 仁學), completed right before he was beheaded by the Manchus in 1898, was one of the earliest examples of Chinese communication theory that grounded transcendental thought in the material infrastructures of information.

Tan was also a leading supporter of communicative efficiency in general and phonetic scripts in particular. He even wrote a preface to a phonetic script proposal in which he briefly elaborated on the merits of simplifying and facilitating education at large.[5] Reading his oeuvre closely, one may recognize the powerful historical moment that connected phonetic scripts in Tan's mind to Buddhist cognitive architecture, neurophysiology, and telegraphy; and it may help us understand Shen Xue's unorthodox approach to script and the brain. Tan was born in the early years of the Qing empire's Self-Strengthening Movement (1861–1895), which sought to integrate the empire into a globalizing yet uneven capitalist economy. Those decades witnessed an ambitious era of industrialization and mechanization that began to transform the Qing society, especially in the coastal regions, as new arsenals, factories, and shipyards were founded for military self-strengthening. Large-scale industrial enterprises were followed by new communications technologies and infrastructures that not only increased the speed and quantity of transmitted information but also precipitated a more significant transformation of the knowledge economy that was felt vehemently at the turn of the century. Growing up in the midst of unparalleled change, Tan was a major defender of industrialization at large, and his foray into a philosophy of communication and mind stemmed from this age of mechanization. The construction of factories, better use of human labor, and more efficient management of time were at the center of Tan's treatise. It was within this industrializing economy that Tan identified the critical role of script for communications networks and productive technologies more broadly. In his words, "when electric wires, postal system, machine manufacturing, simplicity of work, and efficiency of script [*wenzi zhi bianjie* 文字之便捷] are taken together as a whole, the achievement of a generation can equal those of dozens of generations."[6] His exposition on the metaphysics of information and brain, in other words, was a philosophical and economic call for increased mechanization in industrial factories and communications technologies. If industrial mechanization could increase efficiency in factory labor, more "efficient" scripts could do the same in clerical and mental labor and facilitate knowledge production by increasing access to education and information. For Tan Sitong, new technologies could transform the production of commodities and knowledge while unifying consciousness and the outside world. Tan, in short, was employing an industrialist logic to rethink communication philosophy and economic development. Script was critical to both.

And that was precisely the point of view that Shen Xue expounded upon in his own proposal for a phonetic script. Shen emphasized the cerebral dimensions of script reform in order to propose a new vision for mental and clerical labor efficiency in a swiftly changing knowledge economy. He supposedly calculated the amount of time it took to send a telegram in a variety of scripts, from Chinese to Manchu to Mongolian to his own phonetic invention. He explained the anatomy of the ear to his readers to demonstrate how phonetic sound waves traveled into the brain. He also drew on theories of aphasia, i.e., loss of the ability of speech, to make unconventional claims about how language animated the brain—all in an effort to convince his readers of the urgent need for script reform. While his statements might have seemed idiosyncratic to some at the time, or to us today, neurophysiological theories of language and writing were his gateway into comprehending a nascent knowledge economy that neither he nor his fellow reformers knew how to cope with. Shen was one of the first reformers to identify the problem of script not as a problem of language but one of *labor* in an industrializing economy of knowledge (see chapter 1).

He certainly was not the last. In subsequent proposals for script reform, from phonetic scripts to simplified characters, "saving brain energy" (*sheng naoli* 省腦力) became a central trope, as the industrializing economy metaphorically turned the brain itself into a factory for manufacturing information and knowledge. Lufei Kui 陸費逵 (1886–1941), later the owner of the Zhonghua Press, wrote in 1909 that Chinese characters had to be simplified in order to save the brain energy of young students.[7] In 1922, Qian Xuantong 錢玄同 (1887–1939), a leading reformer in early Republican China, despondently noted that he was not even forty years old, but his nerves were exhausted due to the use of Chinese characters.[8] Others similarly blamed the Chinese characters for their "waste" of brain energy when the nation needed it the most. Of paramount importance for script reformers was the relationship between mental work and the technologies of knowledge production, in particular the script itself.

Shen Xue, Tan Sitong, Lufei Kui, Qian Xuantong, and dozens of other script reformers that populate the pages of this book were responding to an ongoing revolution in communications and information that was radically transforming the earlier practices of writing and literacy, and of cognitive work at large. They were living in a precarious age of information, one that started long before computers, and one that fundamentally altered the established practices of knowledge production, hence the acute sense of alienation from a millennia-old writing system. In a nutshell, script reforms were not an outcome of language reforms or phonocentrism; they stood at the forefront of a new era in China that redefined the meaning of information, communication, and mental labor.

Scripts in the Age of Information

This book steps away from phonocentrism and language reforms as explanatory frameworks for understanding script reforms. Following the concerns of turn-of-the-century reformers, I contend that script reforms emerged out of a modern political economy of information that fundamentally transformed the Chinese knowledge economy by instituting a new mental and clerical labor regime in China. Alphabetizing and/or simplifying the Chinese script was an attempt to fulfill the demands of this economy that was structured around new technological practices and infused with the industrial values of efficiency and productivity. This book thus calls for a new narrative for scripts that is centered on the global information age and its intimate link to nineteenth-century industrialization and capitalism. The material transformations of this age, I argue, were central to the emergence of script reforms, not only in China but across the world.

Tracing the roots of the "information age" to nineteenth-century industrialization is certainly not a new endeavor, but the uneven conditions in which it globalized should be underlined. The global information age emerged out of the industrial age of capitalism, and the two co-evolved in the decades since, as fossil-fueled technologies changed production, transportation, and communication practices.[9] The examples are all too common: steam-powered ships and railways transformed the speed of information transmission, and the invention of electric telegraphy in the 1840s instigated a new age of instantaneity, collapsing time and space. As metal replaced wood, a formidable print revolution commenced as well. The invention of the iron hand press around 1800 and more advanced technologies in the following decades transformed the social and economic world of printing in the West. Apart from their immediate impact on the organization of labor in print shops, they enabled an exponential increase in the output and circulation of information in the form of books, journals, and newspapers, and transformed the social and cultural practices of knowledge production as print capitalism expanded over the globe.[10] Concomitant with these changes was the transformation in the managerial and bureaucratic practices of the nineteenth century. The regulation of movement, from the production and shipment of commodities to global migration practices, necessitated new accounting techniques, bureaucratic procedures, clerical labor, and paperwork. The sheer amount of paper output in the United States alone increased five hundred times from the beginning to the end of the nineteenth century. As Kenneth Cmiel and John Durham Peters noted, "an information-hungry society needed paper in the same way an industrializing society needed coal."[11] The analogy between paper and coal is a reminder that the information age unfolded within an industrializing knowledge economy.

Writing in the early 1980s, James Beniger was among the first to identify the birth of the information age as an outcome of industrial capitalism.

According to Beniger, the industrial production of commodities, their national distribution through railways, and the increased use of communications technologies to manage the flow of goods and services precipitated a *crisis of control*, for they generated a growing amount of information and therefore the necessity to manage, process, and control that information. The rise of modern bureaucracies, the invention of new storage and retrieval technologies, scientific theories of factory management, and even school education were all manifestations of information-processing technologies that attempted to resolve an ever-present crisis of control in modern societies.[12] Beniger's emphasis on "control" and his use of "information" as a universal governing principle have rightly been criticized, but his recognition of the information age as both an immediate outcome and an inseparable component of industrial capitalism should not be overlooked.[13] Especially for a twenty-first-century audience steeped in the contradictions of information capitalism that promises more freedom through information access while increasing surveillance and control, Beniger's framework offers a historically grounded interpretation of the entanglements between information and capital since the nineteenth century.[14]

While the majority of scholarly works on the subject center on Euro-American histories, the intimacy between information and capital was critical in the making of a global—and globally uneven—information age. We must not forget that the entry of new information technologies into the non-Western world followed the same routes as Western capital, indicating both the overlapping histories of the two and the uneven conditions that fueled their spread throughout the world. The iron hand press and the movable metal type, for instance, reached China as well as the Middle East, South Asia, and Southeast Asia via evangelical missions supported by imperial economic ambitions in the early nineteenth century. Biblical texts were soon accompanied by a proliferation of translated Western sciences; and as Chinese entrepreneurs and companies embraced print capitalism, new publications began flooding an "information-hungry" market of knowledge in the early twentieth century.[15] A similar trajectory is observed in telegraphy as well. The global expansion of telegraphic networks dovetailed with Western endeavors to penetrate and control non-Western markets. The first non-Euro-American telegraph line was established in the Ottoman Empire during the Crimean War (1853–1856) by the British and the French; and, immediately after, it spread throughout the world. In the early 1870s, telegraphy entered the Qing, wiring the empire anew in the following decades, as treaty ports and their immediate hinterlands turned into centers of both capital accumulation and telegraphic transmission.[16] The spatial overlap between the two attested the link between the two critical flows of the age: capital and information.

The impact of the globally uneven information age was acerbic across the non-Western world, for it ushered in a new political economy of knowledge that challenged the earlier sociotechnical practices of communication. The sense of alienation from script that Chinese reformers were struggling with was felt across the globe. For instance, Vietnam under French colonial rule departed from the Sinitic world as it changed its script from Chinese characters and *chữ nôm* to the Latin alphabet in the early twentieth century. On the other end of Eurasia stood the Turkish Alphabet Revolution in the 1920s, which culminated in replacing the Arabic alphabet with the Latin alphabet after decades of experiments with different kinds of scripts. Central Asian republics under the Soviet Union went through two consecutive alphabet revolutions, one in the 1920s that changed their scripts from Arabic to Latin, and another one in the 1930s that changed them again from Latin to Cyrillic. Mongolia went through a similar process as well, and so did Albania, among others. Even countries that eventually kept their scripts, such as Japan or India, witnessed remarkable discussions about them. There was a global synchronicity in script reforms because they were all precipitated by the metamorphosis of communication practices in the global age of information.

It is impossible to disentangle the information age in China and the rest of the world from the industrialist mantra that prioritized labor efficiency and productivity in human-machine ensembles. Chinese telegraphy offers a particularly potent example for understanding the script reformers' concern with labor efficiency in an industrializing economy. Morse code was originally invented in the 1840s to encode the twenty-six letters of the English alphabet in dots and dashes, but once the telegraph entered the Qing Empire in the 1870s, the alphabetic Morse code's incommensurability with the nonalphabetic Chinese characters questioned the very possibility of telegraphic communication in Chinese. Eventually, the French harbormaster in Shanghai decided to assign a four-digit number to each Chinese character in order to bridge the technological gap between the alphabet and Chinese characters. Chinese telegraphy thus required a two-step process: a

INTRODUCTION

given Chinese character first had to be translated into numbers, and then those numbers had to be retranslated into dots and dashes to fit the electrified channels of communication. The result, according to script reformers, was inefficiency in labor time. The amount of clerical labor time required to locate a Chinese character in a telegraph codebook, translate it into numbers, and retranslate it into Morse code was not even comparable to the amount of time it would take to transmit a phonetic script. The added labor also cost more money: until the 1930s, the sender of a telegram was obliged to pay the telegraph clerk for the added labor involved in translating the characters into numbers, and the receiver was obliged to pay again in order to retranslate the numbers back into characters.[17] The intrinsically Western communications infrastructure, in other words, imposed a particular clerical labor regime that questioned the foundations of the Chinese knowledge economy, i.e., the script itself (see chapter 1).

Telegraphic labor was only one component within a larger political economy that threatened and transformed the Chinese knowledge regime. Industrial print's capacity to increase the output and circulation of information was unrivaled; translated Western sciences challenged what had suddenly become "traditional" Chinese sciences; imperial modes of knowing and learning were breaking down; and mass literacy was emerging as a modern political desire. Even the civil service examination system, the backbone of imperial bureaucracy since the Song dynasty (960–1279), was abolished in 1905. A new economy of knowledge put increased pressure on the use of mental and clerical labor, forcing the reformers to redefine its meaning for knowledge production. It was not that there was too much to know. Rather, the meaning of knowledge was no longer quite the same. The global age of information and capital was deterritorializing the Chinese knowledge economy, disassembling the institutionalized practices of knowledge production, and de-skilling mental and clerical laborers. The major problem that reformers and revolutionaries confronted from the turn of the century onward was how to reterritorialize the economy, reassemble the institutions, and re-skill the laborers.[18] Script was at the center of this reassembly as it had to confront the infrastructural, technological, and epistemic transformations in a modernizing knowledge economy.

The impact of this economy was painful especially at the script level, for the Chinese writing system was unlike phonetic scripts. As it developed from its earliest known form circa 1200 BCE to the nineteenth century, the

Chinese writing system thrived precisely because it could not be reduced to the representation of any spoken language. As a writing *system*, it was able to accommodate linguistic differences, hence its adoption across Japan, Korea, and Vietnam. Within the longer history of writing, Chinese was neither an exception nor an anomaly. In fact, if there is an anomaly to be addressed, it would be the historical emergence of the alphabet itself. Because, as historians of early writing have demonstrated, none of the earliest writing systems in Mesopotamia, Mesoamerica, the Nile River, and the Yellow River were invented to record speech. While the origins of writing are still clouded in mystery, it is safe to argue that all these writing systems developed in conjunction with the bureaucratic and administrative apparatuses of early states. As such, writing systems had the flexibility and capacity to develop characteristics that never appeared in spoken languages.[19] They carried within them written marks and vestiges from earlier ages that were not based on speech but still required labor and expertise to learn and master. The traditional Chinese writing system serves as an elaborate example in this greater world history of writing. It possessed a grammar and syntax that could exist solely in written form; and the characters themselves were composed of a complex set of logographic, phonetic, and semantic elements, which endowed them with a generative capacity that could be used across a diverse linguistic landscape in East and Inner Asia.[20]

The nineteenth-century transformations, however, imposed a new order that was tied to a specifically Western historical experience and intertwined with a political economy of information and knowledge that was structured by alphabetic technologies. The reformers thus identified the nonphonetic quality of the Chinese script as the main obstacle facing the modernization of China's knowledge economy. Their globally disadvantaged position compelled them to identify the phonetic script as the primary means to discipline bodily and mental labor time under a new economic regime that challenged, changed, and regulated the transmission of information. What thus turned the Chinese writing system into a so-called backward script was the temporality of information and capital that was modeled on an alphabetic labor time. The historical emergence of "phonocentrism," in other words, must be traced to the turn-of-the-century clerical and mental labor regime that was grounded in the political economy of the global information age.

INTRODUCTION

Scripts, Contradictions, Ideologies

Exploring the history of script reforms from a material perspective demands a renewed engagement with the history of epistemological transformation in China. In writing the history of modern Chinese knowledge regimes, some historians have identified an "epistemic break" and contended that the semicolonial or hypercolonial conditions that China was subjected to by Western and Japanese empires heralded a fundamental break with earlier regimes of knowledge.[21] One cannot dispute Western colonialism's epistemic violence, but diagnosing a break, I believe, sterilizes the complexity of historical transformation in colonized, semicolonized, or hypercolonized spaces. It might instead be more helpful to ground epistemology in political economy, and rethink knowledge regimes as economic regimes that also rely on material and labor practices for their constitution.

Let me elaborate further on the analogy between knowledge and economy, for the reassembly of the two regimes followed similar paths. Western capital's transformation of non-Western economies materialized through its entry into a dialectical relationship with the preexisting conditions and practices. Marx called these practices "historical presuppositions," and Raymond Williams, in a slightly different context, named them "residual elements." For both Marx and Williams, these "presuppositions" or "residues" were not archaic components that would naturally dissolve under capital's transformation of society; they continued to be present and effective throughout that transformation.[22] The precision of this statement is especially seen in economies that transitioned from failing imperial orders to nation-states, where capital accumulation took place through weaving the existing labor practices and technologies into the dough of a modern age. The so-called traditional labor regimes and technologies of production in China most often proved to be crucial for accumulating capital in the nineteenth and twentieth centuries.[23] The same process was true for knowledge regimes as well. Sean Hsiang-lin Lei's designation of twentieth-century Chinese medicine as "neither donkey nor horse" can indeed be applied to modern scientific culture in general, for epistemic and material hybridity was a necessary condition for building new knowledge regimes.[24] Therefore, the transformation of knowledge regimes in China signals less of an epistemic break than a reassembly of matter and knowledge during its deterritorialization and reterritorialization. What thus deserves historical attention is the dialectic between the global age of information and the historically specific conditions in China, and the myriad contradictions at the linguistic, social, economic, and epistemic levels that this dialectic engendered.

Chinese script reforms offer a particularly good example for understanding the material contradictions generated by a modernizing knowledge regime and demonstrate how these contradictions gave birth to ideological animosities that were critical in the making of that regime. Economy and ideology, matter and knowledge, script and language, "base" and "superstructure" were inseparably intertwined. The alphabetic labor time that the Chinese reformers sought, for instance, was grounded in a Western historical experience, alien to the predominant literary and governmental culture in China. It thus generated inescapable problems that reformers had to confront, starting with the linguistic arena. A standardized phonetic medium of communication could in theory facilitate the flow of information and capital by disciplining and homogenizing the minds of the population, but the path to such an enormous shift in the information order was fraught with contradictions regarding both the place of language in a nation-state and the relationship between language and script. If China *had* a phonetic script, what language would that script represent in the aftermath of a multilingual imperial order? Who had the authority to determine a national language? And in the event of choosing a single language to represent the nation, what would be the fate of multiple regional languages, from Cantonese to Hokkien to Shanghainese, among others?

Chinese scripts did not follow language politics, as historians in the past have argued; they came prior to them, defined them, structured them. Some of the proposed phonetic scripts in the late Qing, for example, contained more than a hundred signs and could represent multiple languages including Mandarin and non-Mandarin. For the reformers who designed them, the physical composition of a script was conducive to imagining and materializing a multilingual nation-state. Other scripts, however, such as the National Phonetic Alphabet or its offspring Phonetic Symbols, which has only thirty-seven syllabic signs, represented only one language, i.e., Mandarin. Using Mandarin-oriented scripts to transcribe non-Mandarin languages was like writing English with fifteen letters; the physicality of scripts had the power to decide who could be represented and who could not, hence the battles that

INTRODUCTION

fill the chapters of this book. From late-Qing scripts to the invention of Pinyin in 1958, and even thereafter, scripts were at the center of both generating and resolving linguistic contradictions in China. To put it differently, the politics of linguistic representation were determined *at the level of script invention*. Scripts were the primary medium for shaping and controlling the politics of language (see chapters 2 and 6).

The contradictions unleashed by the global information age were not limited to phonetic scripts and language politics, as many of the reformers realized early on that abandoning Chinese characters—the "residual elements," in the words of Raymond Williams—would generate more problems than solutions. Instead of brushing the characters aside, they sought to rationalize, reform, and incorporate them into the economy, affirming a hybrid information regime that could be reduced neither to the phonetic scripts nor to the characters. The mass literacy campaigns in the 1920s and 1930s, for instance, called for a reassembly of the Chinese characters themselves, without a complete overhaul of the script. The movement gave rise not only to ideological differences around the meaning of literacy and communication in a modernizing society (see chapter 3), but also to polarizing debates around the simplification of Chinese characters (see chapter 4). Spearheaded in part by Chinese psychologists searching for mental efficiency, the "rationalization" of characters involved the use of statistical methods to reduce the number of characters in the Chinese corpus as well as cutting-edge technologies that measured the speed of eye movements in reading Chinese texts—all in order to define what an "optimum" script looked like in the information age.

And what *did* an "optimum" script look like? Was there a "scientific" method to simplify or phoneticize the characters? Could one reduce the amount of labor put into the production and recognition of a given character without sacrificing its meaning? Was there even a correlation between the number of strokes and the amount of time it took to learn? In other words, what exactly did efficiency in reading and writing mean within a Chinese knowledge economy, and who had the authority to determine the efficiency of a script in a hybrid information regime?

Efficiency was not unlike the philosopher's stone; its promises were so magnificent that its ontology went unquestioned. Indeed, "efficiency" was such a powerful benchmark to claim superiority that the comparisons between the Western alphabet and Chinese characters primarily revolved (and continue to revolve) around issues of speediness, convenience, ease, usability, and so on. The main problem that needs to be addressed, however, is not whether the alphabet is more efficient than the characters or vice versa, but the historical conditions that turned "efficiency" into a normative marker of superiority in the first place. After all, it was only with the institution of a new political economy of information that the Chinese script suddenly turned out to be "inefficient."

Script efficiency as a historical problem was not simply a technical issue of mechanical adjustment; it was laden with ideological conflicts around information politics in a modernizing society. What historians of technology recurrently point out about the politics of technological artifacts is thus applicable to Chinese scripts as well.[25] By the 1930s, there were in fact many different script proposals in China, all searching for "efficiency" in labor while espousing radically different ideological positions toward building a nation-state. Scripts, for instance, could be nationalist like the National Phonetic Alphabet, using nativist graphics to search for linguistic sovereignty (see chapter 2); socialist and internationalist like the Chinese Latin Alphabet, discarding the characters and bringing China closer to the latinized world of the Soviet Union (see chapter 5); fascist like Phonetic Symbols, imposing a native culture of knowledge on the society (see chapter 6); and imperialist like Pinyin, annihilating the indigenous worlds of the non-Han nationalities (see chapter 7). Scripts, in other words, were never neutral instruments for increasing efficiency in information transmission; they embodied and naturalized ideologies.

Scripts, as such, were worldmaking technologies. They had the capacity to change the patterns of thought, not in an Orwellian sense, but in the way that learning a script required an established literary and governmental culture. In learning a script, as David Damrosch reminds us in his study of the cuneiform, "one absorb[ed] key elements of a broad literary history: its terms of reference, habits of style, and poetics, often transcending those of any one language or country."[26] This was true for Mesopotamian cuneiform as well as twentieth-century Chinese scripts. Scripts determined the patterns of access to the production of literary and scientific knowledge; and their reform had the intrinsic power to change those patterns and institute new habits of style and terms of reference. That is what turned the script into one of the most contentious issues in the search for a Chinese modernity.

INTRODUCTION

The materiality of scripts thus compels us to reconsider their ontology. In her critique of the slippage between script and language, Lydia Liu astutely observed that language reforms in China and the world have "in reality sought to eradicate one or another foreign script, resulting in a *code switch* that happened more radically at the level of script than it did at the level of language."[27] From Vietnam to Turkey to China, those "code switches" stand as testimonies to the insufficiency of defining scripts merely as instruments to represent languages. Scripts comprised the primary arena of contestation across the world from the late nineteenth century onward because they were the "codes," not metaphorically but literally, for engineering a new society in the operational, technological, and ideological sense of the term. Scripts were never merely passive carriers of information; they were existential artifacts and "ontological shifters."[28] They were technopolitical products that structured the flow of information while enabling and limiting different forms of human experience. Akin to electricity grids and transportation systems, scripts were the infrastructural media of information societies, emerging out of and embedding within them ideological fantasies.[29] Their materiality was integral not only to print and telecommunications, but also to state propaganda, empire building, mass literacy, and radical thought. Fairly often, they were coopted by political parties as governmental instruments to impose social and linguistic orders, such as the GMD's use of Phonetic Symbols or the PRC's use of Pinyin; but at other times, they became the allies to fight against fascism and unite in the name of socialist internationalism, as in the case of the Chinese Latin Alphabet. Chinese scripts in the global information age invite us to reconsider the physicality of communication, for the politics of their materiality were as crucial as the politics of signification for understanding humans' place in the world of language, technology, and society.

Toward a Global History of Information and Scripts

Codes of Modernity is the product of yet another "turn" in academia: the informational turn. It is possible to locate the origins of this turn in the birth of information theory and cybernetics in the 1940s and the interdisciplinary Macy Conferences of the 1950s. The Cold War decades were arguably the most generative in incorporating cybernetics into social sciences, most clearly evidenced by Donna Haraway's socialist-feminist cyborg manifesto and Gregory Bateson's explorations of the ecologies of the human mind.[30] Information theory, in that regard, played a critical role in the scholarly and literary debates over politics, activism, and the posthuman, especially in the 1970s and 1980s.[31] More recently, however, the expansion of global information capitalism compelled social scientists to examine the troubled entanglements between technologies, surveillance systems, systemic racism, and gender inequality.[32] Departing from the earlier age of cybernetic theory, this unapologetically critical literature employs "information" as an analytical category to scrutinize social and political power structures that are embedded in the algorithms, databases, and classification systems that comprise the digital infrastructure of our everyday lives. This critical lens on present-day information culture, I propose, should also be expanded to scrutinize pre-digital information cultures, for scripts before the age of computers still embedded within them ideological dreams and biases.

The informational turn has entered the historiographical arena, too, as the organization and management of information has itself become a field of historical inquiry in recent years. What particularly sets the informational turn in historiography apart from earlier theoretical ruminations on information theory is the emphasis on the historicity of "information" as defined through socially, culturally, and technologically contrived practices of knowledge production and transmission. From investigating the materiality of premodern scholarly knowledge management to exploring the intimacies between information and state building across the globe, historians have turned "information" into a lens to rethink distinct imperial and national histories and show the multiplicity of "information societies" in world history.[33]

This historiographical framework has inspired a new wave of literature on information history in China, too, which this book draws on and departs from.[34] Arguably the most important example of this scholarship is Thomas Mullaney's work on Chinese typewriters. Writing against Orientalist discourses that deemed Chinese characters backward and incompatible with modernity, Mullaney found an alternative history in the technologization of Chinese characters in general and the invention of Chinese typewriters in particular. The Chinese script not only managed to survive the colonial

INTRODUCTION

onslaught of the alphabet, he contended, but it even surpassed the alphabetic paradigm by becoming a world script in the digital age. The Chinese typewriter thus encapsulated, according to Mullaney, something distinctly "Chinese" about information history—a history that he narrated through a plot of defiance (of Orientalism), heroic exploration (of trying to invent a typewriter), and ultimate victory (of the final technologization of characters). While acknowledging his achievements in opening a space for Chinese information history, my book takes issue with that romantic narrative.[35]

Celebrating the differences of world scripts may allow scholars to question the Eurocentric narratives of information histories, but as the historical studies on information proliferate, this might be the right time to pause and ponder what a global history of information should look like, and how it should incorporate non-Western histories in it. Sinocentric (or any non-West-centered) perspectives, like Mullaney's, without a doubt serve as potent instruments to decenter Euro-American histories and help conjure a more robust and inclusive understanding of information histories. But one cannot disregard the implicit tendency of nation-based histories to efface the multiplicities and heterogeneities *within* the civilizational, imperial, or national units of analyses. What, after all, are the essential components of a "Chinese" information history? Is it meaningful to dismiss alphabetization as an outcome of Orientalism and argue for a celebratory history that solely relies on the technologization of Chinese characters? At what point does celebration morph into fetishization? The difficulty to overcome, I believe, is to generate a historical narrative that can highlight the differences between heterogeneous information histories without reifying civilizational narratives and without erasing the ruptures and inconsistencies within national narratives.

I find it difficult to reduce modern Chinese information history to a technical history of adapting Chinese characters to Western technologies like the typewriter, not only because it disregards the hybridity of the information regime in China in which characters and Pinyin eventually came to coexist, but also because the ideological issues that surrounded scripts in a modernizing knowledge economy went well beyond technical tinkering. In the twentieth century, there were many different scripts in China for Chinese languages. Some of them were native inventions, like the National

[19]

Phonetic Alphabet or simplified characters, and others were imported from the outside world, such as the Chinese Latin Alphabet. But regardless of their differences, they were all central to ideologically driven programs that were forged through transnational networks in the global information age.

Searching for a Chinese (or any non-Western) information history requires tracing these technological and political networks that spanned the globe from China to the United States to the Soviet Union to the Middle East to Inner Asia. The chapters of this book thus follow Chinese scripts to various corners of the world to offer a global method for studying scripts. Chapter 1 lays out the political economic forces that precipitated script reforms, while each of the following chapters focuses on the transnational dimensions of a separate Chinese script. These transnational networks not only offer a new historical narrative for Chinese script reforms, but they also lay bare the global conditions under which the Chinese information society was shaped.

Chapter 2 narrates the history of the National Phonetic Alphabet (NPA), or *bopomofo*, which was invented by the nativist scholar Zhang Taiyan 章太炎 (1869–1936) in the early 1900s as a response to Chinese anarchists in France and Japan who endeavored to adopt Esperanto as the national language and script. The NPA, I further demonstrate, could not have enjoyed the popularity that it did without the Western missionaries in the early 1920s who used their global evangelical networks and printing technologies to promote the new alphabet in and outside of China. The unexpected overlap of global technological and ideological networks, and their ironic twists and turns, I argue, is precisely where we should look to see the invention and evolution of Chinese scripts in the twentieth century.

Similar transnational genealogies are observed in other Chinese scripts as well. Chapters 3 and 4 examine the reassembly and simplification of Chinese characters in the 1920s and 1930s, which were intimately tied to American behavioral psychology and statistical techniques of increasing efficiency in clerical and mental labor. Chapter 3 shows that the circulation of scientists and reformers across the Pacific not only instigated well-known literacy movements, but also gave birth to contested linguistic experiments, such as Hong Shen's 洪深 Basic Chinese (*jiben hanzi* 基本漢字), which sought to eliminate redundancy in communication by proposing 1,100 "basic" Chinese characters that sufficed to express any idea in Chinese. Chapter 4 demonstrates that, in addition to such experiments, the same transnational circuits were also integral to the historical rise and fall of the movement to

INTRODUCTION

simplify Chinese characters, as Chinese educational psychologists in the United States, along with native reformers in China, were all heavily invested in applying statistical methods to the physical composition of characters. The variegated history of mass literacy and simplification, in short, was rooted in the transnational circulation of behavioral and linguistic sciences that searched for efficiency in reading, writing, and knowing. Their instantiation in Republican China exposed deeper political and ideological conflicts that the chapters of this book describe.

The global dimensions of Chinese scripts went beyond Euro-American geographies. Chapter 5 explores the history of the Chinese Latin Alphabet (CLA), the least understood of all Chinese scripts, to stretch the boundaries of modern Chinese history to include Russia, Central Asia, and the Middle East. The first Chinese Latin Alphabet, invented by Chinese Muslims in Central Asia and known as the New Dunganese Alphabet, was in fact a copy of the Unified New Turkic Alphabet, designed in the 1920s by Russian and Turkic revolutionaries to replace the Arabic alphabet used across Central Asia. The movement to latinize the Arabic script had originated in the Ottoman and Russian empires in the 1850s and 1860s, as it stemmed from similar concerns of labor efficiency in a new media ecology governed by the telegraph and industrial print. Decades of Arabic script reforms culminated in a large-scale latinization project in the 1920s, strongly supported by the socialist ideologues of the Soviet Union, who considered the Unified New Turkic Alphabet (UNTA) as the future scientific alphabet of humankind. In the late 1920s and early 1930s, the UNTA was exported beyond the borders of the Soviet Union to places as diverse as Iran, Mongolia, and China in order to instigate a world revolution and build a common socialist civilization made up of letters. Chinese latinization was thus part of a larger Eurasian history that included Soviet psychotechnicians, futuristic visions of human-machine integration, young Chinese Muslim revolutionaries in Tashkent, and dissident Chinese communists in Moscow and Vladivostok.

Tracing the history of Chinese latinization from the socialist shores of Baku to the hypercolonial streets of Shanghai is an attempt to rethink the transnational dimensions of revolutionary thought in the global information age and challenge our notions and assumptions about the boundaries of modern Chinese history. Arif Dirlik once pointed out the radical visions that global history may offer as long as it excavated the multiplicity of networks and imaginations that transcended the West/non-West divide. For him, radical historiographies had to confront modernity "with all its hegemonic assumptions" while investigating alternative modernities.[36] The recent scholarship on the Bandung Conference, Afro-Asian solidarity movements, and the Little Red Book's impact on the globe demonstrates the historiographical enthusiasm to search for an alternative place for Chinese revolutionary thought and practice in world history.[37] This is a historiography that takes seriously the anticolonial struggles and utopian visions, and it shows that while the infrastructures, technologies, and the post-Enlightenment ideals that conquered the world in the nineteenth century may have been European in origin, they were inflected by actors who did not always fit within the neat boundaries of Western and non-Western national histories. Unearthing these transnational networks, such as those of the CLA, enables parallax visions to uncover new histories that upset ethno-national ideologies, and bring back to light the pasts that have been erased in "homogenous, empty times."[38]

The Chinese Latin Alphabet also alerts us to the history of script reform as a counterhegemonic practice. Chapter 6 follows the CLA as it crossed the border from the USSR into the Republic of China in the 1930s, where it served as a political technology to fight against the GMD's leviathan efforts at building a propaganda network via Phonetic Symbols—a nativist script that was put into effect nationally with militarist aspirations. In the hands of left-wing writers, the CLA challenged the ideological power of the party-state so deeply that all latinized publications were banned in 1936. Such counterhegemonic examples, I propose, must be especially highlighted in global information histories, because without them, information history turns into a mere technocratic history of management and efficiency, hiding the ideological struggles that constituted it in the first place.

Despite its subversive origins, the CLA metamorphosed into Pinyin in the 1950s and became an instrument of empire building in a socialist China. Chapter 7 traces that paradoxical metamorphosis. Soviet-style script reform in the early years of the PRC was in fact as central to the revolution as land reform. Indeed, there were hundreds of new phonetic scripts that Chinese revolutionaries proposed in the first decade of the new regime; and in 1958, Pinyin emerged victorious. That is why it came as a shock when Zhou Enlai 周恩來 (1898–1976), the first premier of the PRC, announced the same year that the state was postponing the project to replace Chinese characters with Pinyin. Instead, characters were officially simplified, and Pinyin was made

INTRODUCTION

an auxiliary phonetic script that only represented Mandarin. The reasons for this abrupt turn still remain a mystery because of limited access to the archives, but even without the archives, previously unexplored questions abound. To begin with, if pinyinization was no longer in the cards, why did it take another three decades to officially cancel script reforms? More importantly, why did the PRC launch an aggressive pinyinization campaign in its multiethnic frontiers in 1958 and attempt to replace existing national "minority" scripts such as Uyghur, Mongolian, and Tibetan, among others, with latinized Mandarin letters? In other words, how do we explain the irony of an anti-imperialist empire in the age of global decolonization?

Codes of Modernity offers some responses to these questions through revealing the radical visions, tragic ends, and dissident struggles of reformers and revolutionaries who tried to stitch together a new social order in the global information age. The century-long history of Chinese script reforms finally came to an end in 1986, when the State Council declared that Pinyin was going to replace neither the Chinese characters nor the minority scripts. The Epilogue suggests that the decision came at the intersection of yet another critical technopolitical moment—a computerizing knowledge economy that changed the infrastructural matrix of the information age on the one hand, and a postrevolutionary era of reckoning with the past on the other. The announcement heralded a new stage in modern Chinese history, as the Chinese Communist Party transitioned from a revolutionary party to a technocratic one and attempted to erase the contradictions of the past while promising a future free from them. The credibility of that promise is today doubtful at best, as rapid information access dovetails with increased surveillance, and discourses of optimization permeate everyday lives to turn daily experiences into exploitable data. The global information age continues to generate its own unresolved contradictions in China and the world as it incessantly interweaves humans, technologies, and capital. Looking back on a longer history of information, one indeed wonders whether codes are the solution to our nightmares or have been the very problem since the beginning.

ONE

Alphabetic Labor Time

Scripts, Wires, and Brains in the Late Qing

LET US START again with Shen Xue, the young medical student in Shanghai whom we encountered on the initial pages of this book. Shen was among the first late-Qing intellectuals to write a proposal for phoneticizing the Chinese writing system. Printed in 1896, his *Primordial Sounds for a Prosperous Age* was an unusual treatise that brought together telegraphic communications, brain sciences, and a Confucian-cum-Buddhist cosmology. Grammar was a cerebral phenomenon, according to Shen, as nouns, adjectives, and verbs corresponded to the natural mechanics of different parts of the brain. Chinese characters were the main culprit in cerebral dysfunction because they caused blood to coagulate in the brain, obstructing the flow of language, much like the characters slowing down the transmission of telegraphic information. For the union between the self and the universe to materialize, a phonetic script had to bridge the distance between language and writing.

In terms of his proposal to replace Chinese characters with a phonetic script, Shen's treatise was certainly not the first. Chinese scholars' search for phonetic scripts had started in the early 1890s, and there were several precedents to Shen. In 1892, Lu Zhuangzhang 盧戇章 (1854–1928), hailing from the southeastern province of Fujian, claimed that learning Chinese characters consumed too much mental energy. His *First Steps at Being Able to Understand at a Glance* (*Yimu liaoran chujie* 一目了然初階) was one of the first attempts to write a Chinese vernacular language, that of Amoy (Xiamen), with a phonetic alphabet.[1] There had in fact been several proposals to phoneticize the Chinese writing system in earlier decades and centuries, going back to the Mongol Yuan dynasty's failed 'Phags-pa Script. As I explain in chapter 2, there were also dozens of missionaries who strived to romanize Chinese languages throughout the nineteenth century. But there was something different about this last decade of the century. The frequency of proposals by Chinese scholars to adopt phonetic scripts unexpectedly increased in the 1890s, especially after Chinese defeat in the Sino-Japanese War (1894–1895), and it peaked in the early 1910s, when there were at least fifty different proposals for phoneticization.[2] When Shen Xue published his proposal in 1896, there were in fact two more proposals. One was by Cai Xiyong 蔡錫勇 (1850–1896), a senior diplomat, manager, and accountant from Fujian, who worked across the Qing Empire; and the other was by Wang Bingyao 王炳耀, a Cantonese pastor working for the London Missionary Society. These three reformers—Cai Xiyong, Wang Bingyao, and Shen Xue—constitute the core of this chapter.

What set Shen's treatise apart from others was his bold probe into the cerebro-mental interface between writing and language. In the long history of Chinese medicine, the brain (nao 腦), although important in pharmacology and sexology, had never been the seat of consciousness, i.e., the sovereign of the body that controlled physical actions, regulated cognition and sensation, and gave rise to thoughts and imagination. *Yellow Emperor's Inner Canon* (*Huangdi neijing* 黃帝內經) from the first century BCE, one of the most authoritative sources on Chinese medical traditions, designated five central internal organs (zang 臟) and six hollow organs (fu 腑).[3] The five central organs corresponded to the five senses (wuguan 五官): the eye was linked to the liver, the nose to the lungs, the mouth to the spleen, the tongue to the heart, and the ear to the kidneys. Among these organs, the heart (xin 心) was central to thought, and the kidneys (shen 腎) to bodily health since they regulated the body's vital energy, qi 氣, that flowed through the organs, bodies, and the universe.[4] Shen Xue's treatise thus went against established tradition, as he devoted a central place to the brain in explaining cognition, language, and thought. While his Western training in Shanghai may explain Shen's medical reorientation, his essay posed a curious question for the contemporary reader: What did the brain have to do with scripts?

The increasing number of script reformers from the 1890s onward, this chapter suggests, was symptomatic of a deeper concern about alphabetic labor time, which emerged out of a mental and clerical labor regime predicated on a European historical experience that came to dominate the global information age from the nineteenth century onward. This new labor regime was particularly precipitated both by an industrializing economy that demanded new practices of bureaucracy and literacy and by telegraphic communications that imposed an alphabetic regime of information transmission. After the Nanjing Treaty in 1842, when British gunboats opened Chinese treaty ports to foreign capital, and after the Taiping Civil War (1850–1864) in southern China claimed millions of lives and signaled a domestic imperial crisis, the Qing Empire embarked on a path of transformation, importing scientific and technological knowledge and building factories and arsenals along with higher-learning institutions. The new industrial, bureaucratic, and governmental apparatuses that came out of the Self-Strengthening Movement increased the need for labor, not only for manufacturing goods, but also for transcribing, recording, and organizing a steadily growing archive of information. To the reformers of the period, such as the industrial manager Cai Xiyong, who invented Chinese stenography, a phonetic script seemed to be an expedient instrument for supplying the new institutions with clerical workers as quickly as possible.

When the Great Northern Telegraph Company of Denmark introduced telegraphy to China in the 1870s, and when telegraph wires surrounded the empire in the next two decades, the alphabet-based infrastructure of telegraphic communications added a new layer of urgency to script reforms. Originally designed for the twenty-six Roman letters of the English language, the American entrepreneur Samuel F. B. Morse's telegraphic Morse code posed the greatest infrastructural obstacle to the quintessentially nonalphabetic Chinese writing system. The technical issue was circumvented, but never really resolved, through assigning four-digit numbers to Chinese characters. The mismatch between the alphabet and the Chinese characters, mediated only through numbers, not only turned out to be an economic burden, but also caused time loss due to the added labor of translating characters into numbers and numbers into characters.[5] For many reformers of the period, such as the Cantonese pastor Wang Bingyao, inventing a phonetic script was the best option for optimizing clerical labor time and increasing the speed of information circulation domestically and internationally.

In the 1890s, then, the expansion of the alphabet-based telegraph network, industrial and bureaucratic apparatuses that began to transform clerical labor practices, and the increasing call for consuming Western scientific and technological knowledge put an unprecedented pressure on the use of mental labor, i.e., on the cognitive power to produce, transmit, and consume information. Following the dynasty's defeat at the hands of the Japanese in 1895, these needs were felt even more acutely, as Qing reformers realized that a much larger clerical and mental labor force was necessary to fuel the industrializing economy. As calls for mass literacy started to occupy a central stage among the scholarly community, a phonetic script was deemed to be the easiest instrument for reducing the labor time necessary for mental and clerical work. In short, for late-Qing scholars, and later for Republican intellectuals and those of the PRC, the economy of literacy did not comply with the modern political economy of information. In a new capitalist and alphabetic world order that upheld the industrial values of efficiency and productivity, the Chinese writing system turned out to be a linguistic coprolite.

Shen Xue's venture into the hitherto uncharted territories of cerebral cognition and information technologies was thus a response to this political economic pressure on the use of mental energy in an industrializing and information-driven world. Shen not only rendered a new articulation of the problem through an encephalocentric imagination of the body, but also offered a potential solution for it through his script. Shen's ideas enjoyed a considerable circulation as well, since Liang Qichao 梁啟超 (1873–1929), one of the foremost intellectuals and reformers of the day, wrote a preface to Shen's treatise and published it in one of the earliest editions of *Shiwubao* 時務報, the prominent Chinese reformist journal, in August 1896. With Liang's endorsement, Shen's treatise was hailed as a milestone in the history of Chinese script reforms.

This chapter is built around three script reformers in 1896, who represent the infrastructural and political economic issues that lay at the heart of two intertwined crises of the late Qing: the information crisis and the cognitive crisis. The first two sections examine the script proposals of Cai Xiyong and Wang Bingyao to chart the impact of industrialization and telegraphy on the use of mental and clerical labor. The third section elaborates on the late-Qing theories of the brain and mental labor through Shen Xue's script proposal, which was both a metaphysical and a material search for cognitive progress. Taken together, these three works demonstrate how script reforms were an immediate product of a new political economy of information that redefined labor time in China—a subject that I return to at the conclusion of this chapter.

Cai Xiyong: Clerical Labor and Script

Cai Xiyong, a script reformer who is venerated as the inventor of Chinese stenography, was a native of Longxi, Fujian. After studying at the Language School in Guangzhou and the Capital Language School in Beijing in the 1860s, he put his skills to use with Chen Lanbin 陳蘭彬 (1816–1895), the first Chinese ambassador to the United States. In 1878, he followed Chen to the United States, Japan, and Peru.[6] After four years spent mostly in Washington, D.C., as an interpreter, Cai returned to China in 1881 and joined the late-Qing reformer Zhang Zhidong's 張之洞 (1837–1909) staff in 1884.

Cai's curriculum vitae was representative of a new stratum of bureaucrats and diplomats bred by the Self-Strengthening Movement initiated by the Tongzhi Emperor (r. 1861–1875). After the devastating impact of the Opium Wars and the Taiping Rebellion, industrialization and technology transfer from the West defined these decades, which altered the cultural, military, scientific, and technological makeup of the empire, at least in the coastal regions. In 1861, Prince Gong established the Zongli Yamen 總理衙門, the first office of foreign affairs, and quickly formed language schools (*Tongwen guan* 同文館) to train officials with knowledge of Western languages, first in Beijing in 1862, and then in other port cities. Cai Xiyong himself had attended one such school as a young boy. The following years witnessed an unprecedented industrial transformation across the empire. In 1864, Li Hongzhang 李鴻章 (1823–1901), a general who had risen to prominence during the suppression of the Taiping, established a gun factory in Suzhou. In 1865, Li joined another major general of the day, Zeng Guofan 曾國藩 (1811–1872), who was also well-known for his role in putting down the Taiping, to establish the Jiangnan Arsenal for manufacturing naval vessels and weaponry. A year later, Zuo Zongtang 左宗棠 (1812–1885), the third famous figure in suppressing the Taiping and the future conqueror of Xinjiang, built the Fuzhou Shipyard. Construction of railways, textile industries, cotton mills, coal mining, and advancements in ironworks marked the following decades in the Qing. By the 1890s, Qing military technologies, and warship construction in particular, were indeed more advanced than their Japanese equivalents, despite Japan's victory in the Sino-Japanese War.⁷ The Self-Strengthening Movement, in short, gave birth to a new human-machine complex in the Qing.

As the empire was industrially and technologically transforming, it was also entering a new world of international diplomacy. Cai was one of the early diplomats who spent considerable time in the United States, and he was an eyewitness to Western industrial development, along with the bureaucratic and legal mechanisms that came with it. After he returned to China in 1881, Cai put his knowledge and observation into practice under the tutelage of Zhang Zhidong, then the governor-general of Guangdong and Guangxi, and a leading figure of the Self-Strengthening Movement.⁸

Zhang Zhidong hired Cai to be the manager of daily affairs at the Guangzhou Foreign Affairs Bureau. As an extension of his duties, Cai also became the head manager of industries and Zhang's chief accountant. Cai was mindful of the elaborate administrative and bureaucratic mechanisms that the expanding industrial base required—not only in terms of workers and office clerks, but also new techniques for recording, collecting, and organizing information. He was involved in the management of all foreign enterprises in the province, such as the Guangdong Torpedo Bureau and the Guangdong Mint. In December 1889, when Zhang was appointed as governor-general of Hunan and Hubei, Cai followed him to Wuchang, where he assumed his position as the manager of official documentation. A few months later, Zhang Zhidong established the Hubei Railroad Bureau, the office that oversaw the construction of the Beijing-Wuhan railroad, and he entrusted Cai with the task of managing the official affairs of that bureau as well. Cai surveyed the land, recruited workers and craftsmen, repaired roads, constructed kilns, oversaw the transportation of coal, purchased new machines, and supervised the establishment of the Hanyang Iron and Steel Factory, which started operation in June 1894. Cai Xiyong thus experienced firsthand the centrality of paperwork in managing humans and machines in rapidly developing industries. He even penned in 1895 the first Chinese guide to European-style double-entry bookkeeping, *A Series of Financial Registers* (*Lianhuan zhangpu* 連環帳譜), published posthumously in 1905 by his son Cai Zhang 蔡璋 (1872–1958).⁹

Apart from his concerns for the state of accounting in China, Cai was also the first to invent a Chinese shorthand. *Transmission of Sounds and Rapid Writing* (*Chuanyin kuaizi* 傳音快字) was Cai's landmark publication in 1896, which came not only after more than a decade of work as an accountant, but also after three years of managing Zhang Zhidong's school, the Hall of Learning for Self-Strengthening (Ziqiang xuetang 自強學堂).[10] It was not surprising that the first Chinese shorthand was invented by an industrial manager. Shorthand or stenography, the recording of linguistic data at the speed of speech, may indeed be considered as a form of linguistic bookkeeping. Just like he introduced double-entry bookkeeping to facilitate the management of financial information, Cai devised the Chinese shorthand to increase efficiency in the management of linguistic information in government affairs, court disputes, political debates, schools, or anywhere the recording of speech was deemed important.[11]

Chinese characters, claimed Cai, consumed too much time to learn and were not suitable to the contemporary needs of information recording. Spending ten years to become literate was a bad investment for all parties concerned. Students spent too much energy on undertaking even basic scribal practices, and the government and industries lacked a sufficient number of literate workers who could organize papers. If each sound that the mouth produced was given a separate sign, wrote Cai, the government could solve the problem of illiteracy in a matter of months. Using his shorthand signs, he claimed, one could record more than two hundred words per minute. Although he may have been exaggerating the efficiency of his own transcription system, speed in learning and writing was for Cai the key to economy in labor. As he noted, with the aid of shorthand, one person could accomplish the work of many, and several days' worth of labor could be reduced to one.[12]

Cai's shorthand was composed of fifty-six signs in total: twenty-four initials (*shengmu* 聲母) and thirty-two finals (*yunmu* 韻母), the combination of which, he claimed, represented all the sounds in Beijing Mandarin, the official language of the empire (*guanhua* 官話). In inventing the signs, his model was David Philip Lindsley (1834–1897), who amended the widely used shorthand of Isaac Pitman (1813–1897) in the United States and claimed to have invented the remedy for "fatigue" in writing.[13] In Lindsley's shorthand, there were twenty-four signs that represented consonantal sounds, which provided the blueprint for Cai's initials (*sheng* 聲). As for finals (*yun* 韻), Cai expanded Lindsley's vocal sounds, which originally numbered seventeen.[14] Every Chinese character, therefore, was represented by the combination of two signs, and four tones were designated by diacritic marks on the right or left side of a sign (figure 1.1).

FIGURE 1.1 *Chuanyin kuaizi*. The first column on the right represents the twenty-four *sheng*, and the first row on top represents eight of thirty-two *yun*.
Source: Cai Xiyong, *Chuanyin kuaizi* 傳音快字 [Transmission of sounds and rapid writing] (repr., Hubei: Guanshuju, Guangxu 31 [1905]), 9.

Cai died two years after he published his work, but his son Cai Zhang, who also studied the shorthand of the Japanese stenographer Kumasaki Kenichirō's 熊崎健一郎, carried on his legacy.[15] In 1910, the first school for training stenographers was founded under the Political Advisory Board (Zizheng Yuan 資政院). The following year, at the request of the director and vice director of the board, it expanded to include more students.[16] Cai Zhang took the lead in advancing and promoting his father's work, which formed the basis of the first Chinese stenography textbook, and in a couple of years, three hundred students graduated from the school. Some worked at the newly formed National Council while others traveled to other provinces.[17]

Signs that corresponded to spoken sounds could, the reformers believed, reduce the necessary labor time for literacy from several years to a few weeks, and give rapid rise to a clerical labor force needed in government offices and industries. Literacy, according to the two Cais, amounted to nothing more than work. In the words of Cai Xiyong, "the brush [could] follow the statements of the mouth without any time to think, and the hand [would] not stop moving" while writing in shorthand.[18] Shorthand, in other words, took the mind out of writing, as the stenographer became a mechanical recorder of speech, a court worker. There was no qualitative side to literacy; it was a technical achievement to satisfy the demands of a new economy. The two Cais' shorthand stood at the intersection of the bureaucratic machinery of the state and the mindless recording of the modern clerk.

Cai Xiyong's original shorthand had a large impact on the history of writing in the late Qing. In Fujian, Li Jiesan immediately published his own proposal for a shorthand the same year, and adapted Cai's signs to the Min vernacular languages in Fujian.[19] Wang Bingyao's use of the Pitman shorthand to transcribe Beijing Mandarin and Cantonese was also very similar to Cai's work, even though Wang did not make any reference to him. What made Cai's scheme immortal, however, was his son Cai Zhang's textbook.

Cai Zhang improved the shorthand after his father's inaugural work. He reduced the number of initials to twenty-two and modified the script so that it could accommodate multicharacter phrases and words, rather than just recording one character or one syllable each time. His textbook was geared toward transcribing the keywords that constituted the modern state's lexicon. After teaching the basic principles of the Chinese shorthand, Cai's textbook introduced the shorthand signs for countries (China, France, America, Australia, Portugal, etc.), and made a smooth transition to a specifically bureaucratic terminology, such as parliament (*guohui* 國會), state system (*guoti* 國體), or state affairs (*guowu/guoshi* 國務/國事). After a swift glance at the provinces of China, including specific administrative terminology such as Muslim Regions (*huibu* 回部) or Special Regions (*tebie quyu* 特別區域), Cai introduced the shorthand signs for governmental offices (Cabinet, State Council, Ministry of Internal Affairs, etc.), and administrative titles (president, vice president, secretary, member of State Council, etc.). He then divided the rest of the lessons into nouns (*mingci* 名詞), adjectives (*xingrongci* 形容詞), and idioms (*xiyongyu* 習用語). Nouns included terms such as provisional constitution (*yuefa* 約法), topic of debate (*yiti* 議題), strategy (*shouduan* 手段), policy (*zhengce* 政策), constitution (*xianfa* 憲法), regulation (*guize* 規則), bank (*yinhang* 銀行), and political view (*zhengjian* 政見). Adjectives included commonly used terms such as special (*tebie* 特別), direct (*zhijie* 直接), easy (*jiandan* 簡單), absolute (*juedui* 絕對), cited (*liejude* 列舉的), specific (*jutide* 具體的), or prerequisite (*qianti* 前提). And lastly, idioms included "administrative guidelines" (*xingzheng fangzhen* 行政方針), "for the benefit of the state and fortune of the people" (*guoli minfu* 國利民福), "definitely disagree" (*juedui bu zancheng* 絕對不贊成), and so on. Cai ended the textbook with long excerpts on legal terms as exercises for the students.[20]

The two Cais' shorthand blurred the line between governmental clerks and literate citizens. Although the difficulty of learning thousands of Chinese characters was part of the rhetoric mobilized to promote phonetic signs, the purely clerical use of the latter suggested the invention of a new *Homo scribens* who worked solely to sustain the growing archive of modern bureaucracy. While the Cais strategically employed the idea of mass literacy, for them, literacy was foremost a matter of fueling the clerical labor force in the shortest time possible, and they considered the phonetic script as the fastest and most efficient medium to achieve that goal. Phoneticization, in other words, was inseparable from the demands of a new information economy.

Wang Bingyao: Telegraphic Labor and Economy of Signs

The same year that Cai penned his influential proposal, Wang Bingyao, a Cantonese pastor, also printed a proposal for phoneticization. Efficiency and speed were the pillars of Wang's phonetic script too, but his reasons complemented Cai's in a different way. Wang was the first script reformer in China to ponder the impact of telegraphic communication and Morse code on the Chinese writing system. Dots and dashes that flowed through electrified wires were at the center of Wang's proposal for a phonetic script.

Wang's proposal was well timed. As the outcome of an industrializing economy, the late nineteenth century also witnessed a communications revolution, especially with the expansion of the Chinese telegraphic network that exacerbated the pressure on the technological use of Chinese characters. Danish and British telegraph companies were the first to wire Shanghai and Hong Kong in 1871, and the web of communications swathed the empire in the following decades. The materiality of information quickly became an arena of conflict in an internationalizing economy of telegraphy based on Morse code, a system of notation that abstracted the Roman alphabet of the English language into dots and dashes.[21] When telegraphy slowly filtered into China, the Chinese writing system posed a grave physical challenge: How could nonalphabetic Chinese characters circulate through electrified wires engineered for the alphabet?

The incongruence of electrical communication and Chinese characters was first addressed in 1851 by Daniel Jerome Macgowan (1815–1893), an American medical missionary and a translator of Western science into Chinese. Macgowan's *Philosophical Almanac* (*Bowu tongshu* 博物通書), published in Ningbo, was the first work that introduced the theory of telegraphy into China.[22] *Philosophical Almanac* crystallized Macgowan's effort to explain the significance of electromagnetic telegraphy and the concomitant electrophysiological conception of the human body. The neologism he introduced, *dianqi* 電氣, captured the semiotic transformation of nature and the human body—he combined *dian* (lightning) and *qi* (cosmic force flowing through nature and human bodies) to signify electricity, the unobstructed force that flowed through telegraphic wires and human bodies.[23] His "electric telegraph," however, was not based on Morse code and thus significantly different from the 1871 telegraph codebook.

Philosophical Almanac's chief aim was to introduce telegraphy to China, and in doing so it translated a variety of scientific ideas and instruments that were connected to electricity. As Macgowan put it, "the main design of this brochure being to communicate to the Chinese the principles of the ELECTRIC TELEGRAPH, it was necessary for its elucidation, that some account should be given of the sciences connected therewith; . . . [the Chinese] are perfectly ignorant of Electricity, Galvanism, and Magnetism."[24]

His colonial pedagogy notwithstanding, Macgowan had the more immediate task of reengineering Chinese characters. "Philological difficulties surrounding the subject," he noted, "have led many into the erroneous belief that this nation can be instructed in the sciences generally, only through the medium of an Alphabetic Language." Macgowan was utterly against the alphabetization of Chinese language, which had been an ongoing missionary effort.[25] Instead he wanted to assimilate the Chinese writing system itself into the telegraphic domain by breaking up the characters into their basic components. Working together with "intelligent natives," whose names he did not deem worthy of mention, Macgowan invented a new telegraphic dial plate that could, he believed, be used to form all fifty thousand or so characters in Chinese with only sixteen Chinese symbols. But due to technical difficulties, he suggested that "it might prove more convenient in practice to employ the Manchu alphabet" (figure 1.2).[26]

Macgowan's Manchu/Chinese "electrical communication of signs," i.e., telegraphy, (*dianqi tongbiao* 電氣通標) was the first interface between the Chinese writing system and the alphabet-based technology of the telegraph. His apparatus, although never put in operation, was surprising on many accounts. Macgowan and his Chinese collaborators thought it possible to use Manchu, the official language of the Qing dynasty that few in the empire actually spoke, to transmit telegraphic messages. To my knowledge, this was the first and last mention of the Manchu alphabet's codification by the missionaries. Secondly, instead of the telegraph key widely used in tapping Morse code, they modeled their system on a dial pad similar to William Cooke and Charles Wheatstone's telegraphic dial pad, which had pointing needles that rotated above alphabetic letters—a machine that was invented in the 1830s and enjoyed limited popularity.[27] Thirdly, for the first time, Macgowan and his Chinese collaborators devised a method to index Chinese characters for electromagnetic communication. It was based on "eight strokes" and "seven place-signs." The eight common strokes were taken from the eight-stroke method that predated the Tang dynasty, known as the "eight principles of *yong*" (*yongzi ba fa* 永字八法), which held that the eight strokes that formed the character *yong* 永 were common to all Chinese characters. Macgowan et alia assumed that the permutations and combinations of these

FIGURE 1.2 Chinese and Manchu telegraphy from *Bowu Tongshu*.
Source: Daniel Jerome Macgowan, *Bowu tongshu* 博物通書 [Philosophical almanac] (Ningbo, 1851), unidentified page number.

eight strokes would be capable of creating any Chinese character (figure 1.3). The seven place-signs, on the other hand, indicated the place of the stroke: middle, up, down, inside, outside, left, and right. For instance, if the needle ticked once toward East, it indicated "up"; if it ticked once toward West, it meant "down"; two ticks East was "left," and so on. The strokes worked in the same logic. Two ticks toward East and one toward West meant 丶, two East and two West was ｜, and so on.²⁸

Needless to say, Macgowan was too optimistic about the composition of Chinese characters. The order of strokes in Chinese characters is not as straightforward as in *yong* 永, so his method turned out to be impractical. But the significance of Macgowan's project lay in his effort to incorporate the Chinese writing system into a global economy of communication dictated by the telegraphic medium. Equally important was his importation of galvanism into China to suggest that electricity was the building block of

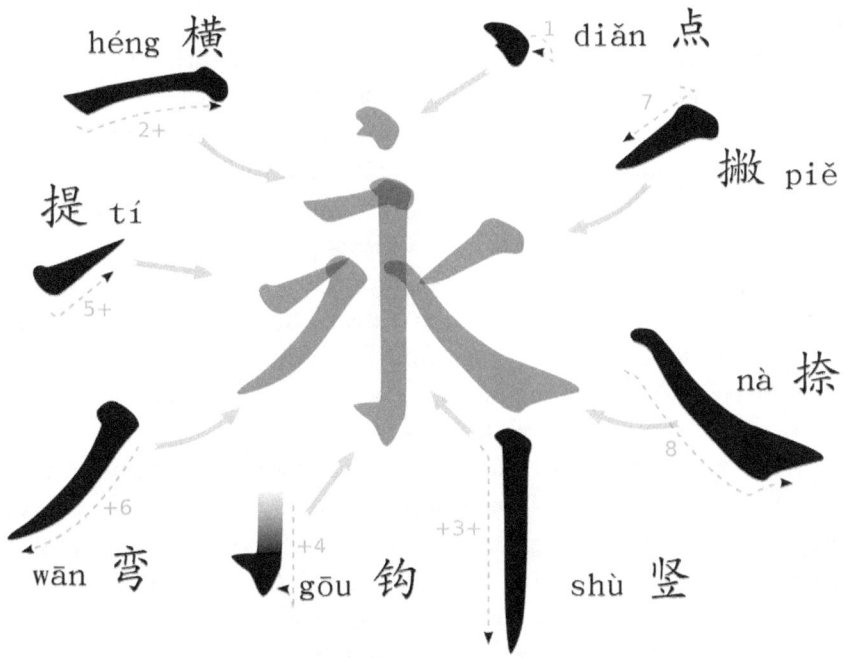

FIGURE 1.3 The eight principles of yong 永.
Source: Wikimedia Commons

human physiology, a position that was embraced in unexpected ways by later reformers of the Chinese script, such as Shen Xue. But let us take the story one step at a time.

The first commercial Chinese telegraph codebook modeled on Morse code was invented by H. C. F. C. Schjellerup (1827–1887), a Danish astronomy professor, in 1871, and was expanded and put in wider use by the French harbormaster in Shanghai, Auguste Septime Viguier (1837–1899). The 1871 telegraph codebook was the blueprint of almost all the telegraph codebooks that were used in China until the advent of the digital age, but it did not come without technical and financial difficulties. Samuel F. B. Morse's telegraph code was based on the English alphabet, in which every letter was represented by dots and dashes. The letter *a*, for instance, was a dot and a dash (• –); *b*, a dash and three dots (– • • •); *c*, a dash, a dot, a dash, a dot

(– • – •); and so on. But the nonalphabetic nature of the Chinese script, which had troubled Daniel Macgowan, demanded a middle stage between Morse code and the Chinese characters, which came in the form of numbers. Viguier assigned a four-digit number to each character, so that a character's number-code could be transmitted via Morse code. To transmit the character *yi* 一, its number (0001) was used; or the character *ya* 亞 was now identified with the number 0077 (figure 1.4). The numbers thus ran from 0001 to 9999, enough to contain 6,000 to 7,000 Chinese characters in common use.[29]

But this coding system caused a major problem for the late-Qing reformers: it required too much labor time to transmit a given character. The telegraph codebook was designed and indexed according to the principles of the *Kangxi Dictionary*'s method of indexing, based on 214 radicals (*bushou* 部首). The 214 radicals were originally invented by the late-Ming literatus Mei Yingzuo 梅膺祚, but they became the sovereign method of indexing Chinese characters under the Kangxi emperor (r. 1661–1722), whose encyclopedic dictionary, the *Kangxi Dictionary* (*Kangxi zidian* 康熙字典), was indexed using this system in 1716. According to the index of 214 radicals, each character contained one radical. The radical for lightning/electricity, *dian* 電, for instance, was *yu* 雨 (which originally meant "rain"). In order to locate *dian* in the dictionary, the dictionary user first had to find the category for *yu* 雨, under which were listed all the characters that had *yu* as their radical, such as snow (*xue* 雪), cloud (*yun* 雲), dew (*fen* 雰), and *dian* 電. The 1871 telegraph codebook was therefore arranged as a dictionary without meanings attached to it, but with the added complexity of four-digit numbers. A telegraph clerk who wanted to locate a given character first had to determine the radical of the character, then find the radical in the codebook, then find the character designated under that radical, and finally translate the four-digit number of that character (which was 6262 for *dian*) into Morse code. The hypothetical clerk was only then ready to wire it away.[30]

The added labor time also cost more money. Until the system was reformed in the 1930s, both the senders and receivers of telegrams had to compensate telegraph clerks for that added labor of locating characters in a telegraph codebook. If one wanted to wire a message from Shanghai to Beijing, for example, they would have to pay the clerk in the Shanghai telegraph office to translate the original message in characters (plaintext) into numerical code; and the receiver of the message in Beijing would have to pay the clerk in the Beijing telegraph office to translate the code back into

FIGURE 1.4 Viguier's *Dianbao xinshu* 電報新書 [New telegraph codebook], 1872.
Source: Wikimedia Commons

characters.³¹ In addition to the problem of labor time, the transmission of telegrams in the form of four-digit numbers was itself too costly. Telegrams were charged according to the number of dots and dashes they involved, and numbers were the longest of all Morse code signs. Let us continue with the example of *dian*, i.e., 6262. If *dian* was hypothetically coded in phoneticized letters, it would be equal to four letters in the Morse code:

d – • •
i • •
a • –
n – •

That's six dots and three dashes. With the dominant four-digit number formula, however, the same character was translated as twelve dots and eight dashes:

6 – • • • •
2 • • – – –
6 – • • • •
2 • • – – –

Chinese characters, as Thomas Mullaney noted, had an economically disadvantaged status when compared to working with an alphabet-oriented information infrastructure.³² Economy in telegraphic communication—both in labor time and in the cost of transmission—acted as the grounds on which late-Qing reformers advocated the phoneticization of the Chinese writing system.

Wang Bingyao was one of those reformers who identified telegraphy as the primary reason for the need to phoneticize the Chinese writing system. Wang was a pastor in the London Missionary Society, and it is noteworthy that although he was well informed about the Roman alphabet for Cantonese used by missionaries since the early nineteenth century, he decided to invent a shorthand rather than follow the Roman alphabet, the reasons of which will become clear in the next chapter.³³ In *A Record of Phonetic Letters* (*Pinyin zipu* 拼音字譜), Wang addressed the problem of codebooks, and claimed that his phonetic script could solve the problem of time loss and money loss in telegraphic communication while helping in the creation of a literate society.³⁴ Wang was writing for a Cantonese population, and his proposal concerned the Cantonese language, spoken in the southern province of Guangdong. It was composed of seventy-five signs—twenty-two initials and fifty-three finals—which in his words was "not difficult to learn even for the dumbest person" (figure 1.5).³⁵ Although Wang devised his system for Cantonese, he added extra signs to represent Beijing Mandarin and vernacular Amoy language as well—a strong indication that he was aware of Cai Xiyong's and Lu Zhuangzhang's script proposals, which were based on Beijing Mandarin and Amoy, respectively. He was indeed in favor of the unification of all languages under Beijing Mandarin. But speakers of different languages needed a method to learn the official language, he noted, which is where his invention entered the picture with its potential to reduce years of strenuous labor to a few days and create a nation (*guo* 國) of knowledge and intellect.³⁶

In Wang's conceptual framework, literacy and telegraphy were both governed by the same laws of economy: neither the time needed to learn Chinese characters, nor that needed to transmit them conformed with the accelerating speed of information. The telegraph collapsed time and space through electrical wires, but in order to encode language in dots and dashes and be telegraphically literate, the minds of the Chinese population needed to abide by the laws of wired communication. The financial and military strength of the West, argued Wang, emerged out of its alphabetic letters, out of "facilitating the path of the written word into the mind [*yi qi lu ru xin* 易其路入心]."³⁷ "If we want to raise China," he wrote, "and especially seek [to have] railroads, machinery, artistry, mining, commerce, banking, postal service, military equipment, and naval ships like in Europe and America, we cannot follow a false path [*buwu qu wei zhi dao* 不務去偽之道]."³⁸ The foundation of progress was the "people's intellect [*minzhi* 民智]," and the technique to *intellectify* the people (*zhimin zhi shu* 智民之述) was none other than a phonetic script that cleared away the obstacles on the path of information into the mind.

When taken together, Cai's and Wang's script proposals indicated what they perceived to be scarcity and inefficiency in clerical and mental labor. The task at hand for both reformers was to invent a script that could reskill the population to produce efficient workers who optimized the use of their

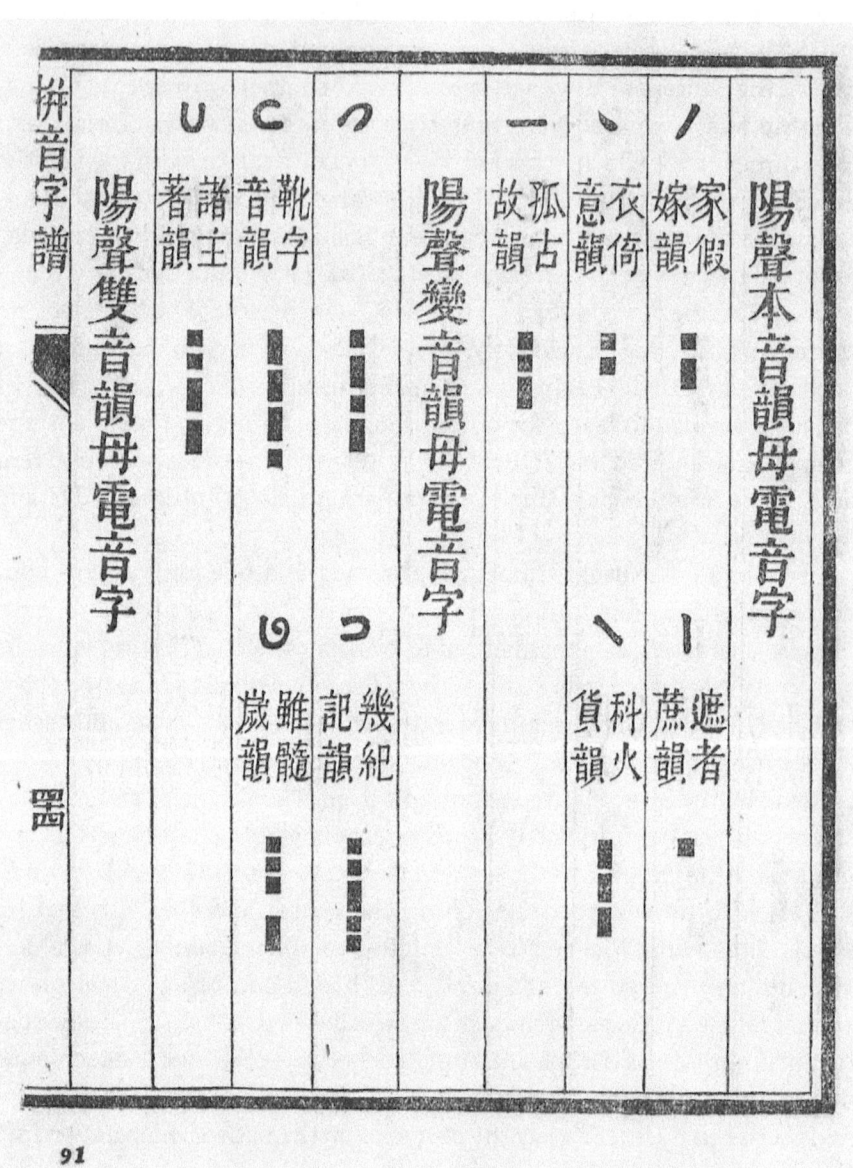

FIGURE 1.5 Wang Bingyao's phonetic script and Morse code.
Source: Wang Bingyao, *Pinyin zipu* 拼音字譜 [A record of phonetic letters] (Beijing: Wenzi gaige chubanshe, 1956), 91.

mental labor in becoming literally productive members of society. For Wang, the telegraphic infrastructure and Morse code were critical forces to engineer a new script, and he was not alone in thinking so. His issue with Morse code was raised over and over again by other late-Qing, Republican, and even PRC intellectuals and technicians. The invention of the Chinese National Phonetic Alphabet (*Zhuyin/Guoyin zimu*) in 1913 and its promulgation in 1918, the subject of the next chapter, were both an effort to reduce the labor time necessary for literacy and an effort to reengineer telegraphic communications. In fact, Phonetic Symbols, the National Phonetic Alphabet's revised and updated version, was experimentally employed in telegraphic communications by the Nationalist Party from 1929 to 1937 in Liaoning Province. The efforts to phoneticize Chinese communication did not end there. In the 1950s, the engineers of the People's Republic of China were as invested in mass literacy as in latinizing telegraphic communications. Most tellingly, Zhou Youguang, the inventor of Pinyin, was heavily invested in a new script partially as an extension of his work on telegraphic reform.[39] Script reforms and the promotion of mass literacy, in other words, were inextricably linked to the dominant communications infrastructure of the era.

Apart from the infrastructural difficulties it imposed on the Chinese writing system, telegraphy also played a significant role in theorizing the body as a repository of information, with the brain as its center. Galvanist theories, which entered the Chinese literary markets via missionary translations, introduced analogies that likened telegraphy to the nervous system, which offered late-Qing reformers scientific venues for concocting new philosophical and political theories that brought together humans and information technologies. Shen Xue was one of them.

Shen Xue: Brain, Script, and Mental Labor

When Shen Xue penned the first Chinese treatise on script and the brain, he was drawing on a growing corpus of translated science, which started with Daniel Macgowan's *Philosophical Almanac* in 1851. As noted, Macgowan and his Chinese associates were the inventors of the term for electricity (*dianqi*), the unseen power that flowed through telegraphic wires and human bodies. As such, *Philosophical Almanac* was the first text in Chinese that proposed galvanist principles for the functioning of the human body.

Electricity was key to understanding both human life and the mechanical transmission of human language.⁴⁰

The same year witnessed the publication of another missionary work that enjoyed wider circulation. Benjamin Hobson and Chen Xiutang published *A New Treatise on Anatomy* (*Quanti xinlun* 全體新論) in Canton in 1851. Hobson was the first Protestant missionary-physician dispatched by the London Missionary Society first to Macao in 1839 and then to Canton in 1848, where he collaborated with Chen Xiutang to write *A New Treatise*. In contrast to *Philosophical Almanac*, Hobson and Chen's work introduced the conceptual and lexical vocabulary necessary to understand the brain as the seat of the mind and soul, and the governor of the body. Defying the traditional Chinese medical and cosmic theories of the mind's place in the body, they started *A New Treatise* with the following remark: "The ancients said that . . . everything comes from the heart. In fact, they did not know that the soul resides in the brain. They also said that the brain was the governing seat of the primordial spirit [*yuanshen zhi fu* 元神之府], [but] they did not know the function of the brain. . . . The brain is the highest sovereign [*zhu* 主] of the body."⁴¹

An encephalocentric conceptualization of the body infiltrated the Chinese minds through governmental metaphors ("governing seat," "sovereign") and neologisms for anatomical parts that did not exist previously in the Chinese vocabulary. The most critical term for propagating a cerebral sovereignty was the medium that connected the brain to the outside world, i.e., nerves, or, in Hobson and Chen's translation, "brain-*qi* tendons" (*naoqijin*): "Divided into branches like ropes, like strings, like threads, they are in general called the brain-*qi* tendons."⁴² Bridie Andrews has noted that the use of *qi* in translating "nerve" was in part a strategic effort to introduce galvanist theories of electricity and the body to China, since in Chinese anatomical vision, every organ had its own *qi*, and they were all affected by the movement of "normal *qi*" in the body.⁴³ In translated anatomy, brain-*qi* tendons connected the self to the outer world.

The following decades advanced anatomical knowledge of the brain in China by translating ideas that had emerged in Western medical writings during the previous several decades. Encyclopedic studies printed in the 1880s, namely Dauphin William Osgood's *A Profound Explanation of Anatomy* (*Quanti chanwei* 全體闡微) and John Dudgeon's *A Complete Investigation of Anatomy* (*Quanti tongkao* 全體通考), were both translations of Henry Gray's

Anatomy, Descriptive and Surgical, originally published in 1858. Osgood's translation was published in Fuzhou in 1881 and circulated in Guangdong, Fujian, and Shanghai. Dudgeon's translation, on the other hand, was printed at the Beijing Tongwenguan Press in 1886, and was sold in the environs of the capital.⁴⁴ Besides the surgical knowledge they sought to disseminate, these encyclopedic works were significant attempts to unify the terminology related to brain sciences and introduce a more sophisticated vocabulary with which to convey anatomical knowledge. *A Profound Explanation of Anatomy*, for instance, defined brain tendons (*naojin*) as "nerves," putting an end to Hobson and Chen's interchangeable concepts of brain-*qi* tendons (*naoqijin*), *qi* tendons (*qijin*), and brain tendons (*naojin*).⁴⁵

Apart from the encyclopedic works, missionaries also published smaller textbooks that circulated more easily. In terms of promoting the conceptual and material link between electricity, the brain, and telegraphic communication, Henry Dwight Porter's textbook *Elementary Physiology* (*Shengshen zhizhang* 省身指掌), also published in 1886, was exceptional. Henry D. Porter arrived from the United States in 1872 as part of the American Board of Commissioners for Foreign Missionaries (ABCFM) North China Mission. Stationed mostly in Shandong, especially in the village of Pengjia, where he founded a small dispensary, Porter led the life of a preacher and medical practitioner until the Boxer Rebellion in 1900. The following year, he returned to the United States, and he died in California in 1916.⁴⁶ His short book on physiology, published in Beijing, was one of the earliest Chinese textbooks on the subject. According to Porter's remarks in the textbook, brain and cognition worked like a telegraph office. Brain-*qi* (*naoqi*) was the electrified *qi* (*dianqi*, electricity) that enabled the *qi* for cognitive functions (*zhijue zhi qi* 知覺之氣). Like the telegraphic cables, the power of *qi* diminished as the distance it traveled increased, and thus electrical batteries (*dianchi* 電池) became necessary, which in the brain were identified by brain cells (*naozhu* 腦珠).⁴⁷ Brain-*qi* originated in the cells, and was carried through "brain cables" (*naoxian* 腦線), i.e., cranial nerves, like electrical cables (*dianxian* 電線), sending and receiving messages: "Ganglions in the brain [*naojie naohe* 腦結腦核] are like telegraph offices [*dianbaoju* 電報局] that receive and transmit speech [*yanyu* 言語]; [and] all human sensations are transmitted through the ganglions in the brain."⁴⁸ In other words, Porter in a curious way collapsed the transmission of speech with the transmission of sensations, both in the form of information.

Translation was both an act of searching for potential semantic hosts in Chinese to accommodate Western concepts and, as Ari Larissa Heinrich suggested, the practice of inventing an entirely new epistemological foundation for understanding the human body.⁴⁹ Regardless of the extent of their circulation in China and their troubled reception during the first decades after publication, Macgowan, Chen, Hobson, Osgood, Dudgeon, Porter, and their Chinese translators, established a new way of knowing the body in China, one in which the circulation of electricity, *qi*, and information was vital for life and consciousness.⁵⁰

By the 1890s, detailed knowledge about the brain and the nervous system, along with the questions it raised about the seat of consciousness, was available in the Qing capital and coastal cities. The increasing presence of the telegraph cables that surrounded the empire at an astonishing speed and the economic problems of telecommunications they precipitated were transformative for late-Qing thought. Instead of reading the missionary writings merely as medical works, late-Qing intellectuals utilized the new theories of the body and technologies of communication to offer solutions to the worsening social and economic problems in the empire. Informed by these medical theories, Shen Xue was the first to define communication as a neurophysiological act of labor.

Shen Xue's approach to the Chinese script combined a translated encephalocentric anatomy with Wang Bingyao's telegraphic concerns and Cai Xiyong's penchant for speed and efficiency in clerical inscription. Shen's radical reassembly of language, writing, and body in China was in part made possible by his native place, Shanghai, which was by the late nineteenth century a center for collecting missionary translations and publications on human anatomy. Shen probably also had access to English publications on topics such as aphasia, which are hard to identify but were most probably stored in missionary collections that Shen made use of during his time as a student of medicine in Shanghai. In addition, Shen was also exposed to Cai Xiyong's shorthand and Lu Zhuangzhang's syllabary, along with missionary romanizations of Shanghainese, of which there were many.⁵¹

A phonetic script, according to Shen, was central to redefining humans' relationship to language and mental work. He was in full agreement with Cai Xiyong and Wang Bingyao, although he never referenced the latter, on the need for a new script to manage the use of time in writing and in telegraphic communication. Shen claimed that he himself tested the speed of writing Chinese in different calligraphies and in different phonetic systems, and noted that in the time that it took him to write 180 small seal characters (*xiaozhuan* 小篆), he could write 200 in clerical script (*lishu* 隸書), 280 in Song font (*songti* 宋體), 300 in regular script (*zhengkai* 正楷), 360 in cursive (*caoshu* 草書), 400 "sounds" (*yin* 音) in English, French, Russian, and German scripts, 320 sounds in Indian script (*yinduwen* 印度文), 340 characters in Japanese syllabary, 360 sounds in the Qing script of Manchu, Mongolian, and Tibetan, 380 sounds in romanized Chinese (possibly, in this case, for Shanghainese), 600 sounds in Western shorthand, 600 sounds in his own phonetic script (*yuanyin xinzi* 元音新字), and 1,800 sounds in the contracted technique of his own script (*yuanyin suobi* 元音縮筆). Even though it is highly questionable that Shen was equally proficient in all these scripts, he argued that the speed (*sulü* 速率) of writing Chinese characters fell far behind that of phonetic scripts.

Echoing the arguments mentioned above, Shen also noted the disadvantage of Chinese characters in telegraphic communication. As noted, a telegraph clerk had to locate the Chinese character in the telegraph codebook, check its number, and translate the number into Morse code. Four-digit numbers, claimed Shen, diminished communication speed and increased labor time for translating the characters into numbers and vice versa. With his shorthand composed of eighteen strokes only, he claimed that he could "send any sound in the world without [the added] labor of translating [into numbers] [*ke bao tianxiayin mian fanyi zhi lao* 可報天下音免翻譯之勞]."[52]

The calculations that Shen supposedly made of the speed of writing and transmitting might have seemed dubious for some of his readers, but his emphasis on labor productivity was historically significant. It was perhaps not a coincidence that he titled his treatise *Primordial Sounds for a Prosperous Age* (*Shengshi yuanyin*), which was surprisingly similar to Zheng Guanying's 鄭觀應 influential work on economic thought, *Words of Warning to a Prosperous Age* (*Shengshi weiyan* 盛世危言), printed in 1894. As Andrew Liu has observed, Zheng's treatise was indicative of a new form of political economic thought in the late Qing that shifted the focus from trade and commerce to manufacturing and production techniques.[53] I would like to add that while Zheng Guanying is remembered for his contributions to political economy, his interest in the material dimensions of production extended into the arena of information and communications as well. He was in fact appointed as the general manager of the Shanghai Telegraph Office in 1881 and thus had direct experience with the global unevenness that governed not only economic relations but also telecommunications. The Qing Empire, according to Zheng, had to stop relying on Western capital to build telegraphic networks and instead train its own clerks and engineers.⁵⁴ Shen did not refer to Zheng Guanying in his treatise, but in his similarly titled book, published only two years after Zheng's, he adopted a parallel language that moved even beyond Zheng's concerns. For Shen, the political economy of information was not solely about machines, electricity, and underwater cables, but also about the labor time necessary for the transmission of written signs.

What made Shen's treatise even more significant, and compelled Liang Qichao to write a preface for him, was his blend of the urgency for optimizing clerical and telegraphic labor with an urgency for a more efficient use of cognitive power. Writing was foremost a physiological phenomenon for Shen. The production of logographic signs was governed by the eye (*xiangxing muzhi* 象形目治), whereas that of phonetic signs was primarily governed by the ear (*erzhi* 耳治). Sounds entered the ear in the form of waves (*tuolang* 脫浪) and hit the eardrum (*ergu* 耳鼓), which then transmitted the waves to four plates (*pan* 盤) through four small bones (malleus, incus, "pearl-bone," and stapes 椎骨砧骨珠骨馬鐙骨); and finally the nerves (*naojin*) recognized this as "sound."⁵⁵ This anatomical process of sound recognition was critical for Shen's purposes because it proved to him that a phonetic letter was the quickest representation of sound as it traveled into the brain. In his own words, "when the labor and rest of mental thought [is studied] from an anatomical perspective [*an tiyongxue xinsi zhi laoyi* 按體用學心思之勞逸]," logographs had to be replaced by phonetic letters, because the cerebral synthesis of the latter was seven times faster than the former.

Shen was most likely exposed to English publications that expounded anatomical visions of script and speech in the earlier decades. In fact, Shen had originally written *Primordial Sounds for a Prosperous Age* in English under the title *Universal Script*, but that manuscript has been lost. The title itself, however, bears significance, for it is surprisingly similar to the missionary search for a "universal alphabet," and Shen might have even derived it from Alexander Melville Bell's *Visible Speech: The Science of Universal Alphabetics* (1867). Despite the similarity, Shen, like many script reformers of the following decades, repurposed the Western project of alphabetization to assert his own vision on writing and language. In the aftermath of the humiliation suffered during the Sino-Japanese War, Shen's physiological script promised hope.

According to Shen's calculations, learning a logogram (*xiangxing* 象形) required seven times more response power (*huifu li* 回覆力) or memory power (*jicai* 記才) than learning a letter. There were five thousand frequently used characters in Chinese, but if one wanted to compose in an ornate literary language, a knowledge of fifty thousand characters was necessary, which in Shen's not-so-reliable calculations demanded seven hundred thousand times more memory power. The exorbitant amount of energy necessary to learn Chinese characters was giving rise to serious neurological problems, too. "The brain requires blood," he noted, "but if the working mind [*laoxin* 勞心] is overused, blood coagulates inside the brain, and the heat exceeds the normal, causing damage to brain and blood." Written signs helped "save memory" (*shengji* 省記), a term that later reformers made frequent use of. Even learning five thousand characters took more than a year for a strong-minded and able-bodied student, and the labor time for learning could not compete with the corresponding time spent by Western children, who could learn the alphabet within several hours. Again, according to Shen's calculations, only an eighth of the population was literate in China, and only 1 percent of the literates were not diagnosed with an illness. The number of people who could study science, administration, and management (*gezhi jingji* 格致經濟), claimed Shen, reached seventy million in the British Empire, a hundred million in America, sixty million in Russia, fifty million in France and Germany. Even in Japan, he speculated, seventy million people had been taught to read in the twenty years since the Meiji reforms. "If China wants to strengthen itself," asserted Shen, "it must start from its script."[56]

The economy of linguistic signs dispelled the extra blood in the brain and allowed cerebral efficiency, according to Shen. But there was more to the connection between language and brain. Linguistic units, in Shen's analysis, were directly connected to parts of the brain. The argument that the faculty of speech was located in the brain was debated by several European anatomists in the nineteenth century, the most famous of whom was the French anatomist and anthropologist Pierre Paul Broca (1824–1880), who in 1861 proposed a particular locale in the brain for the faculty of speech, which later came to be known as "Broca's area." At the time Shen was writing, however, none of those theories had been translated into Chinese. The latest translated work on the encephalon was Henry Gray's monumental work, which predated Broca. When Shen argued for the interconnection between speech and brain, then, he might have consulted missionaries or works in

English, for aphasia occupied an important place in building his theory of writing and the mind. But even so, he was less interested in the minute details of aphasia (which by the 1890s was heavily debated in Europe and the United States) and more involved in inventing a hybrid theory of Chinese traditional grammar and translated brain sciences.

The first step in his theory was to find an imagined ground of commensurability between classical Chinese and modern-English grammatical terminologies. In his semiotic world of Chinese and English grammar, any speech was composed of "living words" (*huozi* 活字), "empty words" (*xuzi* 虛字), and "real words" (*shizi* 實字), which respectively corresponded to "verbs" (*fubo* 浮勃), "adjectives" (*ajidihu* 阿及底胡), and "nouns" (*nang* 囊).[57] Living, empty, and real words mutually constituted each other and were interchangeable. "Smell" (*xiang* 香), for instance, oscillated between living and real words, because "to smell" (living word/verb) was different from "a smell" (real word/noun). "Clothes" (*yi* 衣) could be used as a real word when saying "to take one's clothes off" (*jieyi* 解衣), or as a living word to say "to clothe someone" (*yizhi* 衣之). "People use words interchangeably in this way," wrote Shen, "but they are not aware that psychological transformation [*xingli bianhua* 性理變化] also takes place in the same way."[58]

This "psychological transformation" was none other than what was seen in patients with aphasia (*ren zhi wang* 人之忘), the loss of speech. In aphasia, Shen noted, the first grammatical category lost was real words/nouns, such as people's names or place names. Then came living words/verbs, the loss of which made it impossible to remember empty words/adjectives.[59] Shen's order of forgetting was slightly different from the general Western scientific beliefs about aphasic progression, which held that nouns were the first to be forgotten, and verbs the hardest to forget. The order of losing nouns, adjectives, and verbs had been a subject of debate since at least the 1850s in Europe. In 1890, James Ross, a prominent British physician, had fused evolutionary thought and nineteenth-century colonial anthropology to claim that "the language of aboriginal man consisted almost entirely of verbs, demonstrative pronouns, and a few adverbs of time and place, and that the names of even common objects are always derivative," which is why, according to Ross, "in the dissolution of language caused by disease, nouns should disappear from the vocabulary of the patient before the parts of speech which have been first developed, and, therefore, most deeply organized."[60] Shen was apparently exposed to some of these ideas, but what they indicated to him was that the three categories were psychologically inseparable, because, in Shen's venture into brain sciences, these three grammatical categories were connected to three parts of the brain.

In the science of anatomy, wrote Shen, cerebellum ("small brain," *xiaonao*) controlled movement (*yundong* 運動), cerebrum ("big brain," *danao*) controlled consciousness (*zhijue*), and pons Varolii ("middle brain," *zhongnao*) controlled will (*lizhi* 立志). These three parts of the brain also corresponded to the three psychological faculties: the faculty of sensation and awareness (*juewu cai* 覺悟才), of memory and thought (*jisi cai* 記思才), and of imagination (*xiang cai* 象才). Moreover, in Shen's hybrid science of linguistic grammar, living words/verbs, empty words/adjectives, and real words/nouns also corresponded to the cerebellum, the cerebrum, and the pons Varolii. In Shen's architecture of cerebral consciousness, then, the cerebellum managed the faculty of consciousness and awareness, and worked through living words/verbs and movement; the cerebrum managed the faculty of memory and thought and worked through empty words/adjectives and consciousness; and the pons Varolii managed the faculty of imagination and worked through real words/nouns and will.

Shen complicated things even further: the Confucian-cum-Buddhist values of "benevolence" (*ren* 仁), "fairness" (*yi* 義), and "faith" (*xin* 信), which filled the universe, also corresponded to the three brain parts, and hence to the three grammatical categories, respectively.[61] The cerebellum, movement, verbs, and benevolence functioned in unity; so did the cerebrum, sensation, adjectives, and fairness; and the pons Varolii, will, nouns, and faith. Language unified not only the three parts of the brain but also the three principles of the universe. A speaking and functioning brain was the cosmos in a microscale.

Shen endeavored to bring together a Confucian-cum-Buddhist view of existence, the unity of form and emptiness, with that of brain sciences, psychology, and the physicality of senses. "Form is emptiness, and emptiness is form," quoted Shen from the *Heart Sutra*, and continued: "When there is no matter, there is no body; when there is no body, there are no senses; when there are no senses, there is no psyche [*xing* 性]. Everything has a sound, a vision, a smell, a taste, and a touch. They can be seen because they have a physical appearance [*xingzhi* 形質]."[62] There was a greater level of existence, the Great Void (*taixu* 太虛), which had neither a mind nor a law, neither a sound nor a smell; the Great Void was immeasurable. But in the realm of humans, things were measurable, as worldly "forms" (*sexiang* 色相) were imprinted in the human consciousness through senses. But, Shen argued, human bodies were limited, and minds were clunky (*renshen youxian, xinling kuairen* 人身有限, 心靈塊然). Only through instruments and tools could human consciousness overcome its own limitations. Since consciousness and material appearances were produced both through the five senses *and* speech that animated the brain, Shen argued that "irrefutably, script [was] the best of all instruments and vessels."[63] "A good script," noted Shen, "is one that favors the self by expediting human functioning [*yi ren wei sulü huiwu zishan* 以人為速率惠吾字善]."[64] A phonetic script and the cerebral efficiency it enabled, in short, were the reconciliation of the human and the cosmos, of the self and the universe. As Shen put it, "the Self is the Heaven, and the Heaven is the Self."[65] The script and the brain were the physical media that brought the two together.

Anyone who read and analyzed Shen's rather convoluted argument could point to inaccuracies and raise questions. For instance, did Shen really punch the clock to calculate the amount of time necessary to write in different scripts? Why did he get rid of the traditional Chinese grammatical category of "dead words" (*sizi* 死字)? Why was the principle of the universe only composed of benevolence, fairness, and faith? And so on. But the central problems that Shen addressed, of the centrality of the brain and the inefficiency of mental labor, were more important than the philosophical coherence of his treatise.[66] Drawing from Western sciences of the brain as well as theories of the mind and cosmos, Shen's script was an effort to resolve the cognitive crisis of the empire.

When Liang Qichao took interest in Shen's text, Liang was himself interested in the notion of cerebral efficiency for children's education, and Shen's arguments struck the right chord. Either right before or after he penned his preface to Shen's work, Liang published "On Children's Education" (*Lun youxue* 論幼學) in 1896. "Every human is born with a cerebrum [*danao* 大腦] and a cerebellum [*xiaonao* 小腦]," wrote Liang. For Liang, still at the early stages of his engagement with the encephalon, the cerebrum governed awareness (*wuxing* 悟性), and the cerebellum, memory (*jixing* 記性). The cerebrum, he contended, was easier to mold than the cerebellum, which explained the difficulties that China was facing in its education system. His reasoning was as follows: Chinese education was based on rote memorization, which worked the cerebellum, the part of the brain that was difficult to change. One did not reach the highest points of human achievement through memory, but through "awareness," which encompassed the capacity for innovation through observation. Western countries became "aware" of the steam engine through observing boiling water, of gravity through observing the interaction between objects. China's system of education, on the other hand, "relied on memorizing ancient geography, ancient palaces, ancient exegeses, ancient nomenclature, and extremely detailed textual research on the origins of Chinese characters." This method of instruction caused daily harm to the brain (*nao rishang* 腦日傷); a new system of education based on observation could instead guide the brain (*daonao* 導腦), strengthening it on a daily basis (*nao riqiang* 腦日強). According to Liang, the most convenient time to start guiding a child's brain was when they were five-six years old, i.e., when the ossification of the sutures in the skull closed the fontanel (*naoxin chuhe* 腦囟初合), and when nerves were activated (*naojin chudong* 腦筋初動).[67]

Working during the years when Qing reformers started to prioritize primary education over higher learning, Liang realized the expediency of script reform for the purpose of training generations of young minds who accessed information easily and rapidly and made better use of the "natural composition" of their brains. Liang's endorsement of Shen Xue's enigmatic treatise on the metaphysics of information and mind was an extension of his own reformist vision of education and the role of the brain and mental work in it. Shen had indeed captured an essential component of the modern knowledge economy. In the following years, even though the metaphysics of information was replaced with the late-Qing and Republican scholars' concern for inventing a national mind, efficiency in mental labor remained the guiding principle that drove and legitimized the reform of the script.

Script Reform and Labor Time

The cerebral mind quickly became a keyword in the late-Qing reformers' vocabulary for a new form of literacy, and even a new form of literature. In 1902, when Liang Qichao penned his landmark publication on the theory of the modern novel in China, he emphasized the novel's emotional efficacy through a neurophysiological terminology underlining stimuli (*ciji* 刺激), nerves (*shenjing* 神經), and the brain (*naojin*).[68] In the following years, the same trope permeated the society at large through newspapers, novels, and textbooks.⁶⁹ In 1904, Mr. Ailuo's Brain Tonic, which promised better brain power to students and adults, hit the market in small bottles—and it miraculously managed to stay there until the 1950s.⁷⁰ In 1905, one of the first Chinese science-fiction novels narrated the story of Mr. Braggadocio's electrical brain.⁷¹ In 1909, Lufei Kui, the future publishing giant, demanded the simplification of Chinese characters in order to save students' cerebral energy (*sheng naoli*).⁷² In 1914, Xing Dao, a phoneticist, campaigned to stop the empty use of cerebral energy (*wufu kongfei naoli* 無復空廢腦力).⁷³ The list goes on.

The pressure that an industrializing economy put on the use of Chinese characters was critical for the late-Qing thinkers' reimagination of the uses and abuses of the Chinese writing system. The central problem was that of mental and clerical labor, of the necessity to optimize labor time in accessing, consuming, producing, and transmitting information. Chinese characters, reformers thought, were not suitable for the economic demands that a modernizing information society imposed on human minds. Reformers like Shen Xue blended the material conditions of work, technologies of communication, and translated sciences to reconceptualize the Chinese body and mind and offer a solution to the escalating social and political, not to mention epistemological and ontological, uncertainties.

The late-Qing script reformers' concern with efficiency in labor time opens an inquiry into the centrality of "time" in rethinking industrializing knowledge economies. The critical place of time in labor relations has been fundamental to understanding industrial capitalism, at least since E. P. Thompson's landmark article on the subject. According to Thompson, the British people's consciousness underwent a deep transformation around the turn of the nineteenth century, as industrialized factories regulated labor through mechanized clocks. In contrast to agricultural task-oriented practices that had their own irregular temporal logic, such as intense work during the harvest season followed by a period of "idleness," the clockwork schedule of industrial capitalism disciplined a new consciousness determined by the value of time.⁷⁴

Since the publication of his work, scholars have questioned some of Thompson's assumptions and offered necessary correctives, such as the persistence of irregular task-oriented time under industrial capitalism. As Vanessa Ogle has observed, even "the proliferation of public time through tower clocks and other devices did not necessarily generate or reflect an ability or compulsion to experience and understand time as severed from natural, biophysical and even heavenly rhythms." Industrial capitalism, in other words, had the power to incorporate within itself previously existing labor practices and adapt to "heterogenous temporal landscapes."[75]

The history of Chinese scripts from the late Qing onward invites us to reconsider the issues of time and labor as they pertain to industrializing knowledge economies outside of Euro-American societies. The birth of Chinese script reforms was intimately tied to the disciplining of labor time through new practices of clerical and mental work. The power of mechanized and standardized time in managing labor, which is usually associated with industrial factories, was also felt in the arena of telecommunications and the management of literacy at large. Cai Xiyong's, Wang Bingyao's, and Shen Xue's decisions to redefine the value of script through labor efficiency were the product of a changing temporal awareness under the new political economy of information and capital.

Yet, even the reformers themselves were not entirely certain about what to do with the previous regimes of temporality that the Chinese characters were intertwined with. As opposed to later figures, whom we will discuss in the following chapters, late-Qing reformers did not propose the complete abolishment of Chinese characters. Instead, they were struggling to find a common ground between a forced information order that operated through an alphabetic labor time and the extant information order that operated through a nonalphabetic one. The industrializing knowledge economy, in other words, was not replacing a previous order; it was entering into a dialectical relationship with it.

The decades that followed evinced the contradictions inherent in this dialectic. Some believed that a phonetic script should replace characters; some sought to rationalize and optimize the use of Chinese characters themselves; and others endorsed the simultaneous use of both. In fact, the present-day coexistence of simplified Chinese characters and Pinyin demonstrates how heterogenous practices of communication eventually inhabited the same information order. The continued use of Chinese characters today demonstrates less the success of Chinese nationalism in defeating Western alphabetic imperialism and more the ability of global capitalism and information technologies to adapt to native heterogeneities.

The years that immediately followed the first proposals for script reform revealed the contradictions of a new information order. Regardless of the colonial and imperial conditions under which script reform started, one thing was certain: the phonetic script in China was there to stay. After the publication of Cai's, Wang's, and Shen's treatises, the number of phonetic script proposals skyrocketed, but all the proposals ran into the same pressing issue. In the absence of a common imperial language, what spoken language was the hypothetical phonetic script going to represent? If Mandarin, then which one? The one spoken in Beijing or that in Nanjing? And what about the mutually incomprehensible languages spoken throughout the empire, such as Cantonese or Hokkien or Hakka, among dozens of others? In other words, what were the political and social implications of a phonetic script in a land of extreme linguistic diversity?

The double helix of labor optimization and the politics of script invention in a linguistically diverse landscape constitutes the DNA of this book. A script was fundamental to building an information society, but it did not unilaterally determine its constitution. Chinese reformers, intellectuals, literary figures, psychologists, government officials, and party members who were invested in new scripts imagined completely different information societies through assembling their political visions and scripts in radically different ways. Each script, as the following chapters demonstrate, had an intrinsic potential to weave new connections between humans, machines, minds, and languages.

TWO

The National Phonetic Alphabet
Scripts and the Birth of Language Politics

IN 1912, the newly founded Republic of China's minister of education Cai Yuanpei 蔡元培 (1868–1940) summoned representatives from all provinces to join the Conference for the Unification of Pronunciation. The conference was a breaking point in the history of Chinese scripts and languages. Immediately after the abdication of the last Qing emperor, the emerging leaders of the nation considered the unification of pronunciation to be one of the most urgent tasks. Dozens of participants from all corners of the fallen empire gathered in Beijing in February 1913 to decide upon a phonetic script and ascertain the phonetic values of Chinese characters. It was a seemingly straightforward task, but the discussions ended up in an impasse. Given the plethora of mutually incomprehensible regional languages or "topolects" (*fangyan* 方言) in China, how could the participants agree upon a "national pronunciation" (*guoyin* 國音)?[1] Over the course of four months, the participants formed camps and alliances against one another, for at stake were their own tongues. Yelling and cursing were part of the daily discussions, and at one point, outbursts of profanity ended up in a fist fight. Some people were so irritated that they left the conference entirely. Even the chairman had to change three times. And in the end, the conference only partially succeeded in what it set out to do. The participants agreed upon a phonetic script, which was eventually promulgated in 1918 as the National Phonetic Alphabet (*Guoyin zimu* 國音字母 or *Zhuyin zimu* 注音字母, hereafter abbreviated as the NPA), but the so-called national pronunciation turned out to be a hodgepodge of various linguistic sounds across China, not representing any given language.

The largely forgotten debates around the invention of the NPA invite us to rethink the ties between the politics of linguistic representation and the materiality of scripts. While language politics and language reforms occupy an important place in scholarship, the link between language and script is either taken for granted or it escapes scrutiny altogether.[2] This chapter builds on chapter 1 and suggests that the birth of language politics should be grounded in the material transformations of the global information age, the impact of which was primarily felt at the level of the script. Language politics, counterintuitive as it may sound, followed script reforms. As alphabets and syllabaries were mushrooming at the turn of the century in efforts to develop clerical and mental labor efficiency, they inevitably represented a variety of regional languages, posing a grave threat to the centralization of state authority in the waning years of the empire. In a linguistic power vacuum, phonetic scripts quickly became political technologies to determine the place of language(s) in an emergent nation, culminating in the 1913 conference and the selection of the NPA as the national script.

This chapter seeks to reverse the conventional wisdom that prioritizes languages over scripts. Language politics were obviously important in the fabrication of a national identity, but it was at the material level of the script that battles over the politics of linguistic representation were waged. There were in fact many contenders for the NPA. There was, for instance, Lao Naixuan's Simple Script (*Jian zi* 簡字) that contained more than a hundred syllabic signs to represent a variety of regional languages and institute the material possibility for a multilingual nation. Others, such as Wang Zhao's Mandarin Syllabary (*Guanhua zimu* 官話字母), however, was designed only for Mandarin, with a limited number of signs, excluding other languages at the physical level of its composition. Language politics, in other words, were grounded in the scripts. The materiality of script was more critical than language itself in defining the latter's place in a nation state.

To further clarify this point about the material politics of language, let me draw an analogy between scripts and urban infrastructures. In the 1920s, Robert Moses, the famous urban planner of New York, designed around two hundred low-hanging overpasses on Long Island parkways. These bridges were unusually low, some of them standing only at nine feet, and while they were harmless at first sight, they in fact had a sinister social effect. Moses had deliberately designed these overpasses to deny entry to poor and Black residents who could only afford public buses that were too tall for passage, so only car-owning middle-class white residents could reach the Jones Beach by the ocean—a state park that was also designed, notably, by Moses. The urban design, in other words, physically encoded a politics of segregation, as Langdon Winner has noted. Racial and social hierarchies were enshrined in the physicality of the infrastructure itself.[3]

Moses's overpasses, still in place, continue to make the news as they cause unfortunate bus accidents even today. For my purposes, they serve as powerful reminders for thinking about the politics embedded in infrastructures and technologies at large. Scripts in the late Qing were not unlike the Long Island bridges, for linguistic inclusion/exclusion was determined at the physical level of the script. The above-mentioned scripts of Lao Naixuan and Wang Zhao, which the following pages describe in detail, encoded the designers' respective multilingual and monolingual politics of language. Scripts, in other words, were technologies that policed the boundaries of language; they determined whom to let in, and whom to leave out. The material politics of scripts shaped, concretized, and structured the politics of linguistic representation.

Under scrutiny in this chapter is thus the physical invention of the NPA and the inevitable linguistic contradictions that it generated under global conditions. In narrating the NPA's history, I move beyond the minute events of the 1913 conference and instead examine the transnational and ideological networks that were critical in its invention and promotion.[4] While the NPA was originally invented by the nativist intellectual Zhang Taiyan 章太炎 (1868–1936) in the early 1900s and adopted as the national script during the 1913 conference, its promotion across China in the 1920s was primarily undertaken not by Chinese reformers, but by Western missionaries—a hitherto unexplored story that demands a revision of the extant narratives about missionary involvement in Chinese script reforms.

Euro-American missionaries have occupied a problematic place in historiography, since they were the first to romanize Chinese languages. Historians in the past have described the missionaries' desire to romanize Chinese either as a project of Westernization and modernization or as a history of Orientalism and colonialism. Stepping away from these former debates, I would like to suggest that the missionaries *did* play an important role in the history of Chinese script reforms and in the birth of language politics, but not for the reasons previously assumed. Missionary romanization should also be situated within the global information age, as it was intimately tied to the history of the industrial printing press and the movable metal type, which structured the missionaries' notions of expediency in communication. But the impact of romanization on local Chinese communities was arguably very limited, and romanized biblical texts did not persist for too long into the twentieth century. Chinese script reformers at the turn of the century surely used missionary works as reference points, but in designing their scripts, their ideological commitments to nativism, transnational anarchism, and Esperanto were much more crucial than previous missionary treatises. Missionaries, in other words, were peripheral to Chinese script reforms until the promulgation of the NPA.

It was only *after* the official promulgation of the NPA that the missionaries became central to the effort to promote it. From its promulgation in 1918 to its revision in 1926, the missionaries were the primary actors who, in the absence of a centralized government, propagated the NPA across a fragmented nation through their print technologies and evangelical networks, and witnessed firsthand the troubles wrought by a script that represented an artificial mix of linguistic sounds. The history of the NPA thus alerts us to the materiality of scripts as well as the centrality of transnational networks in the unfolding of script reforms and language politics in twentieth-century China.

Industrial Print and Missionary Romanization

Missionary romanization has occupied a difficult place in the historiography on Chinese script reforms. John DeFrancis, most notably, tried to establish a direct link between seventeenth-century Jesuit romanizations, nineteenth-century Protestant romanizations, and twentieth-century Chinese language and script reforms in an effort to argue that the alphabetic West enlightened the Chinese minds.[5] Scholars coming after him were more careful to paint a more critical portrait of romanization, stressing the missionaries' ties to transnational circuits of imperialism and colonialism.[6] None of the scholarly works on the topic, however, described the actual entanglements between the missionaries and Chinese reformers in the early twentieth century, which challenge our previous assumptions about the place of missionaries in the history of Chinese scripts.

Prior to describing these entanglements, I would like to historicize nineteenth-century romanizations of Chinese languages within a global moment of missionary romanizations that were as much an extension of Western colonialism as of industrialized print. Protestant romanizations were qualitatively different from early Jesuit romanizations. The Jesuits' works in the seventeenth and eighteenth centuries were meant to inform a specific group of European scholars on Ming-Qing culture through the Roman alphabet. In contrast, the Protestant spirit of alphabetization in the nineteenth century emerged out of an industrialist and evangelical desire to carry the Bible to the minds of the Chinese populace in the cheapest and most efficient way possible. Nineteenth-century missionaries' interface with non-Western languages and cultures was shaped by the technology of the movable metal type, as they were the primary harbingers of industrial printing presses. Many of them were printers and typographers themselves, especially in the first half of the nineteenth century. The Lutheran undertones of reenacting the Pentecost around the world notwithstanding, the missionaries were transparent about their search for economy in print, and their projects to romanize languages followed a similar economic logic: the majority of the missionaries believed that a phonetic alphabet, in particular the Roman alphabet, was the most efficient way to represent spoken languages because it economized the transmission of evangelical knowledge from the missionary presses to the minds of the local populace.[7]

The romanized translation and dissemination of evangelical texts followed the nineteenth-century industrialist discourse of efficiency in print, which started with the invention of the iron hand press around 1800. Compared with wooden frames, the durable property of the iron hand press not only changed the bodily and social labor involved in printing, but also enabled long-distance transportation of the new machines. As historian Nile Green has noted, the primary agents in the globalization of industrialized print were the evangelical societies that carried the new technology across the world from Hawaii to Persia to the Malay Peninsula.[8] A Washington and an Albion iron hand press arrived in Canton in the 1830s at the request of the ABCFM missionaries, and the following decades witnessed the import of more advanced print technologies to China.[9]

The intimate connection between missionaries and printing should be underlined if we are to fully understand the history of romanization in China and across the world. With the import of iron hand presses to the "lands of the heathen," missionaries posed themselves as leading printers with the technical know-how to cast movable metal types. In the first half of the nineteenth century, before the onset of colonial and semicolonial orders, the missionaries in South Asia and Southeast Asia cast metal types in the local scripts in order to "communicat[e] intellectual, moral and religious truth in the most inviting form."[10] In the 1820s, the Baptist Mission Press's type foundry in Calcutta was among the first to experiment with printing in a variety of scripts and languages, including Arabic, Persian, Bengali, Oriya, Burman, and Gujarati. The same Baptist missionaries were also the first to cast metal types for Chinese characters only fifteen miles away from Calcutta, in Serampore, in the early 1800s. Peter Perring Thoms (d. 1851), a translator for the East India Company, brought an improved version of these types to Macao in 1815 to be used by Robert Morrison (1782–1834), the first missionary from the London Missionary Society to arrive in Canton. Morrison's famous *A Dictionary of the Chinese Language* was printed with these fonts, and in the following years, two other missionary dictionaries used the same fonts to print Chinese characters.[11]

Until the 1850s, missionaries were romanizing languages for bilingual publications and showed no concerted effort to disseminate information among local people solely through romanized letters. The shift from working with local scripts to romanizing local languages took place midcentury, following the intensified British imperial ambitions across the world. In 1854, a series of alphabetic conferences were organized in London by missionary linguists to determine a common Roman alphabet for the British imperial subjects. Unlike the missionaries of the previous decades, some of the participants were adamant in equating the Roman alphabet with civilization and the non-Roman scripts with barbarity. Friedrich Max Müller (1823–1900), one of the leading missionary linguists, even referred to local languages as "diseases" of the mind and posited the Roman alphabet as the only cure.[12] In *Proposals for a Missionary Alphabet*, which he penned for the conferences, Müller adopted a physiological approach to the problem of linguistic transcription. Sounds, he noted, were guttural, palatal, labial, lingual, and dental, produced through varying physiological assemblies of the speech organs. As such, "how can these principal sounds," he asked, "be expressed by us in writing and printing, so as to preserve their physiological Value, without creating typographical Difficulties?"[13] According to Müller, the solution to all problems was the creation of a "Physiological Alphabet." Speech, according to this formulation, was an act of physiological labor, mechanically produced by organs, and each letter of the so-called Physiological Alphabet was the inscription of a given physiological form. Müller's alphabet was therefore not only the transcription of organ clusters but also a powerful mechanism to tame the organs of speech, to give them the "correct" shape, to discipline the labor of speech, and cure the disease of the mind.

Müller's theory of the alphabet was not only physiological but deeply ideological. Formulated at a critical moment, *Proposals for a Missionary Alphabet* naturalized both the colonial ideology of British imperialism and the linguistic ideology of valorizing speech under a capitalist world order that was transforming labor relations not only in the production of commodities but also of information, language, and thought. The industrial printing press was indeed a powerful tool for justifying both colonialism and capitalism, for the mechanical precision it allowed turned "efficiency," the core value of industrialism, into a normative marker of superiority. The missionary use of the alphabet in the nineteenth century followed a similar industrial logic that put efficiency in the production of information and the rectification of thought at the forefront. That efficiency, many of the alphabetizers believed, could only be achieved with a phonetic alphabet.

The extent to which Müller's ideas resonated with missionaries on the ground is hard to determine. Some of the missionaries in China admired the Chinese writing system itself. The missionary lexicographer Robert Morrison, for instance, noted that Chinese writing "darts upon the mind with a vivid flash; a force and a beauty, of which Alphabetic Language is incapable."[14] But the faith in the Roman alphabet's convenience for evangelical missions was certainly pervasive across the world, even among those who admired the Chinese characters. The missionaries in China were most of all invested in carrying the biblical message to the minds of the people in the most expedient way possible. The coastal provinces in particular, where the number of missionary societies was growing since the 1850s, were home to speakers of diverse languages who did not possess phonetic scripts. Even though the missionaries in China never called their alphabets Physiological Alphabets, their phonetic projects carried with them the conceit that a phonetic script was the most efficient medium of writing, economizing both printing and the transmission of biblical knowledge. With the global missionary force behind alphabetization and the increasing presence of the missionaries in China, the invention of phonetic scripts became central to missionary work.

From midcentury onward, missionaries were particularly active in the coastal provinces of Guangdong, Fujian, and Zhejiang, but made their way into inner provinces as well. By the end of the empire, they had romanized around twenty local languages in China including Shanghainese, Hokkien, Cantonese, and Hakka, among many others.[15] The one major problem they faced, however, was the problem of standardization. In the absence of a centralized network of missionary activities, different societies were following their arbitrary orthographies to romanize local languages. Instead of having one Roman alphabet for China, which could in theory expedite evangelical activities, they had many that contradicted one another. By the 1870s, missionaries recognized the impossibility of devising a standard Roman alphabet for all languages in China—there were simply too many of them. What *could* be done was to devise a standard alphabet for all the vernacular variations of Mandarin.

As opposed to diplomats like Thomas Francis Wade (1818–1895), whose transcription of Beijing Mandarin, Pekingese, became the international standard in the twentieth-century English-speaking world, missionaries were invested in representing multiple vernacular languages. In fact, their plan to standardize a Roman alphabet for Mandarin was partially a response to Wade's romanization method. As a diplomat, Wade was primarily concerned with expediency in international communications, not with evangelizing in local languages. So he designed his Roman alphabet in the 1860s specifically for Mandarin as it was spoken in Beijing, which had only four tones. But Mandarin as spoken in the south showed significant differences. Not only did the pronunciations of the words differ from place to place, but some places also used a fifth tone (*rusheng* 入聲). Unheard in northern Mandarin, the fifth tone was a constitutive part of speech in the southern provinces as it designated a glottal stop, and Wade's romanization was incapable of representing it. One major problem was the letter "h." Missionaries preferred using the letter *h* at the end of a word to signify the fifth tone. Wade, on the other hand, was using *h* as an integral part of his four-tone Beijing pronunciation. Wade's *shih*, for instance, could stand for "lion" 獅 (*shih* in the first tone), "stone" 石 (*shih* in the second tone), "history" 史 (*shih* in the third tone), or "city" 市 (*shih* in the fourth tone).¹⁶ But when the use of "h" was not reserved for the fifth tone, it only made it confusing for the southern vernacular languages. Missionaries were especially troubled by this, and the China Inland Mission (CIM) openly challenged Wade in 1867 by devising a new orthography and using *h* only for the fifth tone. In the following decades, the CIM's orthography was deliberately used by other missionaries as well; and even after Wade's romanization de facto became the standard in international communication and literature, missionaries still continued using the CIM's orthography.¹⁷ The politics of the letter *h* indicated a much larger problem of representation in China's linguistically diverse landscape, and they anticipated the problems that the Chinese reformers themselves were to face soon.

Missionaries were deeply committed to the representation of regional vernacular languages. Immediately after the publication of Wade's *Self-Taught Language Lessons* in 1868, the missionary societies convened multiple times to design a standard Roman alphabet that could rival Wade's romanization and represent Mandarin as spoken both in the north and in the south. After long debates and failed attempts, they finally published *The Standard System of Mandarin Romanization* in 1904, which fixed the phonetic values of letters through a mix of previous romanization schemes. It was potentially revolutionary, for it had the capacity to put an end to almost a hundred years of Western debates in standardizing romanization. The gospels of Matthew and Mark and *Pu Tung Wen Bao*, a monthly periodical published in Standard Romanized Mandarin, quickly followed. The main idea of the Standard System was to use the same letters for different phonetic values. For instance, 江 was transcribed as *giang* in which the first letter *g* could accommodate the phonetic value of the northern *djiang* and the southern *kiang*. In some cases, two spellings were provided for one character: 希 and 西 were both pronounced as *hsi* in Beijing, but the latter was *si* in Nanjing, so the system retained both pronunciations.¹⁸ While its impact among Chinese reformers is hard to ascertain, *The Standard System of Mandarin Romanization* was allegedly the most-purchased book of the Educational Association from 1904 to 1907.¹⁹

Despite its success in the eyes of missionaries, the Standard System in fact became obsolete almost as soon as the publication describing it came off the press—not because Francis Wade reigned supreme, but because Chinese scholars repurposed the phoneticization movement and championed it in a very short period of time. By the time missionaries began propagating the Standard System, Chinese script reformers had already embarked on their own path to devise a phonetic Chinese script. Supported by major intellectuals of the age, such as Tan Sitong, Liang Qichao, and Zhang Taiyan, the movement quickly acquired a native character. From the early 1900s to late 1910s, Chinese script reformers pushed missionaries off the stage as they repurposed their works for new ends. The missionaries came back in the 1920s, but under radically different conditions.

The 1913 Conference and the National Phonetic Alphabet

Just as missionary romanization was losing strength, Chinese script reforms were taking off. Around the turn of the century, Chinese reformers confronted the pressures of a modernizing political economy of information that began to transform the social and economic practices of communication and literacy. It was around then that Chinese script reformers started to selectively utilize missionary works, but they mostly stepped away from the Roman alphabet. The main similarity between missionary romanization and late-Qing scripts was not the graphics but the inevitability of confronting a diverse landscape of languages. Scripts thus served as the physical medium for defining the possibility of linguistic representation in the first place.

Late-Qing reformers' attempts to distance themselves from the Roman alphabet can be detected in many scripts. Lu Zhuangzhang, for instance, one of the first script reformers in the late Qing, was himself involved in the compilation of *English and Chinese Dictionary of the Amoy Dialect*, printed in 1883 by the missionary John MacGowan.[20] Lu was thus not a stranger to alphabets, but curiously enough, in his proposal to alphabetize Amoy and other Min vernaculars, he undertook the effort to invent pseudo-Roman signs. And while revising his system in the following years, he abandoned even those and settled on completely non-Roman signs.[21] Lu was not alone in distancing Chinese regional languages from the Roman alphabet. Wang Bingyao, the Cantonese pastor of the London Missionary Society who invented a Chinese telegraphic code in shorthand, was strictly against the use of the Roman alphabet. As I briefly quoted earlier, he saw the Roman alphabet as an invading force that harmed the foundations of the nation and contaminated the national essence (*guocui* 國粹). "Using other nations' systems of writing for [transcribing] the local sounds of our own nation [*benguo tuyin* 本國土音], even though it might be easy to carry out under current circumstances," noted Wang, "means allowing the foundation of our nation to be easily transformed." Script reform, in other words, could not come at the expense of the national foundation. Wang, in order to preserve the "essence of the central lands [*zhongtu zhi ben* 中土之本]," chose the phonetic signs accordingly, not giving in to the Roman letters of the much-admired Western nations. Shorthand was a better option because it was invented as a speedy technical instrument to record speech, and as such it did not carry the imperialist baggage of the Roman alphabet.[22] Similarly, Shen Xue, despite his close contacts with the missionaries in Shanghai, opted for a shorthand. Li Jiesan, a reformer from Fujian, adopted shorthand for the Min vernaculars.[23] Others were inspired more by Japanese kana than the Roman alphabet and invented scripts distinct from both—for example, Wang Zhao's Mandarin Syllabary, which was almost selected as the National Phonetic Alphabet.[24] The growing sense of anxiety among reformers to preserve the "national essence," especially after the defeat in the Sino-Japanese War, manifested in non-Roman graphics.

The years that followed witnessed an explosion in the number of script proposals, as each inventor claimed to have found the key to speed and efficiency in writing. But as the number of proposals increased, the politics of linguistic representation became more complicated. Even before the 1913 conference, language politics had already taken center stage in late-Qing script reforms. Many were thinking of a linguistic order in which a new phonetic script could be used both nationally and regionally. Lao Naixuan 勞乃宣 (1843–1921), a polymath from Zhejiang, was one of the leading advocates for multilingualism in the early 1900s. He wanted to invent a script that would have enough signs to represent all the major regional languages in China (which did not include the non-Han regions). Beijing Mandarin, for instance, only needed fifty initials and twelve finals, according to Lao's calculations, but Nanjing Mandarin would need fifty-six initials and fifteen finals. Wu languages and dialects needed sixty-three initials and eighteen finals, whereas Min and Cantonese required eighty-three initials and twenty finals. Lao's script, known as Simple Script, was thus attentive to the voiced consonants (*zhuoyin* 濁音) of the south along with the fifth tone, which had been bothering missionaries for decades. He was also careful to designate extra signs for the different tones of Min and Cantonese languages. With a total number of 116 initials and 20 finals, the Simple Script strived to be as inclusive as possible.[25] Yet, the democratic tendencies of Lao's script were a potent source of anxiety for many who considered multilingual representation a recipe for political disaster and ultimate disintegration. Lao quickly became a persona non grata among Shanghai's literati circles.

Nevertheless, his language politics resonated with many who participated in the 1913 conference, where major questions regarding script and language came to a head. Eighty-two scholars representing all provinces were summoned to Beijing by the Minister of Education Cai Yuanpei to devise a phonetic script and determine the pronunciation for 6,500 characters that were commonly used in governmental and telegraphic communications. The 1913 conference was never meant to be a democratic assembly. Not even once were all participants present at the same time, and some provinces were much better represented than others. Seventeen scholars hailed from Jiangsu, for instance, and nine from Zhejiang. In contrast, there were only three from Sichuan and one from Xinjiang.[26] Still, the uneven representation did not make the debates any easier. There were personal rivalries among script inventors, and the tension between monolingualism and multilingualism permeated each discussion.

The impossibility of reaching a peaceful agreement was clear from the selection of Wu Zhihui 吴稚晖 (1865–1953) as the chairman and his archenemy Wang Zhao 王照 (1859–1933) as the vice-chairman of the conference, for the personal backgrounds and politics of the two figures could not be more disparate. Wu Zhihui, a young radical from Jiangsu, had a long career in script and language reforms that spanned the decades from the 1890s to the 1940s. His first foray into script invention was the idiosyncratic "beansprout alphabet" (*douya zimu* 豆芽字母), which he designed with the help of a missionary in Shanghai in 1895.[27] In the early 1900s, Wu left for France, where his short-lived, yet passionate, acquaintance with anarchism commenced. Embracing an alphabetic modernism as the solution to China's problems, he and his friends turned to the universal values of science and started propagating what they believed to be the most scientific language for all humankind: Esperanto.

Arguably the most successful of all artificial languages, Esperanto was invented in 1887 by the Polish ophthalmologist Ludwik Lejzer Zamenhof (1859–1917) and it spread throughout the world in the early years of the twentieth century following the publication of *Fundamento de Esperanto* in 1905. At a time when linguistic differences challenged international (and even national) communications, many truly considered Esperanto to be the language of hope. From the early twentieth century to the start of the Second World War, many intellectuals and activists from diverse national and linguistic backgrounds saw it as an opportunity to break free from the chains of linguistic imperialism and imagine a new internationalist world order that communicated in Esperanto. In the early 1900s, anarchists in Europe and Japan embraced the language, whence it reached the minds of the Chinese dissidents living in Tokyo and Paris, like Wu Zhihui. Shō Konishi carefully pointed out that, for Japanese anarchists, Esperanto was an alternative to the state-centered vision of an international global order; it was a communicative instrument that "ostensibly without culture or territorial belonging, enabled the free and spontaneous formation of transnational societies and associations."[28] For Chinese anarchists, however, Esperanto offered even more than transnationalism. In the absence of a "Chinese language," the anarchists posed Esperanto as an actual contender for becoming the national language. Liu Shipei 劉師培 (1884–1919), a Chinese anarchist in Tokyo, noted that the ease of learning Esperanto was of paramount importance for China, where mutually incomprehensible languages erected the biggest obstacle to linguistic unification.[29] Chinese anarchists in Paris were even more spirited than their counterparts in Tokyo, as their journal *New Century* (*Xin shiji* 新世紀; *La Novaj Tempoj* in Esperanto) lent major support for the cause of Esperanto. With its phonetic script, nontonal structure, and alleged precision with words, Esperanto seemed to be the scientific remedy that late-Qing reformers were looking for all along.

While its star briefly shone bright, only a few reformers in China took Esperanto as a serious alternative for a national language. The extent to which Chinese anarchists themselves learned Esperanto is also questionable. Regardless, anarcho-Esperantism lost its appeal in the following years as global revolutions produced an urgency for national linguistic engineering virtually everywhere in the world.[30] When the revolution hit China in 1911, even anarcho-Esperantists like Wu Zhihui turned to more practical solutions to solve the crisis in communication. Wu was still a major supporter of complete phoneticization and representation of regional languages, but by the time the 1913 conference was convened, he had already abandoned his Esperantist stance and admiration for the Roman alphabet. Still, his phonetic dream moved one step closer to reality when he was selected as the chairman of the conference. What made matters difficult for him was the vice-chairman, Wang Zhao, who was the most prominent figure in script reform and a staunch supporter of Beijing Mandarin as the national language.

Wang Zhao was among the most famous script reformers in the early 1900s, and his Mandarin Syllabary was one of the strongest candidates for the National Phonetic Alphabet. A native of Zhili Province in the north, Wang used to be a supporter of the Hundred Days of Reform in 1898, which necessitated his escape to Japan, where he befriended renowned intellectuals such as Liang Qichao and Kang Youwei. In 1900, he disguised himself as a Buddhist monk and scuttled back into the empire. In Tianjin, he started working on his Mandarin Syllabary. He was well connected with the intellectuals in the capital, one of whom, Wu Rulun from the Imperial University of Peking, endorsed his phonetic script in 1901, which won Wang popularity not only among elite circles in Tianjin and Beijing, but also in the royal court.[31] Publications started to come out in Mandarin Syllabary, sometimes accompanied by Chinese characters, and sometimes standing alone.[32] Wu Rulun, inspired by the national language movement simultaneously taking place in Japan, was especially motivated by the potential of the Mandarin Syllabary to serve as the foundation for a national language in China.

But what exactly was that language? As Elisabeth Kaske has perspicuously identified, the original name for Wang's syllabary was Northern Vernacular Syllabary (*beifang suhua zimu* 北方俗話字母), which was designed for northern vernacular languages in general. It was later that Wang changed the name to Mandarin Syllabary, which represented Mandarin as spoken in Beijing in particular.[33] As such, the national language that the Mandarin Syllabary endorsed was that of Beijing alone, which is most likely why scholars in the capital and the court were endorsing it. But if it were to be taken as the standard, it would be impossible to represent the distinct linguistic sounds of other provinces, as the number of physical signs would simply not be sufficient to do so. The conflict between the Mandarin Syllabary and other scripts was not unlike the one between Wade's romanization and missionary romanizations—their targets were different linguistic communities.

That is why Wang Zhao and Wu Zhihui despised one another. They had different visions for the future of a national alphabet *and* a national language. From the start of the conference, Wang's Beijing centrism was indisputable, and the ideal script for him was, obviously, his own Mandarin Syllabary. Wu Zhihui, on the other hand, was from Jiangsu, which made him naturally attuned to the voiced consonants of the south. As for the script, he would probably be content with anything but the Mandarin Syllabary, as long as it could represent the southern sounds.[34] They both had followers. Wang's followers sought an alphabet that could work in conjunction with the Chinese characters, as in Japanese, and they agreed with Wang that Beijing Mandarin should become the national language. Wu's followers, some of whom were his compatriots from Jiangsu, advocated for the importance of voiced consonants, although they did not see eye to eye in terms of the preferred graphics. According to the recollections of one participant, there were forty to fifty script inventors at the conference, and each reformer bragged about his own script.[35]

Given the exorbitant number of potential scripts, including very strong candidates such as the Mandarin Syllabary, one might wonder why Zhang Taiyan's relatively less-known Syllabary to Record Sounds (*Jiyin zimu* 記音字母) was eventually selected as the National Phonetic Alphabet. A major voice in the preservation of the "national essence," Zhang Taiyan was an intellectual giant at the time, and he designed his script as a response to the anarcho-Esperantists in France. He had been a strong critic of the anarchists and Esperanto since the beginning, arguing that their scientific crusade against the Chinese characters was groundless. He was still of the opinion that China did need a phonetic alphabet, but, according to him, that did not have to come at the expense of characters themselves. Writing from Japan, he was among those who saw the Japanese indigenous phonetic scripts, *hiragana* and *katakana*, as a model for China.[36]

Infuriated by the Esperantists and allergic to the Roman alphabet, Zhang invented his own phonetic script in 1907, composed of thirty-six initials (*niuwen* 紐文) and twenty-two finals (*yunwen* 韻文). Each sign was a derivative of the ancient forms of Chinese characters, as found in the seal script (*zhuanwen* 篆文) of first century BCE. The initial for *d* as in *dao*, for instance, was 刁, which was the seal script of *dao* 刀. 𠄎 was the seal script of *nai* 乃, and stood for the initial *n*. Finals followed the same logic. 𠃋 Stood for *ao*, for it was the seal script for *yao* 幺. Therefore, using Zhang's phonetic script, *dao* could be written as 刁𠃋, *nao* as 𠄎𠃋, and so on.[37] This script will look familiar to Taiwanese readers, for its revised version became the official National Phonetic Alphabet in 1918, and it was renamed Phonetic Symbols (*Zhuyin fuhao*) in

1930. Using the present-day Taiwanese system of transcription, *dao* is written as ㄉㄠ, and *nao* as ㄋㄠ.

The graphic interface of Zhang's script reflected his nativist politics. For Zhang, language, customs, and history were the pillars of national unity. The Poles, he noted, lost their language at the hands of Russia; the Eastern Romans lost their customs to Turkic invasions; and Chinese history was destroyed by the Manchus.[38] Only a revival of language, customs, and history could save the Chinese essence. His phonetic script thus served as a tool for the selective restoration of an imagined national essence that could revitalize the Chinese "race" (*jidong zhongxing* 激動種性).[39] As for the national pronunciation that his script was supposed to represent, Zhang called for the spoken language of Hubei, which he thought to be the closest to classical pronunciation.[40]

There was nothing particularly more "efficient" or "speedy" about Zhang Taiyan's script. The final selection of his script as the National Phonetic Alphabet was merely the product of contingent circumstances. The strength of Zhang's script was in its equal distance to all others, and it was able to speak to the concerns of different groups. It could be used as a stand-alone script, which won the hearts of the alphabetizers; it could also be written alongside characters like Japanese kana, which persuaded the alphabet-on-the-side faction. Further, it was not based on the Roman alphabet, which was welcomed by the anti-Romanists. Even more importantly, repurposing the graphics of ancient characters for phonetic purposes satisfied the ubiquitous nativist contingency at the conference. Besides, when everyone else was trying to become the next big inventor, Zhang's physical absence from the conference, coupled with his formidable intellectual presence, undoubtedly helped his script as well—especially since his disciples from Zhejiang did their utmost to promote it.[41] On March 13, twenty-nine out of forty-five delegates present voted for a revised version of Zhang's script with twenty-four initials and fourteen finals. With the addition of diacritical marks, a further twelve signs to represent southern voiced consonants were also incorporated into the script, despite Wang Zhao's vehement opposition.[42] There were thus fifty-two clusters of signs in total in the first National Phonetic Alphabet. Southern sounds, in other words, were still in the picture (figure 2.1).

The National Phonetic Alphabet was ready, but its language was not. Wang Zhao was already bitter because his script lost to Zhang's and he was even

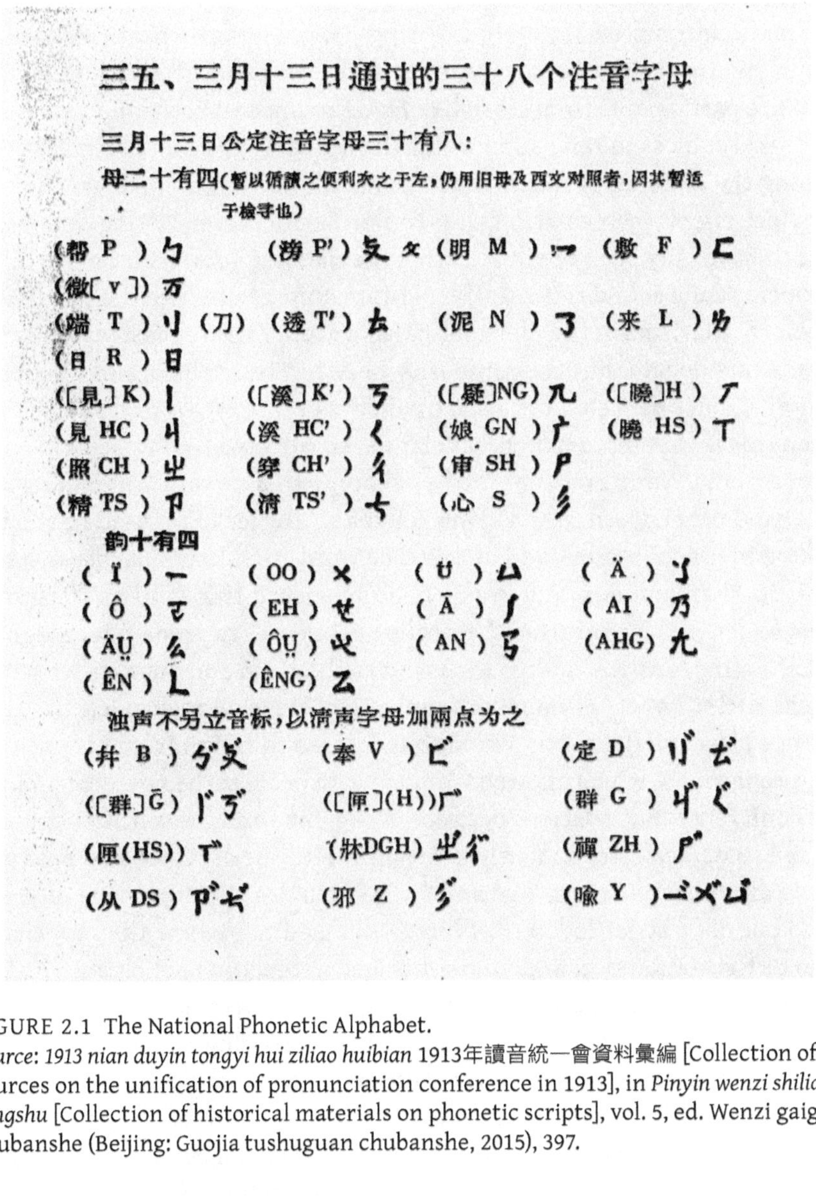

三五、三月十三日通过的三十八个注音字母

三月十三日公定注音字母三十有八：

母二十有四（暫以循讀之便利次之于左，仍用旧母及西文對照者，因其暫适于檢寻也）

（帮 P）ㄅ	（滂 P'）ㄆ	（明 M）ㄇ	（敷 F）ㄈ
（微[v]）万			
（端 T）ㄉ（刀）	（透 T'）ㄊ	（泥 N）ㄋ	（来 L）ㄌ
（日 R）日			
（[見]K）ㄍ	（[溪]K'）ㄎ	（[疑]NG）兀	（[曉]H）ㄏ
（見 HC）ㄐ	（溪 HC'）ㄑ	（娘 GN）广	（曉 HS）ㄒ
（照 CH）ㄓ	（穿 CH'）彳	（审 SH）尸	
（精 TS）卩	（清 TS'）ㄘ	（心 S）ㄙ	

韵十有四

（I）一	（OO）ㄨ	（U）ㄩ	（Ä）ㄝ
（Ô）ㄛ	（EH）ㄜ	（Ā）ㄚ	（AI）ㄞ
（ÄU）ㄠ	（ÔU）ㄡ	（AN）ㄢ	（AHG）ㄤ
（ÊN）ㄣ	（ÊNG）ㄥ		

浊声不另立音标，以清声字母加兩点为之

（并 B）ㄅ〝	（奉 V）ㄈ〝		（定 D）ㄉ〝
（[群]Ḡ）ㄍ〝	（[匣](H)）ㄏ〝		（群 G）ㄐ〝
（匣(HS)）ㄒ〝	（牀DGH）ㄓ〝		（襌 ZH）尸〝
（从 DS）卩〝	（邪 Z）ㄙ〝		（喻 Y）一ㄨㄩ

FIGURE 2.1 The National Phonetic Alphabet.
Source: 1913 nian duyin tongyi hui ziliao huibian 1913年讀音統一會資料彙編 [Collection of sources on the unification of pronunciation conference in 1913], in *Pinyin wenzi shiliao congshu* [Collection of historical materials on phonetic scripts], vol. 5, ed. Wenzi gaige chubanshe (Beijing: Guojia tushuguan chubanshe, 2015), 397.

more alarmed that Beijing Mandarin might lose to the southerners as well. The numerical supremacy of the Zhejiang-Jiangsu group in particular, which numbered twenty-six in total, was troubling for Wang Zhao. He started to mobilize participants from his native Zhili Province and other northern and central provinces to raise support for the use of Beijing Mandarin in determining the national pronunciation of characters. In March, he was able to convince twenty-three participants to sign a petition requesting each province to have only one vote in selecting the national pronunciation. While a democratically sound request, the petition aimed to reduce the power and scholarly charisma of the Zhejiang-Jiangsu group. The request was granted after some debate, but the animosity between the Beijing and Zhejiang-Jiangsu cliques persisted until the final days of the conference. Sometimes, when words were not enough, scholars even resorted to physical violence. At one point, Wang Zhao got into a debate with a certain Wang Rongbao, which did not end well. When Wang Rongbao returned to his seat, he started talking to his colleagues, and uttered the word "rickshaw" (*huangbao che* 黃包車) in Shanghainese. But Wang Zhao misheard the word as "bastard" (*wangba dan* 王八蛋). Infuriated, he rolled his sleeves to prepare for a fight.[43]

Escalating tensions pushed many out of the room and put further strain on the definition of "national pronunciation." Wang Rongbao left the conference after the fight. And Wu Zhihui decided to resign from his position as the chairman, which allowed Wang Zhao to become the new chairman of the conference. But relations between Wang Zhao and the southerners continued to deteriorate, and only a few days after he assumed the position, Wang also resigned from it. Wang Pu 王璞 (1875–1929), a protégé of Wang Zhao but not a strict follower of him, was asked to become the new chairman of the conference, and, under his leadership, the participants finally voted on the national pronunciation, which was a win neither for the Beijing clique nor for the Zhejiang-Jiangsu clique. According to the finalized version of the national pronunciation, initial consonants were sometimes in accordance with the Beijing pronunciation and sometimes not. Voiced consonants were also preserved in some cases.[44] The national pronunciation turned out to be so ad hoc and artificial that no commoner from any province would be able to understand it. Esperanto might have been a better solution. Still, the conference was officially over on May 22, 1913. Implementation of its decisions now rested on the shoulders of the Ministry of Education.

The acrimonious debates over the invention of a phonetic alphabet for an emergent Chinese nation demonstrate the centrality of scripts in defining the exclusionary dynamics of language politics. From Wang Zhao's Mandarin Syllabary to Zhang Taiyan's Syllabary to Record Sounds, the physical design of scripts embedded the politics and biases of their inventors, hence the literal blows that were exchanged during the conference. The final shape of the NPA as it was ratified by the participants reflected the absence of a central authority, which, on the one hand, enabled a democratic discussion of linguistic representation, but, on the other hand, resulted in a completely artificial set of linguistic sounds. This artificial character of the National Phonetic Alphabet constituted the greatest obstacle to its promotion across the nation in the following years.

Missionaries and the National Phonetic Alphabet

The resolutions of the 1913 conference were inconclusive at best, and the political turmoil that China plunged into right after the declaration of the republic did not make the promotion of the NPA an easy task. Cai Yuanpei, the mastermind behind the conference, resigned before the conference had even started, due to ideological conflicts with President Yuan Shikai. From 1913 until the death of Yuan in 1916, the fate of the NPA was unclear, and missionaries and foreign representatives in China were still putting their bets on Wang Zhao's Mandarin Syllabary for the future of Chinese phoneticization. But after Yuan Shikai's death in 1916, the Ministry of Education started promoting the NPA and finally promulgated it in November 1918.

For many of the reformers, the invention of the NPA signaled the end of an informational crisis and the beginning of modern progress. The remarks of Li Jinxi, a May Fourth intellectual, are especially poignant in this regard. Writing immediately after the government's promulgation of the NPA, Li noted the infrastructural and economic reasons behind the invention of the new script. The NPA was not only going to "double the progress with half the labor" in education, but also provide a final solution to the problem of the telegraphic code, which, in the words of Li, was a matter of life or death: "Suppose there is an accident to the permanent way, or to a bridge on the railway, where rescue must be immediate else lives may be lost. In sending a telegram to the next station to stop a train, time is of the utmost importance, for a minute or even a second's delay may involve untold lives and property. Who can estimate the amount of loss that might accrue from the old way of sending a telegram?"[45]

Li's observation is a reminder of the concerns around labor time that had prompted script reforms in the first place. Indeed, while language politics came to define the 1913 conference, one of the most urgent tasks of the conference was to select a script that could transcribe around 6,500 characters that were commonly used for telegraphic transmission—that is why the conference was primarily concerned with "national pronunciation," not "national language." Li made this clear, too: "French is used in telegraphing on the Peking-Hankow Railway, and English on the Peking-Mukden Railway. They are compelled by force of circumstances to employ languages other than Chinese. Similarly at sea, if a steamer encounters some danger and wishes to send out a telegram for help . . . speed is of the highest importance. If a message has to be translated [from text into four-digit numbers] for dispatch, and retranslated [from four-digit numbers to text] on receipt, it undoubtedly hinders business." Echoing a generation of script reformers, Li noted that the invention of a common phonetic script with a common pronunciation was the most practical solution to these pressing issues. For him, the National Phonetic Alphabet was thus of vital importance. As he succinctly put it, "circumstances made it necessary, and it simply had to be made and promulgated."[46]

Li's optimism was shared by other reformers as well as the central government. In April 1919, the Preparatory Committee for the Unification of National Language (Guoyu tongyi choubeihui 國語統一籌備會) was formed and linguistic unification commenced, despite the artificiality of national pronunciation. In 1922, the Preparatory Committee prepared the typeface for the NPA to standardize its dissemination, which reflected the scientific spirit of the day, as the strokes in each letter followed a standardized geometrical angle (figure 2.2). The second stroke in m ㄇ, for instance, formed a 90-degree angle; in z ㄗ, a 60-degree angle was in order; in ou ㄡ, a 45-degree angle, and so on.[47] The scientific universalism of the NPA attracted Western typewriter companies as well. In 1924, Burnham C. Stickney, an assignor to Underwood Typewriter Company, received a patent for his Chinese Phonetic Typewriter.[48] Other May Fourth intellectuals were also excited about the new alphabet. Wu Zhihui believed in the power of the NPA so much that he was corresponding with his fellow reformer Qian Xuantong solely in the NPA,

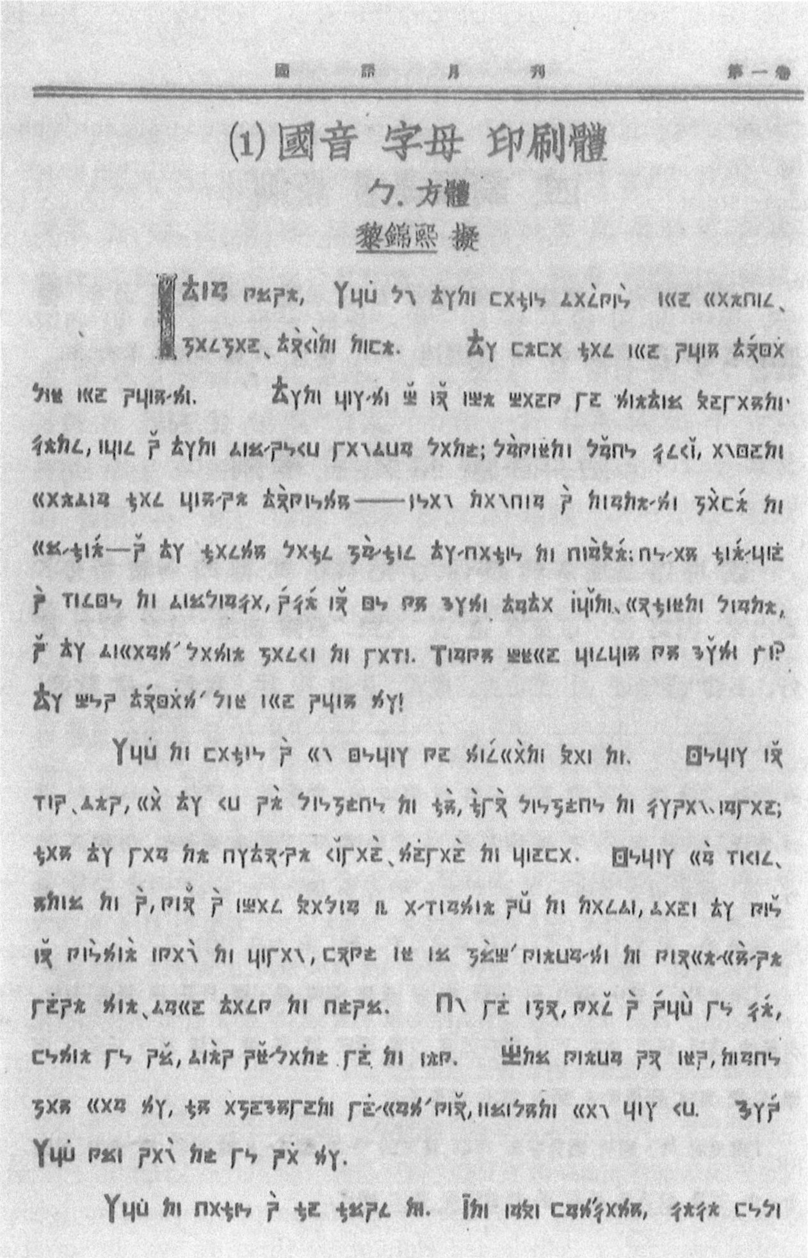
國語月刊 第一卷

(1) 國音字母印刷體

ㄅ. 方體

黎錦熙 擬

FIGURE 2.2 An article written and printed solely in National Phonetic Alphabet. *Source*: Li Jinxi, "Guoyin zimu yinshuati" 國音字母印刷體 [National Phonetic Alphabet typeface], *Guoyu yuekan* 1, no. 7 (1922): 52.

without using any Chinese characters.⁴⁹ In short, the 1920s were the dawn of an alphabetic age in China . . .

Or so it seemed. The educational and technological infrastructure necessary for script reform and language unification was conspicuously absent in the 1920s. The fonts were ready, but the Ministry of Education lacked the funds to subsidize printing presses, publish and distribute textbooks, train and dispatch teachers speaking one common language, and thereby raise a new generation of monolingually skilled minds. Chinese characters were still the dominant medium of instruction and communication, and without a strong centralized government, the NPA simply could not take off in the 1920s. Even the Shaanxi warlord Yan Xishan 閻錫山 (1883–1960), who wanted to employ the new script to build his own state, was unable to train enough teachers.⁵⁰ A countrywide propaganda for the NPA needed more than intellectual acumen.

That is when missionaries came back onto the scene. As a matter of fact, they had never truly left. Missionaries had been following the native scripts with particular enthusiasm, even though their input did not matter during the 1913 conference. Observing the increasing volume of script inventions since the 1890s, many of the missionaries had already begun to step away from the Roman alphabet and lean toward native inventions. Some of them were especially drawn to Wang Zhao's Mandarin Syllabary as it was the most popularized script since the early 1900s.

Sidney G. Peill (1878–1960) from the London Missionary Society was one of the first to recognize the strategic value of native inventions. Born in Madagascar to missionary parents, Peill was dispatched to north China in 1906. Employed as a medical missionary in Zhili, Peill realized the significance of literacy for missionary work in hospitals. Men and women from the countryside would spend three to four weeks in the hospital, which in the eyes of Peill was long enough to teach them the fundamentals of the Christian faith, but too short to make them literate and self-sustained in their studies.⁵¹ The solution for him, as for many other Christians during the preceding several decades, was a phonetic script. In the midst of native script inventions, he singled out the Mandarin Syllabary as his favorite. Together with his unnamed associates, Peill added eight more finals to Wang's script and clarified some pronunciation problems, ending up with fifty initials and twenty finals in total (figure 2.3).⁵² Peill was so certain of the Mandarin Syllabary's future victory that he even printed John's Gospel in the Mandarin

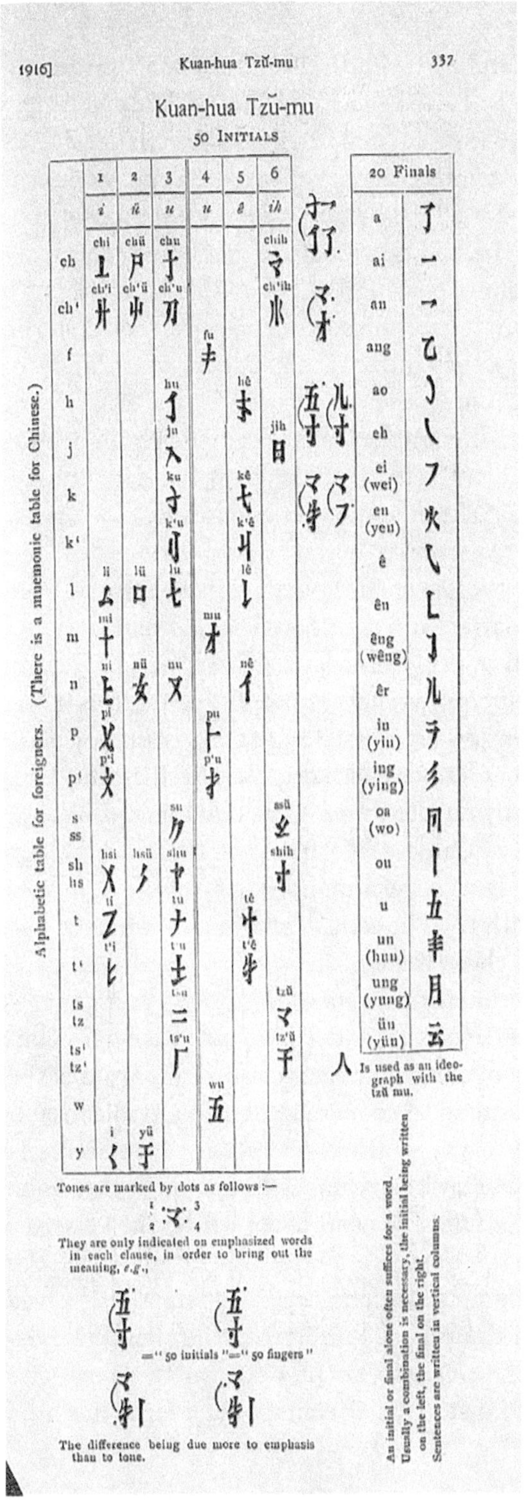

FIGURE 2.3 Peill's Mandarin Syllabary.
Source: "Kuan-hua Tzŭ-mu" [Mandarin Syllabary], *Chinese Recorder* (May 1916): 337.

Syllabary in 1916. Faith in the Mandarin Syllabary was in fact so high among the foreigners that Walter Caine Hillier, a British diplomat in China who later became a professor of Chinese at King's College, invented a typewriter, a linotype machine, and a Braille system for the blind based on the Mandarin Syllabary. The Remington Standard Typewriter Company adapted a typewriter for the same script, and the Linotype Company was ready to supply linotype machines in 1915 to enter a new market of knowledge in China.[53]

Once missionaries realized that the Chinese reformers had selected the NPA over the Mandarin Syllabary, they shifted their support accordingly. In October 1918, right before the promulgation of the NPA by the Ministry of Education, the missionary establishment decided to form the Phonetic Promotion Committee (PPC) to shoulder the final mission to alphabetize China—but this time, on Chinese terms.[54] The missionaries' embrace of the NPA lay at the intersection of two major trajectories. To start with, missionaries were never exclusively committed to the use of the Roman alphabet per se. Even before Peill, there were missionaries who considered the Roman alphabet an alien script for China and invented syllabaries that were easier to write with a Chinese brush.[55] Their reluctance to invent non-Roman scripts in the second half of the nineteenth century mainly stemmed from the typographical problems that came with them, since each script required casting new types, which could be financially burdensome.[56] The unexpected wave of native phoneticization in China by Chinese reformers was therefore a blessing for the missionaries. Having sensed the propitious wind of the NPA, they were quick to veer toward it with the Phonetic Promotion Committee and they selected Sydney Peill as its chairman.

The changes in the world missionary movement were also significant for the institutionalization of the PPC. Starting with the World Missionary Conference in Edinburgh in 1910, disparate Christian missions around the world had come to an understanding to cooperate. Continuation committees were subsequently formed to ensure the cooperation between different missions. In China, this regulatory body came to be known as the China Continuation Committee (CCC), under the auspices of which the Phonetic Promotion Committee came to life in 1918.[57] John R. Mott (1865–1955), the chairman of the Edinburgh Missionary Conference, was personally involved in the creation of the China Continuation Committee at the Shanghai Missionary Conference in 1913. The purpose of the CCC was to coordinate between different missions and distribute the missionary force in China more equally throughout the provinces in order to bolster evangelization. Even though the committee was not adequately representative of the missions, it still established a framework for the fragmented missionary work in China, and, more importantly, twenty-two of its sixty-five members were Chinese.[58]

One of the objectives of the CCC was to work with the Chinese government, especially in educational improvement. As Francis L. H. Pott, an American Episcopal missionary from Shanghai, noted, "the present Ministry of Education cannot do much for primary education. Our attitude must be such as to ensure the Government that we are not setting up a rival system, but that we want to help in this critical time in Chinese history. We must adopt, as far as possible, the Government curriculum and their school period."[59] The missionaries achieved their goal, for they were already in touch with some of the leading figures in the phoneticization movement. As a matter of fact, the formation of the Phonetic Promotion Committee *preceded* the official promulgation of the NPA, which proved the strong tie between the missionaries and the Chinese reformers. The PPC had on its advisory board figures like Wang Pu, the last chairman of the 1913 conference, and future Republican educators, such as Guo Bingwen 郭秉文 and Yan Jialin 嚴家麟.[60] Chinese scholars of the alphabet not only approved and supported the missionary movement, but also in part relied on it, for the organizational power of the CCC was central to the promotion of the NPA. The printing presses of the missionaries had been running for this purpose for decades and, given the government's lack of funds to propagate the system, they were the alphabet's best chance.

Sidney Peill began his duty as the chairman of the PPC in October 1918.[61] Given his extensive work with the Mandarin Syllabary and knowledge of native scripts, he seemed to be the best choice for leading the project. But after a few months of trying to promote the NPA, Peill grew increasingly frustrated with it. In a letter to Susie J. Garland, the secretary of the PPC, he noted that young boys and girls who learned the Mandarin Syllabary in a fortnight could not read the NPA even after a few months of study. Wang Zhao would have been proud to hear this:

> Dr. Warnhuis [vice-chairman and treasurer of the PPC] . . . told the secretary of the London Missionary Society . . . that I had said the Chu Yin [sic, NPA] was the best system for illiterates!! Also he said that I was teaching Chu Yin at my own

station instead of Kuan Hua Tzu Mu [sic, Mandarin Syllabary]!!! . . . That Chu Yin was being read fluently by the patients in my hospital!! . . . IN THE CHU YIN CLASS 105 HOURS OF INSTRUCTION ENDED IN COMPLETE FAILURE. . . . IN THE KUAN HUA TZU MU CLASS, 26 HOURS OF INSTRUCTION RESULTED IN COMPLETE SUCCESS IN EVERY CASE . . . NO ONE CAN BE MORE THOROUGHLY DISAPPOINTED THAN I AM TO FIND ALL MY YEARS CONFIRMED THAT CHU YIN TZU MU IS NO ADEQUATE SUBSTITUTE FOR KUAN HUA TZU MU.[62]

Fuming with anger and disbelief, Peill resigned and continued publishing in the Mandarin Syllabary instead.[63] With or without him, however, the momentum of the NPA in the first few years was dazzling. In 1919 alone, pamphlets describing the NPA's thirty-nine symbols and the Hundred Surnames were printed and sold in the thousands. In the following years, missionaries supplemented phonetic primers with phonetic cardboard games, syllabary charts, phonetic dictionaries with pictures, as well as scripture readers, beatitudes, and biblical parables. Evangelization was still the primary goal of missionaries, but now they could do it while working with the government (figures 2.4 and 2.5).

Despite a countrywide promotional campaign, linguistic problems ensued that the NPA could not overcome. China's linguistic diversity and the artificiality of national pronunciation constituted the greatest obstacles in the wide dissemination of the alphabet since the beginning. In certain places, such as in Eastern Shandong, Hankou, and in Wu regions, missionaries were adapting the NPA to local sounds, reportedly with "good success."[64] Especially in Shanghai and Suzhou, the PPC reported that it received an adaptation of the NPA in Wu languages from the members of the Ministry of Education. The technical details of this "adaptation" are not clear, but the report noted that these signs were not yet officially promulgated.[65] It is highly probable that these signs were based on the original NPA of the 1913 conference. Regardless of the details, however, it was significant that missionaries were still trying to enhance the NPA to enable the representation of non-Mandarin vernacular languages, and there were government officials who supported the plan. These enhanced versions of the NPA were printed by the missionaries themselves in the 1920s.

Not every language was as lucky, however. A report from Andong, Northern Jiangsu, noted the following in 1921: "In regard to the Chu-yin-tsi-mu [sic, NPA], its chief merit (universality) is also its chief difficulty. The words

FIGURE 2.4 "Illustrated posters to advertise the Phonetic Script and to show how the Bible meets the need of the individual and the nation." Courtesy of the Burke Library, Columbia University, Union Theological Seminary, PPCR.

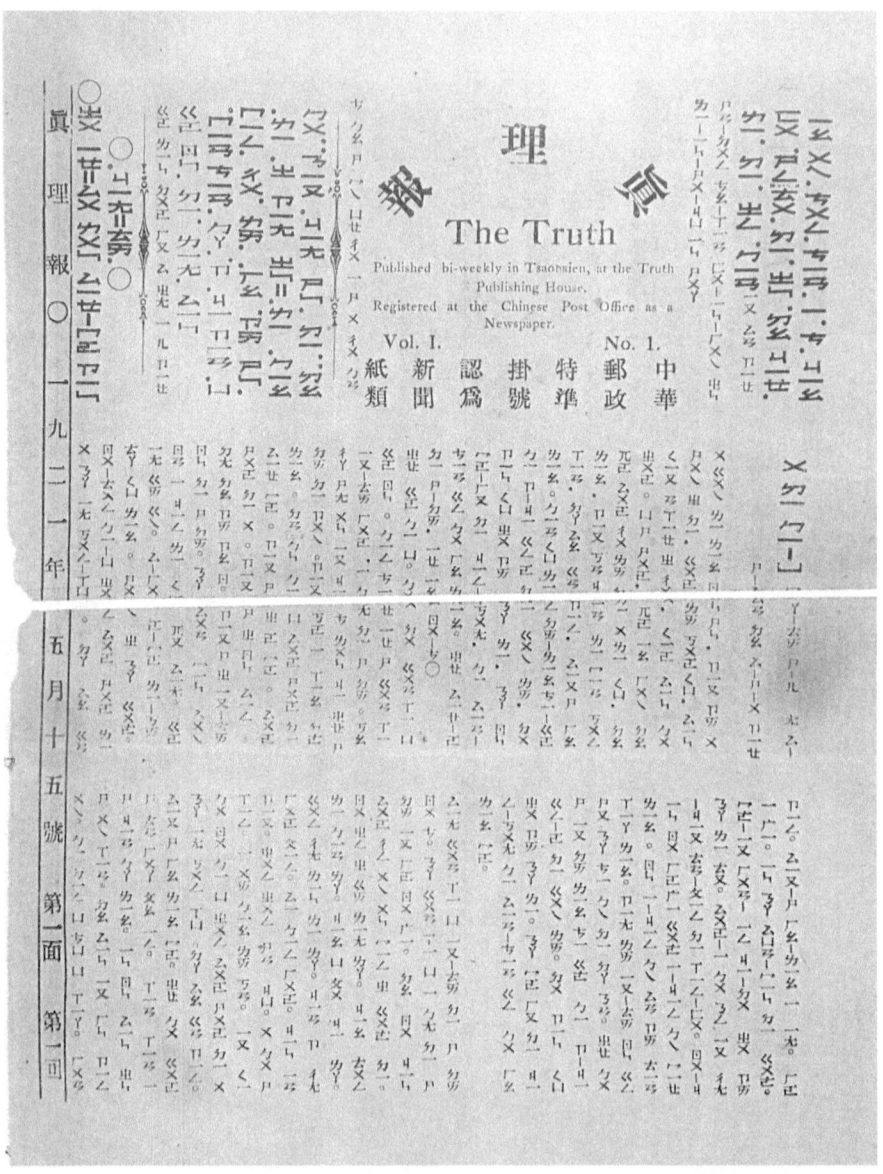

FIGURE 2.5 *The Truth*: Biweekly periodical published in the NPA (1921). Courtesy of the Burke Library, Columbia University, Union Theological Seminary, PPCR 1-1-9.

THE NATIONAL PHONETIC ALPHABET

Antung people stumble over most are those that are not exactly phonetic according to their way of pronouncing. Any system will meet with the same difficulty as soon as it is taught in districts where the pronunciation varies."[66] It was a correct statement. In Henan, too, the students of the alphabet did not have a good grasp of the national pronunciation, and therefore did not understand what was being read.[67] As late as 1925, Peill still noted the difficulties of disseminating simple medical information in the villages of northern China, for the alphabet was not compatible with the vernacular language.[68]

Besides the long-standing problem of vernacular languages, printing also stood as a physical challenge. The PPC was in touch with Commercial Press and Zhonghua Press, the two largest publishing houses at the time, to help produce large print runs. The missionaries were counting on the government's ability to build an educational infrastructure to teach the NPA, but the lack of strong government support was problematic for the success of the movement. For mass production, Dr. Fong Sec, then chairman of the PPC, urged Commercial Press to buy a Monotype machine, but the agents of the Monotype company in Shanghai were reluctant to invent a machine for the NPA. The company asked for a down payment without offering a timeline for delivery, and Commercial Press was unwilling to make the investment.[69] The nationwide success of the movement relied primarily on the government, but the financially challenged government was not willing to spend any money. The only institutions that consistently funded the movement were the Milton Steward Evangelistic Fund, the Women's Boards of Foreign Missions, and the British and Foreign Bible Society. Therefore, the furthest the movement could go was to print the New Testament.

The initial years of excitement were illusory. Funds were not enough to print and circulate primers, the government lacked the power to train teachers, and, perhaps most importantly, the artificiality of the national pronunciation turned out to be the largest impediment to the NPA's dissemination. Since the official announcement of the national pronunciation in 1918, there was already a general dissent within the Preparatory Committee toward it. In 1926, after years of failing to promote it, the commission decided to reverse its earlier policy and adopted the Beijing pronunciation as the new national pronunciation (*xin guoyin* 新國音).[70] This change landed a significant blow not only to southerners but also to missionaries. The Phonetic Promotion Committee's records show that in the second half of the

1920s, missionary involvement was considerably less than in the early years. In 1930, when the GMD, eager to build a party-state, reappropriated the NPA and changed its name from the National Phonetic Alphabet to Phonetic Symbols (Zhuyin fuhao), the alphabet became the main instrument of linguistic unification and government propaganda, as I will explain in chapter 6. In the following years, the party-state's expanding governmental apparatus determined a new future for Chinese scripts and languages, one in which missionary involvement was neither needed nor desired.

* * *

The transnational history of the NPA raises some important issues that challenge previous scholarship that described the history of alphabetization and phoneticization in China as the product of nineteenth-century social Darwinist discourses and evolutionary thought. Thomas Mullaney's work on the Chinese typewriter in particular stressed the Orientalist genealogy of alphabetization in China. Citing nineteenth- and twentieth-century Westerners who saw Chinese characters as "incompatible with modernity," Mullaney located the origins of Chinese alphabetization in Orientalist-cum-Darwinist discourses that were presumably pervasive among nineteenth- and twentieth-century Euro-American scholars. A history of Chinese typewriters, Mullaney argued, posed a definitive challenge to these Orientalist pretensions, as it showed that the Chinese information technologies were eventually built on Chinese characters themselves.[71]

The entanglement between missionaries and Chinese reformers in the history of the NPA, however, suggests a different framework for understanding the history of alphabetization in the information age. From nineteenth-century romanizations to the promulgation of the NPA, missionaries had an indisputable presence in Chinese script reforms, but it is hard to reduce their motivations to Orientalist discourses. The primary aim of missionaries was to reach the minds of the local communities in the quickest way possible, and their assumptions about the so-called efficiency of the Roman alphabet stemmed from a particularly European historical experience that the missionaries wanted to replicate in China, without recognizing the historically distinct conditions of the Chinese languages and characters. But unlike Max Müller's overtly racist attitude toward local languages and scripts in India, many of the missionaries in China had an ambiguous relationship with the Chinese writing system. Some even romanticized the Chinese characters as being better than the alphabet, which was reminiscent of seventeenth-century European philosophers' transcendental ruminations about Chinese writing. After the 1850s, while romanization was well under way, some missionaries were still skeptical about the value of the Roman alphabet, either preferring to use the Chinese characters or inventing new phonetic scripts that could be written with the Chinese brush. For many missionaries, phonetic scripts were not necessarily superior to the Chinese characters; they were seemingly more expedient for evangelical purposes among vernacular linguistic communities. But regardless of their stance, we should bear in mind that neither missionary works nor Orientalist discourses about Chinese characters had any serious impact on Chinese reformers until the late nineteenth century.

Chinese reformers' appropriation of missionary works and Western discourses of progress must be grounded in the historical specificity of the decades from the 1890s to the 1920s. As already noted, reformers' primary concern was what they perceived to be inefficiency and scarcity in mental and clerical labor in an industrializing economy that imposed alphabetic labor time as the benchmark for efficiency. The so-called backwardness of Chinese characters stemmed from a modernizing political economy of information transmission and knowledge production, the impact of which was especially clear at the turn of the twentieth century. Early Republican reformers' plan to unify language, and to invent the NPA to do so, was a product of the late-Qing search for efficiency to facilitate the flow of information in an emergent nation. The reformers, in other words, did not invent the NPA because of an internalized self-Orientalizing belief in the backwardness of Chinese characters, but because of the historically specific circumstances in the global age of information. That is why even staunch nativist reformers like Zhang Taiyan had to surrender to a phonocentric hegemony and invent phonetic scripts in order to become part of an international world order. The NPA was invented precisely for that purpose, and with it, a hybrid information culture began to form in China—one that included both Chinese characters and a newly minted Chinese alphabet.

The politics of linguistic representation were particularly thorny and continued to dominate the debates around scripts in the decades to come. But apart from language, the politics of efficiency manifested in other fields as well. One of the immediate outcomes of the NPA was reformers' awareness of the sociotechnical ecology that scripts were embedded in. An alphabetic re-skilling of the population, it turned out, required not only the invention of a national pronunciation and language but also printing technologies, schools, curricula, teachers, and textbooks. In an environment where Chinese characters were still the dominant medium of communication, the supposed superiority of the alphabet came under intense scrutiny. As a result, the infrastructural and linguistic imbroglio in the early 1920s prompted a new movement that supported stepping away from alphabetization and instead rethinking information politics through the reform of the Chinese characters themselves.

THREE

Basic Chinese

Cognitive Management and Mass Literacy

CHINESE SCRIPT REFORMS, as the previous two chapters have shown, were at the forefront of a global information age that challenged the sociotechnical practices of communication in China. The response to this challenge came in various forms, as some reformers called for replacing the Chinese characters with a phonetic script, some aimed to follow the Japanese model and have an auxiliary phonetic script, and others embraced Esperanto as the ultimate solution. But while the proposals showed a great deal of variety, the reformers all shared a common desire: to increase efficiency in mental and clerical labor and expedite access to information. Script reforms, in a nutshell, were taking place within a new economy of knowledge.

The precondition for developing a modern knowledge economy was mass literacy, a goal that all script reformers were aiming for since the late nineteenth century. By the 1920s, mass literacy had become one of the central projects for all reform-minded intellectuals. The leaders of the movement, such as James Yen (Yan Yangchu 晏陽初, 1890–1990) and Tao Xingzhi 陶行知 (1891–1946), along with many other May Fourth intellectuals, believed that illiteracy plagued close to 90 percent of the population and constituted the greatest obstacle to building a nation. The extant literature on the history of mass literacy has rightly taken issue with these estimates. Evelyn Rawski, for instance, suggested that 30 percent to 45 percent of men and 2 percent to 10 percent of women "knew how to read and write" in the late nineteenth century.[1] A recent wave of scholarship, moreover, has stepped away from determining the number of literate people and instead emphasized the significance of the mass literacy campaigns as a *political* project that was tied to ideas of nation building and citizenship.[2] While informed by these works, this chapter approaches the history of mass literacy from yet another perspective: mass literacy as a matter of communication engineering and information management.

Mass literacy, I would like to suggest, was a new way of structuring information and labor during an age of industrializing knowledge economies. The development of mass literacy in China was directly linked to the question of script, but it was not always tied to an alphabet. Many of the reformers, even while they worked toward alphabetizing China, were simultaneously trying to rationalize the Chinese writing system itself according to the modernist principles of efficiency and productivity. The duty at hand for reformers was to reduce the number of Chinese characters from a frequently used set of ten thousand (especially used for telegraphic communications) to a most frequently used "basic" set of one thousand, which could in theory make a subject literate enough to fulfill basic needs, such as accounting, letter writing, and reading simple texts. While there were imperial examples for literary primers that used around a thousand characters, such as *The Thousand Character Classic* (*Qianzi wen* 千字文), the method of selecting the most frequently used characters was different in the modern period.[3] As opposed to imperial primers, modern textbooks were composed of characters carefully selected through a statistical analysis of large sets of linguistic databases, such as newspapers, novels, journal articles, short stories, and so on. The making of textbooks and literary primers, in other words, was an act of communication engineering that involved new scientific approaches to the collation and management of information.

Bracketing the debates over phonetic scripts, this chapter examines the rationalization of Chinese characters themselves. The issue of labor efficiency in a modernizing economy of knowledge was critical in this process, compelling us to focus once again on the conditions generated by a new political economy of information. On the one hand, these conditions gave rise to phonetic scripts such as the NPA. On the other hand, the search for efficiency in mental and clerical labor also led to a movement to reform the Chinese characters themselves, both through statistically measuring them, which is the subject of this chapter, and through simplifying them, the subject of the next one.

The project to engineer a basic set of Chinese characters was one component of a wider measurement movement in Chinese education, and it was closely tied to the measurement movement that American behavioral psychologists spearheaded in the United States. Indeed, the Chinese mass literacy movement in the 1920s and 1930s was deeply intertwined with Euro-American theories of psychology, language, and communication engineering. Some of the leading figures of the mass literacy movement were first-generation Chinese psychologists who were trained in the United States and appropriated the Western methods of communication engineering for the instruction of Chinese characters for the masses. Psychological and linguistic research conducted by Chinese psychologists and educators was therefore remarkably similar to the research undertaken by their American mentors, who prioritized industrial efficiency in mental labor. Chinese educational psychologists and their experiments were at the forefront of creating a "basic" Chinese, the exact definition of which turned out to be a highly contested subject.

This chapter further expands the global history of Chinese script reforms by unearthing the transnational scientific networks behind the mass literacy movement. It in particular investigates the intertwined history of mass literacy and cognitive optimization in China and the United States in the 1920s and 1930s. I start with a brief overview of Taylorist psychology in the United States to explain how the scientific premises of American behavioral psychologists resonated with Frederick Taylor's *The Principles of Scientific Management* (1911), which preached the use of scientific methodologies to increase efficiency and productivity in industrial economy through disciplining the bodies and minds of workers. American psychologists, the mentors of the first generation of Chinese educational psychologists, approached the question of the human mind from a similar perspective and discarded the value of qualitative experience for the purpose of inquiring into the mechanics of increased efficiency and productivity in mental work. Their scientific approach to language and writing was indicative of the industrializing knowledge economy in the United States, with its demand for a bigger and more efficient mental labor force. In other words, the psychological enterprise was a scientific attempt at cognitive management.

American psychologists' involvement in the cognitive management of the nation was an inspiration for Chinese psychologists, who experimented with the Chinese writing system using similar tools. The second section explores the Sino-American measurement movement, which included not only statistical measurements to increase Chinese literacy but also intelligence tests to quantify mental capacities for the purpose of organizing cognitive labor at massive scales. The two kinds of measurements were indeed closely related—the psychologists who translated and implemented intelligence tests in China also concocted frequency analyses of Chinese characters. The third section focuses on James Yen's Thousand-Character Primers (*qianzi ke* 千字課), which were an especially famous product of this era. Composed of a basic vocabulary of around one thousand characters, Yen's primers built on Chinese psychologists' character-frequency analyses in order to expedite mass literacy campaigns in the countryside, in cities, and among armies. Indeed, Thousand-Character Primers were a peculiar microcosmic specimen of the Chinese knowledge economy. They championed efficiency in learning and were ideal for the creation of mental laborers who could be indoctrinated by national and moral values while acquiring the necessary skills for accounting and letter writing, i.e., for basic knowledge work.

I devote the last section to a little-known work of a well-known literary figure, Hong Shen 洪深 (1894–1955), who published *The Use and Instruction of 1100 Basic Chinese Characters* (*Yi qian yi bai ge jiben hanzi shiyong jiaoxuefa* 一千一百個基本漢字使用教學法) in 1936. Hong Shen's Basic Chinese was a cogent critique of James Yen's primers, which were by then backed by the GMD's right-wing ideologues. Much like James Yen and Chinese psychologists, Hong's book was also a product of transnational scientific networks. He was in particular inspired by Charles K. Ogden and Ivor A. Richards's Basic English, a linguistic (and later, imperial) project that sought to eliminate redundancy in language by reducing English vocabulary to a basic set of 850 words that could communicate all meaning that the English language was capable of producing. For Hong, the communication philosophy of Basic English offered a way to rethink the purpose of literacy in Chinese. Hong's Basic Chinese was an effort to save literacy from being solely a project to satisfy the demands of a knowledge economy tied to the politics of a party-state. For Hong, James Yen's primers only helped create passive participants who mindlessly partook in an ideology that reproduced an unequal system. Hong's Basic Chinese, on the other hand, employed cognitive efficiency in a critical way and argued that his limited vocabulary could help create active political agents instead of passive participants by instilling in the subjects' minds an awareness of the socioeconomic contradictions of global capitalism and imperialism. In the highly politicized and polarized environment of the 1930s, Hong's project, despite its extremely limited circulation, provided an alternative way to think not only about the meaning of literacy, but also the place of characters within a new knowledge economy at large.

Taylorist Hands and Minds: The Scientific Principles of Cognitive Management

In 1911, Frederick Winslow Taylor published one of the most influential texts of the twentieth century, *The Principles of Scientific Management*. In Taylor's words, the United States of America in the early twentieth century was plagued by "national inefficiency" in all matters of daily life, and the remedy to this epidemic was the development of a management culture based on scientific principles. Efficiency and productivity were the passwords to a new industrial system that could eliminate labor waste through the employment of scientific methods in managing the human-machine ecology. A colleague of Taylor, Frank Bunker Gilbreth (1868–1924), elaborated on Taylor's principles with his motion studies, fatigue studies, and time studies, all of which used laboratory methods and "measures supplied by psychology" to optimize the output of what he called "the human element" in industrial production.[4] Gilbreth treated motion, fatigue, and time as engineering problems, the mechanics of which could be best understood in a laboratory setting, where the human element's physiological movements could be recorded. Scientific inquiries into the psychophysiology of labor, in Taylor's and Gilbreth's formulations, could increase industrial productivity and cure the plague of inefficiency once and for all by disciplining the bodies and minds of the laborers, and synchronizing them with the tools of production.

Clerical labor was part of this industrial economy. The rising need for clerical labor in various industries, combined with a movement for public education and mass literacy, put pressure on language and its inscription as the primary means for supplying industrial and educational demands, which were sometimes inseparable indeed. "The industrial world is becoming more and more definite in its requirements for industrial training," noted Gilbreth, "[which] is making it possible for all types of schools to give their pupils a training which enables them to fit into working conditions without the customary, preliminary jolt, and months and years of judgement." This training consisted of making every student "finger-wise," i.e., "training his muscles so that they respond easily and quickly to demands for skilled work."[5] "Finger training" was a central component of "motion economy," which sought to save energy and time to increase productivity. Gilbreth even curated a Fatigue Museum to draw attention to the problem of fatigue-caused reduction of output in industries as well as in schools and showcased different kinds of chairs that helped reduce workers and students' fatigue.[6] This industrialist approach to education was already gaining currency as one of the most "innovative" trends in American public education since the early 1900s, best exemplified by the infamous and highly controversial Gary Plan in Indiana, which was praised by the Rockefeller Foundation as the future of American education, but despised by others who claimed that it trained children "to be an efficient cog in the industrial machine."[7]

The complexity of the debates about American public education aside, the industrialist view of education resonated finely with the early twentieth-century American psychology of education. Motion studies, finger training, and the scientific measures that Gilbreth drew on were already put under scientific scrutiny by American psychologists at leading institutions such as Columbia University's Teachers College, Brown University, the University of Chicago, and Stanford University, among others. Indeed, American psychologists played a leading role in building what I would like to call the scientific principles of cognitive management, which experimented with bodily skills for clerical labor and with cognitive skills such as memory, language acquisition, and learning in general for the purpose of optimizing mental labor. A mechanical understanding of the mind was crucial for quantifying cognitive skills and increasing efficiency in intellectual work of all sorts, for children as well as for adults. Studies of language and writing came at the forefront of these experiments. Cognitive management inquired into the mechanics of language acquisition and endeavored to formulate a psychological theory of literacy that was capable of training a mental labor force prepared for the demands of an industrial knowledge economy. The underlying motivation in cognitive management was increased efficiency in the financial management of education and the reconceptualization of students as workers—not only as potential future laborers for industries, but as mental laborers and knowledge workers whose acquisition and production of information had to be economized. Psychology of literacy and learning, in other words, followed the same assumptions about efficiency and productivity that Frederick Taylor had championed in *The Principles of Scientific Management*.

The psychological experiments regarding literacy took different shapes. Charles H. Judd (1873–1946), a eugenicist psychologist at Yale who was among the pioneers of the scientific measurement movement in education, measured the "complex muscular movement[s]" of hands, fingers, arms, and shoulders to understand the "division of labor" in the production of writing.[8] Edmund Huey (1870–1913), who shared Judd's concerns, conducted similar experiments for reading at the turn of the century.[9] He compared horizontal and vertical reading, calculated the speed of silent reading, experimented with the importance of "irs and as etter of ord in ensin eanin" (first and last letters of words in sensing meaning), and used ophthalmological tests to determine the best form of typography to optimize the physiological energy of the eye. His findings culminated in the magisterial *Psychology and Pedagogy of Reading* in 1908, which became a landmark volume in the development of the psychology of literacy.[10] These studies were later echoed by Chinese psychologists as well.[11]

The psychology of learning quickly evolved into a field of its own, dubbed educational psychology, and was spearheaded by Edward Lee Thorndike (1874–1949) at Columbia University's Teachers College, where most of the Chinese psychologists received education. Thorndike was one of the leading figures in behavioral psychology, which concerned itself with what was measurable and quantifiable, and thus eliminated subjective experience from psychological equation. An extremely prolific academic, Thorndike ventured into virtually every field that related to the psychology of learning, from intelligence tests to theories of mental fatigue. Like his contemporaries, he had an early penchant for standardizing handwriting, a field that flourished after his seminal invention, the graphometer. In 1910, pioneering the studies in the scientific management of education, Thorndike developed a scale for measuring the quality of handwriting, called a graphometer, to be employed for children from the fifth to the eighth grade and for adult women. On his scale, which went from 0 to 18, typewriters occupied the highest ranks (15 to 18), and he believed that children who reached the quality of 13 should be taught to write with a typewriter, for the effort to increase one's writing quality from 13 to above 14 required serious labor and was thus uneconomic.[12]

A rival handwriting scale was soon invented by Leonard P. Ayres (1879–1946), the director of the Division of Education of the Russell Sage

Foundation from 1908 to 1920, whose statistical studies aimed to increase efficiency and rational calculation in the decisions of the Council of National Defense during the First World War.[13] Ayres was a statistician by training, and during his tenure at the Russell Sage Foundation, he also put his knowledge to practice in linguistic statistics and the scientific management of education. He was one of the first figures to have come up with a Basic English vocabulary, composed of a thousand most frequently used words, which influenced not only the famous Basic English of Ogden and Richards, but also Chinese linguists and psychologists. In 1912, Ayres published *A Scale for Measuring the Quality of Handwriting of School Children*, which adopted "legibility" as the criterion.[14] Thorndike had used the judgements of readers to come up with a scale of general merit, while Ayres measured "the amount of time required to read with a given degree of accuracy a given amount of matter written in the handwriting being studied."[15] Soon, new handwriting scales were invented by various psychologists for practical use in schools, although none of them reached the fame of Thorndike's or Ayres's.[16]

Be it "merit" or "legibility," both scales, along with many others that were invented later, shared a common assumption about the purpose of writing. Manifestations of individual psyche in writing simply did not matter for behavioral psychologists and statisticians. The value of writing lay in the capacity of the individual to produce a standard form of legible writing, accountable data. In contrast to a contemporaneous movement known as graphology, which analyzed personalities through specimens of handwritings, Thorndike and others eliminated "personality" from the hand's movement on paper.[17] There was no mind-body dichotomy, just motor skills necessary for recording information; there was no introspective imagery, only letters on the paper. Writing, in other words, lost significance as a mental process, and became an automated motor skill that behavioral psychology helped optimize. What was left of penmanship was machinery.

Cognitive Management: Intelligence Tests and the Educational Measurement Movement

When first-generation Chinese psychologists, such as Chen Heqin 陳鶴琴 (1892–1982), arrived at the Teachers College at Columbia University, psychology of efficiency was the trademark of the discipline, with numerous studies on handwriting, word counts, speed of writing, typing, reading, and, most importantly, the measurement of intelligence.[18] The use of intelligence tests, first invented by Alfred Binet (1857–1911) and Théodore Simon (1873–1961) in France in 1906, reached its zenith in the United States during the First World War, and they were managed by the same psychologists who championed the rationalization of writing, like Edward Lee Thorndike. It was not a coincidence that the Chinese psychologists who devised the first literacy tests, analyzed character frequencies, and experimented with punctuation marks and the simplification of Chinese characters were also deeply involved in the promotion of intelligence tests for the reorganization of cognitive labor on a national scale.

The complex history of the quantification of intelligence has been the subject of countless works that explained intelligence tests' intimate relationship with eugenics, philosophical inquiries, and the highly racialized techniques of phrenology, cephalometers, and anthropometers.[19] While in agreement with these works, I would like to suggest that the invention of scales to measure human intelligence was also a product of the industrialist desire to optimize mental labor through reorganizing it on a mass scale according to innate cognitive skills. Alfred Binet's works provide the best example, although they have been glossed over in previous studies. The earlier publications of Binet, the famed inventor of the first intelligence scale, show that he was concerned more with *travail intellectuel* than the quantification of intelligence.[20] He was especially troubled by the problem of mental fatigue. His book *La Fatigue Intellectuelle* (1898) was one of the first to make mental work and fatigue a central problem in experimental psychology. It might thus be fruitful to reconsider the invention of intelligence tests as the product of an information age that redefined humans' relationship to knowledge work and mental labor. The measurement of intelligence was part of an intellectual movement to *manage* the mind, both in terms of optimizing physiological givens, such as the eyes and the hands, and of creating the optimum social environment that corresponded to the participants' "naturally" determined mental capacities.

Intelligence tests became popular in the United States, especially during and after the First World War, when they were entangled with the American military-industrial complex. But anthropometric testing had a longer history in America. Having grown out of nineteenth-century phrenology, anthropometry enjoyed popularity especially in post–Civil War America, and was complemented by mental tests in the 1890s.[21] It was not until 1916, when Stanford psychologist Lewis M. Terman completed the revision of the Binet-Simon Intelligence Scale, known as the Stanford-Binet, that the use of intelligence tests became widespread in the United States. The Stanford-Binet also introduced the most famous concept in intelligence tests: the intelligence quotient (IQ), the ratio between mental age and chronological age.[22] Terman's IQ turned intelligence into a standardized, universal, and quantifiable measure applicable to humans of all ages and races. Even more importantly, its invention coincided with the onset of the Great War, and the scientific universalism of psychological tests turned IQ tests into an integral part of American military management. In 1917, one of the subcommittees formed under the Psychology Committee of the National Research Council, headed by Major Robert M. Yerkes, prepared procedures for the psychological examination of new recruits in the army.[23] Given the number of officers, "group mental tests" were devised to measure up to five hundred people at one sitting. Apart from the Army Alpha Test, which was used for literate recruits, an Army Beta Test was also devised to measure the mental capabilities of illiterates or non-English speakers.

The statistical work for these mental tests was undertaken by psychologists whom the reader is now familiar with, such as Lewis M. Terman from Stanford, Edward L. Thorndike from the Teachers College at Columbia University, and others. Major Yerkes was especially satisfied with the results: "The service of psychological examining in the army has conspicuously advanced mental engineering, and has assured the immediate application of methods of mental rating to the problems of classification and assignment in our educational institutions and our industries."[24] After the successful employment of the Army Alpha Test, the National Research Council devised a new system of mental tests for educational institutions. The General Education Board complied, and in 1920, complete scales were finalized and issued by the same psychologists.[25]

When the first generation of Chinese psychologists arrived in the United States, they found themselves in the midst of a booming discipline and were impressed by the American advancements in mental engineering. Intelligence tests, they believed, had implications for settling disputes over racial differences, creating a better army, reforming social problems, devising better employment strategies, and creating a scientific system of education.[26]

Rather than using the test to justify racial bias and segregation, as was happening in the United States, Chinese psychologists used intelligence tests to argue for racial equality in intelligence, and even for measuring the IQs of Chinese historical figures.[27] A telling example of this concern was Lin Chuanding's (1939) work, *A Historiometric Study of Thirty-Four Eminent Chinese*, which used a complicated—and rather inadequate—set of biographical data to calculate the IQs of "Chinese geniuses," all of whom were famous historical figures, such as Li Bai and Liang Qichao. Even the title of Lin's book mirrored similar American studies, especially James McKeen Cattell's statistical work on "eminent men."[28] At stake was the cognitive sovereignty of the Chinese nation, and the universal methodology offered by intelligence tests became the ground on which Chinese psychologists claimed an equal status with Western nations.

The historical need to optimize mental labor was at least as important as refuting racism-induced Orientalist misconceptions about intelligence. The first Chinese intelligence test was devised by Chen Heqin and Liao Shicheng 廖世承 (1892–1970) in 1922 to satisfy educational needs. Chen and Liao were among the first generation of Chinese educational psychologists who gained a degree in the United States. Chen Heqin, a native of Zhejiang, graduated from Tsinghua in 1914, and pursued higher degrees first at Johns Hopkins and, starting in 1917, at Columbia University's Teachers College, where he studied with the leading behavioral and educational psychologists of the period, such as Edward Thorndike, Paul Monroe, and John Dewey. Also an active manager of kindergartens, Chen prolifically experimented and published on educational and children's psychology throughout his long career that spanned six decades in mainland China. A pioneer in the field of psychology, he also took part in the mass literacy movement under the GMD, and later under the Chinese Communist Party (CCP) in the 1950s. Liao Shicheng, on the other hand, was a colleague of Chen from Tsinghua who pursued a higher degree in educational psychology at Brown University. Together with Chen, he played a leading role in the development of psychology as a discipline in China in the 1920s. Chen was invited by Guo Bingwen 郭秉文 (1880–1969), the president of Southeastern University in Nanjing, to teach psychology at Southeastern University and Nanjing Teachers College, where Chen Heqin and Lu Zhiwei 陸志韋 (1894–1970), another psychologist from the University of Chicago who translated the revised Binet-Simon Intelligence Tests into Chinese, formed the first department of psychology.[29] When Liao Shicheng joined them in Nanjing, Chen and Liao set out to write the first Chinese intelligence test.

Given the priority accorded to education, it was not surprising that the calculation of human intelligence came to be intimately connected with the psychology of literacy. Chen and Liao claimed that there were two kinds of intelligence tests. One measured natural intelligence, the other, one's abilities. Natural intelligence depended on the amount of peripheral nerves in one's brain. It was completely innate and had nothing to do with the environment.[30] The "abilities" to memorize, observe, imagine, and create, on the other hand, were not predetermined, and could be improved with the right tools, such as new primers or new writing systems. Intelligence tests sorted out the naturally inclined from the naturally disinclined; literacy tests devised techniques to increase one's ability to learn. Implemented on a national scale, psychological experiments could offer the organizational tools to manage cognitive labor on a mass scale.

The blueprint for Chinese mental tests came from the above-mentioned American psychologists, as the two academic cultures were closely intertwined. Chen and Liao devised different tests for use depending on the subject's age or level of literacy.[31] They believed in the necessity to separate school classes according to levels of intelligence, create a special class for gifted students, and use tests for school entrance examinations—all practices being carried out in various ways in American institutions, such as Columbia University's "freshman tests." The first mental tests for entrance examinations were put in effect at Nanjing Teachers College in 1920. In 1921, Peking Teachers College also started using intelligence tests; and soon, Peking Women's Teachers College followed.[32] The educational measurement movement and the development of intelligence tests intensified when William McCall (1891–1982) from Columbia University's Teachers College visited China in 1922–1923 to devise an intelligence test in collaboration with Chinese educators and psychologists, some of whom he knew from Columbia. McCall was one of the most ardent supporters of the psychological measurement movement, which, he believed, had a particular philosophy—one that he condensed into fourteen theses and explained in detail in his magnum opus, *How to Measure in Education* (1922). The first of his theses was Thorndike's famous dictum: "Whatever exists at all, exists in some amount." McCall despised "quality" in education: "There is never a quantity which does not measure some quality, and never an existing quality that is non-quantative [sic]," he noted, "even our halos vary in diameter." Personal initiative, judgment of relative values, leadership, poetic appreciation, and every other product of "mental machinery" could be quantitatively measured, McCall argued.[33]

McCall stayed in China for a year and worked with the National Association for the Advancement of Education (Zhonghua jiaoyu gaijin she 中華教育改進社), headed by Tao Xingzhi, another graduate of the Teachers College at Columbia University and a pioneering figure in the promotion of mass literacy. Tao and McCall both had strong faith in the value of adopting scientific measurements to take progressive leaps in education, and they were further aided by other psychologists, including Chen Heqin, Lu Zhiwei, and Liao Shicheng.[34] Under the direction of Lu Zhiwei, the revised Binet-Simon Intelligence Test was devised, and 1,400 male and female students between the ages of three and twelve were selected from cities and districts surrounding Nanjing for the first implementation of the test. In the following years, intelligence tests were used in schools in Beijing, Nanjing, and Shanghai as a measure for mental classification, and, during the war, in the army and the police force.[35]

The intimate connection between intelligence testing, mass literacy, and industrialization is recognizable in the achievements of James Yen. A colleague of Tao Xingzhi, James Yen spearheaded the establishment of the Chinese Mass Education Association (Zhonghua pingmin jiaoyu cujin hui 中華平民教育促進會) in 1923 and initiated the Mass Education Movement (MEM). Beginning in 1927, James Yen and the Chinese Mass Education Association started employing intelligence tests to separate classes, form groups for different purposes, chart the future accomplishments of any given student, determine what student was fit for what kind of industry, measure how hardworking a student was (depending on their level of intelligence), and discover "genius."[36] As newly drafted soldiers were coming into the territories where the movement was flourishing, James Yen and his colleagues also started visiting the barracks and giving intelligence tests to soldiers to train appropriate officer-teachers for the army. In one instance, James Yen noted that sixty of the best officers were selected as teachers for the division, given a "rather strenuous process of mass-education methods of teaching," which included the use of projectors and cards instead of books. "This mass method [without books]," James Yen wrote in a letter, "has proved most effective with the soldiers and aroused a tremendous amount of interest among the whole Division.... One of them remarked that if all the soldiers could be given a chance for mass education China would have an entirely different type of army."[37]

The measurement movement in education continued uninterrupted in the following years, as measurements offered the know-how to manage education and spread literacy. Intelligence tests were just one aspect of the greater measurement movement that aimed to reorganize cognitive labor on a national scale and economize it through adjusting the tools of learning to mental skills. Quantification of intelligence was a powerful method for the organization of labor according to age and innate cognitive skills, but it did not help develop one's abilities, which was the territory of education. The penchant for measurement that fueled the MEM was also instrumental in changing the patterns of studying and learning, as the prophets of modern education deemed economy of time in learning a prerequisite for expanding literacy. The dominant obstacle, however, was the overwhelming number of Chinese characters. On what basis was the number of Chinese characters going to be reduced to economize their acquisition and increase the mental productivity of literate subjects? Who was going to choose the characters? And who could confirm that a given set of basic Chinese characters was more appropriate than thousands of other potential sets? With the onset of the MEM, psychologists and educators all saw the vast number of Chinese characters as a psychological barrier to mental efficiency. The leaders of MEM and Thorndike-trained Chinese psychologists were among the members of the crisis-resolution team.

Knowledge Work: James Yen, the Mass Education Movement, and Thousand-Character Primers

The measurement movement in education utilized psychological techniques of measurement to reorganize mental labor on a mass scale and create a social and educational environment that would be most suitable for cognitive optimization. Cognitive management through psychological experimentation was simultaneously accompanied by statistical analyses of characters to devise the most efficient method to sync the population with the information that surrounded it. The end result was Thousand-Character Primers (*qianzi ke*). Just as intelligence tests were aiming to reorganize society based on cognitive skills, Thousand-Character Primers were providing the necessary informational fuel to create knowledge workers to satisfy the needs of a growing knowledge economy.

One of the first systematic attempts to reduce the number of characters was undertaken by the above-mentioned James Yen, who employed intelligence tests in the classrooms and the barracks. Indeed, James Yen's Mass Education Movement was sponsored by the Rockefeller Foundation's China Program from 1934 to 1945.[38] From one perspective, the MEM's philosophy of education was not much different from what Gilbreth wanted to achieve in public education, i.e., economizing education while creating productive laborers for new industries. Familiarity with new technologies and the acquisition of the necessary skillset for becoming an efficient worker were the main pillars of the MEM's philosophy, too. With its commitment to the scientific principles of cognitive management, the MEM was an unprecedented effort to prepare the biggest mental labor force that would drive the engines of the Chinese industrial knowledge economy forward.

James Yen is remembered as a pioneer in mass education and rural reconstruction. A native of Sichuan, Yen worked in France and studied at Yale, and, on his return to China in 1920, he launched the MEM to turn all Chinese into literate citizens. James Yen's fame is largely due to the Ting Hsien Experiment, the Rockefeller-supported rural reconstruction experiment in Ding County, Hebei Province, which demonstrated that life in rural China could be socially, culturally, and economically developed through an implementation of Yen's liberal philosophy of education. The Ting Hsien Experiment ran from 1926 to 1937, and later became a model for rural reconstruction across the world in France, Mexico, the Philippines, the United States, Cuba, Colombia, and Ghana.[39] James Yen and his MEM enjoyed popularity not only among the higher echelons of the GMD—Generalissimo Chiang Kai-shek himself invited James Yen to foster rural reconstruction across China—but also among the international community. Most remarkably, Pearl Buck took a personal interest in Yen's rural experiments, which she popularized in the English-speaking world with *Tell the People: Talks with James Yen About the Mass Education Movement* (1945).

James Yen's long career started in Boulogne, France. Dispatched by the YMCA as part of an effort to provide services to Chinese migrant laborers in France during the war, James Yen arrived in Boulogne in 1918, and his initial contact with illiterate Chinese laborers ignited his lifelong desire to expand literacy.⁴⁰ This was the first time that James Yen devised a Thousand-Character Primer. The primer was influenced by the traditional *Thousand Character Classic* but involved a list of characters that were more applicable to vernacular use. James Yen's Thousand-Character Primer later became the foundation on which he launched the Mass Education Movement in China, and by the end of the 1920s, he upgraded his primers according to the statistical work undertaken, as fate would have it, by Chen Heqin, the Columbia graduate who brought intelligence tests to China.

Chen Heqin was the first to do a comprehensive statistical word count in Chinese, taking his American counterparts as his model. Apart from Leonard P. Ayres's study mentioned above, others had undertaken similar counts, the most comprehensive of which was Edward Thorndike's word count in English with a total database of 4,565,000 words, within which he had counted 10,000 individual words. Chen Heqin was inspired by these examples and conducted the first systematic character count of Chinese in a similar manner.⁴¹ He created a database of 554,478 characters from various newspapers, journals, primary school textbooks, novels, and other miscellaneous publications, and counted 4,261 most frequently used individual characters. In 1928, he listed these characters according to their frequencies, and published his findings. Inspired by Chen's examples, other such studies followed. In 1929, Ao Hongde 敖弘德 conducted a very similar study and came up with 4,339 characters, supplementing Chen's list with 78 more.⁴² In 1930, a certain Wang Wenxin 王文新 further analyzed 601,345 characters from student essays and books in order to "economize learning" (*jingji xuexi* 經濟學系). By then, the Department of Educational Research at Zhongshan University had already calculated that the time necessary to learn all the characters encountered in Chinese education was 362,880 minutes. Wang wanted to maximize the learning ability of students by separating the number of characters according to different school grades and determining how many characters should be taught from first through sixth grade. He collected a total of 207,246 characters from student essays written in sixty-four schools in Guangdong, Guangxi, Zhejiang, Jiangsu, and Hebei provinces. He added another 303,941 characters to the list by including language textbooks published by Commercial Press, Zhonghua Press, and World Press. Wang was even precise in the labor time involved in the calculation of character frequencies: it took him and ten other secretaries 314 days and 4 hours to count

511,187 characters in total. At last, they counted 2,954 characters used in student essays, and 4,279 characters used in textbooks.[43]

Wang's precision with the amount of labor he and his coworkers had put in reflected a highly performative component in the scientific practice of counting. Chinese psychologists and educators who were using new techniques to optimize the Chinese writing system were also self-consciously carving out a space for themselves in the new professional division of labor in social sciences. The technical know-how and the immense amount of labor that the psychologists exerted in counting, measuring, and displaying information empowered them as a new class of social scientists who claimed to possess the knowledge to change China—a position that is not unlike that of the emerging class of digital humanists in the twenty-first century.

Based on Chen Heqin's character frequencies, James Yen devised his primers with an idealized vision of what a literate subject meant for the development of a modern nation-state. Mass literacy entailed the standardization of mental labor as well as the indoctrination of the individual with a certain subject position in modern society. James Yen concocted three different primers—for rural farmers, urban workers, and soldiers—with different contents that would impose more than reflect a presupposed set of moral behaviors for these three groups of people. The primers for soldiers, for instance, included among their basic vocabulary the phrase "the army must be followed with loyalty" (*congjun yao zhongxin* 從軍要忠心), whereas those for farmers taught the evils of opium smoking, with a vocabulary that included "poison" (*du* 毒) and "smoke" (*yan* 煙).[44] Yen's primers, in other words, reflected his desire to create subjects who would be literate enough to recognize their duty for the state, become morally aware of their place in society with respect to their social class, and handle basic clerical work such as accounting and recording.

James Yen's literate students, whether children or adults, were in certain respects similar to the workers that the Gary Plan in the United States was intended to create. Frederick T. Coats from the Rockefeller Educational Board had summed up the purpose of Gary Plan as follows: "We do not desire to make poets or orators of these people. We do not cherish even the humbler ambition to raise up among them statesmen, lawyers, scientists or medical men, of whom we have an abundant supply."[45] To what extent were James Yen's primers different from the Rockefeller ideal, especially given that his

Mass Education Movement was funded by the Rockefeller Foundation? Was the Mass Education Movement and the measurement movement that it held in high regard a means to enlighten the people, or was it complicit in producing cogs in the industrial (and, in this case, rural and military) machine?

It would be unfair to claim that James Yen was operating solely with the support of American dollars, especially because he actively resisted the demands of the U.S. State Department after the establishment of the Joint Commission on Rural Reconstruction in 1948, which requested that Yen emphasize agricultural and rural industrial developments over education.[46] Nevertheless, not everyone was satisfied with the basic characters that James Yen used in his primers, and the most coherent critique was articulated by Hong Shen, a rival literary engineer of Chinese.

Basic Chinese: Hong Shen and Radical Knowledge Work

In 1936, Hong Shen, an acclaimed author, dramaturge, and film director, published *1100 Basic Chinese Characters*. Hong had studied in the United States after receiving a degree at Tsinghua University in 1916. After a stint at Ohio State University, he decided to study drama at Harvard under George Pierce Baker before going back to China in 1922 and launching his career as a playwright. In 1930, Hong joined the League of Left-Wing Writers, a group of famed literary figures who advocated a socialist future for Chinese literature. In the early 1930s, while he was enjoying a prolific writing career, Hong developed a keen interest in Basic English, a linguistic project created by Charles K. Ogden and Ivor A. Richards. Invented in the 1920s and 1930s, B.A.S.I.C. (British, American, Scientific, International, Commercial) was composed of only 850 words that could express all meaning in the English language. Soon after its invention, the promise of efficiency and speed it offered turned Basic English into a medium of Anglo-American linguistic imperialism, swiftly permeating colonized and semicolonized spaces around the world. It was such a powerful instrument of imperial expansion that H. G. Wells's *The Shape of Things to Come* (1933) imagined a totalitarian government in the twenty-first century that ruled the world via Basic English. Writing around the same time as Wells, Hong Shen was in fact a teacher of Basic English in China in the 1930s. While instructing the imperialist medium, however, he repurposed its methods to engineer a similar project for Chinese in order to respond to the politics of mass literacy in China in the 1930s. The ironic end product was *1100 Basic Chinese Characters*—a project that used the techniques of Western linguistic imperialism to concoct an anti-imperialist philosophy of literacy that particularly critiqued James Yen's primers. Hong's Basic Chinese was a political manifesto for a different form of communication engineering, which came at a time when James Yen was collaborating with the GMD as the party was strengthening its grip on political power and increasing censorship on any publication that was even remotely antiestablishment.

First, a brief background on Basic English. According to Ivor A. Richards's account, the idea of a Basic English arose while he was coauthoring the book *The Meaning of Meaning* with Charles K. Ogden in the 1920s. Ogden realized that when describing a given word, the same words would come up over and over again, which suggested that a limited number of words, a subset of English, could semantically produce all that the language was capable of expressing. Basic English, in the words of Richards, was going to be "an all-purpose language and serve trade, commerce, technical education, as well as news, the diffusion of science, politics, general knowledge, and the discussion at simple levels of all the common affairs of man."[47] Invented primarily by Charles K. Ogden, Basic English sought to eliminate the redundancies of English, replace verbs with "operatives," and reduce its vocabulary to 850 words, all in order to turn English into an international language that would supersede all other languages, including the artificial ones such as Esperanto.[48] "What the world needs most," noted Ogden, "is about 1,000 more dead languages—and one more alive."[49]

On the one hand, Basic English was a statistical project that relied on word counts, measurement of redundancies, and formulation of an optimum number of words to be used in communication. It was therefore highly informed by the word-frequency analyses conducted by American statisticians and psychologists. Ogden, in his narrative of the history of Basic English, especially acknowledged the works undertaken by Edward L. Thorndike and John Dewey.[50] On the other hand, Ogden and Richards were also concerned with meaning in language, and with the connection between thought and language.[51] They did not want to simply create language machines, but humans who would be able to express their thoughts accurately using a limited vocabulary. Basic English aspired to become the sole token of linguistic exchange in the world, and it had a significantly stubborn history in China.

As the two men were working on a basic vocabulary for English, Richards made a trip to China that cemented his desire to finalize Basic English. When he was a visiting professor at Tsinghua University in Beijing, he noted the aspiration of the Chinese students to read the most complicated pieces of English literature, despite their difficulties in learning the basic elements of the language. The number of English words taught at Chinese schools reached seven thousand, which produced confusion rather than clarity. Richards saw Basic English as the solution to the limited communication between the English-speaking world and China. China, in other words, became the main target and market for Basic English.[52]

According to Ogden, 850 words were enough to express anything in English, with the exception of scientific subdisciplines, for which a supplemental list of words would be necessary. There were only sixteen verbs in Basic English: give, get, take, put, come, go, keep, let, make, say, see, send, do, have, be, and seem. The only auxiliaries allowed were "will" and "may." In order to eliminate semantic redundancy, certain less frequently used words were dropped to leave room for more frequently used words. There was no need for "difficult," when "hard" sufficed. Who needed "husband" or "wife," when "male," "female," "man," and "woman" were already in use? Was "kid" or "child" necessary when one could simply say "son" and "daughter?" The core of 850 words signified efficiency by means of semantic precision. Basic English was certainly an ambitious project in linguistic engineering that relied on a mechanistic idea of communication. And yet, it was not quite clear why certain words were chosen over others: "umbrella" was apparently essential for Basic English, whereas "dance" was unnecessary.[53]

While eliminating redundancy in word use could in theory facilitate the acquisition of language, the technical precision of the project posed English as the scientific heir to a long-forgotten Babel, and its promise of efficiency in communication turned it into an imperial tool. "Empires of the futures are the empires of the mind," claimed Winston Churchill in 1943, referring to Basic English.[54] That same year, the British War Cabinet started promoting Basic English, since it could save the English language from falling prey to pidgins in regions across the world that were still under British occupation. Linguistic engineering, in other words, turned out to be a precision weapon for the empire. As a matter of fact, every single letter of the acronym BASIC (British, American, Scientific, International, and Commercial), as John D. Peters once noted, was imperial.[55]

Its imperialist impulse aside, Basic English had a long and complicated career in China. Richards's interest in promoting it in China continued through the 1930s, and the Chinese Ministry of Education thought highly of the project, since it could save a significant amount of time and money in teaching English to children. Some of the Chinese political figures even thought that Basic English was an expedient complement to Chinese, for the latter was only appropriate for "poetical and literary fancies." As the Chinese diplomat W. W. Yen (Yan Huiqing 顏惠慶) noted, "just as the picturesque sedan chair must give way to the ugly railway car . . . so an artistic but inelastic language must adapt itself to more modern requirements." Yen's self-deprecating remark gave an even stronger ammunition to Basic English, and Ogden did not fail to quote Yen at length to promote his project in China and across the world.[56] The war that started in 1937, however, brought an abrupt end to the ministry's plans, as guns and bombs silenced Basic English. But the teaching Basic English still continued in Yunnan and Tianjin with the financial support of the Rockefeller Foundation.[57]

Basic English was conducive to the development of Hong Shen's *1100 Basic Chinese Characters*, but Hong's project had a more radical component that Basic English or even its first cousin, James Yen's Thousand-Character Primers, lacked. All the projects mentioned—Basic English, Thousand-Character Primers, and Basic Chinese—shared a common technoscientific origin that championed linguistic efficiency to optimize mental labor, and they all highlighted the need to simplify linguistic complexity to increase intellectually productive output in the shortest amount of time. Their political goals, however, were very different. Basic English was an imperial project to turn English into an international language. James Yen's primers, on the other hand, aimed to standardize mental labor according to his philosophy of education, which held that workers, farmers, and soldiers were the pillars of a modern Chinese nation, and thus had to be cultivated as such in the shortest time possible. Hong Shen's Basic Chinese, in contrast, was an effort to elicit political awareness through engineering a new set of Chinese characters that differed from James Yen's.

Before examining Hong's Basic Chinese in detail, it is important to acknowledge the origins of the project and highlight the contradictions embedded in Hong's primer. On the one hand, as a member of the League of Left-Wing Writers, Hong's choice of characters represented an anti-capitalist and anti-imperialist vision for literacy that was at odds with James Yen's

GMD-supported mass-literacy campaign. On the other hand, as a teacher of Basic English, Hong himself occupied a problematic place in the imperial expansion of the English language, as he never publicly critiqued the imperialist undertones of Basic English. Calling him an agent of the empire would be too harsh, but his awe of the scientific principles of Basic English cannot be disregarded. Even the title itself bears the traces of this contradiction. Once translated into Chinese, B.A.S.I.C. was no longer an acronym for empire, but a basic (*jiben* 基本) tool for mass literacy. Hong was able to domesticate the empire, but only at the cost of retaining its fundamental values of efficiency, speed, and productivity. Within the globally uneven circumstances, this contradiction was in fact not an anomaly, but a manifestation of the modern condition in China.

Hong Shen's critique of Yen's primers was sharp. A simplified Chinese as formulated and practiced by Yen and his primers concealed a cognitive complicity in the extant system of thought. The primers not only advocated well-defined boundaries between different social classes, but also presented a simplified linguistic pattern that served to reproduce a wider cognitive one. The frequent use of characters represented a particular cognitive structure, along with a socioeconomic and political system, that words helped produce and reproduce; and as long as the same frequent characters were taught in schools, there was no way to snap out of the habitual patterns of communication. Statistical reduction of language was complicit in reproducing an extant cognitive system, for it treated frequency as inherently more meaningful than rarity.

Hong Shen perspicaciously addressed this problem when he published *1100 Basic Chinese Characters* in 1935. He admired statistical linguistics and communication engineering as much as James Yen and Ogden and Richards, but he was more invested in changing the patterns of thought rather than reproducing them, and in creating subjects who were aware of their own socioeconomic conditions rather than a docile population that conformed with the system. First of all, Hong believed that the words in James Yen's primers were not enough to represent one's emotions and thoughts, nor were they enough to read a newspaper and understand the world. There were a lot of characters that signified "things" (*shiwu* 事物) but not enough that referred to life behaviors (*shenghuo xingwei* 生活行為). He acknowledged that Yen's primers were still a big improvement from the traditional *Thousand Character Classic*, which was extremely redundant from a modern linguistic perspective, but still too narrow. The primers were good enough to express one's simple thoughts, but not enough to understand the "struggle for survival" (*shengcun jingzheng* 生存競爭). Although Hong maintained a certain distance from the Chinese Communist Party, he believed that a socialist terminology allowed a critical view of the conditions of social existence that James Yen's vocabulary was unable to convey. Using James Yen's primers, wrote Hong, one would not be able to understand "Imperialism's Economic Invasion of Semi-Colonies" (*diguo zhuyi duiyu cizhimindi de jingji qinlüe* 帝國主義對於此殖民地的經濟侵略) or "International Contradictions and the Second World War" (*guojijian de maodun he di er ci shijie dazhan* 國際間的矛盾和第二次世界大戰). All that James Yen's primers enabled was letter writing or daily bookkeeping and accounting (*jizhang xiexin* 記帳寫信); reading books, newspapers, government proclamations, or literature was still off-limits. In practice, noted Hong, "the outcome of studying Thousand-Character Primers is no different than the earlier outcome of studying the *Thousand Character Classic* in villages!"[58]

Hong Shen's critique targeted the very premises on which James Yen et al. had devised and revised their primers. Yen's primers aimed to economize the time necessary to create literate subjects who were designated as citizens with particular duties to the nation. Using Yen's primers, sons and daughters could communicate with their families through simple letters on the one hand; and on the other hand, they could work as financial and bureaucratic scribes for the nation-state. The cognitive world that James Yen's primers manufactured was inhabited by the ideal literate subjects who worked for an existing economy of thought. Hong Shen, on the other hand, wanted to turn people into politically aware subjects rather than bookkeepers or letter writers. For Hong, word frequencies reflected the extant economy of thought, and sticking to them simply helped reproduce it without questioning its conditions of existence. In order to escape from statistical boundaries, Hong chose his 1,100 characters very carefully. "My wish," said Hong, "is to use these thousand characters to lead the common people [*yiban minzhong* 一般民眾], to organize them, and to enable them to become progressive and powerful citizens [*gongmin* 公民] of the modern age who seek survival through struggle."[59]

Hong's semantic usage of words was similar to Basic English. Just like Ogden and Richards, Hong was against the use of nonbasic words if the same meaning could be delivered with the use of basic words. For instance, he eliminated "younger sister" (*mei* 妹) from his vocabulary, because younger sister could be represented by "female younger brother" (*nüdi* 女弟). The words for "husband" (*fu* 夫) and "wife" (*qi* 妻) were simply "male" (*nan* 男) and "female" (*nü* 女), just as in Basic English. Using Hong's basic characters, one had to say "I am his younger brother" instead of "he is my elder brother" because "elder brother" (*ge* 哥) was not part of the basic characters. There was no "island" (*dao* 島), but "a small mountain in the middle of a sea." No "monk" (*heshang* 和尚) but "one who has removed hair and is pursuing (religious) practice."[60]

In contrast to Basic English, however, in choosing his basic characters, Hong was motivated by a terminology that could upset the economic structures of thought. Although he took out the simple words such as "monk," "younger sister," "husband," and "wife," he deemed it necessary to keep the character *zhi* 殖, not only because people had "reproductive organs" (*shengzhiqi* 生殖器), but because China was a "semicolony" (*ci zhimindi* 此殖民地). Departing both from Yen's and from Ogden and Richards's projects, he introduced a conceptual vocabulary that could help adult learners grasp the socioeconomic conditions that they inhabited, such as "imperialism" (*diguozhuyi* 帝國主義), "contradiction" (*maodun* 矛盾), law (*falü* 法律), "economy" (*jingji* 經濟) and, of course, "efficiency" (*xiaolü* 效率).[61] The masses needed to know about the contradictions of modern life and "imperialism's economic invasion of semi-colonies."[62] For Hong, in contrast to James Yen, literacy meant political participation in the world, rather than the passive reproduction of a nationally determined economy of knowledge. The distinction he drew between the two kinds of literacy was nothing less than that between clerical workers and political actors.

While carefully selecting basic characters, Hong was also motivated to include regional differences of language and behaviors into his list of characters. Eleven hundred characters could be sufficient, at least according to Hong, for political thought across the Chinese-reading nation, but some characters were used more than others in real life in different parts of the country. Shanghai's culinary culture, for instance, featured crabs (*xie* 蟹), and it was common for people in Shanghai to recognize that character. "Crab" could therefore be included in literary primers published for a Shanghainese audience, but it would not make any sense, according to Hong, to have it in primers in Shandong. In contrast, people in Shandong usually slept on brick beds on fire pits (*keng/kang* 坑/炕), so including that character in primers specific to Shandong would conform with the lifestyle of the region. Similar differences could also be observed in the common vocabularies of people living in the countryside and the city, and primers had to show variance depending on the locality in which they were distributed. To account for such differences, Hong suggested literary primers should include an added list of 150 "special characters" (*tebie zi* 特別字), which could vary from place to place.[63]

While Hong never explicitly mentioned the political reasons for his attention to regional differences, it is not difficult to detect the alignment between his regional focus and the politics of the left-wing Chinese Latinization Movement in the 1930s. As chapters 5 and 6 will explain in detail, Chinese latinization began in the 1920s in the Soviet Union as an extension of the larger Soviet nationality policies and the Soviet Latinization Movement that swept across Eurasia. When Chinese communists living in the Soviet Union collaborated with Russian linguists to devise the Chinese Latin Alphabet in the late 1920s, their main goal was to make it available for all languages in China, such as Shanghainese, Cantonese, and Hokkien, among others. This was a deliberate move to fight against the homogenizing tendencies of the GMD-led National Language Movement (Guoyu yundong 國語運動) centered only on Mandarin. While Hong Shen was writing his primer, left-wing printers and publishers were already latinizing a variety of regional languages in China in an effort to push back against Mandarin and the GMD. Meanwhile, James Yen was revising his primers to include the Mandarin pronunciation of each character transcribed in Phonetic Symbols (*Zhuyin fuhao*), bringing his literacy campaign ever closer to the ideological power of the party. As such, Hong's anti-capitalist, anti-imperialist, and anti–James Yen primer was also conspicuously anti-GMD.

The ideological drive behind Hong Shen's Basic Chinese compels us to think beyond his immediate opponent, James Yen, and instead situate Hong and his work within a global history of information and communication. His literary experiment, after all, was not only a response to Yen but also an extension of Ogden and Richards's Basic English. As John Durham Peters elaborates, Basic English was conjured upon the principle of "rational[izing] social relations," and as such, it was built on a particular theory of communication, which Ogden and Richards defined as "a use of symbols in such a way that acts of reference occur in a hearer which are similar in all relevant respects to those which are symbolized by them in the speaker."[64] Their idea of communication, as Peters notes, was purely psychological, and meaning emerged out of a contact between minds that operated through symbols. The behaviorist conceit that prioritized disembodied mental efficiency was embedded in the words of Basic English. Hong's Basic Chinese, on the other hand, was almost anti-psychological. His philosophy rested on an irreducibly social and political *context* for communication. He did not inquire into how meaning emerged through mental contact, but rather into how meaning could become socially and politically meaningful. Basic Chinese, in other words, was different not only in content but also in its very premise for what constituted political meaning in communication.

Hong's *1100 Basic Chinese Characters* had an ambiguous reception in China, and its impact was minimal. Yuen Ren Chao, a leading Chinese linguist, claimed that it was a valuable addition to the efforts to promote mass literacy.[65] Eugene Shen, a Stanford psychologist, on the other hand, thought that Hong's replacements were simply "ridiculous."[66] Valuable or ridiculous, Hong's primer did not reach the masses as James Yen's did, partly because it did not have financial supporters like the Rockefeller Foundation, and partly because it was an experimental project on literacy. Still, his commentary on communication raised a critical question: How could linguistic and script efficiency upset the extant patterns of communication and thought, and act as the foundation for an alternative cognitive future?

* * *

Early twentieth-century scientists and literary figures in China were living in the midst of profound uncertainties regarding the future of the nation and national communication. Their relentless efforts to reduce the number of characters in order to educate the masses were the outcome of deeper anxieties generated by the demands of the global information age in which all that was solid, to quote Marx, was melting into air. New pressures on language and writing engendered new contradictions, new possibilities, and new limits for the communication engineers of modern China whose lives and minds were deeply intertwined with the global currents of scientific thought and practice, especially with American behavioral psychology and the belief in statistical efficiency embedded in it.

Acknowledging the interconnected histories of American and Chinese communication engineering in the 1920s and 1930s and underscoring the divergent practices of James Yen, Chen Heqin, and Hong Shen demonstrate the close link between mass literacy and the management of Chinese characters. Character-frequency analyses, intelligence tests, literary primers, and Basic Chinese were all manifestations of the modern age of information that redefined the meaning of mental and clerical labor while naturalizing the industrial value of efficiency in knowledge production. Mass literacy as a communication engineering project was ideologically contrived not only at the level of party-state building, but even at the basic level of counting, selecting, and discarding characters. The history of mass literacy is thus indicative of the ideological nature of information and script engineering at large.

Information ideologies aside, the management of Chinese characters that I described in this chapter also poses a conundrum in the history of Chinese script reforms. On the one hand, as the first two chapters described, the impact of alphabetic labor time was formidable in China. From the turn of the century onward, many reformers began inventing phonetic scripts, and ultimately Pinyin was officially adopted as a national alphabet in the mid-twentieth century. On the other hand, Chinese characters were never abandoned. Textbooks, novels, poems, and scientific articles were all printed in Chinese characters, almost never in an alphabet. How, then, should we understand the historical conditions of an informational hybridity that eventually came to define the Chinese knowledge economy?

The twentieth-century rationalization of Chinese characters demonstrates the persistence of so-called traditional technologies in the modernization of the Chinese economy. One may offer similar examples for the continued use of traditional technologies in different industries, such as their employment in nineteenth-century Chinese tea production. Andrew Liu's work on the history of tea has drawn attention to the social logics of accumulation in the tea-producing regions of China. One of his remarkable findings was that as Chinese tea competed with Indian tea in a globalizing capitalist economy, tea producers relied on traditional instruments and practices, such as incense sticks, to increase labor efficiency. A millennia-old technology used for timekeeping, burning incense sticks in tea factories offered a method to regulate and discipline labor time during a period of increased competition in the world market. The accuracy of incense sticks was not comparable to mechanical clocks, but "the *social context* of the tea factory," as Liu puts it, "endowed these pre-mechanical labor processes with an industrial, distinctively modern character."[67]

What incense sticks were for the accumulation of capital in the nineteenth century, Chinese characters were for the accumulation of knowledge in the twentieth. China's entry into a global market of commodities and knowledge did not obviate preexisting technologies of production; on the contrary, it relied on them by reconfiguring them. The use of incense sticks for regulating labor within the social context of a tea factory was not unlike the statistical management of Chinese characters for increased labor efficiency within the social context of the Chinese knowledge economy. In other words, what some reformers in the twentieth century thought of as an archaic means of production—i.e., Chinese characters—turned out to be the most constitutive part of a modern knowledge economy in China.

Stuck between an alphabetic order imposed from outside and a nonalphabetic one that grew from within, the Chinese script was taking shape within the dialectics of the global information age. In the 1920s and 1930s, the number of characters was eventually reduced to fuel cerebra, but the future of the script was still far from certain. On one side of the table were the "simplifiers" who wanted to reduce the number of strokes in Chinese characters to simplify manual and mental labor. On another side were the supporters of the NPA who believed in the merits of a phonetic alphabet but were not certain about how to accommodate the characters. On a third side were "romanists" who thought that the Roman alphabet was a better choice than the nativist graphics of the NPA. On yet another side were "latinists," the communist revolutionaries who believed in an internationalism founded on latinized (not romanized) letters. And on the fifth side of this strange pentagonal table sat the more-conservative nativists who were content with the Chinese characters as they were. The future of Chinese script relied on the geometry of balance between these different sides.

FOUR

Simplification of Chinese Characters
Mining, Counting, Seeing

HUMANS ARE READING animals. At least that is how the young psychologist Zhang Yaoxiang 張耀祥 (1893–1964) defined them in his master's thesis completed at Columbia University's Teachers College. One of the first modern psychologists of China, Zhang was a colleague and friend of Chen Heqin and other psychologists we encountered in chapter 3. His thesis, completed in 1919, was on the psychology of reading Chinese, and he started his study with the following words: "The increasing part played by reading in the life of civilized man is a striking characteristic of modern culture.... The man of to-day may be defined as a reading animal.... When everybody reads, and some do scarcely anything else, and the amount to read increases daily, it is highly desirable that reading should be made as easy and rapid as possible."[1] Reading was merely "a psycho-physiological operation" for him, an operation that could be optimized via reorganizing the page.

Zhang was one of the first psychologists to experiment with the direction of reading, punctuation marks, extra signs, side signs, numbers, and the absence/presence of paragraphs, in an effort to design the best writing practice to increase and facilitate mental input. His work on rethinking the components of a printed page was indeed reminiscent of the Fordist assembly line. Punctuation marks divided sentences into pieces to help the working mind assemble them, auxiliary signs designated proper nouns and names to help the mind distinguish them, and indented paragraphs ordered the flow of information to help the mind digest them. In Zhang's hands, new devices of inscription functioned as cognitive tools for reconstructing the technospatial architecture of the page, and ultimately increase efficiency in mental labor.

For many of the psychologists and reformers in the 1920s and 1930s, Chinese characters proved a particularly obstinate hurdle on the path to building a new architecture for writing. The number of strokes, they believed, was the main obstacle that stood between nation and information, and the only way to overcome this issue was to simplify the characters. The simplification of Chinese characters was in fact partially an outcome of the National Phonetic Alphabet's failed promise. Rather than offering a solution to the problem at hand, the NPA posed even larger problems that the reformers could not immediately address. On the one hand, the promotion of the NPA required a technological and political infrastructure that the nascent republic did not possess. On the other hand, the artificial national pronunciation that the NPA represented from 1918 to 1926 was a source of dismay for many of the reformers, for no one understood anything written in the NPA. While reformers were still in favor of adopting a phonetic script in the long run, they turned to the simplification of characters as a temporary relief.

Qian Xuantong 錢玄同 (1887–1939) was representative of this new reformist tide in the 1920s. A May Fourth radical, Qian was an advocate of the NPA and one of the most adamant supporters of an alphabetic future for China. "I still haven't reached forty, but my nerves are already abnormally fatigued," he wrote, blaming the Chinese characters. The antiquated composition methods, old-fashioned thousand-character classics, and especially the characters themselves, with their convoluted number of strokes, caused either idiocy or neurasthenic collapse. For the sake of sanity, at least according to Qian, the script needed adjustment. But he was realistic about the social and intellectual environment in which he worked. As a dedicated alphabetizer, Qian was committed to "curing the essence" (*zhiben* 治本), i.e., eliminating Chinese characters in order to save Chinese minds. As a participant in the promotion of the NPA, however, he saw that the only manageable alternative at the time was to "cure the signs" (*zhibiao* 治標), i.e., simplify the characters. In 1922, along with his colleagues at the Preparatory Committee for the National Unification of Language, Qian famously declared that the course of action was going to be the reduction of the number of strokes in characters.[2] And thus the simplification of characters officially commenced.

SIMPLIFICATION OF CHINESE CHARACTERS

Character simplification was an *informational* project, not a linguistic one. Without a doubt, it was interwoven with linguistic concerns, such as the *baihua* movement that advocated a rapprochement between spoken and written language, but the reduction of the number of strokes in a character did not have anything to do with spoken language per se. The reformers were instead concerned with labor time in the manual production and mental acquisition of characters. Fewer strokes, they believed, could increase efficiency—a modernist belief that was not different from what had instigated phoneticization in the first place. But much like the linguistic conflicts unleashed by phonetic scripts and divergent theories of literacy generated by frequency analyses, simplification also engendered new contradictions in considerations about the place of characters in a modernizing knowledge economy.

During the years that followed the publication of Qian's article, the reformers found themselves in a conundrum. Even if simplification could in theory increase efficiency in writing and reading, what exactly was the method to reduce the number of strokes in a given character without sacrificing its meaning? What was the relationship between strokes and semantics? What did it even mean to "see" a character? Could character strokes be abstracted into statistical data to scientifically manage simplification? Or did the Chinese characters defy scientific understanding?

In the initial years of simplification, reformers called for using *suzi* 俗字, characters that were already in circulation and were simplified by common people. The search for *suzi*, I would like to suggest, was one of the largest text-mining projects in republican China. Reformers sought to locate and extract characters with fewer strokes from an enormous range of literary texts, including historical novels, plays, classics, dictionaries, letters, account books, medical prescriptions, handwritten notes, speeches, and mimeographed publications. In the hands of reformers, historical and daily texts turned into databases to search and retrieve (*soucai* 搜採) simplified characters from in order to put them back into circulation. Text mining received an even greater boost when Lin Yutang 林語堂 (1895–1976), one of the most influential liberal scholars of the period, publicly endorsed the simplification project in 1933 and called intellectuals from different professions to mine for *suzi*. But the result was complicated, for one character could have multiple *suzi* that were entirely different from one another. Which one, then, was best for standardizing simplification? And who had the authority to choose one *suzi* over another?

The moment of doubt was the cradle of innovation. The absence of a well-defined trajectory in simplification allowed creative proposals to surface with different claims about the psychological, social, and political practices of reading and writing. Some of the most influential proposals complemented the text-mining project by drawing on the works of Chinese psychologists who had been trying to respond to urgent questions, such as the link between stroke counts, learning speed, and the psycho-physiological process of recognizing characters. As debates proliferated among reformers, so did the number of proposals; and the increasing number of simplified characters turned standardization into a politically charged campaign. What began with a handful of scholars in the 1920s evolved into a social movement by the mid-1930s and prompted an ideological polarization among the reformers, as different versions of simplified characters embodied disparate information politics. Eventually, the Ministry of Education promulgated a preliminary set of 324 simplified characters in August 1935, but was compelled to suspend the project only five months later, when it realized the political cost it could bring to the GMD. The history of character simplification thus demonstrates how the search for efficiency in reading and writing was inevitably entangled with ideological positions regarding the place of characters in the Chinese knowledge economy.

Text Mining in Republican China

Before Qian Xuantong et al. announced it as the antidote to neurasthenia in 1922, calls for simplifying characters were already circulating in reformist circles. Lufei Kui 陸費逵 (1886–1941) was one of the first proponents of simplification. In the aftermath of the abolition of the civil service examination system in 1905, Lufei proposed simplification as part of an educational reform that aimed at reducing the necessary labor time to produce literate minds. Writing in the inaugural issue of the *Journal of Education* (*Jiaoyu zazhi* 教育雜誌) in 1909, he noted the amount of mental labor simplification would save among the students (*sheng xuezhe zhi naoli* 省學者之腦力).[3] He defended the use of *suzi* that were already in circulation among the populace, for they would be easily embraced by the people and help save strokes.

SIMPLIFICATION OF CHINESE CHARACTERS

Deng 燈, for instance, was commonly written as *deng* 灯, and it saved ten strokes. Writing *yu* 与 instead of *yu* 與 could also save ten strokes; *ti* 体 instead of *ti* 體 saved sixteen; *dian* 点 instead of *dian* 點 saved eight; *dui* 对 instead of *dui* 對 saved nine, and so on. Even his own name, Lufei argued, consumed too much energy, so he proposed to write it with half the number of strokes.[4]

When Qian Xuantong published his milestone article in 1922 on the simplification of characters, he introduced another possible trajectory. Apart from the simplified characters that were already in use, he noted that there were hundreds of examples of simplified characters in historical novels, account books, medical prescriptions, songbooks, and other miscellaneous materials dating from as far back as the Song and Yuan dynasties. In the past, Qian noted, simplification had followed a few basic steps. If the character was too complicated, then the number of strokes was reduced while keeping a similar "form" (*xing* 形), such as in *shou* 壽 simplified as *shou* 寿. In other cases, a certain component of a character served as a simplified synecdoche, as in *sheng* 聲, which was simplified as *sheng* 声. In certain characters, only one part of the character caused complication, in which case only that part was simplified, as in *bian* 邊 turning into *bian* 边. Other characters allowed a replacement of their phonetic component, as in *yuan* 遠, in which the phonetic component *yuan* 袁 was replaced with the homophonic *yuan* 元 to become *yuan* 远. Some of the characters, Qian believed, could be taken directly from old works, such as *li* 禮 simplified as *li* 礼. Some could use phonetic loan characters (*jiajiezi* 假借字), such as replacing *gan* 乾 with *gan* 干. And lastly, some could be replaced with alternative characters, such as using the simple character *xiang* 响 instead of *xiang* 響.[5] In short, Qian wanted to excavate the multiple pasts of Chinese as a way to illuminate the future and he called for a historically informed *suzi*. With this, simplification turned into a large-scale text-mining project.

In 1928, Hu Huaichen 胡懷琛 (1886–1938), a scholar of Chinese classics, published one of the first methodological works for simplifying characters and suggested supplementing *suzi* with simplified characters found in old works, such as *Shuowen jiezi* 說文解字, and with the invention of new characters, such as those found in vernacular works and in Japanese. *Shuowen jiezi* was the first Chinese dictionary, compiled by Xu Shen 許慎 (ca. 58–148) in the second century. For Hu, it offered a native database for the simplification project, for one could see many of the characters in their simplified forms: *qi* 气 instead of *qi* 氣; *yun* 云 instead of *yun* 雲; *bing* 冫 instead of *bing* 冰, and so on. Apart

[121]

from classical examples, Hu also advocated for the use of "new characters" (*xinzi* 新字) used in vernacular literature. Novels written in the vernacular language of Suzhou, for instance, made use of characters such as 勥 (a combination for *wuyao* 勿要 [unnecessary]). In writing new characters, Japanese was also an inspiration for Hu. Japanese authors shrank "steamboat" (*qichuan* 氣船) to one character combining *zhou* 舟 (boat) and *qi* 气 (steam), and "electric wire" (*dianxian* 電線) to one composed of *mi* 糸 (thin thread) and *dian* 電 (electricity).[6] Why wouldn't Chinese follow the same route?

It was a similar desire that motivated Liu Fu 劉復 (1891–1934) and Li Jiarui 李家瑞 (1895–1975) to mine *suzi* from Song, Yuan, Ming, and Qing texts, but their study was not as didactic as Hu's. Rather, they aimed to show the complexity involved in the simplification project by building the largest list of *suzi* hitherto published. Their widely acclaimed work, *A Record of Common Characters Since the Song and Yuan Dynasties* (*Song yuan yilai suzi pu* 宋元以來俗字譜), published in 1930, was geared toward finding the historical precedents to the simplification project, and it was much more ambitious than Hu's.[7] Liu and Li made use of twelve works in total, composed of a mix of classics, novellas, popular history books, poems, and plays, all of which had been widely circulating among the populace since the Song dynasty. *Biographies of Exemplary Women* (*Gu lienü zhuan* 古列女傳), for instance, contained 349 *suzi*; *Thirty Zaju Plays from Yuan Editions* (*Gujin zaju sanshi zhong* 古今雜劇三十種) had 963; the popular play about the Tang general Xue Rengui's conquest of the East offered 304, and so on. Liu Fu and Li Jiarui listed 1,604 characters with 6,240 *suzi* variants, which showed that there were roughly four *suzi* for each character. What set this study apart from other projects was that Liu and Li did not try to devise a proposal to standardize *suzi*. Theirs was merely a compilation to show the variations in *suzi* throughout the centuries. In doing so, they pointed at but avoided the hardest problem: Given the historical varieties, how could *suzi* be standardized?

Some responses were quite radical. Chen Guangyao's 陳光堯 (1906–1972) proposal, for instance, was enticing, distinctive, and bizarre, when compared to the examples above. One of the pioneers of the movement who advocated simplification throughout his life, Chen combined all the tools at his disposal to invent new simplified characters, rather than selecting them from earlier works. He boldly rewrote "President Sun Yat-sen's Will" (*Zongli yizhu* 總理遺囑) in his own simplified script, utilizing a mix of methods. In simplifying *guo* 國 (country), for instance, he placed *tu* 土 (soil) in the middle of *wei*

□ (enclosure) (figure 4.1).⁸ It is not clear, however, how legible the new script was, even to the literate eye.

Lin Yutang was ambiguously attracted to Chen Guangyao's proposal. Lin was one of the most prolific liberal intellectuals of early twentieth-century China and the famous inventor of the Ming Kwai Chinese Typewriter.⁹ In 1933, after Chen Guangyao's simplified characters were gaining some popularity, Lin initiated a movement for simplification in his popular biweekly journal, *Analects (Lun yu* 論語*).* While paying homage to Chen's endeavor, Lin was skeptical of its efficacy and instead publicly endorsed *suzi*. A firm believer in simplification, Lin saw it as the product of a natural process of evolution that had been at work since ancient times. Wasn't Li Si's "seal script" (*xiaozhuan* 小篆) in the Qin dynasty one step above the earlier *zhouwen* 籀文? And didn't Cheng Miao take a great leap forward in inventing the "official script" (*lishu* 隸書), which was a simplified form of the seal script? Why would anyone be opposed to the use of *suzi* that were already in common circulation and saved strokes in writing, such as *qie* 窃 instead of *qie* 竊, *ling* 灵 instead of *ling* 靈, *hao* 号 instead of *hao* 號, *wan* 万 instead of *wan* 萬?¹⁰

With Lin's support, *suzi* reached the height of their popularity and replaced alternative projects like Chen Guangyao's. *Suzi* saved strokes, facilitated the recognition and reproduction of a character, and eliminated the need to invent new characters. Most importantly, this was a bottom-up project, for *suzi* were already in use by the common people. What remained to be done was first an ethnographic search to hunt down *suzi*, and then to standardize and popularize them. As for the characters that did not have a *suzi* equivalent, Lin agreed with Qian Xuantong and others that examples from old works and different kinds of Chinese calligraphy could provide a solution.¹¹

Lin's journal served as a platform to allow others to contribute to the project and reach the wider public. Immediately after Lin called for the use of *suzi*, he started receiving dozens of proposals for simplified characters, several of which he published in his journal. The ethnographic search for *suzi* in daily life encouraged reformers to leaf through mimeographed publications, letters, account books, and all sorts of written materials they could find on the streets and in libraries. As was the case with Liu Fu and Li Jiarui's *suzi* from historical texts, however, there were multiple *suzi* equivalents of Chinese characters. If there were six different *suzi* for one character, who had the authority to decide on one? On what basis could *suzi* be selected for standard use?

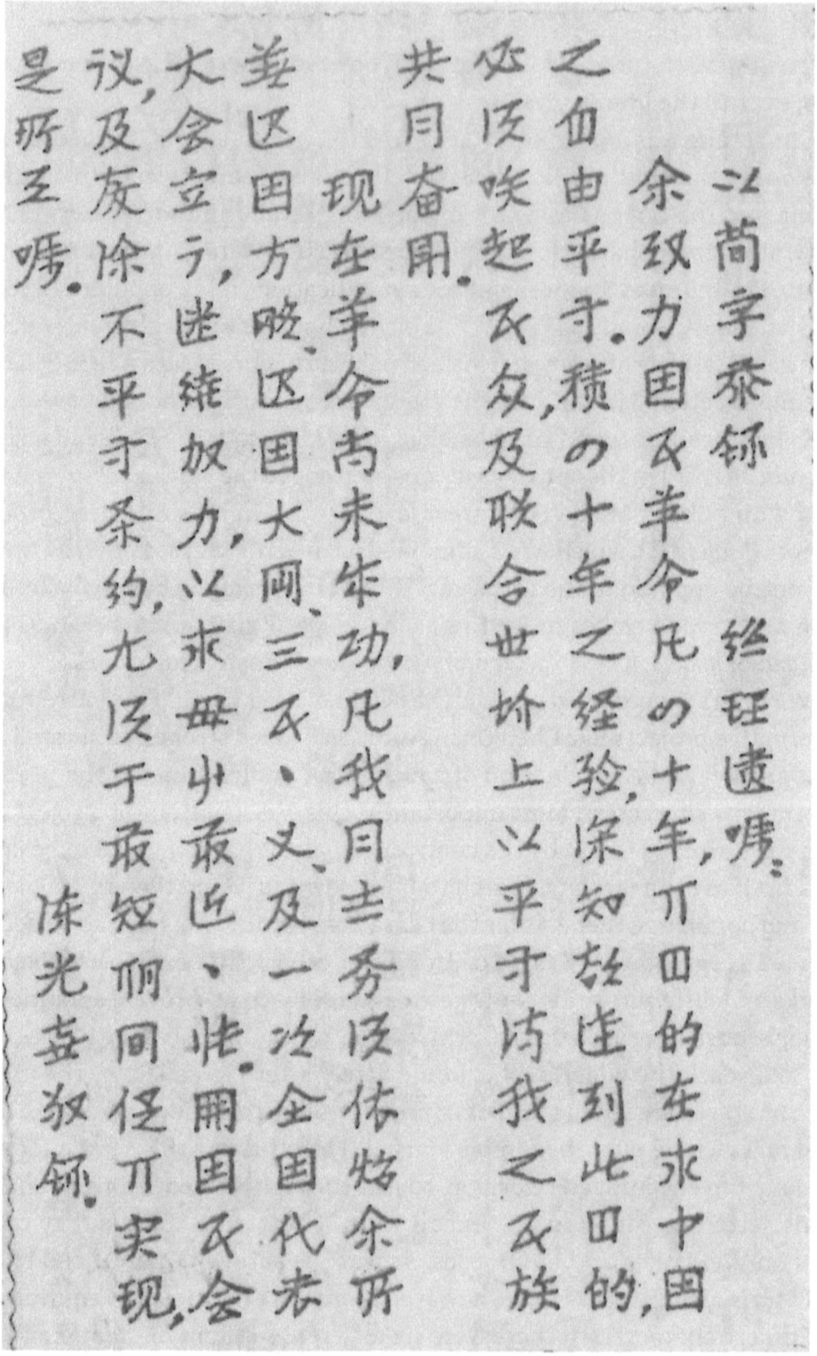

FIGURE 4.1 *The President's Will* by Chen Guangyao.
Source: Chen Guangyao, "Jianxie zongli yizhu jie" 簡寫總理遺囑解 [An explanation for writing the President's Will in simplified characters], in Lin Yutang, "Wode hua—tichang suzi" 我的話-提倡俗字 [My word—promote suzi], Lun yu 29 (November 1933): 216.

Lin Yutang's call for *suzi* proposals opened a new chapter in the simplification of characters, since people from different occupational backgrounds with different ideas about the trajectory of simplification could voice their concerns and submit their original proposals. Two of the most famous proposals that Lin deemed worthy of analysis were by Xu Zemin 徐則敏 and Du Dingyou 杜定友 (1898–1967), who advocated two different approaches to simplification, and were informed by different psychological debates circulating in China and the United States on reforming the Chinese characters. These two proposals were not only influential within the movement at large, but they also represented different methods of "seeing" Chinese characters, and different opinions about the paths of efficiency.

Counting the Strokes: Statistics and Character Simplification

The first generation of Chinese psychologists were at the forefront of efficiency studies, but even they could not unanimously agree upon a scientific methodology to reform Chinese writing. The two proposals for *suzi* that Lin Yutang shared with the public in *Analects* demonstrated both the significance of psychological studies on the reformers and the divergent epistemic practices among the psychologists themselves. The first proposal, by Xu Zemin, an educator from Zhejiang, was based on earlier statistical studies of U.S.-trained Chinese psychologists who spearheaded the measurement movement in Chinese education. Drawing heavily on statistical counts and experiments, their works reflected an epistemology of writing that saw Chinese characters as an amalgamation of strokes. The number of strokes, they believed, could be correlated with the amount of time needed to learn a character, and thus offer a method for reform. Du Dingyou, on the other hand, was a pioneer in library sciences, and drew inspiration from gestalt theories to argue for writing as a historical and psycho-physiological process that generated "habits" that could not be reduced to stroke counts. The divergent theories showed psychologists and reformers wrestling with a capricious science of writing that raised more questions than it answered.

Liu Tingfang 劉廷芳 (Timothy Tingfang Lew) (1891–1961) was the first psychologist to conduct a study of learning Chinese characters. A Protestant Christian born into a missionary family in Wenzhou, Zhejiang, Liu attended St. John's College in Shanghai before moving to the United States in 1910.

After brief stints in Tennessee and Georgia, he completed his undergraduate studies at Columbia University, studying theology for two years, and then started his doctoral work in 1916 at Columbia's Teachers College. He finished it quite hastily in 1920 and returned to China to take part in the New Culture Movement. He originally planned his doctoral study in three parts: a study of the learning process, a photographic study of eye movements in reading Chinese, and a word count of Chinese characters used in daily life. Although the tasks of recording eye movements and word counts were later undertaken by other psychologists, Liu was the first to write a psychological study of Chinese character acquisition.

Liu was among the reformers who wanted to articulate a *Chinese* response to the information age and believed that Chinese characters could be rationalized to conform with the demands of the knowledge economy, like Chen Heqin and Hong Shen. He began his work on the psychology of characters with a critique of the phoneticization movement, which was in full swing by the time he was writing and publishing: "The prophetic voices among [scholars, scientists, and educators] which first led the nation out of its slavish obedience to the ancient style into a wholesome appreciation of the practical conversational style of literary expression, are now solemnly calling it to go into a yet newer world in which the use of the old ideographs will be abandoned. This is, therefore, a time for people to 'stop, look and listen.'"[12]

The main problem, according to Liu, was to determine how the "bonds" formed in the learning of Chinese characters. What was the mental process by which the form (*xing* 形), sound (*sheng* 聲), and meaning (*yi* 義) of a character bonded with one another? In articulating the question, Liu was drawing on the Han-dynasty scholar Xu Shen's *Showen jiezi*, which was the first treatise to theorize Chinese writing according to the trilateral structure of form, sound, and meaning, since every character had a form that corresponded to a sound and a particular meaning. But in posing the question in terms of "bonds," Liu was *psychologizing* Chinese writing.[13]

Liu's study was not prescriptive. He wanted to understand and provide a remedy for the psychological complexity of interacting with Chinese characters. His test subjects came from different backgrounds, and their number and linguistic capacities varied according to the experiment. Some were Chinese adults who were studying at Columbia University, some were American students and psychologists from Columbia, and others were Chinese children from New York's Chinatown who were familiar with Chinese languages to varying degrees. The purpose was to determine the characters that were easy to learn, the causes that affected the facility of learning, the differences in learning the sounds and meanings of characters, and the methods that subjects used as memory aids. He chose his characters from the Commercial Press' *New Dictionary* 新字典 (1912), a landmark publication that contained around 30,000 characters, 9,586 of which were designated as commonly used and the rest as obsolete or very rarely seen. Liu first analyzed the 9,586 characters and charted a graph that showed the distribution of characters according to the number of strokes (figure 4.2). The analysis showed that nearly 80 percent of all characters required between seven and eighteen strokes, with the record belonging to characters with twelve strokes, which amounted to 829 in total.[14]

In order to identify the main factors that played into learning characters, Liu chose twenty-six rare characters that varied in complexity from one stroke to forty-seven strokes, roughly representing the variety of stroke numbers in common characters.[15] The Chinese subjects were shown twenty-six cards, each with one of these characters. If the subject informed the experimenter that they had seen the character before, that character was put aside, thereby assuring that the test was undertaken with characters that were seen for the first time by the subjects. The subjects were then taught the sound and meaning of the character, and, after six months, they were tested again to determine how well they remembered them. The number of recitations and the time it took the subject to remember the sound and the meaning of a character and to reproduce a character in written form were recorded to see how the differences in remembering the sound, meaning, and form of the character played out depending on the number of strokes.

The results showed a great diversity in the nature of associative aids subjects used in learning Chinese characters. Liu counted thirty-nine ways for the formation of the form-sound bond, and forty-two ways for the form-meaning bond. In forming the bonds in question, some used the meaning, some the sound, some a synonym, some the radical, and some an "unexplainable" part of the character.[16] Given this variety, Liu asked, how could the characters be simplified? Did the number of strokes have any effect on the process of learning or not?

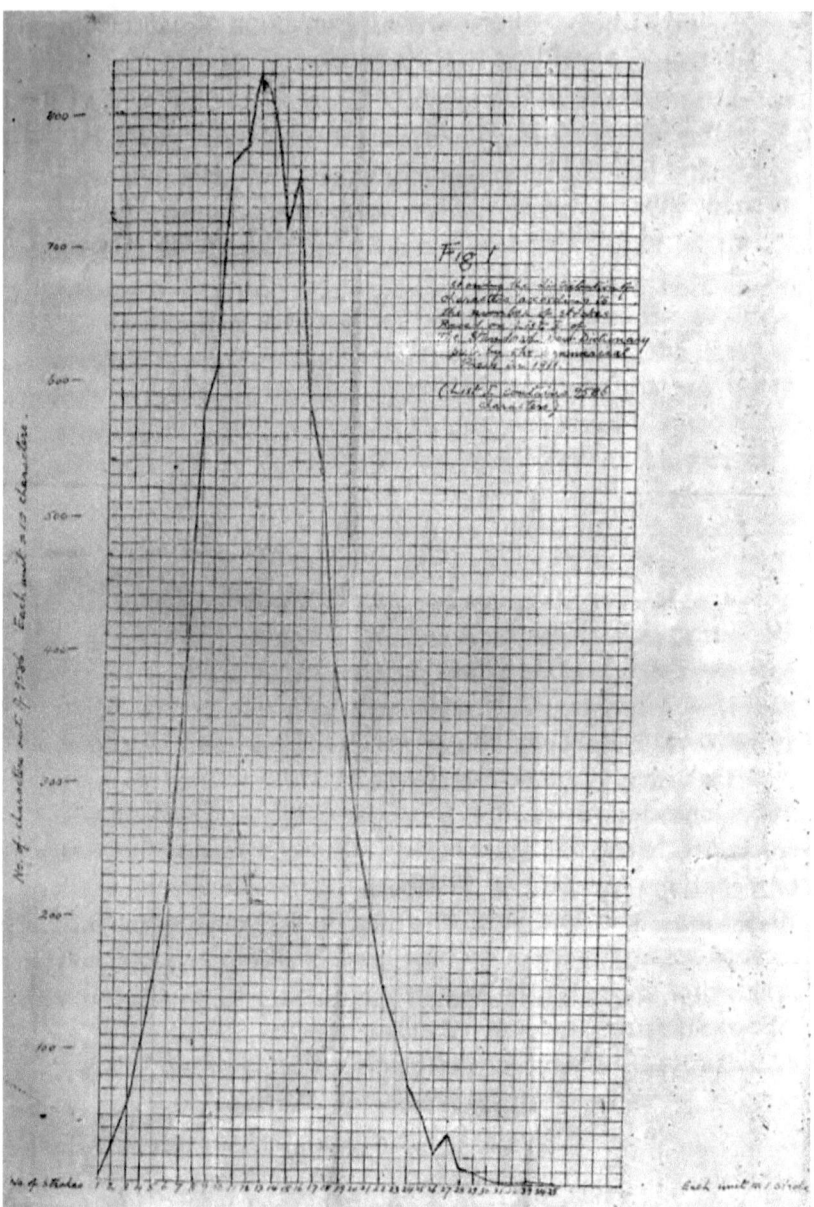

FIGURE 4.2 The distribution of characters according to the number of strokes. Each vertical unit corresponds to ten characters, and each horizontal unit corresponds to one stroke. The graph reaches its apex at 12 strokes, with a record of 829 characters. *Source*: Timothy Tingfang Lew, *The Psychology of Learning Chinese: A Preliminary Analysis by Means of Experimental Psychology of Some of the Factors Involved in the Process of Learning Chinese Characters* (Peking, 1924[?]), 23.

He then correlated the number of strokes with the rate of acquisition of sound, meaning, and form of a character, and tested it with all the different subjects, but the findings were again unexpected. An increase in the number of strokes did not result in a correlated difficulty of learning either the sound or the meaning of a character. But, if only meaning was taught to a beginner, then characters with more than ten strokes were more difficult to learn than those with ten strokes or fewer. In learning the form of a character, it was usually the case that the characters with a medium number of strokes were easier than the extremes, and the ones with the highest number of strokes were more difficult than those with fewer strokes, but those with very few strokes were not necessarily easier than the rest. Furthermore, the characters with a higher number of strokes were harder to learn but easier to recognize than those with fewer strokes. The reason for this unpredicted outcome, wrote Liu, was that the number of strokes was not the only nor the most important element in learning a character. Dozens of associations made between the form, sound, and meaning of a character played a big role in the acquisition of characters.[17]

In the following years, other psychologists' findings followed Liu's. In 1928, Cai Lesheng 蔡樂生 (Loh Seng Tsai) and Ethel Abernethy, two psychologists at the University of Chicago, also experimented with the number of strokes to determine whether the level of difficulty in learning characters decreased with the reduction of strokes. The experiment consisted of thirty Chinese characters paired with random English words. Three series were used, comprised of ten characters each. In the first series, there were three strokes for a character; in the second, there were six; and in the third, twelve. Twenty-one American graduate students who had no experience with Chinese characters served as research subjects. Each pair was shown for three seconds, and immediately after the showing of each character in each series, a test of recognition was given. Twenty-four hours later, a test of retention followed. And finally, a test of reproduction.

Cai and Abernethy claimed that the difficulty of retaining and reproducing a character increased with the number of strokes, but in the recognition of a character, the difficulty was in fact independent of the number of strokes, for characters with an equal number of strokes showed great differences in the time required to learn them. They thus concluded that in recognizing a character, the "patterns of characters," i.e., character forms (zixing 字形), were more important than stroke counts.[18] In short, neither Liu's nor Cai and Abernethy's research offered evidence for the reformers' claim that simplification facilitated learning. The composition of a given character had intrinsic visual qualities that were indispensable for recognizing it. But given that retaining and reproducing a character were also part of the labor involved in learning, wasn't it still necessary to reduce the number of strokes? And if so, what would be the methodology of reduction?

Ai Wei 艾偉 (1890–1955), Xu Zemin's mentor and a psychologist who taught Chinese at the School of Foreign Service at Georgetown University, formulated the most cogent response. In 1928, following the American psychologists and Liu Tingfang's pioneering works, he studied the psychology of learning characters, using James Yen's Thousand-Character Primer as his dataset. Of its 1,232 characters, Ai determined, 87 percent were composed of between five and seventeen strokes. He experimented with 148 American students from George Washington University and Georgetown who had no knowledge of Chinese characters. His main goal was to measure the time needed to reproduce the characters correctly, depending on the number of strokes. He prepared cards with different characters, and showed the cards to subjects eight times, each time for eight seconds; after each display, he asked them to reproduce what they saw (figure 4.3).[19]

His results showed that characters with ten or fewer strokes were much easier to learn than characters with more than ten strokes; yet, the rise in the number of strokes did not necessarily correlate with the difficulty of reading. On average, the characters with thirteen strokes were harder to memorize than those with seventeen strokes, which led Ai to conclude that the arrangement of strokes, i.e., the form of the character (*zixing*) was a significant component in assessing the difficulty of learning.[20] He proposed a practical solution to the problem at hand: eleven to fifteen strokes could form easy as well as hard characters depending on the character form. The hardest characters to learn were those composed of thirteen or more strokes, those with more than ten strokes on either side (such as *liu* 劉 or *luan* 亂), and those that had three or four parts to them (*yi* 疑 or *sha* 殺).[21] Simplification was a meaningful psychological enterprise as long as the forms of characters were maintained while their complicated components were simplified.

Xu Zemin's proposal for simplification, which was eventually published in Lin Yutang's *Analects*, followed Ai Wei's studies. Little is known of Xu,

SIMPLIFICATION OF CHINESE CHARACTERS

FIGURE 4.3 Reproduction of characters with different stroke numbers.
Source: Ai Wei, "Hanzi zhi xinli yanjiu (wei wan)" 漢字之心理研究(未完) [A psychological study of Chinese characters (to be continued)], Jiaoyu zazhi 20, no. 4 (1928): 15.

except his work on simplification and Chinese education at large, but his was one of the most ambitious and statistically driven studies at the time. In 1930, before he made it into *Analects*, Xu carried out a statistical study of stroke counts based on Chen Heqin's, Ao Hongde's, and Wang Wenxin's word counts, and he used Ai Wei's study to argue for a psychologically convenient reduction of strokes. Xu chose 800 out of the frequently used 2,400 characters, and compared them with all the characters and their stroke counts in the *Great Zhonghua Dictionary* 大中華字典, which had 42,239 characters in total.[22] His analysis was even more meticulous than Liu Tingfang's, who had used only 9,586 characters for his own work.

Xu's purpose was to decrease the number of strokes in the most frequently used characters, so that learning characters could conform with student psychology. He replicated Ai Wei's findings that characters with ten strokes or fewer were easy to learn. Among the characters with ten to fifteen strokes, the level of difficulty depended on other factors. Those that had more than fifteen strokes were simply too difficult. Based on Ai's findings, Xu calculated that among all 42,239 characters, 22.46 percent were easy to learn, 37.83 percent were difficult, and 39.71 percent depended on other factors. Among the frequently used characters, the results were not that encouraging either. Difficult characters still accounted for 18.34 percent, and the ones whose difficulty depended on other factors added up to 39.16 percent. In other words, even the frequently used characters were not that easy to learn. Simplification of characters was thus necessary, especially of the 18.34 percent of characters that were identified as difficult. Characters with more than eleven strokes, Xu wrote, must be simplified to have fewer than eleven, and those that already had fewer than eleven strokes should still be simplified further. If the average stroke number of the most frequently used one thousand characters could be taken down to around six, it would increase the speed of learning by reducing the required time by half.[23]

To devise a proposal for simplified characters, Xu combined Ai Wei's psychology with the *suzi* movement, which had been steadily progressing, and collected a large amount of *suzi* examples from various sources. He asked university students to write the *suzi* variants for 2,400 frequently used characters and searched for *suzi* in handwritten notes, letters, account books, and mimeographed publications of public speeches as well as in dictionaries and cursive-style calligraphy. Older books from the Qing dynasty and Liu Fu and Li Jiarui's collection of *suzi* from the Song onward also expanded the limits of Xu's *suzi* collection. In 1931, he published a list of 2,500 simplified characters, and when Lin Yutang endorsed the project, he selected 550 examples from his list to serve as a model for simplification. In 1934, Lin published them in *Analects*.[24] Some, though certainly not all, of Xu's characters will look familiar to the contemporary readers of simplified Chinese (figure 4.4).

Xu's proposal was a peculiar specimen, as he combined statistical knowledge with the ongoing search for *suzi*. Scientific experimentation was just an ally in the larger movement to simplify characters, for simplification clearly could not be based on science and experimentation alone. There was

FIGURE 4.4 A Sample from Xu Zemin's 550 *suzi*.
Source: Xu Zemin, "550 suzi biao" 俗字表 [A list of 550 suzi], *Lun yu* 45 (1934): 40.

more to learning Chinese characters than stroke numbers and the mechanics of acquisition. There was something in the *form* of characters, in the patterns of their constitution, that statistically driven psychologists alluded to but could not fully comprehend. Understanding the psychology of reading needed more than experiments and graphs; it required a phenomenological approach that could demonstrate the historically and socially embodied qualities of writing and seeing the characters. The second influential proposal in Lin Yutang's *Analects*, devised by Du Dingyou, sought to offer an alternative to the science of reading and writing.

Seeing the Characters: Habits and Character Simplification

A native of Guangdong, Du Dingyou received his degree in library sciences at the University of the Philippines. After his return to China in 1921, Du became a pioneer in Chinese library sciences, and was well-known for the novel methods he invented for simplifying the indexing of Chinese characters in libraries. A fervent critic of indexical innovations that relied solely on numbers, such as Wang Yunwu's famous Four-Corner Method (*sijiao haoma* 四角號碼), Du spent his early career trying to understand the interface between characters and the reading eye.[25] While not a psychologist himself, he was a proponent of the discipline as he found psychological experiments to be crucial for paving a way for reform in information management. He even published a textbook on psychology in 1925, which had almost twenty editions in six years.[26]

Du's interest in library sciences and indexing coincided with the period of reform in Chinese characters, and he offered his contribution to the simplification project. Before he came to terms with *suzi* in the 1930s, he had avant-garde ideas for reform. In the 1920s, for instance, he suggested that Chinese characters provided a unique opportunity to *combine* multiple characters into one, and thereby reduce the number of strokes and increase the density of input. He took classical literary style as his model. In classical texts, certain characters were indeed the combination of two characters. For example, *gai* 盍 was a combination of *he* 何 and *bu* 不, meaning "why not?" Du wanted to carry out the same principle for modern usage and invent new characters accordingly.[27] His favorite example, coming from his own occupational interest, was "library," which in modern Chinese was written in three characters, *tu-shu-guan* 圖書館, but he proposed to write it as one 圕, a *shu* 書 (book) inside a *wei* 囗 (enclosure), pronounced as *tuan*. Du's contemporaries praised this effort to economize writing through combining and shrinking characters, and Du started creating more examples.[28] But in the following years, he abandoned his avant-garde designs, and started working on a more practical project that took him to the territories of *suzi* and habits.

SIMPLIFICATION OF CHINESE CHARACTERS

In the early 1930s, Du was especially troubled by the problem of indexing Chinese characters in libraries. Deeply annoyed by popular indexing methods built on numbers and strokes, Du sided with the psychologists who had long been addressing the issue of character form. As Liu Tingfang, Cai Lesheng, and Ai Wei had all pointed out, the problem of efficiency in reading could not be resolved merely through a calculation of strokes; character forms were in many cases more important. Du concurred. Character forms were significant, he noted, because they conformed with the psychophysiological "habits" (*xiguan* 習慣) of reading Chinese. Chinese readers had been interacting with Chinese characters for thousands of years and had developed a particularly Chinese habit of "seeing" the characters.

Du's formulation of the question in terms of habits echoed earlier psychologists' work on the direction of reading Chinese. Since 1919, the change of the writing direction from vertical columns to horizontal lines was a fiercely debated subject. Many of the reformers, both psychologists and educators, believed that horizontal reading was intrinsically more efficient than vertical reading; but when this claim was put to test, every single result showed that vertical reading was in fact faster! Psychologists such as Zhang Yaoxiang, Du Zuozhou, and Eugene Shen (Shen Youqian), who recorded physiological reaction times and eye movements in their studies, all argued that this unexpected result simply reflected the old habits of reading, and that it could not be used as decisive evidence to argue that reading vertically was objectively more efficient (figure 4.5).[29]

Zhou Xiangeng 週先庚 (1903–1996), or Siegen K. Chou, took it upon himself to resolve this conundrum of habits. Zhou was a psychologist at Stanford from 1925 to 1930, and he later held several appointments in the psychology departments of Tsinghua, Beijing, and Southwestern University. During his brief stint at Stanford, he became highly skeptical of earlier research on the direction of reading and added further dimensions to the study of efficiency. Instead of comparing sentences written horizontally and vertically, he turned them upside down, wrote them from right to left, tilted them ninety degrees, and experimented with all possible directions characters could be written and arranged in. He further replicated his experiments with English words and sentences. In the end, he came up with a new conceptualization: the gestalt of reading Chinese characters.[30]

The gestalt of reading Chinese was a derivative of word-gestalt studies in Euro-America, according to which the perception of a word written in

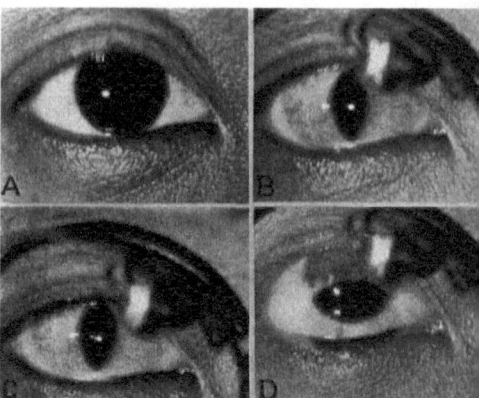

FIGURE 4.5 Measuring eye movements in the reading of Chinese.
Source: W. R. Miles and Eugene Shen, "Photographic Recording of Eye Movements in the Reading of Chinese in Vertical and Horizontal Axes: Method and Preliminary Results," *Journal of Experimental Psychology* 10 (1925): 346, 351.

English letters was not so much based on the individual letters but on the gestalt of the word, which was bigger than the sum of its parts. He took the example of an English poem. When the poem was turned upside down, the words did not look the same, although their similar structures were still vividly discernible. Its mirror image, similarly, required a different orientation for the reader, but since the sequences of individual letters were not altered, it did not make a big difference in the perception of the word-gestalt. Yet, instead of turning each word upside down, if one turned the mirror image of each individual letter upside down, then the experience of reading was completely different (figure 4.6). The word-gestalt no longer had its original characteristics. If the order of the letters were changed even more radically, the word-gestalt would lose almost all of its properties.

Zhou followed the same order of distortions in his experiment of Chinese sentence-gestalt. He changed the order and position of characters for his experiment (figure 4.7). And his findings were, again, unexpected. It turned out that leftward horizontal reading was indeed 5 percent faster than rightward reading. Moreover, leftward reading was also 4 percent faster than the traditional downward reading. Leftward horizontal reading,

SIMPLIFICATION OF CHINESE CHARACTERS

> Being a brain is not to live in gladness
> So long as conscious mammals rant and rave:
> For thoughts askew provoke my cells to madness
> And force me fast toward a luckless grave.

FIGURE 4.6 The original poem (*top*); poem turned upside down (*middle left*); the poem's mirror image (*middle right*); the mirror image of each individual letter turned upside down (*bottom*).
Source: Siegen K. Chou (Zhou Xiangeng), "*Gestalt* in Reading Chinese Characters," *Psychological Review* 37, no. 1 (January 1930): 54–55.

in other words, was the fastest. But instead of taking this finding at face value and arguing for the necessity to write horizontally in a leftward direction, Zhou suggested that reading efficiency was not necessarily an outcome of line arrangement. It had "something intrinsic in the sequential order of eye-movement pauses." The eye-movement pauses in the linear width of each English word was different from the order of eye-movement pauses from top to bottom. "Words or letters follow one another," he wrote. "The word 'follows' implies a meaning that is both spatial and temporal. When two or more words or letters stand together on the page . . . they are only spatially following one another. But so long as they are intended to be read . . . they are not only spatially following one another but temporally as well."[31]

Similarly, in Chinese downward reading, the perceptual process followed a spatiotemporal order: first came the bottom side of the first character and then the top side of the next. In other words, the temporal-spatial sequence of written letters/characters followed an intrinsic physiological order, and thus "the general preference in reading efficiency," wrote Zhou, "is not for a certain absolute reading-direction nor for a certain absolute character-position exclusively but rather for a certain relative

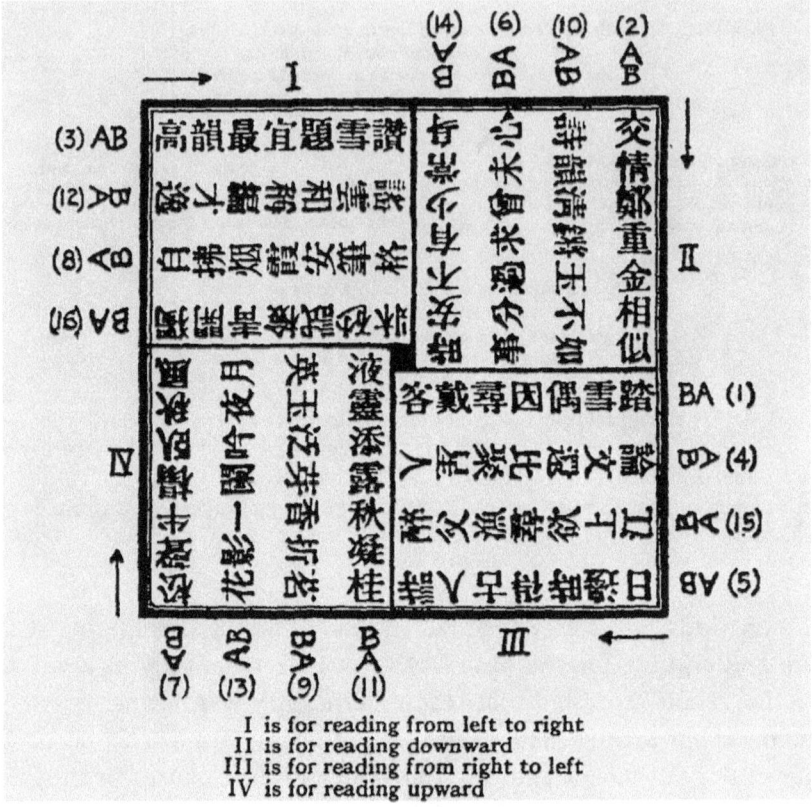

FIGURE 4.7 Experimenting with the directions of reading Chinese.
Source: Siegen K. Chou (Zhou Xiangeng), "Gestalt in Reading Chinese Characters," Psychological Review 37, no. 1 (January 1930): 60.

temporal-spatial sequence resulting from the direction-position combination. It is this temporal-spatial sequence that constitutes the *Gestalt* of a line of Chinese characters."[32]

The physiological process of reading from top to bottom, argued Zhou, like his colleagues, was a deep-rooted, habitual phenomenon: "Chinese adult readers find their reading efficiency preference most strikingly for the primary *Gestalt* of 'bottom-to-up' sequence irrespective of the reading direction, primary in the sense that it had been the only traditional sequence for centuries until about a decade ago." Efficiency, in other words, could not be artificially fabricated. The gestalt of the spatiotemporally configured reading units and "the phenomenal and reaction patterns and configurational dispositions and capacities *within the reader*" determined reading efficiency. Responding to earlier comments that habit cannot be the exclusive and exhaustive explanation, Zhou argued that "[habit] can be . . . *the* exclusive and exhaustive explanation in the sense that the age-long and life-long traditional practice in vertical downward reading of upright characters has entirely outdone, eclipsed, and obliterated the hypothetical influence of all other possible factors."[33]

Zhou's reconsideration of habit in terms of spatiotemporality of writing provided an alternative to a mere calculation of speed and statistical analyses. The physiology of the human subject, according to Zhou, was not enough to account for efficiency. It was the spatial configuration of the written word and the historically developed interaction between writing and the human subject that played the most significant role in determining efficiency. Habits, in other words, were not obstacles, but necessary components of mental and literate life. They could not be changed according to a unilateral calculation of physiological reaction time.

Du Dingyou's own work on indexing Chinese characters wrestled with the issue of character forms and habits, and, in many ways, it echoed Zhou's patterns of thought. A habit, according to Du, was a deeply ingrained psychophysiological process, and it could not be changed with the wave of a hand. But in contrast to Zhou, who used habits as a reason for sustaining the status quo, Du used them as a springboard to reform Chinese information management. Du was not an experimental psychologist like Zhou and others, but his amateur interest in incalculable habits gave rise to some of the most original research on the psychology of reading Chinese.

In his magnum opus on indexing Chinese characters, Du devised eight ways of "seeing" a character, which corresponded to Chinese people's "psychological and physiological habits" (*xinli he shengli shang de xiguan* 心理和生理上的習慣) of reading.[34] According to Du, Chinese characters were first of all visual constructions. They were composed of radicals (*bushou* 部首) and character roots (*zigen* 字根), and these two components were habitually indispensable in seeing and reading a character. The characters for his name, Du Dingyou 杜定友, for example, were written vertically, horizontally, and diagonally (figure 4.8). A reader of Chinese visually perceived the vertically written character *du* 杜 from left to right—according to habitual sight, a reader's eye followed the spatial and temporal order by seeing the radical

次第	名稱	定　　義	圖　形 (陰面為部首)	舉例
1	縱	凡字可以直判為數組者以左邊第一組為部首		杜
2	橫	凡字可以橫判為數組者以上邊第一組為部首		定
3	斜	凡字可以斜判為數組者以左上第一組為部首		友
4	載	凡字可以斜判為數組而左下部有一長捺或長鉤承載上部者以左下部為部首		述
5	覆	凡字可以橫判為數組而第一組有一撇一捺遮蓋其他各組者以上部為部首		公
6	角	凡字可以內外判為數組而外部包蓋其他各組之一角或兩角不成正方形者以外部為部首		開
7	方	凡字成四方形者以方框為部首		圖
8	整	凡字不可分判者依全字筆順排列		史

FIGURE 4.8 Du Dingyou's eight forms for characters.
Source: Du Dingyou, *Hanzi xingwei pai jian fa* 漢字形位排檢法 [An arrangement method for Chinese character forms] (Shanghai: Zhonghua Press, 1932), 2.

木 before the character root 土. If a character was horizontally written, however, like *ding* 定, then the Chinese viewer perceived it from top to bottom, i.e., 宀 (radical) came before 疋 (character root). When a character was written diagonally, as in the case of *you* 友, perception of the left side preceded perception of the right side. As for his favorite character, "library" 圖, habit demanded that the eye read it rectangularly—first the enclosure 囗 (radical), then the treasure inside, the book 書 (character root).[35] The ways of seeing, much like the gestalt of reading, coincided with the visual structure of the

SIMPLIFICATION OF CHINESE CHARACTERS

Chinese characters, in which the radical and the character root were equally important.

Du's theory of seeing was specifically aimed against rival indexing schemes, but it was also the basis of his proposal for simplification. Two years after he published the eight forms of seeing Chinese characters, Du published a list of four hundred simplified characters. As long as the number of strokes could be reduced without harming either the visual form of the character or the psycho-physiological habit of reading it, Du saw no problem with simplification. He was especially in support of *suzi* and was closely following the other proposals. Remaining true to his earlier indexing project and the extant *suzi*, Du decreased the number of strokes in radicals and in character roots in order to retain the forms mostly intact—except the popular *suzi* that completely replaced complicated forms, such as *zhi* 只 instead of *zhi* 祇 (figure 4.9). His faithfulness to *suzi* helped to put his proposal at the forefront of the simplification project. Some of Du's characters will also be familiar to readers of Chinese, even more so than Xu's.[36]

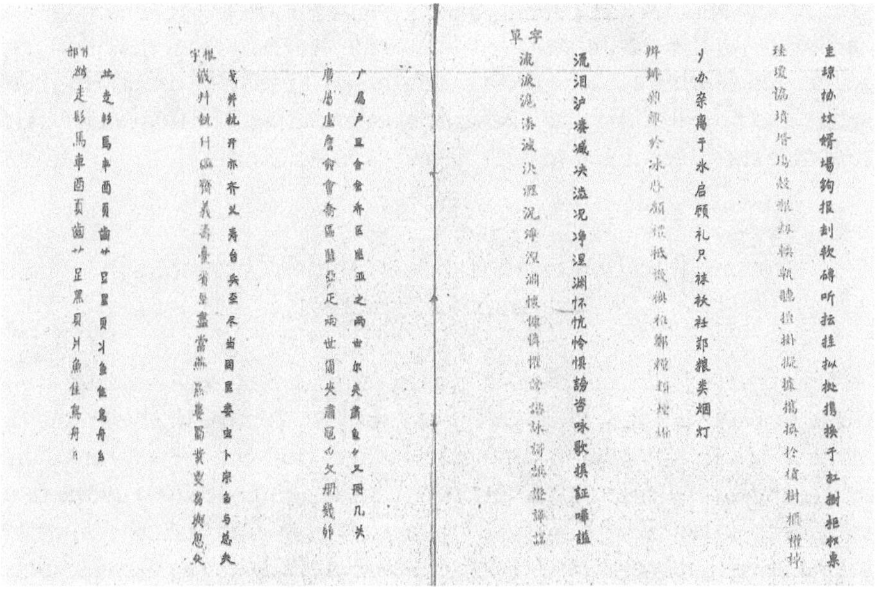

FIGURE 4.9 Du Dingyou's proposal for simplified characters.
Source: Du Dingyou, *Tushuguan bian muyong jianzi biaozhun zibiao* 圖書館編目用簡字標準字表 [A standardized list of simplified characters for use in library catalogues] (Shanghai: Zhongguo tushuguan fuwushe, 1934).

[141]

As opposed to statistical analyses that put faith in numbers, Du's version of simplified characters was an experiment in understanding the psychology of reading as a historically and socially constituted practice. The identification of strokes as the basic units of a character was misleading, according to Du. Strokes, after all, were not alphabetic letters, and statistical works that counted strokes were wrong in assuming that the two were somehow commensurable. Reforming Chinese information management, either for indexing or simplifying characters, necessitated the adoption of categories that were intrinsic to the composition of characters themselves. For Du, radicals and character roots were the indivisible components of characters, which the reading eye had interacted with for thousands of years, developing a mutually constitutive habitual practice that could only be reformed from within.

Taken together, Xu Zemin's and Du Dingyou's proposals offered different epistemic methods for simplifying Chinese characters. But regardless of their differences, they were both products of transnational scientific networks that extended from China to the United States, and they were both printed and endorsed by Lin Yutang, the leading name in the simplification debates. With the debates gradually maturing, it seemed that the reformers could soon reach a consensus over the standardization of simplified characters and propel China into a new age of information. The final step was to convince the government to put the project into action.

Simplification as Apocalypse: "Native Characters" vs. "Handy Characters"

Du's proposal in 1934 was the last in a list of influential schemes, including those of Hu Huaichen, Chen Guangyao, and Xu Zemin. In the following months, Wu Zhihui, Qian Xuantong, and others from the Preparatory Committee put all the proposals together and made a final decision on the first standardized set of 324 simplified characters. In August 1935, the Ministry of Education finally approved the first set and promulgated its use in schools. After more than a decade of work, Chinese characters were finally and officially simplified. But in January 1936, only five months after the ministry's approval, the Central Executive Committee of the GMD decided to postpone the project indefinitely. Especially given that the government had close ties with the Preparatory Committee, which fully supported the movement, the abrupt decision to cancel the project was surely surprising. What was the problem with simplified characters?

The GMD had an ambiguous position regarding the simplification of characters. Since the Shanghai massacre in 1927, when GMD forces brutally suppressed the communists in Shanghai and severed ties with the CCP, there was an increasing influence of fascist ideology among the higher echelons, with an emphasis on "native culture." In February 1934, Generalissimo Chiang Kai-shek initiated the New Life Movement (NLM), which was the GMD's counterrevolutionary project to nazify the party under the image of a Chinese führer, and discipline citizen behavior by intervening in daily life to build and mobilize a new nation. The NLM was officially launched in Nanchang, Jiangxi Province, on February 19, 1934, but the plan to emulate German and Italian fascism was already underway before that date.[37] A crucial element in the nazification of party politics was the reinvention of a traditional vocabulary and culture as the essence of the Chinese nation. The new public morality (*gongde* 公德) consisted, on the one hand, of a modern hygienic vocabulary that focused on orderliness and cleanliness, and of a traditional conceptual vocabulary based in Confucian morality on the other: "propriety" (*li* 禮), "righteousness" (*yi* 義), "integrity" (*lian* 廉), and "sense of shame" (*chi* 恥). Modernity was equated with embracing native traditions, and reviving a "native morality" (*guyou daode* 固有道德).[38] What Dai Li, the head of intelligence and Chiang Kai-shek's right arm, had written as the purpose of espionage in 1934 was true for the New Life Movement at large: "to construct a psychology [*jianshe xinli* 建設心理] through recuperating China's native virtue [*guyou zhi dexing* 固有之德性], and to turn the people's minds toward the correct revolutionary path [*geming zhi zhenggui* 革命之正軌]."[39] "Nativeness" was critical for imagining the past and ordering the present for a "new life." Similar to the Third Reich's revival of classicism, the GMD's purpose was to discipline the people's minds and bodies by reviving native glory and inventing a new architecture of being in modern space and time.

The ideological commitments of the GMD played a critical role in the history of scripts reforms, including character simplification. The biggest anathema for the leaders of the NLM was the abandonment of Chinese traditions, and script reform fell within this category. Even before the official announcement of the NLM, script reformers who might not have necessarily agreed with the fascist turn in politics anticipated the kind of issues "nativeness" as a political project could pose for the simplification of characters. In January 1934, just a month before Chiang initiated the NLM and a year and half before the Ministry of Education promulgated 324 simplified characters, Qian Xuantong recognized the dangers of nativist thought and published a new article, titled "A Proposal for Mining the *Native and Thus More Appropriate* Simplified Characters" (*Soucai guyou er jiao shiyong de jiantizi an*).[40] Placing the emphasis on "native and thus more appropriate," hoped Qian, could convince the party that simplification was not against native culture.

Qian's concerns were justified, for immediately after the declaration of the NLM, Chiang Kai-shek ordered Wang Shijie 王世傑 (1891–1981), the minister of education, to investigate simplified characters and determine whether they conformed with the ideological position of the party. On June 4, 1934, Wang wrote a long letter, and explained that the simplification of characters was necessary for expanding literacy, and that they were based on "native" characters—in other words, characters were not created anew. Wang quoted in detail a letter he had received from Wu Zhihui in 1934, who was then the head of the Preparatory Committee. In his letter, Wu conceptualized the project as being as "native" as possible. In the words of Wu Zhihui, progressive dynasties had simplified writing piecemeal, and the GMD was going to be the last in this long chain of simplification. There were three pillars of the movement, all of which spoke to the ideological vision of the GMD—national revival (*minzu fuxing* 民族復興), cultural progress (*wenhua gaijin* 文化改進), and linguistic unity (*yuyan tongyi* 語言統一):

> From now on, writing Chinese characters will recuperate the two-thousand-year practice of simplifying characters. In January [1934], this committee has therefore penned "A Proposal for Mining the Native and Thus More Appropriate Simplified Characters," and passed a resolution to first search and select appropriate characters to use as simplified characters, which is going to be edited as *A Record of Simplified Characters* [*Jianti zipu* 簡體字譜], and [the committee] will organize a commission to select these characters. As of now, the committee is in the process of selection. The simplification of Chinese characters is certainly

not a fundamental reform. Therefore, we search and select the characters with less strokes from the cursive script [*caoshu* 草書], running script [*xingshu* 行書], and other scripts [*bieshu* 別書].⁴¹

Wu Zhihui's endorsement was carefully articulated, as he likely recognized the danger that simplification was in and reconceptualized it as a project that had been progressing for two millennia. With Wu's letter in hand, Wang Shijie proposed the following: firstly, characters were going to be selected according to their earlier use; they were not going to be reinvented. Secondly, after the publication of the first set of simplified characters, the Ministry of Education was to solicit ideas from all sides and slowly increase the number of simplified characters. And lastly, the use of simplified characters was going to be limited in scope. For the time being, only general school textbooks, general reading materials, and primary school textbooks were going to be published with them.⁴²

Wu Zhihui and Qian Xuantong were clearly nervous about the outcome of the NLM, which explains the title of Qian's article a few months prior. Theirs was an endeavor to save the simplification movement from falling prey to the conservative voices inside the GMD, hence the choice of the description "native, and thus more appropriate." The movement was too big to abandon, and an enormous amount of labor had been exerted by reformers. Nativeness had not been the primary objective of the movement, but given the unprecedented emphasis on native culture, it did not hurt to redefine the simplification movement according to the party line, since text mining was after all a "native" project. At least for the time being, the party could get behind the movement.

Nativeness was not the only obstacle, however. By 1934, the simplification movement was already out of the hands of the few people who had initiated it. The members of the Preparatory Committee had been supporting the project since the beginning, but Lin Yutang's public endorsement through *Analects* had taken the movement to a different level. *Suzi* and the populism that they evoked were embraced by a large number of scholars, writers, and intellectuals with different political views and different opinions regarding the ultimate future of Chinese characters. In 1935, the momentum of simplified characters was almost too big to stand up against, but the movement was no longer unified.

While the Preparatory Committee was trying to rescue simplification by reformulating it as a nativist endeavor, a separate group of reformers composed primarily of leftist intellectuals embarked on a different path. They also wanted to simplify characters, but they fervently opposed nativism and certainly did not see simplification as the culmination of an imperial progression. For them, simplification was a necessary first step toward a future abandonment of characters altogether and an eventual embrace of a latinized China. As the next two chapters will explain in detail, latinization started as a socialist project in the USSR and reached its zenith in China in the early 1930s. Leftist writers unanimously agreed that the USSR-backed Chinese Latin Alphabet was the only option China had for the future.[43] Yet, many of the leftist writers were aware of the technical problems an abrupt alphabetic transition could engender. That is why they put their efforts into simplification. But both the politics *and* the method of simplification, they claimed, had to be different. The movement thus assumed a new life when Chen Wangdao 陳望道, along with other leftist script reformers, championed it in 1935. As the chief editor of *Taibai* 太白, Chen saw merit in *suzi* and the simplification movement, for it closely resonated with the leftist project of creating a "language of the masses" (*dazhongyu* 大眾語).[44] Chen joined hands with his comrades and with supportive liberal scholars to promote a different set of simplified characters that did not map onto the Preparatory Committee's project.

In February 1935, on the pages of *Shenbao*, intellectuals from diverse backgrounds jointly announced that they had cast typesets for three hundred simplified characters, or, in their own words, "handy characters" (*shoutouzi* 手頭字), the characters in the hands of the masses (figure 4.10). Among the two hundred supporters of the "handy characters" were a variety of people from different backgrounds, including the psychologists and educators hitherto mentioned, and some famous leftist and liberal figures: Hong Shen, Zhang Yaoxiang, Liu Tingfang, Yu Dafu, Hu Yuzhi, Chen Wangdao, Lin Handa, Guo Moruo, Cai Yuanpei, Tao Xingzhi, Zheng Zhenduo, Ye Laishi, Lao She, and many others. In spite of the liberal voices in the project, the use of the term "handy characters" (*shoutouzi*) instead of "simplified characters" (*jiantizi*) was a political decision that signaled leftist involvement. Most of the characters were in fact the same as or very similar to the simplified characters prepared by the Preparatory Committee,

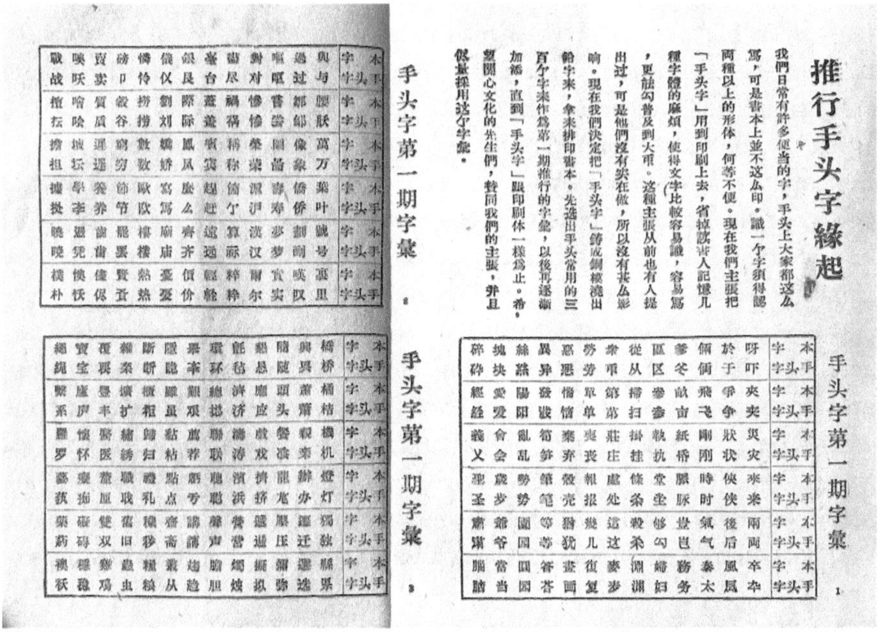

FIGURE 4.10 A selection from the three hundred handy characters.
Source: "Tuixing shoutouzi yuanqi" 推行手頭字緣起 [The origins of carrying out handy characters], *Xinsheng zhoukan* 2, no. 6 (1935): 22.

but some who signed the announcement, which read more like a short manifesto, claimed that the "handy characters" were indeed different from "simplified characters."

Pan Guangrong 潘廣鎔, a leftist and a latinist, explained the difference as follows: "All handy characters are of course simplified characters ... [but] not all simplified characters are handy characters, because some of them are not simplified according to habits [of writing]."[45] Pan only wanted handy characters that reflected the writing habits of the masses (*dazhong*). He was annoyed by the scholastic side of the project that involved thumbing through old dictionaries, characters, and calligraphic styles, which others had been praising along with the use of *suzi*. The character for "masses" (*zhong* 衆), for instance, was simplified as *zhong* 众 by Qian Xuantong and others, but according to Pan, it had to resemble the character 禹 without the three strokes at the bottom (冂 and 一), which, Pan claimed, conformed more with the masses'

[147]

daily use, indicating that handy characters were by the masses and for the masses. He further noted that handy characters were the first step toward an ultimate latinization, a crucial difference that set handy characters apart from simplified characters. In addition, Pan was also proud to show the agency of the self-appointed representatives of the masses involved in casting handy-characters typesets. The Preparatory Committee's demand that the government cast typesets for them was passive, according to him. The handy-characters team did not wait for the government to comply; they came, they cast, and they printed.[46] Importantly, the handy characters were cast in metal, as the manifesto noted: "We advocate the use of 'handy characters' to print so that the trouble imposed on the reader's memory by several forms of characters may be reduced. . . . Others have advocated the same earlier, but none put it into practice, and thus they had no impact. Now, we have decided to melt copper molds and cast typesets to print 'handy characters' in books."[47] Not surprisingly, neither Lin Yutang nor Wu Zhihui nor Qian Xuantong were among the people who signed the manifesto for handy characters.

The simplification movement was not solely leftist by any means, but the leftist involvement (or hijacking) of the project demonstrated the inherently politicized nature of proposals for reducing character strokes. For instance, Zhang Shuhuang 張樹璜, a scholar from Hunan known for his works on National Learning (guoxue 國學), was furious. Zhang was against simplification projects of all sorts, but, writing shortly after the manifesto, he proclaimed that "handy characters" foretold nothing less than "national suicide" (zisha minzu 自殺民族).[48] Zhang was not alone in his animosity. The simplification project as a whole was already on precarious grounds, and handy characters did not help its case, as they heralded a future devoid of characters in toto.

A few months later, in August 1935, the Ministry of Education promulgated the first set of 324 simplified characters, officially proposed by the Preparatory Committee.[49] However, the officially published 324 characters had some peculiar characteristics. Only 193 of the characters were the same as the handy characters that were already cast and in use for printing, signaling the sharp difference between the two schemes.[50] Moreover, the ministry's characters were lithographed, which indicated that the ministry had still not issued an order to cast typesets for the characters (figure 4.11). In terms of practical implementation, handy characters were winning the race,

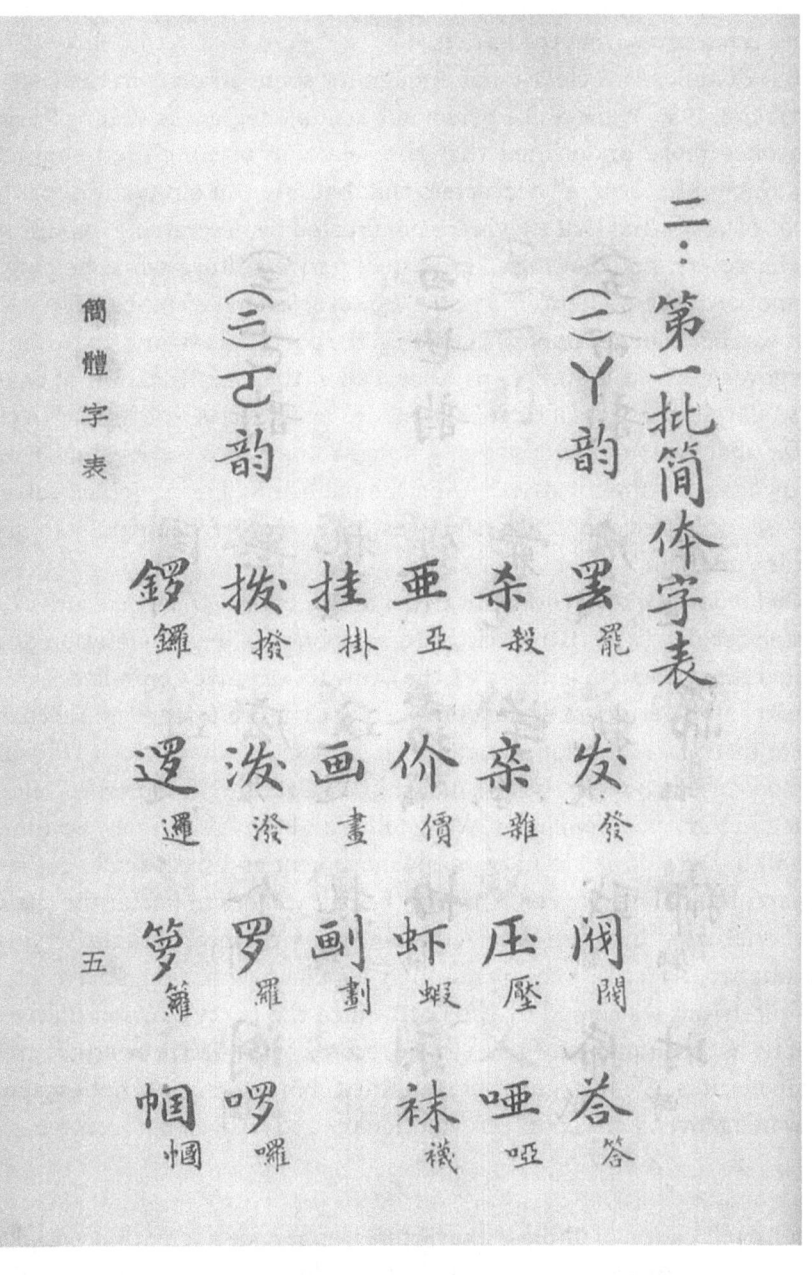

FIGURE 4.11 A sample from the Ministry of Education's 324 simplified characters. *Source:* Jiaoyu bu, *Jianti zibiao di yi pi* 簡體字表第一批 [A list of simplified characters, first batch] (Jiaoyu bu, 1935).

while the government and the Preparatory Committee were trying to distance themselves from the leftists.

But distance was clearly not enough for some officials in the GMD. On October 8, 1935, Wang Shijie personally sent a telegram to Chiang Kai-shek and once more underlined that the selection of simplified characters was limited to "native" characters that had been in circulation for thousands of years, and that they were not created from scratch. Simplification of characters, noted Wang, "respect[ed] native culture while helping the promotion [of characters]."[51] By then, however, even the emphasis on nativeness was not enough. Opposition within the party was strong. In November, the governor of Hunan, for instance, called the simplification of characters "self-destruction of national essence" (zihui guocui 自毀國粹).[52] In cities as far apart as Taiyuan and Hong Kong, committees were established to lobby against simplification.[53] Even the publishing houses joined forces to oppose simplified characters, since casting new types would put a financial burden on them.[54]

On January 17, 1936, the Political Committee of the Central Executive Committee decided in its fifth meeting to postpone the implementation of simplified characters. On January 22, the Central Executive Committee sent the order to all government agencies to postpone the project; and on February 5, the Ministry of Education complied.[55] It is not clear what exactly transpired behind closed doors in the five months between the characters' promulgation and their postponement. Wang Shijie and the Preparatory Committee did all in their power to narrate the movement as a native one, but it was apparently still disliked by many in the party. More importantly, the support that simplification received from left-wing intellectuals, who were simultaneously leading the increasingly popular latinization movement, was definitely not welcomed by the GMD, since the party's raison d'être was strictly anti-communist. Although the records of the GMD's meetings are not available, it is safe to argue that simplified characters could not escape the New Life Movement's counterrevolutionary and nativist persecution.

* * *

The simplification of Chinese characters was at once a scientific, social, and political movement. Much like the Mass Education Movement's intimate relationship with experimental psychology, simplification was also informed in various ways by psychological theories that ranged from statistical calculations to the phenomenology of seeing characters. Common to all reformers was an endeavor to articulate a native response to the information age that transformed the demands on manual and intellectual labor. In contrast to alphabetization, character simplification was a project to domesticate global forces and change from within.

While character simplification involved a wide range of actors, we should remember that it was initiated by a search for mental and clerical labor efficiency in a modernizing political economy of information. Indeed, simplifying the characters was akin to what Schumpeter called "creative destruction," through which industrial capitalism "revolutionizes the economic structure *from within*, incessantly destroying the old one, incessantly creating a new one."[56] The innovations in Chinese information technologies under a republican knowledge economy mirrored this process, as the simplifiers sought revolution *from within*. Their ultimate goal was not unified, as some considered simplification as an end in itself while others saw it as a step toward latinization. But regardless of their divergent ambitions, script reformers creatively embodied "the spirit of informationalism," inventing new indexing methods, experimenting with punctuation marks, and simplifying characters in order to revolutionize the Chinese knowledge economy.[57] And yet, character simplification, just like the invention of phonetic scripts and the statistical frequency tests, was also inevitably tied up with information politics, which eventually led to the demise of the movement itself.

Despite their seemingly radical stance, the simplifiers were radical only within the bounds of the native system. Anything more radical than simplification was certainly beyond the paternalist toleration of the GMD. After all, the party cultivated a severe aversion to simplification after the leftists promoted it as the first step toward ultimate destruction, i.e., latinization. Latinization was without a doubt the most popular movement in Chinese script reforms, and it was part of a much larger latinization movement across Eurasia, from Turkey to Mongolia. While the Chinese simplifiers were wrestling with text mining and fascist politics, half of Eurasia was buzzing with latinization and the revolutionary destruction that it called for. Chinese communists and left-wing intellectuals soon joined the rest of the continent. Why, they asked, should China keep its native characters when even the Russians were willing to latinize the Cyrillic alphabet? Why not join the revolution, destroy the millennia-old tradition, adopt a radically new script, and fundamentally transform the material interface with language and information? In order to understand the power of these questions in the 1930s, the next chapter takes us on a journey to the other end of Eurasia, where latinization started as a revolutionary project—Baku, Azerbaijan.

FIVE

The New Dunganese Alphabet
Latinization Across Eurasia

THE CHINESE LATIN ALPHABET (CLA), commonly known as Sin Wenz 新文字, was arguably the most controversial Chinese script designed in the global information age. Finalized in 1931 in Vladivostok, a major city on the Pacific coast in Far Eastern USSR, the CLA was the only major Chinese script to have originated outside the borders of republican China. Yet, its lasting impact on the Chinese society was remarkable. In the midst of battles over script that ranged from the National Phonetic Alphabet to the simplification of Chinese characters, the CLA posed a radically different alternative: its socialist designers called for an utter destruction of the Chinese characters and their replacement by latinized letters. The power of the CLA and the society that it envisioned for China was formidable in the 1930s. Hundreds of figures from a variety of political backgrounds espoused the CLA over other scripts, and their support continued even after the GMD officially banned the promotion of the CLA in 1936, soon after it suspended character simplification. The popularity of the CLA grew after the establishment of the PRC, until it was replaced by Pinyin in 1958.

How did the CLA's radically destructive design become so coveted among Chinese reformers and revolutionaries from the 1930s onward? What did it offer that other scripts did not? This chapter is an attempt to provide a revisionist history of the CLA's origin to rethink the particular moment in which it promised a powerful alternative for Chinese reformers and revolutionaries. Scholars have previously pointed out that the latinization of Chinese started in Moscow through a collaboration between Chinese dissidents and Russian linguists and philologists. Much credit is given to Qu Qiubai 瞿秋白 (1899–1935), a young communist who moved to the Soviet Union after the Bolshevik Revolution and took part in the Chinese Latinization Movement. While he was in Moscow, the common narrative goes, he collaborated with the Russian linguist Vsevolod Sergeevich Kolokolov (1896–1979) in designing the CLA and published his proposal in 1930 under the Russian title *Kitaiskaia Latinizirovannaia Azbuka* (*Chinese Latinized Alphabet*), which was ratified in Vladivostok a year later and entered China thereafter. The CLA, up until now, has been narrated as Qu's work of art.[1]

However, a close reading of the CLA's letters themselves, as they were ratified in 1931, reveals a different origin story, for they were in fact not entirely the same as Qu's letters from a year prior. The phonetic values of letters as they were used in the CLA will be quite jarring to the modern reader of Pinyin. *Yuyan* 語言 (language), for example, was transcribed as *yjan* in the CLA. *Ladinghua* 拉丁化 (latinization), to give another example, was latinized as *latinxua* in the CLA. The Chinese Latin Alphabet, in other words, used letters with unusual phonetic values: *j* of the CLA gave a *y* ([ɥ] /[j]) sound; *x* gave a *h* ([x]/[h]) sound; *y* gave a *ü* ([y]/[ü]) sound, and so on. Where, then, did these letters come from? And what can they tell us about the origins of the CLA?

This chapter revises the history of the CLA by starting with the First All-Union Turcology Congress that convened in Baku, the capital of the Soviet Socialist Republic of Azerbaijan, in 1926, where the revolutionary participants decided to latinize the Arabic script in use across the Caucasus and Central Asia. The reason for this geographical reorientation brings me to the historical argument of this chapter: latinization was a Turkic project, the beginnings of which dated back to the 1860s in the Ottoman Empire and Russian Transcaucasia. The political economy of information that transformed mental and clerical labor regimes was not unique to China—it was truly global. The modern impulse to create literate subjects and turn them into efficient knowledge workers was also ubiquitous in Central Asia, the Ottoman Empire, and the Russian Empire from the second half of the nineteenth century onward. In each, the innovations in printing technologies, the inauguration of telegraphic communications, mass education movements, and the expansion of bureaucratic apparatuses for information management proved to be challenging for the local systems of writing, precipitating new techniques to increase mental and clerical labor efficiency.

The first calls for Arabic script reform started in the 1850s and 1860s in Istanbul, Tbilisi, and Tehran. Pressured by new communications and information infrastructures that arrived with Western imperial penetration, especially by the telegraph and the movable metal type, reformers contended that the Arabic script was an inefficient medium in a new age of information. The similarities between Arabic and Chinese script reformers were indeed striking. The main problem, according to some of the Arabic script reformers, was the multiple glyphs used for most letters, since Arabic letters took different shapes depending on their place in a word. This caused problems both for telegraphic communication, which was based on an epistemology of writing in separate letters, and for letterpress printing, which required casting multiple metal sorts for each letter. New communication technologies, in other words, turned the Arabic script into an "uneconomic" technology in the eyes of reformers. Some of them also emphasized the need to reform the script in order to avoid "mental confusion" (*teşviş-i zihni*) and "waste of thought" (*sarf-ı efkar*), which echoed the Chinese reformers' concern with efficiency in mental labor.[2] While Qing and Ottoman intellectuals had little to no contact with one another, their employment of a similar vocabulary in describing their scripts bespeaks the political economic forces of the global information age that challenged communication practices across the non-Western world in very similar ways.

By the 1910s, there were a number of script proposals in the Russo-Ottoman space, and in 1922, following the Bolshevik Revolution and the fall of the Ottoman Empire, the Azerbaijanis in Baku championed the movement by inventing the latinized New Turkic Alphabet (*jeni turq əlifbası*), which was particularly praised by Russian intellectuals and revolutionaries. "Latinization," in the alleged words of Lenin, was "the great revolution in the East!"[3] Only four years after the promulgation of the New Turkic Alphabet in Baku, the First All-Union Turcology Congress convened in the same city under the auspices of the Central Committee of the Soviet Union. Its goal was to resolve the problem of the Arabic script in the USSR, which was used widely across Central Asia among Uzbeks, Kazakhs, Turkmens, and other nationalities. Heated debates around the future of the alphabet ended in a majority vote that approved of latinization, and shortly after the Congress, Russian and Turkic revolutionaries devised the Unified New Turkic Alphabet (UNTA) to latinize the Arabic letters of Turco-Muslim nationalities. But the ambition of the revolutionaries was even greater. For them, the UNTA was not only a new script for Central Asia but the new internationalist medium to build a socialist civilization that went beyond the borders of the USSR. Following its invention, the UNTA immediately became the blueprint for latinizing non-Turkic languages as well, such as Kurdish, Persian, and Mongolian. It was within this Eurasian context that the UNTA was exported to China, too.

The first version of the Chinese Latin Alphabet, before its ratification in 1931, was known as the New Dunganese Alphabet (*novyi dunganskii alfavit*), and its letters were largely based on the latinized letters of the UNTA. The New Dunganese Alphabet was invented by and for the Dungans, i.e., Chinese Muslims living in Central Asia and speaking a language close to northern Mandarin. What distinguished the Dungans from the Han Chinese was the script they used to transcribe Mandarin sounds, which was in Arabic letters. Known as Xiao'erjin 小兒錦, also known as Xiao'erjing 小兒經, the Arabic script used by the Dungans turned out to be a convenient starting point for latinizing Chinese, since the UNTA was specifically designed to latinize the Arabic letters at large. In 1928, the New Dunganese Alphabet thus replaced the Arabic script of the Chinese Muslims with the latinized script of the UNTA, and later it also became the basis on which the Chinese Latin Alphabet was finalized in 1931. Hence the "strange" phonetic values of the CLA that I mentioned earlier: *j* of the CLA gave a *y* sound because it carried within it a secret Arabic *ya* ى, the historical traces of which have been erased in scholarship. X carried a secret *ha* ح, *y* a secret *waw* و, *c* a *che* چ, and so on. The New Dunganese Alphabet, and later the Chinese Latin Alphabet, were therefore an outcome of Mandarin *as written in the Arabic script*. In contrast to the extant literature that insists on tracing the origins of script reforms to the Jesuits or Protestant missionaries or Euro-American Orientalists, an archaeology of the CLA demonstrates that Chinese latinization was the product of a transnational Eurasian history. Before we can understand the CLA's power in China, the subject of the next chapter, we must situate it within the Soviet search for labor efficiency and the revolutionary internationalism of latinization across Eurasia.

The First Turcology Congress and the Scientific Organization of Labor

Identifying the origins of the CLA's letters takes us on a transnational journey across Eurasia and into the latinization of the Arabic script in the Socialist Republic of Azerbaijan. The majority of the CLA's letters were indeed identical to the letters of the Unified New Turkic Alphabet, devised immediately after the First All-Union Turcology Congress, which convened in Baku in 1926. The oil-rich town of Baku was a center for transnational reformist thought since the late nineteenth century, as it stood at the intersection of the Russian, Ottoman, and Persian empires. Following the Bolshevik Revolution, the city also became a center for socialist thought and, in 1920, it hosted the First Congress of the Peoples of the East—an anti-imperialist congress organized by the Comintern and convened with the participation of communists from all around the world. A turning point in the history of postcolonialism, the First Congress of the Peoples of the East was an effort to generate new patterns of producing knowledge about the colonized East.[4] The same anti-imperial spirit was palpable in the First Turcology Congress as well, convened only six years later in the same city. Under the leadership of the Azerbaijani reformer S. A. Agamalyogly (Səməd ağa Ağamalıoğlu, 1867–1930), the Congress brought together more than a hundred figures from across the Soviet Union and the world with a single purpose: to latinize the Arabic script of the Turkic nationalities. It was in this Congress that the CLA's letters were born.

The question of the Arabic script that the congress addressed had been a contested issue in the Ottoman and Russian empires since the mid-nineteenth century. Pressured by a new media ecology comprised of the telegraph and the movable metal type, reformers in the Russo-Ottoman space proposed to write Arabic in separate letters and represent vowels as they appeared in colloquial speech, which they believed could facilitate print, telegraphic transmission, and literacy. What began as a search for efficiency, however, generated insurmountable problems regarding imperial identity, the politics of linguistic representation, and the place of Islamic learning in modernization. Much like the late-Qing debates, conflicting opinions around reform and revolution increased during the turn of the century as communication infrastructures expanded and calls for educational reforms intensified. While Chinese reformers were busy designing the

National Phonetic Alphabet, reformers in the Russo-Ottoman space were trying to invent their own scripts for asserting national identities, some of which were inspired by revised Arabic letters, and some by the Latin alphabet. Following the Bolshevik Revolution and the fall of the Ottoman Empire, the latinist Azerbaijanis in Baku triumphed over their competitors and invented the New Turkic Alphabet in 1922—a watershed in the history of global script reforms (figure 5.1).

The New Turkic Alphabet crystallized amidst an industrialist modernity that promised mechanical efficiency and cultural progress. The simultaneous emergence of the New Turkic Alphabet of the Azerbaijanis, the National Phonetic Alphabet of the Chinese, and the Taylorist writing experiments of the Americans is a reminder of the global synchronicity that was characteristic of the information age. Scratching the surface of any national history of writing technologies, we may find the same modernist principles in effect. Raja Adal, for instance, also noted the prevalent discourse of speed and functionality in his comparative analysis of Egyptian and Japanese script styles during the same period, demonstrating the striking commonalities between cultures that rarely had contact with one another.[5] But similarities did not beget a uniform outcome, as the demands of the information age were negotiated differently in separate historical contexts. The search for efficiency and productivity was especially controversial in the Soviet Union, where socialist revolutionaries claimed that they could surpass the production levels of Western capitalist regimes while creating a new proletarian culture. Lenin's support for the New Turkic Alphabet was crucial within this larger context, as the principles of latinization seemed to conform with the universalist principles of socialism and in particular with the principles of the Scientific Organization of Labor.

Scientific Organization of Labor (Nauchnaia Organizatsiia Truda, hereafter NOT) was coined by Aleksei Gastev (1882–1939), an aficionado of Frederic Taylor and the leading Russian figure in the efforts to optimize labor efficiency in the USSR's industrial production. Originally a poet, hailed as "the Ovid of engineers, miners, and metal workers," Gastev was an industrial romantic, for whom the machines were extensions of the human body, not unlike McLuhan's definition of media.[6] After the October Revolution, he turned his attention from poetry to industrial production and formed the Central Labor Institute (TsIT) in 1920, where he put into practice his theories about the place of the human in an age of mechanical production. The

Эта таблица была подлинно в следующем виде:
Jeni turq əlifbasının duzuluzu.
يڭی تورك الفباسنڭ دوزولوشی.

A a a آ	B b be ب	C c ce ج	Ç ç çe چ	D d de د
E e e ٱ	Ə ə ə أ	F f ef ف	G g ge ڲ	H h haz (ح) ه
I i i اٍ	Ļ ļ Ļ ى (داری)	J j je ى (آی)	K k ka ق	L l el ل
M m em م	N n en ن	ᶇ sagır nyn	O o O (تو) او	Θ θ θ او (سوز)
P p pe پ	Q q qu ک	Ǫ ǫ qu گ	R r er ر	S s es س
T t te ت	U u u و (اوتو)	V v ve و	X x xe خ	Y y y و (اوزون)
Z z ze ز	Ż ż ze ذ	Ʒ ʒ ʒe ش	, apostrof	مﻌﻠﻮم mə'lym

FIGURE 5.1 The New Turkic Alphabet in Azerbaijan (1922).
Source: F. Agazade, *Istoriia vozniknoveniia novogo tiurkskogo alfavita v ASSR, s 1922 do 1925 god* [A history of the development of the New Turkic Alphabet in ASSR, from 1922 to 1925] (Baku: Komiteta po provedeniiu novogo tiurkskogo alfavita, 1926), 10.

goal of NOT was to "process man," as the slogan of the TsIT ran: "Mankind learned how to process things; the time has come to thoroughly process man."[7] Gastev did not draw an artificial distinction between the human and the machine, nor did he envision a future where machines would replace human labor. For him, the machine was the ideal for the human itself. The central concept he used to define the creation of a new work culture under socialism was *ustanovka*, variously translated as "setup," "arrangement," or "installation." Under Gastev's TsIT, proletarian work culture was the rearrangement of humans and machines, the installation of a network in which the boundary between the two was no longer clear. The highest stage of human civilization—socialism—signified nothing less than a seamless communication between the machine and the human, an ultimate mechanization of the human body and mind.

For Gastev, the mechanization of labor was among the most significant achievements in the psycho-physiological culture of the proletariat. The modern complex systems of machinery, composed of instruments and laborers, claimed Gastev, "establish particularly connected collectives, and give birth to particular types of people, whom we must embrace just as we embrace the machine.... *History really demands the brave design of human psychology that depends on historical factors, like machinism.*"[8] Emancipation of the human mind, in other words, demanded mechanization and automatization: "In order to become a strong cognitive worker," wrote Gastev, "one must arrange a colossal memory; in other words, one must build a voltage [*napriazhenie*] that can quickly and in various ways encompass the diverse automations of memory; and then, these automations can be included in newer and newer combinations ... and thus the human-thinker can score victory after victory. The automation of man is not in conflict with his organic creativity."[9]

Reminiscent of late-Qing reformers Shen Xue and Tan Sitong, Gastev's *Homo machinus* was also a *Homo informaticus* whose speaking and writing skills were automated in modern industrial life. In Gastev's human-machine complex, the movements of bodies and instruments were in sync with the flow of information from the machine to the body and from the brain to the instruments and back. The circulation of electricity through the telegraph lines, telephone, and radio was for Gastev a confirmation that electricity and information animated modern existence.[10] The factory was a laboratory of this world, buzzing with the electrified flow of information. In this massive, mechanized complex of biomechanical integration, the cognitive laborer's memory could also be automated through the mechanization of language and writing. There was no room for ambiguity in mechanized semantics, the fuel for optimum cognitive work. The "word" (*slovo*), claimed Gastev, should be created in the image of the crude language of commercial letters, the language of telegrams, or the simple dialogues of people in train stations and banks. Language had to be "short, exact, categorical." The same was true for writing as well. "If we want to reach that stage of splendor in which every official, every active and thinking person can possess the art of stenography," wrote Gastev, "then we must exhibit at least the demand that every person, who calls himself cultured, could learn to write distinctly and legibly and at the same time bring the speed of his own writing to thirty words a minute."[11]

While the Gastevian principles of NOT did not go unchallenged, the emphasis on psycho-physiological economy, speed, and mechanization was embraced by both revolutionary scientists and artists who strived to create a new proletarian culture of being and thinking. The differences in theoretical approaches notwithstanding, NOT's impact in the 1920s was visible across many disciplines and fields. Psychotechnicians were trying to organize the social institutions based on cognitive skills; neurophysiologists of labor wanted to determine the optimum patterns of physical movements; performance artists were measuring the most efficient use of the human body; futurist literary figures of the Left Front of the Arts were welcoming NOT's techno-humanist call; and, most importantly for our purposes, script reformers were seeking the optimum integration between the alphabet and the human.[12]

The First All-Union Turcology Congress convened when NOT was at the height of its popularity in the USSR. The search for an economy of written signs, the elimination of semantic ambiguity, and the physiology of labor in writing, typesetting, and typing were all problems that resonated with NOT. Script was an instrument of production that could be reengineered to enable an integration between humans and technologies of writing—between hands, eyes, fingers, typewriters, printing presses, and the telegraph. The First Turcology Congress and the subsequent latinization across Eurasia followed the early Soviet intellectuals' search for human-machine integration, which generated a new arena of information politics that extended from Baku to Vladivostok.

For some, the optimum integration between the human and the machine demanded a mathematical calculation of phonemes. Nikolai F. Iakovlev (1892–1974), who was later appointed as the president of the Techno-Graphic Commission of the All-Union Central Committee of the New Alphabet, took mechanization to the extreme by inventing a mathematical formula for alphabets: $A = (C + V) - (\pm C' \mp V') + 1$, in which A stood for alphabet, C for the total number of consonant phonemes, V for the total number of vowel phonemes, C' for the number of consonant pairs, V' for the number of vowel phonemes that could be used with a hard or soft consonant, and the 1 at the end for an extra sign that could help distinguish between the hard and soft consonant. While Iakovlev built his formula based on the specificities of Russian, his Turcologist followers tried to adapt his "economy of signs" to Kyrgyz and Uzbek as well.[13]

Iakovlev was also one of the fiercest critics of the imperial Russification that took place through the cyrillization of the Arabic script, something the famous Orientalist Nikolai Ilminskii (1822–1891) and others attempted to do at the end of the nineteenth century. Latinization signified the complete abandonment of Russian colonialism, and Iakovlev did not shy away from summoning the philologists to latinize even Russian itself. The Latin alphabet, after all, was an affirmation of the break with a colonialist past, and moreover, it was a better fit for the modern man's (*sovremennyi chelovek*) physiological movements of the hands and eyes in writing and reading—the speed of writing in Latin as opposed to Cyrillic was 14–15 percent faster, and it was four times faster to read Latin than Cyrillic. Besides, the money that could be saved in printing Latin letters instead of Cyrillic was around 11–12 percent, according to Iakovlev's calculations.[14] The jury, however, was still out on the latinization of Russian. And when Lenin allegedly told Anatoly Lunacharskii, the commissar of education, that the Russian population was not yet prepared for latinization, the project was suspended indefinitely.[15] For Iakovlev, it remained as a future ideal. But in the meantime, there were dozens of other languages that awaited latinization.

Lev I. Zhirkov (1885–1963), a linguist and an Iranologist who participated in the congress, did not go so far as to formulate the mathematics of writing, but he believed that the theoretical perspective offered by NOT provided the solution to the problem. The technical perfection of the alphabet had certain norms. Its convenience to the eye of the reader came at the top of the list. Second, its reproduction on a given surface had to be easy across

THE NEW DUNGANESE ALPHABET

the technological instruments (such as the printing press, pen on paper, or the typewriter). And third, its simplicity was a necessary quality for educating the masses. The Arabic script, Zhirkov commented just like all the others before him, did not conform to any of these rules—it was categorically impossible for the Arabic script to conform with the principles of NOT.[16]

While NOT offered a justification for latinization, the principles of efficiency and productivity were not always in favor of it. Galimjan Sharaf (1886–1950), a member of the Tatar delegation, disagreed with Zhirkov and others who clearly had a bias against the Arabic alphabet. A strong proponent of Arabic letters, Sharaf delivered a long speech at the congress to claim that the Arabic alphabet *did* comply with NOT. Communication technologies such as the telephone, the telegraph, or the radio transmitted information only in space, noted Sharaf, but the alphabet (*shrift*) was the "instrument for communicating human thoughts and mental achievements through both space *and* time."[17] A change in the alphabet was a break in the flow of information both spatially and temporally, and the principles of NOT, argued Sharaf, presented the solid ground on which to keep the flow *as it was*. According to Sharaf, it was true that the Arabic script had defects, but instead of throwing it out, would it not be better to try to change it from within?[18] To start with, diacritical marks could be placed on vowels to signify exact sounds and help the Arabic alphabet reach phonetic accuracy. In fact, according to his calculations through comparisons between Yakut, Bashkir, Tatar, and Azeri, Latin letters worked only with 47–56 percent of the sounds in Turkic languages; for the rest, either the letters had to be given new phonetic values or new letters had to be invented. The Arabic script, on the other hand, needed only 15 percent more signs to achieve linguistic accuracy.

Sharaf was also able to formulate an articulate response to those who claimed that writing in separate letters increased reading speed. Words, he said, were not cognitively recognized as a combination of letters, but as "hieroglyphs." If the letters of the word *can* جان (spirit), for instance, were written separately as ج ا ن, it would not be decipherable to the literate mind, for that separation would eliminate the "hieroglyphic" quality of the word, replacing the real word with an unsettling replica. The reason people had a difficult time reading Turkic languages in the Latin alphabet was not because they did not know the letters of the alphabet, but because the "hieroglyph-word" (*ieroglif-slovo*) was not recognized when written in latinized letters. What mattered in reading was the form of the word—a statement that was

THE NEW DUNGANESE ALPHABET

very similar to the Chinese reformers' arguments for the significance of character forms (*zixing*). As for the problem of "dots" above or under letters creating confusion, Sharaf saw no difference between the Arabic letters ب پ ث ت and the letters in the New Turkic Alphabet that were again optically very similar to one another: *o, ө, q, ol, g, e, ә*.

The Arabic script was also physiologically suitable to the productive movements of the hand, according to Sharaf. In writing Latin letters, although the line was written from left to right, the movement of the hand followed a counterclockwise direction, such as in *o, b, e*, etc., which was the reason for writing the line from left to right. In Arabic, the movement was in the reverse order, hence, while the letters و ر س followed a clockwise direction of the hand in production, the line itself followed an order from right to left. The order of the line and the manual movements were thus in conformity; technically, there was nothing wrong with the direction of writing. Moreover, certain words saved more physical energy when written in Arabic letters, such as the word *balta* (axe). When writing the word in Arabic بالتا, the hand made only eight–nine movements including the dots, at least according to Sharaf's calculation, but in Latin letters, it took thirteen–fourteen, demanding 30–35 percent more effort. In other words, the physiology of the hand and the manual movements in the production of a letter followed the principles of NOT, too. The latinists were right, Sharaf claimed, in pointing out the typographical issues surrounding the Arabic script—the number of words in Arabic letters that fit into a line could not compete with those in Latin letters; the diacritical marks slowed down the speed of typesetting; and the number of yearly publications in Arabic script did not match those printed in the Latin alphabet. However, the reform movement in Arabic letters was already in progress in Kazan since the late nineteenth century, noted Sharaf, and printers had already started achieving remarkable results.[19] In sum, reforming the Arabic letters was a better solution for increasing labor productivity while keeping the temporal flow of information from the past to the future unobstructed.

Sharaf's arguments were cleverly conceived. Employing the same mechanical discourse as the Russian linguists to argue *for* the Arabic script was an excellent rhetorical strategy. But it was not at all welcomed by the latinists.[20] Rather than the physiological aspects of alphabetic production, the geography of the Arabic alphabet and the plausible connections between Pan-Turkism, Pan-Islamism, and the Arabic script proved to be the bigger problem that Sharaf did not touch upon. Galimjan Ibrahimov (1887-1938?), a colleague of Sharaf from Kazan and also a supporter of the Arabic script, spoke at the congress in favor of alphabet reform from within. For Ibrahimov, the Arabic alphabet was necessary for maintaining the temporal dimension of the nation and preserving the access to historical information created by the forefathers—an argument that again brings to mind the Chinese simplifiers. If the nation was a closed information system, the alphabet was the key to its database, and without the key, there was no cultural access. Furthermore, Ibrahimov was himself a firm believer in the cultural-literary federation of Turkic languages:

> I'm using the principle of the cultural and literary federation of Turkic languages with caution. We cannot build one Turkic language—neither the phonetics nor the morphology nor the socioeconomic status [of the languages] permit that, but we, as Turkic people, [also] cannot be isolated from each other.... I insist: integration [*neotorvannost'*] will be reached in a federation, not a confederation, but a federation of Turkic languages, in which each language will be autonomous with its own structure, but the general base, general rules, and general lines in all Turkic languages will be taken into consideration.[21]

Ibrahimov's call for a Turkic federation was especially criticized by the chairman of the congress, Agamalyogly. Agamalyogly had been at the forefront of latinization since the early 1920s. Immediately after the invention of the New Turkic Alphabet in 1922, he was the one who traveled to Moscow to meet with Lenin and show him the alphabetic achievements of Azerbaijan. It was to him that Lenin allegedly said that "Latinization [was] the great revolution in the East!"[22] As an uncompromising latinist, Agamalyogly was especially disturbed by Ibrahimov during the congress. He dismissed Sharaf's arguments as "absurd theoretical reasoning" and wrote that Ibrahimov's cultural-literary federation "smelled of Pan-Turkism."[23] Ibrahimov's "Arabism," according to Agamalyogly, meant a bodily relationship (economic and political) with the Soviet Union, but a spiritual relationship (ideological and literary) with all Turkic countries. "My sweet comrade," he noted, "none of this differs from what our mullahs say every day in mosques."[24] In reality, Ibrahimov was unlike earlier reformers—like Ismail Gasprinskii—who tried to invent a common language for all the Turkic peoples. But his defense of the Arabic alphabet and his demand that the common lexical and grammatical elements that comprised all Turkic languages should be preserved and developed in order to create a "cultural and literary federation of Turkic languages" did not sound innocent at a time when late-imperial Pan-Turkic ideals were still embraced by many Turkic intellectuals.

Beside his quest for semantic standardization and economy in thought and reading, Agamalyogly was clearly on a crusade against Islam since the early 1920s—an ultra-secularist stance that was common to Turkic revolutionaries. He deliberately constructed a narrative of Islamism versus secularism and positioned the latinists as the progressive partners of the Soviet Union, and the arabists as the obsolete Pan-Islamists. He portrayed the state of affairs before the October Revolution as shaped by the dominance of mullahs, fanaticism, primitive economy, and the absence of schools.[25] Literacy, mechanization, productivity, and emancipation from superstition and religion were the building blocks of socialism in Central Asia—ideas that were later immortalized in Dziga Vertov's film *Three Songs About Lenin* (1934). Agamalyogly's was thus a conscious rhetorical effort to win the Soviet Union on the side of the latinists. Besides, didn't Lenin himself tell Agamalyogly that latinization was the "revolution in the East?"

Drawing a clear distinction between arabists and latinists, Agamalyogly was also capitalizing on an existing fear among the Soviet intelligentsia. There was indeed a strong Pan-Islamist intellectual current among the Turco-Tatars in the Russian Empire as well as among Arab and Ottoman intellectuals in the rest of the Islamic world before the fall of the Ottoman Empire and the Bolshevik Revolution. Even the Japanese Empire financially and militarily supported it across Eurasia, and Pan-Islamism did not simply cease to exist in the immediate aftermath of empires.[26] Agamalyogly was a charismatic leader, a persuasive speaker, and a pragmatic intellectual who knew how to manipulate public opinion in ways that would serve the interests of the latinists.

The defense of the Arabic alphabet was almost a lost cause, despite all the arguments in favor of technological efficiency and NOT. Pan-Islamism/Turkism was too serious of a problem, Agamalyogly was too strong of a figure to stand up against, and latinization was too revolutionary to abandon. Technology and politics were inseparably bound in an effort to invest in a linguistic infrastructure that, even if not rational or economic at all, was an investment "in a new humanity, a new being, a new cosmos."[27] As the Russian linguists all pointed out, the Latin alphabet for Turkic people was not going to be limited to the Turkic people, but was going to be the universal script for all the nations and nationalities. If the Arabic script were to remain, it would be limited to the Turco-Tatars at best and pose an obstacle to the internationalist flow of information in the future. While Sharaf and Ibrahimov had the Turco-Tatars in mind, Zhirkov, Iakovlev, Agamalyogly and others thought about the entire world. When the decision to latinize was put to a vote in the congress, 101 voted for latinization, 7 voted against, and 9 were impartial. For Sharaf, it was a big defeat. And Ibrahimov, perhaps sensing that the fate of the Arabic script had already been decided even before the congress, first raised his hand "for," then "against," and finally abstained from voting.[28] Latinization had officially begun.

From the Unified New Turkic Alphabet to the New Dunganese Alphabet

Immediately after the Turcology Congress, Agamalyogly traveled to Moscow to join the Third Session of the Central Executive Committee of the Soviet Union, where the All-Union Central Committee of the New Turkic Alphabet (Vsesoiuznyi tsentral'nyi komitet novogo tiurkskogo alfavita) was formed. The official seat of the committee was in Baku, but its executive bureau was in Moscow. Even though the decision to latinize was taken in the First All-Union Turcology Congress, the latinization's execution in the Turkic world required solving related technical problems, foremost of which was the final shape of the latinized letters themselves and the creation of a unified alphabet for all the Turkic people.[29]

Things moved fast. The Unified New Turkic Alphabet (*unifitsirovannyi novyi tiurkskii alfavit*) was the first important step in the installation of a common informational materiality and a shared psycho-physiological process of knowledge production for all the nations in the world. The first plenum of the All-Union Central Committee of the New Turkic Alphabet was convened in Baku in June 1927, again headed by Agamalyogly. The UNTA was created in the first plenum and finalized and put into practice after the second plenum, convened in Tashkent in 1928.[30] Agamalyogly, Zhirkov, Iakovlev, and others who were present at the First All-Union Turcology Congress also joined the plenums. The letters *b*, *d*, *f*, *h*, *e*, *m*, *n*, *p*, *r*, *s*, *t*, *v*, *x*, and *z* did not pose any difficulty, but it was not easy to reach consensus on other letters.

THE NEW DUNGANESE ALPHABET

The Scientific Council of the New Turkic Alphabet, for instance, proposed that c should be used for ç (ch) ҷ, and ç for c ҵ, because the letter c statistically occurred more in Turco-Tatar languages, saving the labor of putting an extra tail under c. Or for sh (in Cyrillic, ш), there were three different proposals: the Scientific Council proposed š, Azerbaijanis proposed ҙ, and the Kazakh Republic proposed the Russian letter itself, ш.[31] Each letter of the alphabet was thus put to vote, and the UNTA was created through a collaboration between Turkic and Russian scholars, some of whom were simply trying to assert national difference, whereas others were trying to find the future alphabet for humankind (figure 5.2).

Many scholars, Turkic and Russian alike, were aware of the implications of the UNTA. It was not only an alphabet for the Turkic people, but one for the global future of socialism. Although some Azerbaijani intellectuals in the third plenum stepped away from unifying all alphabets, the UNTA had already become the blueprint for all Turkic and non-Turkic people after the first plenum in 1927.[32] Iakovlev was enthusiastic about this global alphabet and believed that the Russians were going to latinize their own alphabet as well, making the UNTA the international system of writing. "That is why," noted Iakovlev, "it seems to me that the only appropriate name for this committee in the future should be 'The Committee of the International Alphabet' or 'International Graphics.'"[33] From then on, the Unified New Turkic Alphabet became the basis on which all the national alphabets were created. Mongolian (Buriat and Kalmyk), Caucasian (Avarian, Darginian, Lezgian, Abkhazian, and others), and Persian (Tadjik, Ossetian, Kurdish, and others) were all latinized based on the letters of the UNTA.[34] In 1930, the All-Union Central Committee of the New Turkic Alphabet changed its name to the All-Union Central Committee of the New Alphabet. The Unified New Turkic Alphabet was now the New Alphabet for All.[35]

Apart from a shared informational materiality that the alphabet provided, the UNTA also helped the Central Committee of the Soviet Union expand its influence into non-USSR lands. The latinization of Tadjik, for instance, broadened the Soviet Union's informatic channels into Iran and Afghanistan. The latinization of Kurdish was aimed more at Kurds living in Iran, Turkey, and Iraq than at the small population of Kurds in Armenia. And the one that proved to be the most successful of all, the latinization of Dunganese, was aimed at winning over the "revolutionary East," China.

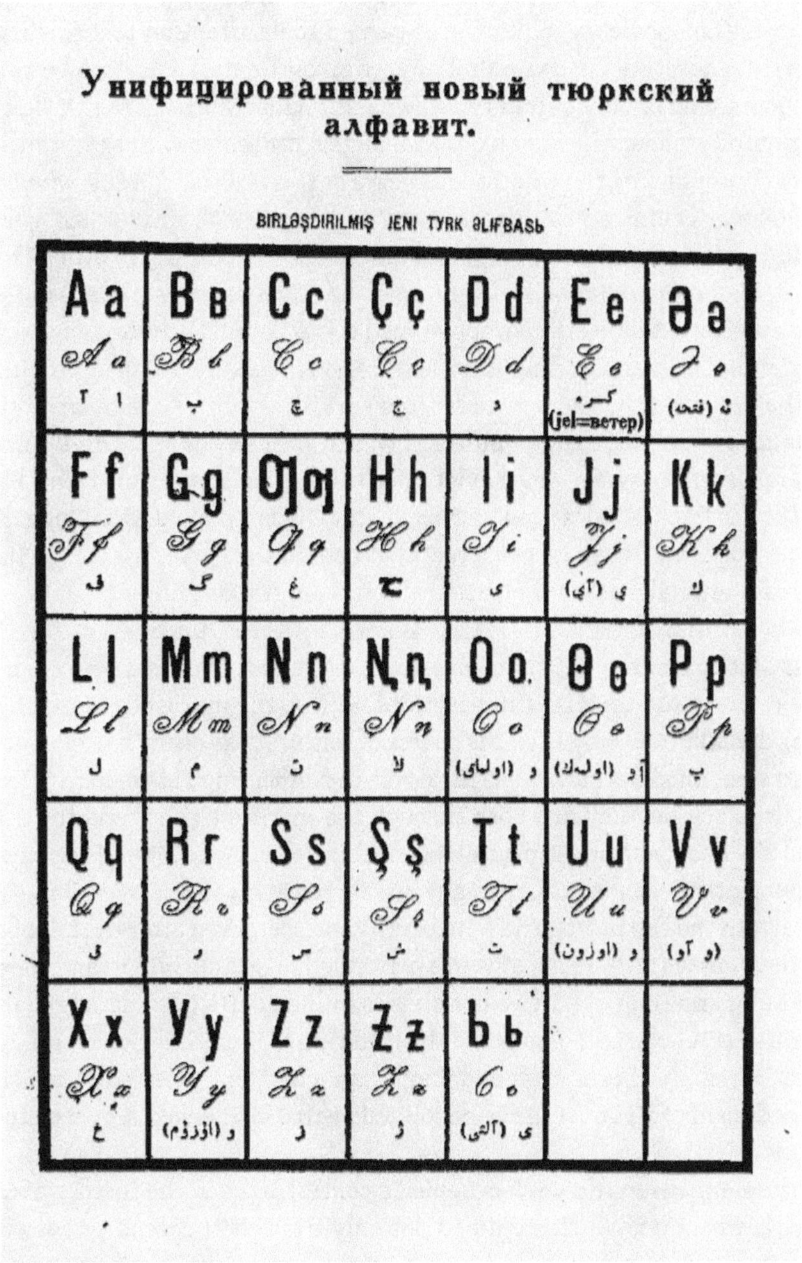

FIGURE 5.2 The Unified New Turkic Alphabet.
Source: Kul'tura i pis'mennost' vostoka [The culture and writing of the East], vol. 2 (Baku: Izdanie VTsK NTA, 1928).

THE NEW DUNGANESE ALPHABET

The UNTA had its most lasting impact in China. Immediately following its invention, Soviet revolutionaries turned their attention to a small diasporic Chinese Muslim community living across Central Asia. Known as the Dungans, who later acquired their own nationality status in the USSR, this community had emigrated from Xinjiang to present-day Kyrgyzstan and Kazakhstan during the tumultuous years of the 1870s and 1880s, when the region was colonized by General Zuo Zongtang 左宗棠 (1812–1885), whose brutality is enshrined in Dunganese folk songs.[36] According to official census data, their population in Kyrgyzstan and Kazakhstan was 14,600 in 1926, and according to the ethnographer Vasil'ev's account, their language was a mixture of vernacular languages spoken in Shaanxi and Gansu provinces in the northwest, with loanwords from Turkish, Arabic, Russian, and other languages.[37] While their population was almost negligible, the Dungans offered a gateway for the Soviet revolutionaries to win over the East. "Although the [UNTA] is used for small nations [narod], such as the Dungans," wrote Iakovlev, "we must not forget that behind that small nation, we have a great national mass in the East—behind them stands China."[38]

The latinization of Chinese thus started with the Dungans, i.e., the Chinese Muslims in the USSR. The presence of Muslims in China, who are usually referred to as *hui* 回, can be traced back to the maritime world of the Tang dynasty (618–907). Over the course of centuries, as historians have demonstrated, Muslims played a critical role in connecting East Asia to Central Asia and the Middle East, both through the maritime route and the overland Silk Road. Acting as cultural intermediaries, they facilitated diplomatic and scientific exchanges, especially during the Mongol rule over China and Eurasia in the thirteenth and fourteenth centuries. Even after the fall of the Yuan dynasty (1279–1368), Muslims continued to occupy important roles in the Ming and Qing dynasties not only as military officials and merchants, but also as scholars who invented the tradition of Han Kitab, which brought together Islamic knowledge and Confucian learning.[39] They were thus the embodiment of an imperial cosmopolitanism that challenged reified cultural boundaries.

The Dungans in the USSR occupied a central place in the history of Chinese latinization, which stemmed not only from their serendipitous position in the Soviet Union, but, more importantly, from their indigenous Arabic script. The crucial difference between Dunganese and the Chinese vernacular languages we have encountered thus far was that the former

THE NEW DUNGANESE ALPHABET

was written with an Arabic script known as Xiao'erjin. Xiao'erjin is colloquially yet rightfully known as the first Pinyin in Chinese history, which used Arabic letters and diacritic marks to transcribe Mandarin sounds. The origin and development of Xiao'erjin are little known, but the earliest examples of using the Arabic script to transcribe Chinese sounds come from a fourteenth-century Persian translation of a Chinese medical treatise, *Tanksukname-i Ilhani*, a product of Mongol-era Eurasian scientific exchanges (figure 5.3). Some scholars also note that the Mongols used a similar (perhaps the same) system in diplomatic exchanges as well, but no remaining examples have survived, and therefore the claim does not stand on any solid ground. Nevertheless, after the fall of the Mongols, Chinese Muslims continued using Xiao'erjin for religious purposes during the Ming and Qing dynasties and the republican period as well, even though the rate of literacy was arguably never very high (figure 5.4).[40] Regardless, the Dungans brought Xiao'erjin to Russian Central Asia in the late nineteenth century, and some of the earliest printed versions of the script came out in

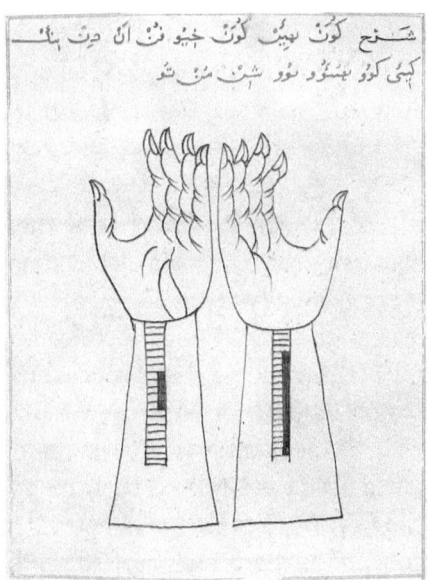

FIGURE 5.3 Chinese words written in the Arabic script in *Tanksukname-i Ilhani der Ulum-u Funun-u Khatai* [The book of rarities of the Ilkhanids on the arts and sciences of China], 1313.
Source: Süleymaniye Manuscript Library, Ayasofya no. 3596.

[171]

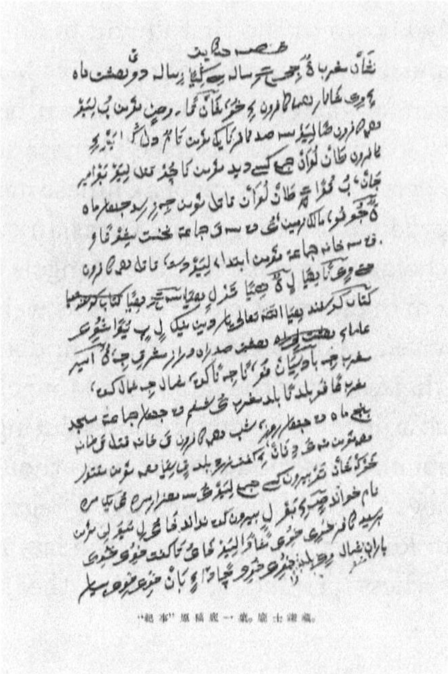

FIGURE 5.4 A twentieth-century manuscript in Xiao'erjin.
Source: Bai Shouyi, ed., *Huimin qiyi* 回民起義 [The Muslim uprising], vol. 3 (Shanghai: Shenzhou guoguang she, 1953).

Tashkent in the late 1890s, which showed that by then the script had lost some of the Arabic letters (ح ذ ر ض غ) but included new ones to represent Mandarin, such as ص with three dots on top.[41]

Once the UNTA was designed, the Dungans concentrated their efforts on latinizing Xiao'erjin accordingly. The first proposal to latinize Dunganese was drafted by the Kyrgyz Committee of the New Alphabet, and the second one by Dungan students in Tashkent, namely Iasyr Shivaza (1906–1988) and Juma Abdullin (?–?), who used the UNTA as their model. In 1928, these students even printed the first Dunganese newspaper, *May 1*.[42] In order to finish the project, Yakub Zhon, the director of the only Dungan school in Frunze, Kyrgyzstan, was summoned to Baku. As he noted in a speech at the All-Union Central Committee of the New Turkic Alphabet, the New Dunganese Alphabet was based on the Arabic script in use, not on other phoneticization projects of Chinese languages.[43] As a matter of fact, Dungan students studying in Tashkent in the 1920s, including the Dungan poet Iasyr Shivaza, had started reforming the Arabic script before latinizing it.[44] The slight differences between the Turco-Muslim Arabic Script and the Dunganese Arabic Script, i.e., the reformed Xiao'erjin, corresponded to the slight differences between the UNTA and the New Dunganese Alphabet (figure 5.5). With the support of one of the leading Russian sinologists, Evgenii Polivanov (1891–1938), the first textbooks and literature in the New Dunganese Alphabet were printed by the above-mentioned students. In the following years, as the New Dunganese Alphabet was undergoing some changes, it provided a blueprint for a greater project to latinize, in the words of Iakovlev, "the great national mass in the East"—China.

The history of Chinese alphabetization in general, and the CLA in particular, is often narrated as a product of Western imperialism and Orientalism from the nineteenth century onward. While it is true that Chinese languages were latinized by Western diplomats and missionaries in the nineteenth century, and while it is also true that those latinization projects were later

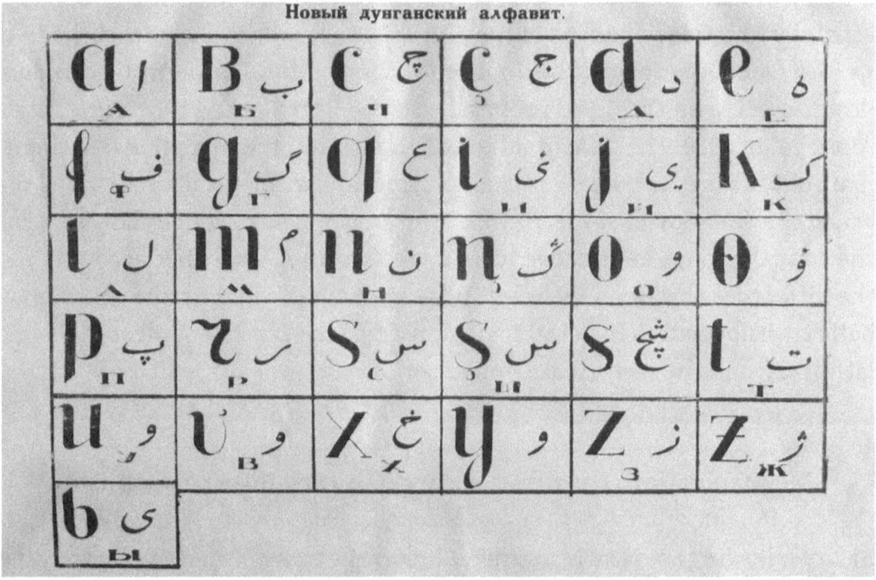

FIGURE 5.5 The New Dunganese Alphabet, 1928.
Source: B. Chobanzade, "Itogi unifikatsii alfavitov tiurko-tatarskikh narodov" [The results of the unification of the alphabets of Turco-Tatar peoples], *Kul'tura i pis'mennost' vostoka* 3 (1928): 24–25.

used by Chinese reformers, the material composition of each script invites us to discover their divergent origins and historicize them within their particular transnational, technological, and ideological conditions. The CLA's immediate predecessor, the New Dunganese Alphabet, was borne out of transnational revolutionary networks that were activated by industrializing knowledge economies. Therefore, the material composition of the New Dunganese Alphabet had nothing to do with the missionaries or diplomats, and everything to do with the latinization of the Arabic alphabet within an internationalist movement in the USSR. The latinization of the Dunganese Xiao'erjin, as Iakovlev noted, was a means to a greater end, for behind the Dungans stood China.

This genealogy compels us to revise the existing literature on Chinese latinization, which put Qu Qiubai, a leading member of the CCP and a longtime resident of Moscow, at the center of the Chinese Latin Alphabet (Sin Wenz). This literature is not entirely wrong. Qu certainly played an important role in devising the CLA, as he published *Chinese Latinized Alphabet* (*Kitaiskaia latinizirovannaia azbuka*) in Moscow in 1930, a year before the CLA was officially ratified in Vladivostok. A closer look at Qu's letters in 1930 and the officially sanctioned version of the CLA in 1931, however, shows that the two were in fact not the same. The finalized version of the CLA was instead a compromise between Qu's 1930 proposal and the UNTA-based New Dunganese Alphabet of 1928. The CLA, in other words, was not the invention of a single man, but the product of larger technological and ideological forces that governed the Sino-Soviet space. At this point, readers may wonder how exactly the New Dunganese Alphabet turned into the CLA, and what accounts for the differences between the two. The next chapter will describe this alphabetic transformation in detail to demonstrate the persistent place of Soviet latinization in the history of Chinese script reforms.

Mechanization, Latinization, and Literary Internationalism

Before following the New Dunganese Alphabet's transformation into the Chinese Latin Alphabet and witnessing the revolutionary organization of society it inspired, I would like to highlight one of the rare examples of latinized literary production that embodied the spirit of internationalism. As latinized letters gained momentum across Eurasia as a new medium that increased the velocity of knowledge circulation between nations and nationalities, they also engendered an internationalist mode of aesthetics and sparked hope for an alternative literary vision that could allow disparate linguistic communities to be mutually constitutive of each other. This vision was perhaps best captured by the Turkish poet Nazım Hikmet (1902–1963), who incorporated China into his avant-garde literary imagination.

Arguably the most controversial poet in Turkish history, Nazım Hikmet was originally from Salonika (present-day Thessaloníki). After a brief stint in the Ottoman Navy, he left for Moscow in 1922 during the Turkish War of Independence (1919–1922). He studied at the Communist University of the Toilers of the East in Moscow for two years before traveling back to the newly established Republic of Turkey in 1924. But when the Turkish courts started prosecuting anyone who could be a potential threat to the new regime, and specifically targeted the communist journals that Nazım Hikmet was publishing in, he escaped to Moscow in 1925 and stayed there until 1928. The Turkish government did not treat him any better once he returned. From 1929 to 1938, he was in and out of prison several times, and he then spent the next twelve years in prisons across Turkey, until 1950. A year after his release, when he was forced to enroll in the army, he fled to the Soviet Union. Stripped of his Turkish citizenship, he stayed in the Soviet Union until his death in 1963.[45]

In 1923, while in Moscow, Nazım Hikmet composed a poem called "To Be Mechanized" ("Makinalaşmak"). He was aware of the linguistic changes taking place during the turbulent years of his youth, as the omnipresent communication technologies and postimperial epistemologies were generating new conceptions of language, technology, script, and the human. In "To Be Mechanized," he was responding to these colossal transformations as a student in Moscow:

> trrrrum,
> trrrrum,
> trrrrum!
> trak tiki tak!
> I want to be
> Mechanized!

As Nergis Ertürk notes in her analysis of the poem, Nazım Hikmet's poetically mechanized opening lines "trrrrrum, trrrrum, trrrrrum, trak tiki tak" were an affirmation of the death of language as mere speech and a tribute to it as machinery, within which meaning was produced through a combination of meaningless letters.⁴⁶ The onomatopoeic constellation of letters to represent the sound of a running motor (*trrrrrum*) or the regular, round-the-clock rhythm of a working machine (*trak tiki tak, trak tiki tak*) was the ideal that Nazım Hikmet strived for in his own desire to become the machine: "I want to be Mechanized!" The mechanization he yearned for also anticipated the death of the organic body, a futurist imagination of an integration between the machine and the human:

> It is coming
>   from my brain my flesh my skeleton!
> I'm going insane
> to take every generator
>   under myself!
> My salivary tongue is licking the copper wires,
> and in my veins
>   motor cars are chasing after locomotives!
> trrrrum,
>   trrrrum,
>   trrrrum,
> trak tiki tak
> I want to be
>   Mechanized!
> I will definitely find a solution to this
>   and I will reach happiness the day
> when I place a turbine in my belly
> and attach a double propeller to my tail!⁴⁷

"To Be Mechanized" was the first Turkish poem to follow Russian futurism's craving for mechanical precision and a union of the human and the machine. Nazım Hikmet was describing a biomechanical man, a technohuman who could transcend his own limits through an integration with industrial machinery. The speeding cars and locomotives in his veins, his tongue licking copper wires, the turbine in his belly, and the double propeller in his back to reach "happiness" echo Donna Haraway's cyborg subjects, "creatures simultaneously animal and machine, who populate worlds ambiguously natural and crafted."[48] A few decades before the cybernetic revolution, Nazım Hikmet was embracing the techno-human subject who could transcend cultural and national boundaries.

Nazım Hikmet penned "To Be Mechanized" amid the fascination with and theorization of the techno-human. Mayakovsky's Left Front of the Arts (LEF), which sought an internationalist aesthetics for all the working classes in the world, had a direct impact on Nazım Hikmet's futurist poetry, of which "To Be Mechanized" is one of the rare examples. LEF artists embraced Gastev's desire for word economy, speed, simplicity, exactness, and unambiguity in the 1920s. Boris Arbatov, a member of LEF, even praised Gastev's poetry for its novelty.[49] In an age when language itself was mechanized, a seamless Gastevian integration of the machine and the organic human promised a future that could be shared by all artists, regardless of cultural and national differences.[50]

The penchant for a biomechanical body and a techno-human language was a key component of Nazım Hikmet and the Russian futurists' political vision for communist literary internationalism. Nazım Hikmet composed "To Be Mechanized" in 1923 (probably in Arabic letters) but published it for the first time in his book of poetry *835 Lines* (*835 Satır*) in 1929 in Latin letters, immediately after the Turkish Alphabet Revolution. *835 Lines* was a fierce attack on the old culture, and part of the literary movement called Down with the Icons (Putları Kırıyoruz), which aimed to define a new paradigm for Turkish literary production. Nazım Hikmet had the leading voice in the movement, and *835 Lines* was his manifesto in content and form. As opposed to the newly established Republic of Turkey's pedantic efforts to create a national language that was distinctly "Turkish," Nazım Hikmet's political vision of a mechanized future with a mechanized body and language yearned for a poetical machinery that transcended the boundaries of the nation-state while still remaining vernacular. He was always in favor of writing with a simplified language that could be translated into other languages without sacrificing meaning. For him, the difficulty of translating the "old icons of literature" into foreign languages was the main indicator of the need to install a new culture of literary production, simultaneously vernacular and international.[51] Nazım Hikmet never wrote openly in defense of latinization, but given his use of the Latin alphabet even when writing his personal letters and diaries (in contrast to his peers, who continued using the Arabic script in their personal correspondences), and given the significance of the movement when he was in Moscow, it would be safe to claim that for Nazım Hikmet—as for the Chinese latinists—the Latin alphabet served the dual goals of internationalism and vernacularism.

His personal life and poetry were also a testimony to this vernacular internationalism. One of his closest friends in Moscow was the Chinese communist Xiao San 萧三 (1896–1983), also known as Emi Siao—the first biographer of Mao Zedong, a leading figure in translating Chinese literature into Russian, the translator of the socialist song "L'internationale" into Chinese, and arguably the biggest name in the Chinese Latinization Movement (his crucial role in it will be discussed in chapter 6). In 1929, a year after his return to Turkey, Nazım Hikmet composed one of his landmark poems in Turkish, "Gioconda and Si-Ya-U" ("Jokond ile Si-Ya-U"), to honor Xiao San's imagined death in Shanghai under the rule of Chiang Kai-shek. Also partially published in *835 Lines*, "Gioconda and Si-Ya-U" was a story of sexual and political liberation and love between Xiao San (transcribed as Si-Ya-U) and the Gioconda from Leonardo da Vinci's famous painting *Mona Lisa* (figure 5.6).

The poem starts with the Gioconda in the Louvre in 1924. She is bored by history, by the museum, and by being a mere historical specimen with a fake smile destined to remain on her face until eternity—"a smile that is even more famous than Florence." Then she sees Si-Ya-U, a Chinese "who doesn't look at all like the Chinese with the queues." She falls in love with Si-Ya-U and starts forgetting the names of the Renaissance masters of art. The Gioconda now wants to see

> the black oil paintings of birds and flowers
> dripping
> from the thin and long reed brushes
> of the Chinese painters with slanted eyes.

Then, one day, the French authorities expel Si-Ya-U out of France, who goes back to China to join the socialist revolutionary struggle. Depressed and longing for her Chinese love, the Gioconda talks to the narrator of the story, and the narrator helps her break free from Louvre to travel to China in search

FIGURE 5.6 The cover page of "Gioconda and Si-Ya-U."
Source: Nazım Hikmet, *Jokond ile Si-Ya-U* [Gioconda and Si-Ya-U] (Istanbul: Akşam Matbaası, 1929).

of Si-Ya-U. She (still in a frame) gets on a plane together with the narrator, and they fly across Africa and the Indian Ocean before reaching the Sea of China. The Gioconda jumps off the plane and lands on a British ship on its way to Shanghai. At last, she arrives in the city. She sees her love from a distance, and just when she is about to approach, Chiang Kai-shek's "executioner" (*cellat*) severs Si-Ya-U's head from his body:

> It was such a day of death
> that the Gioconda from Florence lost in Shanghai
> her smile that is even more famous than Florence.

With the fake smile, a reminder of patriarchal authority, erased from her face, the Gioconda steps out of her frame and joins the revolutionary struggle on the streets of Shanghai. Finally, the French authorities capture the Gioconda and burn her on the stake:

> The Gioconda was painted red with flames
> she laughed with a smile coming from her heart
> the Gioconda burned as she was laughing.[52]

Nazım Hikmet's poem was a work of literary internationalism par excellence.[53] The Gioconda was an object of Western patriarchy and an apolitical woman famous for a smile that she did not even like. She fell in love with a Chinese revolutionary who did not fit the Orientalist portrayals of a backward China—instead, the China of the poem had a unique culture with a revolutionary potential. She then got on a plane with the Turkish narrator, who helped her escape from the museum, and flew over colonized Africa and the Indian Ocean, mapping out the future revolutionary spaces. When the Gioconda finally reached Shanghai, she lost her love at the hands of an executioner but became a true communist revolutionary and sacrificed herself on the stake with a smile that truly came from her heart. The Gioconda was finally free.

"Gioconda and Si-Ya-U" retained certain similarities to "To Be Mechanized." This was a long poem that had an elaborate story line with multiple protagonists, geographies, and technologies. Nazım Hikmet used a diverse narrative style (the Gioconda, the narrator, and a sailor on the British ship all spoke with their own voices) to decenter an I-narrative, and non-Western

THE NEW DUNGANESE ALPHABET

geographies to decenter Eurocentrism. In "Gioconda and Si-Ya-U," Nazım Hikmet did not turn himself into a machine, but he did incorporate the new techniques and technologies of representation into his authorial vision. To begin with, the story unfolded in a temporally diachronic and globally synchronic progression of scenes that the reader could "watch" as if watching montaged scenes from a movie. This cinematographic approach was not surprising given Nazım Hikmet's admiration for Vsevolod Meyerhold and Sergei Eisenstein, and his personal friendship with Sergei Tret'iakov, who also helped Nazım Hikmet translate one of his poems, dedicated to Meyerhold, into Russian.[54] Nazım Hikmet wrote each scene in the story as if the figures were acting on a stage or in front of a camera. Indeed, one scene was most probably informed by the documentary film *Shanghai Document* (*Shankhaiskii Dokument*) directed by Yakob Bilokh and released in 1928 (figure 5.7). When the Gioconda reached Shanghai, right before she saw Si-Ya-U, she had an ethnographic moment in the streets:

> The Chinese juggler
> Lİ
> is screaming at the top of his lungs
> His hand that looks like a yellow, skinny spider
> is throwing the thin and long knives in the air
> And again
>   once more
>   once more
>   once more
>   five
>   once more.
> The knives bolt and flow one after another
> in the air, as they draw circles with thunder.

Bilokh's *Shanghai Document* billed itself as an eyewitness account of China after the communist defeat in 1927, which provided a convenient decorative setting for the imagined death of Xiao San. Nazım Hikmet translated (or transmediated) the image of China, captured with cinematographic technologies and camera and montage techniques, into his Turkish poem. What is more significant, however, is that he brought in the new vision provided by the technologies of representation into his communist internationalist

FIGURE 5.7 "Bednotu obsluzhivaiut ulichnye fokusniki" [The street jugglers serve the poor], *Shankhaiskii Dokument* [Shanghai document] (1928), 12:49.

narrative style, and through them, envisioned a world without a center—a world that witnessed fascist brutalism (Si-Ya-U's rolling head), but that was still full of hope for what was offered by technology (the planes in the air) and human agency (the Gioconda out of her frame).

Nazım Hikmet's poem circulated only in Turkey; it never reached Xiao San. In fact, the two friends did not meet again until 1951, when a chance encounter in Berlin brought them together for the first time since Moscow. After the serendipitous reunion, Xiao San immediately invited Nazım Hikmet to Beijing to participate in the Asia-Pacific Region Peace Conference in 1952. Convened during the Korean War, the conference welcomed Nazım Hikmet, for Turkey was fighting against China and North Korea on the side of the United States for the sole purpose of joining NATO, which it did in 1952. Nazım Hikmet represented the voice of a Turkish dissident who had taken refuge in the USSR, and in his speech, he condemned Turkey for being an American colony.[55] The same year, his poems were translated from Russian into Chinese for the first time, with Xiao San writing a preface for them, and in the following years, more translations followed.[56] After a short stay in

Beijing, Nazım Hikmet went back to Moscow, and the two friends probably never met again.

Nazım Hikmet and Xiao San's decades-long friendship is a glimpse into the literary internationalism that started in the early days of the Soviet Union. They were both vernacularists and internationalists, a seeming contradiction that they managed to overcome through imagining a common socialist and techno-human existence that came before cultural differences. Nazım Hikmet and Xiao San stepped out of the dichotomous world order of the colonizer and the colonized to imagine a new internationalism that inspired literary imaginations across Eurasia. It was in the 1920s, when Xiao San and Nazım Hikmet met for the first time, that the seeds of literary internationalism were planted. Their search for an internationalism that could transcend cultural boundaries, "install" a new culture of intellectual labor internationally, and use the new technologies of representation to envision new global spaces and political futures was indeed intimately connected to the "great revolution in the East"—latinization. For the revolutionaries of the era, a common Latin alphabet had the potential to provide the means for vernacularizing and internationalizing all nations and nationalities while creating a socialist mode of literary existence. Just like Nazım Hikmet's imagined world without a center in "Gioconda and Si-Ya-U," the Latin alphabet was going to knit the nations together and form a socialist network through letters.

* * *

Latinization across Eurasia began as part of an anti-imperialist moment that sought to change the medium of producing knowledge about the colonized East. The choice of the term "latinization" (*latinizatsiia*) as opposed to romanization was indicative of the anti-imperialist universalism in Soviet thought in the 1920s. As opposed to the "Roman" alphabet, which, apart from having an unfortunate semantic resemblance to the Romanov dynasty, had been an instrument of Western colonialism, the "Latin" alphabet represented a scientific universalism that could be shared with the entire world by designing a common psycho-physiological interface with language and facilitating the flow of information across different linguistic orders.[57] Fueled by a futurist desire for human-machine integration and an internationalist one to disseminate revolutionary ideas across borders, latinists were the agents of the "great revolution in the East," which sought nothing less than to create a Eurasian socialist network of nations and nationalities. It was within this moment that the Chinese Latin Alphabet was born, initially as the New Dunganese Alphabet. The invention of the New Dunganese Alphabet was thus critical in the global history of Chinese script reforms, for young Chinese Muslim revolutionaries' latinization of Xiao'erjin linked the Arabic script reforms that had been in progress for decades to the latinization of Chinese.

The material links between the Middle East, Russia, Central Asia, and China force us to confront the truly global scale of the information age, shaped by political economic forces that redefined the place of script in the construction of a new economy and culture of knowledge. The deterritorialization and reterritorialization of knowledge economies across Eurasia generated new possibilities for connecting the world in radically new ways, from the export of the UNTA to literary internationalism. The alleged speed and efficiency aside, what came with latinized letters was a new way of imagining the place of language and literature in the world. Nazım Hikmet's fictional biography of Xiao San was a work of poetry as much as a product of the 1920s, which created the conditions for an internationalist literary cross-pollination that lasted for decades. For revolutionaries like Xiao San and Nazım Hikmet, latinization offered a literary technology for an internationalist culture in which non-Western literatures that were until then unrelated, like Turkish and Chinese, could come together to create something new, like "Gioconda and Si-Ya-U."

Latinization offered even more than literary internationalism to Chinese intellectuals and revolutionaries, as the next chapter will explain. The years that spanned the First All-Union Turcology Congress in 1926, the invention of the New Dunganese Alphabet in 1928, and that of the Chinese Latin Alphabet in 1931 witnessed pivotal transformations in China. In 1927, the GMD forces massacred communists on the streets of Shanghai, severing the already weakened ties between the GMD and the CCP. The onset of the Nanjing decade (1927–1937) saw an increased centralization of the party-state and the rise of a fascist ideology that sought legitimacy in an imagined native culture. As already discussed, the Chinese characters themselves occupied a central place in this nativist imagination. When even the simplification of Chinese characters was anathema to the party, latinization was sacrilege. In 1930, while Chinese and Russian revolutionaries in the USSR were trying to change the New Dunganese Alphabet into the Chinese Latin Alphabet, the

THE NEW DUNGANESE ALPHABET

GMD decided to rename the National Phonetic Alphabet "Phonetic Symbols" (*Zhuyin fuhao*), which reflected the political vision of the party: a unified language (Mandarin) that coexisted with the native treasure (Chinese characters). It was the GMD's paternalist statism that compelled the Chinese revolutionaries to configure an alternative system of language and information in the 1930s. That system came in the form of the Chinese Latin Alphabet.

SIX

The Chinese Latin Alphabet

A Revolutionary Script

THE YEAR 1931 was one of significance. Three years after the invention of the New Dunganese Alphabet, Chinese communists and Russian linguists gathered in Vladivostok at the First Chinese Latinization Conference to finalize and ratify the Chinese Latin Alphabet (CLA) or Sin Wenz; the goal was to get rid of Chinese characters by replacing them with the Latin alphabet. The conference convened at a critical moment in Chinese history. Since its consolidation of power in 1927, the GMD was anxiously watching the latinization movement gather momentum in the Soviet Union and was wary of the movement's implications for its party-state–building efforts in China. In 1930, it renamed the National Phonetic Alphabet "Phonetic Symbols" (*Zhuyin fuhao*) and promulgated it only as an auxiliary script to promote literacy in Chinese characters—the quintessential elements of a native culture (*guyou wenhua*) that was treasured by a growing fascist ideology. Phonetic Symbols not only sought to preserve the Chinese characters, but it also ran counter to decades of debates around multilingualism, for it represented one language only, Mandarin as spoken in Beijing. Thus, when the Chinese Latin Alphabet was finally approved in Vladivostok in 1931, the purpose of the revolutionaries was both to join the internationalist movement in the USSR and to push back against the GMD's linguistic and political hegemony enshrined in Phonetic Symbols. In the 1930s, then, there were two major competing phonetic scripts for China, which, graphically and ideologically, were as different from one another as they could possibly get:

THE CHINESE LATIN ALPHABET

Chinese Latin Alphabet (Sin Wenz):
A B C Ch D E F G I J K L M N Ng O P R Rh S Sh T U W X Y Z Zh
Phonetic Symbols (*Zhuyin fuhao*):
ㄅㄆㄇㄈㄉㄊㄋㄌㄍㄎㄏㄐㄑㄒㄓㄔㄕㄖㄗㄘㄙㄧㄨㄩㄚㄛㄜㄝㄞㄟㄠㄡㄢㄣㄤㄥㄦ

This chapter situates the popularization and subsequent demise of the Chinese Latin Alphabet within the larger history of the global information age and the particular history of Sino-Soviet information politics in the 1930s. What made it possible for the Latin alphabet to travel from Baku to Vladivostok to Shanghai was the political economy of information that transformed the practices of writing, reading, and thinking across the world. The common vocabulary of reformers and revolutionaries was a testimony to this shared global experience. While late-Qing reformers were trying to "save brain energy" through phoneticizing or simplifying Chinese characters, Ottoman intellectuals were trying to eliminate "waste of thought" through reforming the Arabic script, and the Soviet latinists' engagements with Scientific Organization of Labor were strikingly similar to American and Chinese psychologists' efforts in cognitive management through statistical analyses of language and writing. The homogenizing power of a modern political economy was manifest across cultural and linguistic divides. Considered from this perspective, latinization was yet another, albeit the most radical, instantiation of the global information age.

Like all the other scripts we have encountered, however, the Latin alphabet also produced its own contradictions. For Soviet revolutionaries, latinization was the ultimate revolution that would bring progress and enlightenment to the socialist world; rarely did they think about the material world of the letters they so believed in. It was only *after* the implementation of latinization across the USSR that they realized the social, technological, and infrastructural dimensions of a latinized world. Soviet instructors themselves, Russian and non-Russian, needed extensive training to learn and teach the Latin alphabet; demand for new typewriters, linotype machines, and typesets was overwhelming; and Soviet bureaucracy had to contend with not one but two scripts—Latin and Cyrillic. By the mid-1930s, what was supposed to create an informational utopia ironically ended up generating an informational crisis. Eventually, amid the rising wave of Russification, latinization died a quick death in 1938, when Stalin ordered the cyrillization of all national scripts. Almost overnight, the nationalities of the Soviet

Union who had latinized lost their alphabets and had to begin rewriting their languages in hastily designed Cyrillic letters.

And yet, while latinization was on its last legs in the USSR, Chinese leftwing intellectuals carried the torch of revolution to China. In the 1930s, the CLA drew support from a wide range of Chinese reformers and revolutionaries who embraced it as a counterhegemonic technology to disrupt the GMD's propaganda network, which was partially engineered through Phonetic Symbols. By the middle of the decade, anti-party intellectuals were using the CLA to latinize regional languages and print textbooks to disseminate socialist principles. Latinization, for them, was a political exercise in what Manuel Castells called "network switching"—it was an attempt to enact counterpower through upsetting the party-state's information regime.[1]

But the CLA also had its internal contradictions that almost no Chinese revolutionary wanted to admit. Like their Soviet counterparts, Chinese revolutionaries were so enamored with the promises of the Latin alphabet that they seldom considered the true cost of destroying Chinese characters. In the middle of revolutionary enthusiasm, there was only one person who recognized the internal contradictions of latinization—or at least only one who left a trail we could follow. That person was no other than Xiao San, the USSR-based leader of Chinese latinization and the protagonist of Nazım Hikmet's avant-garde poem we examined in the previous chapter. At a time when the bright light of latinization was fading away in the Soviet Union, Xiao San began questioning the cognitive dimensions of the Latin alphabet. His self-reflections, which I turn to at the end of this chapter, not only offer a glimpse into the contradictions of latinization itself but also help us discern the phenomenological limits of script reforms at large.

The Chinese Latin Alphabet, Gwoyeu Romatzyh, and Phonetic Symbols

Qu Qiubai, the young Chinese communist and one of the early members of the CCP, is generally acknowledged as the inventor of the CLA. But as mentioned in chapter 5, the letters of the CLA tell a different story. When examined closely, the differences between the CLA as it was proposed by Qu in 1930 and the CLA as it was ratified in 1931 take us into two separate geographies. The letters, on the one hand, demonstrate Qu's engagements with the ongoing phoneticization efforts in China, as the extant literature has already identified. But on the other hand, they reveal the persistent role of the Unified New Turkic Alphabet and the New Dunganese Alphabet in the material composition of the CLA. So, who invented the CLA, if not Qu Qiubai?

The invention of the CLA began immediately after that of the New Dunganese Alphabet in 1928, and their histories were intimately connected.[2] Chinese Communists in Moscow enthusiastically embraced latinization as part of revolutionary internationalism. Among them were well-known figures who later took office under the PRC: Wu Yuzhang 吴玉章 (1878–1966), Lin Boqu 林伯渠 (1886–1960), and Xiao San. Their involvement, especially Xiao San's, in the promotion of the CLA has largely been overshadowed by Qu Qiubai, who drafted the first proposal for the CLA in February 1929 with V. S. Kolokolov (Ch. Guo Zhisheng 郭質生, 1896–1979), and published the first article on it in the Russian-language journal *Problemy Kitaia* (*Problems of China*) in 1930, together with a book titled *Kitaiskaia latinizirovannaia azbuka* (*Chinese Latinized Alphabet*) that came out the same year in Moscow.

Qu Qiubai's *Chinese Latinized Alphabet* was a potent response to the linguistic and political developments in China under the GMD. In the 1920s, Yuen Ren Chao had invented the first romanization scheme for Beijing Mandarin—not to be confused with latinization. Chao was arguably the most prominent linguist in China, and his peripatetic life that took him from Cornell University to the Bell Labs to a professorship at University of California, Berkeley, has been the subject of earlier works. Chao was involved in script and language reforms since his days as a college student at Cornell in the 1910s, and he was in close contact with leading Sinologists and phonologists at the time, such as Bernhard Karlgren (1889–1978).[3] Chao's Roman alphabet for Mandarin grew out of these early interactions, along with the ongoing Chinese efforts to promote the National Phonetic Alphabet, which was already promulgated by the government. Chao's alphabet was in effect a romanized version of the National Phonetic Alphabet. In November 1926, endorsed by many linguists and reformers, Chao's National Language in the Roman Alphabet (Gwoyeu Romatzyh, hereafter, GR) was recognized by the Preparatory Committee as the Second Phonetic Alphabet for Mandarin; and in 1928, a year after the massacre of communists, it was officially recognized by the GMD as well (figure 6.1).[4] When Qu Qiubai, Kolokolov, and others were inventing the Chinese Latin Alphabet in Moscow, GR was the enemy.

國語羅馬字拼音法式
——國音字母第二式(續)——
聲 調 拼 法 (二)
(結合韻母)

	(陰平)	(陽平)	(上)	(去)
ㄧㄚ	ia	ya	yea,-ea	yeh,-iah
ㄧㄛ	io°	yo°	yeo,-eo°	yoh,-ioh°
ㄧㄝ	ie	ye	yee,-iee	yeh,-ieh
ㄧㄞ	iai°	yai	yeai,-eai°	yay,-iay°
ㄧㄠ	iau	yau	yeau,-eau	yaw,-iaw
ㄧㄡ	iou	you	yeou,-eou	yow,-iow
ㄧㄢ	ian	yan	yean,-ean	yann,-iann
ㄧㄣ	in	yn	yiin,-iin	yinn,-inn
ㄧㄤ	iang	yang	yeang,-eang	yanq,-ianq
ㄧㄥ	ing	yng	yiing,-iing	yinq,-inq
ㄨㄚ	ua	wa	woa,-oa	wah,-uah
ㄨㄛ	uo	wo	woo,-uoo	woh,-uoh
ㄨㄞ	uai	wai	woai,-oai	way,-uay
ㄨㄟ	uei	wei	woei,-oei	wey,-uey
ㄨㄢ	uan	wan	woan,-oan	wann,-uann
ㄨㄣ	uen	wen	woen,-oen	wenn,-uenn
ㄨㄤ	uang	wang	woang,-oang	wanq,-uanq
ㄨㄥ	ueng	weng°	woeng	weng
-ㄨㄥ	-ong	-orng	-oong	-onq
ㄩㄝ	iue	yue	yeue,-eue	yueh,-iueh
ㄩㄢ	iuan	yuan	yeuan,-euan	yuann,-iuann
ㄩㄣ	iun	yun	yeun,-eun	yunn,-iunn
ㄩㄥ	iong	yong	yeong,-eong	yonq,-ionq

FIGURE 6.1 Gwoyeu Romatzyh (GR), the national language in Roman alphabet.
Source: "Guoyu luomazi pinyin fashi—guoyin zimu di er shi" 國語羅馬字拼音法式-國音字母第二式 [The transcription method for Gwoyeu Romatyzh—the second National Phonetic Alphabet], *Guoyu yuebao* 1 (1927): 1–2.

Qu Qiubai despised GR. Since the earliest days of phoneticization, the four tones of Mandarin were an obstacle for devising phonetic letters for Chinese, but Yuen Ren Chao claimed to have found the solution, which was the reason both for other linguists' veneration and for Qu Qiubai's condemnation of it. Chao suggested using the letters themselves to show the four tones. The sound *ia*, for instance, was written as *ia* if it was in the first tone, *ya* in the second tone, *yea*, *-ea* in the third tone, and *yah*, *-iah* in the fourth tone. It was ingenious indeed, for the tones were incorporated into the phonetically written words. But the problem, for Qu Qiubai, was that it could be used *only* for the officially recognized Beijing Mandarin, which had four tones. What about the Chinese languages, asked Qu, that had more than four tones, such as those in Zhejiang, Fujian, or Guangdong? How could the GR accommodate languages that had six tones, eight tones, or more? Reminiscent of Gramsci's critique of language and hegemony, Qu argued that GR's hegemonic undertones disqualified it as a national phonetic writing system, for it imposed standardization at the expense of linguistic diversity. Indeed, the biggest difference between romanization (GR) and latinization (CLA) was that the former sought to standardize Chinese based on one language, Mandarin as spoken in Beijing, whereas the latter wanted to allow disparate vernacular linguistic communities free expression. GR, in the words of Qu, was not a "Romanized [*luomazide* 羅馬字的] Chinese script" but a "disgusting [*roumazide* 肉麻字的] Chinese script."[5] "Romanization" was "bourgeois latinization," and the choice of Beijing Mandarin as the language of the nation reflected the "exploitative practices" of the ruling class.[6] For the latinists, even if Mandarin could become the national language, all linguistic communities must have the innate right to have an alphabet to represent their own tongues.

Qu Qiubai was not entirely correct in accusing Yuen Ren Chao's GR of representing the ruling class. Chao was the biggest name in Chinese linguistics and the first to systematically work on Chinese regional languages. It was in part thanks to his pioneering linguistic work that the latinists were able to devise new alphabets later in the 1930s. Moreover, Chao himself was a believer in the future alphabetization of China, although he never had a clear stance regarding the alphabetization of what he called "non-Mandarin dialects," i.e., the mutually incomprehensible regional languages across the nation.[7] But regardless of Chao's own politics, Qu Qiubai's theory of language also rested on questionable grounds, for he took multilingualism as the sole path toward eliminating class differences in language. As Jing Tsu has noted, Yuen Ren Chao's consideration of "dialects" was indeed more nuanced than Qu Qiubai's ideas on linguistic representation. For Chao, there were dialects even within a given linguistic community that still represented class differences, such as the "dialects" of educated elites and that of immigrant laborers.[8] Multilingual representation, in other words, did not necessarily eliminate class differences, even if it did in principle offer a cultural technology for the "masses."

Even though Qu condemned Chao's "bourgeois" proclivities, the letters for his proposed Chinese Latin Alphabet indeed owed a lot to Chao's GR. In 1930, when Qu published *Chinese Latinized Alphabet*, it was surprising that the letters he chose for it were significantly different from the New Dunganese Alphabet. Composed of twenty-three initials (*b, p, m, f, w, d, t, n, l, r, g, k, ń, h, zh, ch, sh, jh, z, c, s, j*) and thirty-six finals, it was much closer to the GMD-approved GR, despite the scathing critique that Qu posed against it.[9] The difference between the two was more political than technical. When Qu was devising his Latin letters as an alternative to the Roman letters approved by the GMD, the main problem he encountered was the representation of "five tones" (*wusheng* 五聲). The fifth tone (*rusheng* 入聲) of the southern provinces, which had troubled missionaries and Chinese script reformers for a long time, was a concern for Qu as well, who was himself hailing from the southern province of Jiangsu, where the fifth tone was integral to speech. But as opposed to previous reformers who tried to represent the fifth tone with an extra sign, such as an *h*, Qu made a strange decision: the tones, he claimed, did not matter. Linking the tones, wrongly, to accents in Indo-European languages, Qu decided to take not only the fifth but all the tones out of his alphabetic system.[10]

Qu's alphabet was thus ambiguous on more than one level. On the one hand, most letters were closer to GR than to the USSR's Unified New Turkic Alphabet (UNTA). For instance, as in GR, Qu made use of digraphs (*zh, ch, sh, jh*), even though digraphs did not exist in the UNTA, which was devised on the principle that each sound should be rendered with one letter. Further, in situations where the use of tones was an absolute necessity, he adopted the GR's technique of representing tones with the letters themselves—as in *mae* 買 (to buy) and *mmae* 賣 (to sell), or *she* 是 (to be) and *sshe* 使 (to cause).[11] On the other hand, it was not clear what language Qu's alphabet was meant to represent. The title of the book, *Chinese Latinized Alphabet*, obscured more than it revealed, and some of the transcriptions made it clear that the sounds the latinized letters stood for were a mix of northern and southern linguistic sounds without a clear rationale (昂, for instance, was transcribed as ńań in Qu's book).[12] Furthermore, Qu's decision to step away from the Soviet Union's UNTA was also enigmatic. Using digraphs such as *ch* or *sh* instead of the UNTA's ҫ or ş was later framed as a practical solution for using typewriters, which seems like a plausible explanation, since UNTA typewriters were not available in the USSR when Qu wrote the *Chinese Latinized Alphabet*—an issue that I will discuss more below.[13] But one wonders whether Qu's decision was part of an effort to resist a possible Sovietization and instead preserve a sovereign place for China. Or perhaps he wanted to distance Chinese latinization from Sino-Muslim latinization? Whatever the reasons might have been, Qu's alphabet went through a considerable change in May 1930, when the Chinese latinists invited Alexander A. Dragunov (Ch. Long Guofu 龍果夫, 1900–1955), who was then working on Dunganese, to help reform the alphabet.

The invitation came at a critical moment. Just a month earlier, in April 1930, the Central Executive Committee of the GMD had changed the name of the National Phonetic Alphabet (NPA) (*Zhuyin/Guoyin zimu*) to Phonetic Symbols (*Zhuyin fuhao*). The change was a deliberate decision to emphasize the immutable place of the Chinese characters themselves. The committee noted that the Phonetic Symbols were like Japanese hiragana, i.e., phonetic equivalents of Chinese characters, "symbols" that were only used to indicate the characters, not to replace them.[14] It was telling that the GMD took the decision to adopt Phonetic Symbols in 1930, right after Qu Qiubai published his essay on Chinese latinization in Moscow and called for a complete replacement of the Chinese characters with the Latin alphabet. The fate of the Chinese script was being decided within a larger Sino-Soviet space.

Resolutely anti-communist and counterrevolutionary, Phonetic Symbols embodied all that the Central Committee could have asked for. They could be learned in "three days" and thus conformed with the modern search for speed in information access. They could be printed next to Chinese characters or be used by themselves. And it was possible to transcribe standard Mandarin as well as non-Mandarin languages with the new alphabet: "[With Phonetic Symbols], there is no sound that cannot be transcribed, and no speech that cannot be communicated [*wuyin bu ke zhu, wuyu bu ke chuan*]."[15] The script's power to transcribe all languages and the possibility to use it even without characters were important at all levels of society and bureaucracy, and were especially significant for propaganda purposes:

> If the party adopts the Phonetic Symbols, it can save strokes and ink in propagating the doctrines [*xuanchuan zhuyi* 宣傳主義] and spreading them to reach large numbers of illiterate masses. If government officials adopt it, common people's concerns and problems will be understood better, for [officials] may accept documents written in Phonetic Symbols by people who do not know Chinese characters, and [they may] issue orders in Phonetic Symbols. If teachers and students adopt it, they may exert the least amount of time and effort, and teach all their family members, servants, colleagues, and friends [how to use Phonetic Symbols].... When [nationwide] mobilization is in order, intelligentsia may do its utmost for propaganda, and like in Japan, [people] may read general books and newspapers with hiragana (i.e., Phonetic Symbols). It will be in no time that the number of literate people will rise from 20 percent to 70 or 80 percent.[16]

The militarist ideology behind Phonetic Symbols guided the GMD's effort to disseminate it. The Central Executive Committee immediately informed all the party offices and cadres about Phonetic Symbols' use to intensify the propaganda of party doctrines (*zeng xuanchuan dangyi* 增宣傳黨義) and ordered all officials to acquaint themselves with the alphabet: Phonetic Symbols was going to be the official alphabet of the regime. The Ministry of Education established the Commission to Promote Phonetic Symbols (Zhuyin fuhao tuixing weiyuanhui 注音符號推行委員會) and started teaching the alphabet to all government cadres in Nanjing, while quickly drafting a plan to spread this activity across the nation. According to the "Method to Promote Phonetic Symbols in Each Province, City, and District," education departments and offices in each province, city, and district were going to set up a Phonetic Symbols Committee, whose duty was to promote the new alphabet and carry out linguistic surveys. They were then going to report the survey results to the Preparatory Committee for the National Unification of Language and prepare booklets for teaching Phonetic Symbols to people of different regional languages (*fangyan*).

That was not all. Each place was going to have new typesets for Phonetic Symbols, so that they could be printed next to the Chinese characters. Even the news was going to be published with Phonetic Symbols. All the road signs, street names, business signs, station signs, school signs, and factory signs were going to be transcribed with them. Propaganda slogans (*xuanchuan biaoyu* 宣傳標語) and advertisements were not going to be left without the new alphabet either, nor were government offices nor organizations nor teams nor schools. "President Sun Yat-sen's Will" (*Zongli yizhu*) and his "Instructions" (*xunci* 訓詞) for the Huangpu Military Academy, as well as all textbooks, were going to be printed with Phonetic Symbols. In official publications and local newspapers, the right side of the text was going to have Phonetic Symbols for the national language, and the left side Phonetic Symbols for other vernacular languages and dialects.[17] In short, the GMD was going to penetrate the minds of the populace through Phonetic Symbols.

Phonetic Symbols turned out to be as large of a problem for Chinese latinists as GR. The promotion of the Chinese Latin Alphabet thus became an absolute necessity for the revolutionaries in the Soviet Union to resist the GMD's program. But for all the reasons described above, Qu Qiubai's Chinese Latinized Alphabet was not mature enough to be officially ratified. The solution, for the time being, was to invite Alexandr Dragunov, a scholar of Dunganese, to help redesign the CLA. As one of the main Sinologists working on the New Dunganese Alphabet, Dragunov was deeply knowledgeable about Chinese languages at large. But for him, the revolutionary alphabet was the UNTA itself, not Qu Qiubai's GR-related Chinese Latinized Alphabet.

Dragunov's involvement significantly transformed Qu's alphabet and brought it much closer to the UNTA. Most of the letters in Qu's alphabet and the UNTA already had the same phonetic values—after all, Roman or Latin, they all used the same letters. The finals, in particular, remained mostly intact with minor changes, such as *ae* turning into *ai* and *uae* turning into *uai*, bringing Qu's CLA even closer to the original GR. But Dragunov replaced some of Qu's initial phonetic values with those of the UNTA. *H* was replaced with an *x* ج to render the phonetic values of [x]/[h]/[ɕ], *c* was given the phonetic value of *che* ج to render [tɕʰ] and [tsʰ], and *j* was given the only value of *y* ی ([ɥ] and [j]). Qu's *jy* (Pinyin: *yu*) was replaced with the single letter *y* ی ([y]/[ü]), *jh* was replaced with *rh* [ɻ~ʐ] (closer to the pronunciation of *r* in the UNTA), and *ń* was replaced with *ng* [ŋ], which did not exist as a digraph in the UNTA. The only initials from Qu's proposal that were significantly different from the UNTA and that remained in the final version of the

CLA were the digraphs *zh* [tʂ], *ch* [tʂʰ], *sh* [ʂ], and *gi* [tɕ], the first three of which were exactly the same as in GR.

So, in the end, who invented the CLA? We do not have stenographic records of the meetings where these letters were discussed. It is not even clear if Qu Qiubai was present at the meetings that finalized the phonetic values of the CLA's letters. He certainly was *not* present when the alphabet was officially recognized in the First Chinese Latinization Conference in 1931. But given the mix of phonetic values that can be traced at once to Gwoyeu Romatzyh, the Unified New Turkic Alphabet, and Qu Qiubai's publication in 1930, it is meaningful to consider the CLA as a compromise between the USSR's UNTA and Qu Qiubai's GR-inspired Latin alphabet. The CLA, in other words, was an artifact of the ideologically charged Sino-Soviet space in which there were multiple scripts vying for dominance. This compromise, especially the five digraphs, was to cause some headaches for the Chinese latinists in the following years. But in the meantime, the final version of the CLA was at last approved in Vladivostok during the First Chinese Latinization Conference in September 1931. For many, it was the dawn of a latinized age.

Revolution in Crisis: The Chinese Latin Alphabet in the Soviet Union

The First Chinese Latinization Conference in Vladivostok was the most significant event in the history of Chinese latinization, as it spelled out the purpose of the Chinese Latin Alphabet. The participants in the conference, including Xiao San, the strongest name in Chinese latinization after Qu Qiubai, stood up against the elitist literary culture that they believed the Chinese characters helped reproduce. "Imperialists and the GMD," noted Xiao San during the Conference, "are trying to extinguish the movement for a proletarian culture . . . banning *baihua*, and propagating against the Latin Alphabet [with] the National Phonetic Alphabet [sic, Phonetic Symbols] as a way to keep the ideographic writing system." In the spirit of internationalism and proletarian revolution, the conference resisted phonetic alphabets that were graphic permutations of logographs, such as Korean hangul, Japanese hiragana, and Chinese Phonetic Symbols. The Latin alphabet, which used to be an instrument of Western colonialism, now became an antiimperialist weapon in the hands of the communists. Secondly, the Conference drafted a highly radical resolution, stating that "the dialect [*kouyin* 口音] of a certain place cannot be made into the standard dialect of the entire country." It instead divided Chinese languages into five main regions—Northern Mandarin, Guangdong, Fujian, Zhejiang, and Hunan and Jiangxi—and claimed that each of these places should be given the right to develop their own local literary cultures.[18] In 1931, the only textbook published in the CLA was that of Northern Mandarin, but the plan was to publish textbooks, compile dictionaries, and thereby codify the non-Mandarin vernacular languages as well.[19]

The initial formulation of this linguistic vision was confusing. According to the nationality policies in the USSR, language was one of the central instruments in the definition of nationalities, and at first glance, the Chinese latinists' determination to give each vernacular language a "culture" of its own seemed like a copy of the USSR's nationality policies. As a matter of fact, even Xiao San, during his speech in the conference, identified these mutually incomprehensible languages as "nationalities" (*natsional'nosti*).[20] At first sight, it seems that Qu Qiubai, Xiao San, and others tried to impose a Stalinist vision on China by implying that different languages indicated separate nationalities. The resolutions of the First Chinese Latinization Conference, however, make it clear that Chinese latinization and the politics of representation that came with it were not simply an imitation of the Soviet regime, but a carefully crafted appropriation of Soviet nationality policies into the local linguistic and political conditions of China. A comparison of the conference resolutions in Russian and Chinese translations clarifies this point. As mentioned above, the resolution in Chinese stated that "the dialect of a certain place cannot be made into the standard speech of the entire country [不能以某一個地方的口音作為全國的標準音]"; but the original resolution in Russian stated that "one out of many local Chinese dialects cannot be used as the standard for the whole country [нельзя употребить один из местных китайских диалектов в качестве стандартного для всей страны]." Possibly because of the lack of commensurability in *kouyin* and "dialect," the Russian resolution was later edited to insert the following correction: "one out of many local Chinese languages or dialects of China cannot be used as the standard for the whole country [нельзя употребить один из местных китайских (языков или) диалектов (в китая) в качестве стандартного для всей страны]."[21] In other words, the resolutions never spoke of a "multinational" system; instead they were careful to emphasize a "Chinese national culture" (*zhongguo minzu wenhua* 中國民族文化) in which latinization would enable a multilingual coexistence, but the represented languages would not be designated as separate nationalities.²² Latinized China was a multilingual vision for one Chinese nation, which was significantly different both from the Soviet model and the GMD model, and also from what the nation turned out to become under the PRC.

Despite the emphasis on linguistic representation, however, the resolution was unclear about how and when exactly this codification was to take place. The Russian draft of the resolution stated that scientific work in Northern Mandarin and in "dialects" was to take place simultaneously (*odnovremenno*); but the printed resolution in Chinese noted that since "70-80% of Chinese people can all communicate in Northern [Mandarin] dialect [*kouyin*], it is going to be used as the standard for now, and textbooks and dictionaries will be compiled in it. The compilation work in the languages and dialects of other places [*qitafang kouyin* 其他方口音] will start later."²³ Bloated statistics aside, the difference between the Russian and Chinese resolutions might have been the result of a practical problem. Even though multilingualism was the primary goal of the CLA, textbook and dictionary compilation for different languages and dialects across China was a scientific enterprise that required meticulous work, preferably done *in* China. Given the geographical distance and the extant political problems between the two countries, Soviet linguists never conducted linguistic work on the ground. Their knowledge about Chinese "dialects" came either from the main journal of the Folklore Movement, *Geyao zhoukan* 歌謠週刊, or from the publications of Chinese linguists, some of whom they would have labelled as "bourgeois," such as Yuen Ren Chao, Liu Fu, Wang Li, Zhou Bianming, and others.²⁴ Early in 1932, they proposed an ambitious plan to conduct work in Chinese languages and dialects—for Shanghai, Guangzhou, Nanjing, Hankou, Fuzhou, Changsha, Nanchang, Shanxi, Gansu, Jiangxi, Hunan, and Hubei— but none was carried through.²⁵ The only non-Mandarin linguistic work that came close to being carried out in the Soviet Union was that of Cantonese by Vasilii S. Pukhov (1908–1937), a Chinese of Cantonese origin working as a language instructor at the Oriental Institute in Leningrad, but the plan was never realized.²⁶ Almost every year, the Scientific Research Commission of the Far Eastern Committee of the New Alphabet (Dal'nevostochnyi komitet novogo alfavita [DVKNA]), which had Xiao San as its president, had dialectological work in its plans, but every year, it was postponed to the next.²⁷

As a matter of fact, even linguistic work in Northern Mandarin CLA was not coming along as successfully as imagined in the USSR. The DVKNA was founded right after the conference with the sole purpose of spreading the CLA in the Far Eastern Soviet Union, where illiterate Chinese population was the largest.[28] The CLA was thus put in practice in the Far East, particularly in Vladivostok, Khabarovsk, Blagoveshchensk, and Artyom, but the social and technical limitations did not facilitate the ambitions of the movement. To start with, there were not enough teachers to teach the CLA.[29] Secondly, the Far Eastern Committee of the New Alphabet was having chronic problems with printing, to the extent that printing simply stopped in July 1932 because of the lack of typesets.[30] There were only three print shops, one in Vladivostok, one in Khabarovsk, and one in Blagoveshchensk, that were supposed to publish works for latinized Chinese, Korean, and for the ethnic minorities of the "Peoples of the North" (*narody severa*), but despite the constant calls from the Chinese, Koreans, and other minorities, by July 1932, they had still not received the typesets they needed.[31]

The material issues that revolutionaries were troubled by are important to recognize. The proponents of latinization were so attracted to the alphabet's modernist promises of progress that they hardly considered the infrastructural and technological materiality of scripts at large. There was in fact a constant discrepancy between their modernist ideals and grounded realities. Almost none of the revolutionary latinists, for instance, had any hands-on experience with printing. They were under the fallacious phonocentric assumption that once scripts phonetically represented languages, efficiency in mental and clerical labor would increase and enlightened knowledge would follow. In reality, however, the new alphabet required a new social and technological infrastructure—typewriters, linotype machines, textbooks, schools, and teachers, among other components. In other words, the internationalism espoused by the latinists required a sociotechnical assemblage that the revolutionaries were not prepared to shoulder.

Latinized typewriters offer a good example of the material limits of internationalism. Conceived of as the "apparatus of indigenization" (*korenizatsiia*),[32] the first latinized typewriter in the USSR, known as Janalif, was invented under the supervision of Mukhammed Ibragimovich Idrisov (1882–1948), a Tatar engineer from Kazan.[33] Following the principles of Scientific Organization of Labor (NOT) and Underwood typewriters, Idrisov tried to optimize "finger work" (*rabota pal'tsev*) in typing by calculating the letter frequencies for each language. In 1929, Idrisov began his work, and devised different keyboard arrangements for twenty different nationalities in total. Only a few national languages that were close to one another in terms of letter frequencies had the same keyboards (such as Uzbek and Uyghur or Chechen and Ingush); others were all different, leading to a sudden proliferation of keyboard designs.[34] This abrupt demand for nationally specific typewriters was not easy to supply, since this was the first time that typewriters were ever produced in Russia, and jamming was only the most basic of the issues.[35] The factories in Kazan and Leningrad were not producing fast enough to meet the demands from the republics. As late as in 1934, standardized keyboards were manufactured only for Azeri, Bashkir, Kazan Tatar, Kazakh, and Crimean Tatar.[36] In order to optimize production and open up room for other nationalities that still lacked their own keyboards, the All-Union Central Committee of the New Alphabet even tried to unify the keyboards of the Turkic languages, although the project did not bear any fruit.[37] In 1936, the committee was still demanding the standardization of keyboards for fifteen more languages, which was never achieved by the typewriter factories.[38] The prospects were even worse for linotype machines. Some Tatar engineers tried to invent them, but they all failed, and the machines were eventually imported from the Mergenthaler Setzmaschinen-Fabrik in Berlin, which also supplied the same machines to the frustrated latinists of the Far East, including those for latinized Chinese and Korean in 1932.[39] Paradoxically, the pivotal technology of internationalism, i.e., the Latin alphabet, turned out to be its greatest obstacle.

Even with linotype machines and partial success with typewriters, the problems continued to grow, not only for the Chinese but for all nationalities in the Soviet Union, for the ideological power of Soviet latinization was wilting. The first major breaking point in the movement came in 1932–1933, when the ethnic, national, and linguistic policies in Ukraine and Belorussia led to a catastrophe. Belorussian, Polish, Ukrainian, and Russian cultures were closer to one another, and in Belorussia and Ukraine, hostility toward Russian culture was considered to be a move away from the Soviet Union toward Poland. The east and the west of the Soviet Union were very different in this regard. In the east, Russophobia was considered to be a result of tsarist colonialism, but in the west, it was considered to be "treasonous irredentism." Language politics were a particularly thorny issue in the nationality policies of the west. The nationalization of languages, the invention of terminologies, and the acceptance/rejection of Polish/Russian words in Ukraine and Belorussia were entangled with greater ethnic and national problems, which resulted in the terror campaigns of 1933.[40]

As an extension of these issues in the west, latinization suffered a huge blow in the east. In 1933, Semen Dimanshtein (1886–1938), the director of the Institute of Nationalities, noted that Russian language no longer had the same class content, and so, to non-Russian peoples, it was different from what it used to be before the revolution.[41] This was the first time that the Russian language was promoted by a member of the All-Union Central Committee of the New Alphabet, and it signaled a policy of Russification that was quickly going to replace internationalism in the Soviet Union. Only two years later, in 1935, the first crucial shift in latinization took place in the Far East, when the Latin alphabets of the Peoples of the North were replaced by the Cyrillic alphabet. As the initial project of an internationalist order was rapidly turning into a network of national languages governed by Russian, latinization started to crack under pressure. And the walls were closing in on the Chinese Latin Alphabet as well.

One of the major accusations against the CLA came from Stanislav Antonovich Vrubel (1904–?), an instructor at the Moscow Sun Yat-sen University, who had not been content with the reformed Chinese Latin Alphabet since the beginning. According to Vrubel, the CLA was closer to the "bourgeois" English alphabet, i.e., GR, than to the internationalist alphabet of the USSR, i.e., the UNTA, as exemplified by the New Dunganese Alphabet. There had in fact always been a subtle tension between Dunganese latinization and Chinese latinization, since Qu Qiubai's first effort was based more on the GR than the UNTA. Even though Dragunov had moved the CLA closer to the UNTA in 1930, the tension between the Dungans and the Chinese was not resolved. In 1932, the New Dunganese Alphabet was slightly reformed in Kazakhstan, and then in 1933, it was reformed again and given the same alphabet as the Chinese Latin Alphabet. But according to reports from 1934, it was rejected by the Dungans, who after all had their own nationality and did not want to be consumed under a greater Chinese identity.[42]

Vrubel's issue with the CLA was a product of this existing tension between the Dunganese and the Chinese alphabets. His main point of attack was the CLA's use of five digraphic signs (*ch*, *sh*, *zh*, *rh*, and *ng*), which were not part of the internationalist alphabet, hence its "bourgeois" English quality. In December 1935, piggybacking on Vrubel's accusations, the People's Commissariat for Education (Narkompros) also announced that the CLA was oriented toward the English alphabet. Within the increasingly politicized environment, a conference was immediately put together in Moscow in March 1936—including Xiao San, Alekseev, Dragunov, Shprintsin, Zhirkov, Laikhter, and others—to debunk the Narkompros's accusations, and keep the CLA as it was.[43] The conference participants articulated a cogent response, claiming that apart from the digraphic signs, almost all other letters were the same as in the UNTA. As a matter of fact, both sides of the dispute were correct. Some of the digraphic signs, after all, *were* coming from the Chinese "bourgeois" Roman Alphabet, but the rest of the letters *were* from the Dunganese/Unified New Turkic Alphabet. This mix of letters did not necessarily signal a deviation from Soviet internationalism; it was rather a compromise that allowed socialist internationalism to reach beyond the USSR. Yet, since 1933, as the Soviet Union's nationality policies were losing their internationalist vision, Vrubel's critique was just one of the problems that Chinese latinists had to face.

The conference in 1936 provided a platform for everyone to voice their dissatisfaction with the Chinese latinization movement in the USSR. For Vasilii Alekseev, one of the leading Sinologists in the USSR and a major figure in Chinese latinization, the new textbooks in the CLA signaled a shift toward Russification. Certain words, he claimed, were simply bad imitations of Russian, such as *shaoshzdi* 少識字的—an awkward literal translation of the Russian word for "illiterate," *malogramotnyi*, which literally stands for "little" (Ru. *malo*, Ch. *shao*) and "literate" (Ru. *gramotnyi*, Ch. *shzdi*). Alekseev also showed dissatisfaction with the translations of foreign country and city names. Why was Paris written in the CLA as "Paris" instead of "Bali," the latter being the transcription of the Mandarin name of the city? Or why was Moscow written as "Moskva," a transcription of the Russian pronunciation, rather than "Moske," a transcription of the Mandarin pronunciation? Why "Roma" and not "Loma?"[44]

Xiao San was also confused about the new terminologies. In 1932, he was given the task of writing a Sino-Russian dictionary, but the final product was nowhere near completion. During the conference, he noted how complicated the question became in the case of the so-called international words, such as "proletariat," "communist," or even the word "international." In some cases, he proposed, it was better to write both the "international" word and the Chinese translation/transliteration in parentheses. When writing "proletariat" in Chinese, for instance, the word "proletariat" could be followed by *uchangiegi* in brackets—a temporary solution until "international words" were established in Chinese. But in the case of other words, he could not provide solutions. For example, would it really be possible to write "kompartiia" (Communist Party) instead of *gungchandang*?[45] He might as well have asked, Is "kompartiia" even international? What, after all, was the delineation between "international" and "Russian" vocabularies?

The conference did not end on a good note, and the participants' complaints did not offer a way out. In the meantime, the literacy movement in the Far East was not faring any better. In June 1937, Naim I. Liubin and Vladimir Baum, members of the Presidium of the Far Eastern Committee of the New Alphabet, sent an angry telegram from Khabarovsk to the Central Committee of the New Alphabet in Moscow and stated that "from 1935 to 1937, the All-Union Central Committee of the New Alphabet has neither guided, nor helped, nor been interested in the work of the Northern and Chinese sections of the Far Eastern Committee of the New Alphabet."[46] There were not enough teachers, there were not enough textbooks, there were not enough print shops and typesets, and, given that Xiao San never finished the compilation of the much-awaited Russo-Chinese dictionary, terminologies were never defined. According to a report written in the same year, students in the Chinese Leninist School in Vladivostok studied the CLA only during their first year, and partly in their second year. There were no textbooks in the CLA for more advanced students, so they were simply studying books written in Chinese characters, "to the extent that the graduates of this school forget the CLA and are not able to use it any further." What made things even worse, and more farcical, was that a certain Comrade Nosov, who was supposed to teach instructors how to teach the CLA, himself did not know the alphabet![47] As the members of the presidium succinctly put it, "the Presidium of the DVKNA regards the work of the DVKNA in the past two years as utterly dissatisfactory."[48] With no support from the Central Committee of the New Alphabet, and amid changing political waves concerning the nationalities, typographical problems, and the tension between Dunganese and Chinese, the Chinese latinization in the USSR turned out to be a fiasco.

Sin Wenz in China

Surprisingly, however, as the Chinese Latin Alphabet was losing steam in the USSR, it was gaining popularity in China, under the name Sin Wenz. From 1932 onward, when the initial challenges in typography were temporarily overcome in the Soviet Far East, there was a steady increase in the number of latinized works. Dictionaries and propaganda materials as well as textbooks in Northern Mandarin, mathematics, geography, and history were published; and in the following couple of years, there was a proliferation in publications as Xiao San, Wu Yuzhang, Lin Boqu, Kolokolov, Dragunov, Laikhter, and Shprintsin, among others, started translating works into the CLA.[49] From 1934 to 1936, Sin Wenz research societies (*xinwenzi yanjiuhui*) were established throughout the nation, in Shanghai, Beijing, Tianjin, Guizhou, Henan, Shanxi, Guangxi, Chongqing, Sichuan, and other provinces; and with the research societies came primers in Sin Wenz.[50] In November 1934, one of those primers came to the attention of the GMD authorities; it narrated the history of latinization as it developed in the Soviet Union and suggested the following exercises:

> *Exercise*: Use Sin Wenz to answer the questions below:
>
> 1) Where are the workers in the Far Eastern USSR from?
>   (Answer: In the Far Eastern USSR, there are a lot of workers from the East. There are Chinese and Koreans.)
> 2) Why are the majority of Chinese working masses [*laoku dazhong*] illiterate?
>   (Answer: Chinese characters are extremely difficult. These difficult characters can be learned only by the bourgeoisie.)
> 3) What should be done to increase the level of knowledge and education among the masses [*dazhong*]?
>   (Answer: The Soviet Union develops national cultures. We use latinization to replace the Chinese characters, for now it is easy to learn [the Latin alphabet].... Long live Latinized Chinese Writing!)[51]

The content *and* the form, which were indeed inseparable, were distressing for the GMD. In February 1935, the Military Political Bureau stated that Sin Wenz textbooks were designed by the CCP Central Committee and were used to train workers in the doctrines of the party. "This," the bureau noted, "is a new turn in propaganda methods used in China. Police forces and military offices around the whole country must all be alert and seize [the publications]."[52]

Sin Wenz was in fact not spearheaded by the CCP—it was much bigger than the party, which at the time was barely trying to survive the Long March. The biweekly *Sin Wenz*, the first journal to be devoted to discussions on Sin Wenz, started publication in 1935 in Shanghai, the center of the movement in China. The number of textbooks and reference works on Sin Wenz was increasing, and Esperantist journals were helping further the cause.[53] The following year, the Shanghai Sin Wenz Research Society even published a manifesto, "Our Views on Promoting Sin Wenz," signed by more than 150 famous figures, communists and noncommunists, including Tao Xingzhi, Hu Yuzhi, Ai Siqi, Nie Gannu, Du Zuoyou, Ba Jin, and even Cai Yuanpei. The manifesto clearly laid out the stakes involved, and echoed the sentiments of the First Chinese Latinization Conference in 1931 with an added emphasis on GR:

> The National Language Romanization [Gwoyeu Romatzyh] venerates the dialect of Beiping as the National Language; nominally advocates the unification of the National Language, but actually it sets up a dictatorship of the Beiping dialect.... What the masses need in the way of a new script is a new phonetic writing, a new writing without the nuisance of tone indication, one that breaks away from the dictatorship of one local dialect.... Right now, the Proposal for Shanghainese Sin Wenz has already been published by experts in Shanghai, and we look forward to criticisms. Proposals for Xiamen and Hakka dialects have been prepared and are currently under examination here [at the Shanghai Sin Wenz Research Society]. Guangzhou, Fuzhou, and Huizhou dialects are being prepared.[54]

After the First Chinese Latinization Conference in Vladivostok, the left-wing manifesto for the CLA/Sin Wenz was the second most significant moment in the history of Chinese latinization. It was striking that the latinists in Shanghai were putting the Soviet plan into action just when the movement was in jeopardy in the Soviet Union. The signatories vowed that they were going to publish higher-level textbooks, novels, journals, and newspapers in Sin Wenz, invent a new stenography method and typewriter, and carry out linguistic simplification to reach out to the masses.[55] As a testimony to the power of latinization in China, the manifesto also demonstrated how the movement had evolved into something that far surpassed the USSR's and the CCP's lead. In fact, the connection between the Soviet Union and the Chinese latinists rested specifically on one figure, Xiao San, who also happened to be the one to give the Soviet latinists the good news that multilingual work in the CLA was finally being carried out. Soviet latinists were happy, and perhaps surprised, to see that the movement was indeed progressing in China, despite its gradual demise in the USSR.[56] It was clear that the success owed more to the efforts that Soviet latinization had inspired in China than to the financial and organizational support provided by the USSR in carrying it out, which, by 1935, amounted to nil.

The latinists' excitement was a threat to the GMD. The support that the CLA received from the society at large attested to the fact that the movement was not simply led by the CCP—it was a social movement, which made it even more dangerous for the GMD. Secondly, the infiltration of Sin Wenz into multiple vernacular languages, which the GMD was itself trying to dominate through Phonetic Symbols, posed an immediate concern, since a direct channel between anti-party intellectuals and multilingual communities could undermine the GMD's consolidation of power. And the GMD had every right to be concerned. In 1936, *Zhongguo Yuyan* (*Languages of China*), a left-wing journal dedicated to Sin Wenz, published an article in Shanghainese written in Sin Wenz.[57] A Sin Wenz textbook in Wuxi was also ready for publication.[58] Meanwhile, Sin Wenz textbooks for Suzhou, Changzhou, Xiamen, Guangzhou, Yangzhou, and Sichuanese languages and dialects were in the pipeline.[59]

Despite the technical difficulties in designating tones (or frankly, the impossibility of it), Sin Wenz in non-Mandarin languages was easier to print than Phonetic Symbols. According to the GMD's order to publish in various tongues, the Chinese characters were printed along with Mandarin Phonetic Symbols on the right side and Phonetic Symbols for regional languages on the left, which posed financial and technical difficulties for the publishers.[60] In Sin Wenz, however, all languages and dialects were simply printed using one alphabet and they were not complemented by Chinese characters, which in theory facilitated the printing business to a great extent. It seemed that Sin Wenz was not only the shortest and the fastest route to the minds of the people, but also the cheapest.

As the reach of Sin Wenz kept expanding, the much-distressed Central Propaganda Bureau issued its final verdict. On April 7, 1936, the bureau wrote a long report to the Central Standing Committee on Sin Wenz. The report first pointed out the larger project behind latinization. Leftist intellectuals, who were the inventors of this new alphabet, claimed that the Chinese characters were too difficult to learn and read, and that they were only used by scholars and officials. According to the leftists, "the exploitation of the scholar-officials [*shidaifu suo boxue* 士大夫所剝削] must come to an end, so that the masses [*yiban dazhong* 一般大眾] may enjoy the merits of being literate." The Central Propaganda Bureau, however, did not agree with the rationale behind the script:

> There are other reasons behind illiteracy in our country. [The reason] is certainly not the difficulty in learning Chinese characters. The evolution of a national writing system has its own historical background, which is related to the national culture. The Chinese characters that are used in our country have a glamorous history spanning thousands of years. Yet, today, [some] advocate their abolition. Wouldn't that destroy our country's native culture [*guyou wenhua*]? Besides, Latinxua Sin Wenz is far from perfect. From a cultural and academic perspective, it has no merits to speak of. Therefore, those who promote it do not do so for the quality of the alphabet itself; they use it as a tool of agitation. When observed closely, new publications that promote this movement and that are written in this alphabet are discovered every day. Eight or nine out of ten publications use it only in name and hide the cunning scheme of agitating class struggle. . . . In order to preserve native culture and wipe out heretical ideas, [the Central Propaganda Bureau] asks the Central Government to instruct all the publishing houses to prohibit all publications that promote the Latinxua Sin Wenz movement, and all the books and journals written in the alphabet. From now on, only researchers with special permits in the education offices [can work on it]. These publications must not be printed again, in order to prevent disorder.[61]

The report made it clear that Sin Wenz was one of the biggest obstacles in the GMD's own circuit of propaganda. Expectedly, the script was banned shortly after. Even though the Shanghai Sin Wenz Research Committee petitioned the Shanghai Social Affairs Bureau in 1937 and claimed that Sin Wenz could help promote education and unify the illiterate masses in a short time during the war, the GMD stayed firm in its decision.[62] The only phonetic script that was officially recognized by the party was Phonetic Symbols, and, during wartime, the party did all in its power to expand the influence of its phonetic alphabet and the doctrines embedded in it, as I will explain in the next chapter.

But that was not the end for Sin Wenz. As a matter of fact, it grew even stronger during the early years of the war, especially in the International Settlement in Shanghai and in Hong Kong, where Cantonese primers as well as latinized primers in other Chinese languages were published.[63] Chen Heqin, the psychologist who made the first statistical frequency analysis of Chinese characters, which we examined in chapter 3, was one of the main supporters of the system, and he even authored a primer for the refugees in Shanghai (in northern Mandarin).[64] During these early years of the war, the CCP also got involved in promoting Sin Wenz, especially in Shaanxi-Gansu-Ningxia, where the party was the strongest.[65]

But despite its impact on China, latinization was gasping for air in the Soviet Union. The technopolitical issues that latinization was entangled with throughout the 1930s resulted in Stalin's abrupt order in 1938 to cyrillize all national languages and put a definitive end to latinization. Shortly after Europe plunged into war, the years of labor put into inventing a Latin alphabet were instantly negated by the simple creation of a Cyrillic equivalent for each Latin sign.[66] The politics of cyrillization, needless to mention, were significantly different from the politics of latinization. The Cyrillic letters for Turkic languages, for instance, showed variations even if the phonetic values were the same, for Stalin aimed to put an end to a potential unity between Turkic nations. The same phoneme [dʒ] (pronounced *j* as in "jump," designated by ç in the UNTA) was given the sign Ч in Azeri and Ж in Turkmen, which signaled the central government's plan to separate the nations from one another while reconnecting them all to Moscow. The death of latinized letters also anticipated the death of postcolonial Turcology. Aleksandr Samoilovich, Evgenii Polivanov, Bekir Chobanzade, and dozens of other Turcologists and philologists were all executed starting in 1937 on false charges of Turkish or Japanese espionage.[67] Those who defended Chinese latinization were not spared either. Pukhov, the Chinese communist from Guangdong, was executed in 1937, and Xiao San's close friend Liubin, a member of the Presidium of the DVKNA, was arrested in 1938. Xiao San himself was not permitted to leave the Soviet Union until he finally received permission in 1939 to go to Yan'an.[68]

A year later, in 1940, Xiao San and other latinists of the Chinese Communist Party officially toned down their support for the CLA/Sin Wenz. A statement signed by ninety-nine people, including Xiao San and Wu Yuzhang, noted the following point:

> We do not at all propose to immediately replace Chinese characters with Sin Wenz, nor to call a halt toward continued modification of the latter. We endorse the script revolution, but we are not attempting in vain to complete it at once. Although characters are incompatible with present needs, and although a phonetic script must be used, Chinese characters do have a long history. They cannot be easily abandoned; instead, they must be slowly transformed. That is the only way to succeed in script reform. What we want to do now is to use Sin Wenz to teach illiterates, so that they will in a short time be able to use it to study politics and science, and also use it to study Chinese characters.[69]

The statement reflected a major change in plans that crystallized at the intersection of both national and transnational conditions. On the one hand, the death of latinization in the Soviet Union dealt a major blow to the Chinese latinists. The house arrests, imprisonment, and executions they suffered under the Great Purge were traumatic, causing them at least to distance themselves from the Soviet-led internationalist agenda. On the other hand, the CCP under the leadership of Mao Zedong was redefining the contours of literary and cultural revolution in Yan'an in the midst of the Second World War. Mao's famous "Talks at the Yan'an Forum on Art and Literature" in 1942 underlined the core value of "massification" (*dazhonghua* 大眾化), which guided the writers and artists in representing the masses while transforming them into a revolutionary class.[70] The absence of any statement regarding script reform in Mao's speech indicated the party's distance from it in defining and practicing revolution in literature and the arts. This was perhaps not that surprising given that the Chinese latinists in Yan'an had already seen the technological and political conundrums of Soviet latinization. Pushing for the same kind of change in the technologically impoverished conditions in Yan'an would have caused more problems than solutions during the creation of revolutionary masses. Thus, the disillusionment from Soviet latinization, the raging Second World War, and the attempt to define revolutionary culture in Yan'an put the Chinese Latin Alphabet in a precarious position; and in 1940, the CCP suspended latinization.

* * *

Latinization across Eurasia was one of the most radical movements in the global history of information. Stretching from the Caspian Sea to the Pacific Ocean, the Unified New Turkic Alphabet had an indelible impact on the information politics of diverse nations and nationalities, including China. The Chinese Latin Alphabet was both a nationally contrived reaction to the GMD's hegemonic attempts to transform Chinese society and a transnationally contrived product of global historical conditions. Its star shone bright as a counterhegemonic technology that not only promised linguistic pluralism, but also offered the material means to change the social and political practices of communication. As such, latinization in China was destined to initiate not only a material and ideological revolution, but also a cognitive one that sought to reprogram the embodied and mental practices of information access and topple the social hierarchy of linguistic sounds. The latinists of China embarked on a radical cognitive journey, perhaps without fully realizing the gravity of its consequences.

There was one person, Xiao San, who did realize the cognitive contradictions that the Latin alphabet could unleash. In 1936, when he came together with other latinists and Soviet Sinologists in Moscow to discuss the future of the Chinese Latin Alphabet, he addressed a variety of issues that must have startled the latinists. In a generous act of self-criticism, he first claimed that Qu Qiubai had been wrong all along in excluding the tones from the CLA. Tones, he realized, were not "accents" as Qu had put it; they were integral to speech. While he did not mention Gwoyeu Romatzyh, Xiao was clearly reckoning its value as a new Chinese script that was attentive to the indispensable place of tones in speech. Second, he noted that the entire project of multilingualism had also been a disaster, and what they should have done instead was to promote Beijing Mandarin and unify language in China—a suggestion that ran counter to everything that the latinists had been fighting for. "We must choose the dialect [that represents] the masses the most," claimed Xiao, going against the resolutions of the First Chinese Latinization Conference:

> We know that the workers and toilers usually get together in the centers, in the cities of the country. Beijing is the old cultural center, and Tianjin, the center of production. In Beijing, Tianjin, and other cities of the north, there is one northern dialect. I think that the Chinese bourgeois Romanists, who fervently stand behind a unified state language, will not be successful, but precisely because of

[one northern dialect], we will succeed to a certain extent in unifying the languages of the northern provinces under one northern language. This is the most common language of China. For countless times, we have tried to put latinization at the forefront, and we said that we should divide the Chinese language into five to seven groups, but the biggest group is that of the north.[71]

His most quixotic remark, however, came last. "The last question," he said, "which might not even be on the agenda right now, is the question of cultural language based on the new alphabet." As a writer himself, Xiao San had been at the forefront of latinization because he believed that the CLA could offer a better technology to write revolutionary literature and reach the masses. "When I started working on latinization," he said, "I wanted to write a literary piece of work based on the most popular colloquial language of the people." But then he added the following remark: "Yet it was painful for me, for *I just could not succeed in writing*.... This is a very difficult and complicated question.... I will talk about this more the next time."[72]

But there was no next time. Xiao San fell silent in the face of probably the largest contradiction that the CLA generated—the discrepancy between universal modernist ideals and embodied realities. If latinization was the revolution, Xiao San's moment of doubt showed the phenomenological limits of that revolution, for the protagonist of Chinese latinization was yearning for the Chinese characters. The CLA could, perhaps, internationalize China and tie it into a socialist network of nations. It could even open new venues of internationalist solidarity and exchange. But Xiao San's shocking revelation showed that there was a hidden value in the centuries-old intertwinement between characters and literary creativity that the Latin alphabet simply could not replicate. Latinized letters could certainly replace Chinese characters with the force of a modern state apparatus, as they had across Eurasia. But was it worth it?

Soviet latinization's greatest source of power—its universalist discourse of progress, efficiency, and productivity—was also its biggest weakness, for it completely disregarded historical specificities. The internal contradiction of latinization was apparent in Lenin's alleged dictum—"Latinization is the great revolution in the East!" Its emergence out of Baku was apparently sufficient to render it the revolution in the "East" that stretched from there to Shanghai. In reality, the Comintern's revolutionary program for the East was built on universalist principles that were woefully uninformed of local conditions. This ignorance became clear in the case of Chinese latinization as well. None of the Russian Sinologists or Chinese communists had adequate knowledge about Chinese languages to implement the multilingual vision they cultivated for China. Every year, the Scientific Research Commission of the Far Eastern Committee of the New Alphabet drafted new resolutions for printing primers and dictionaries in a variety of Chinese languages; but every year, it had to postpone them to the next. Chinese latinization turned out to be a revolutionary dream that ignored the historically and socially embodied practices of reading, writing, and thinking.

Still, when left-wing intellectuals brought it south of Vladivostok, the Chinese Latin Alphabet enjoyed enormous popularity as a subversive political technology. Its initial strength did not come from the CCP, but from the left-wing writers' opposition to the GMD-backed Phonetic Symbols and GR and their insistence on engineering an alternative communication network. It was only with the GMD's prohibition of the CLA in 1936, the Japanese invasion in 1937, and the death of Soviet latinization in 1938 that the CLA began to lose its momentum in China. But even with all the odds against it, the CCP did not cancel or ban latinization; it merely suspended it. The revolutionary history of the CLA was still not over.

SEVEN

The Empire of Pinyin

ONCE WE RECOGNIZE the Eurasian revolutionary history behind Chinese latinization, Pinyin presents as a grave anomaly. Invented in 1958 by a former Wall Street banker, Zhou Youguang 周有光 (1906–2017), Pinyin was markedly different from the Chinese Latin Alphabet/Sin Wenz. Pinyin turned Sin Wenz into *xin wenzi*; *yjan* into *yuyan*; *latinxua* into *ladinghua*; and *pinjin* into *pinyin*. Not only were the phonetic values of Pinyin letters different, but so were their political promises. The purpose of the Chinese Latin Alphabet in the 1930s was to build a multilingual nation while establishing an alternative communication network that rivaled that of the GMD. And in the 1950s, since the GMD's Phonetic Symbols and propaganda warfare no longer constituted a threat, the CCP could in theory carry out its alphabetical and multilingual mission through the CLA. Yet, when Zhou Youguang and his colleagues devised Pinyin, it turned out to be something entirely different from what the latinists were previously imagining. Pinyin represented only one language, Mandarin, just like Phonetic Symbols; the CCP made it clear that it had no intention of supporting a multilingual nation. In addition, Pinyin was officially announced as an auxiliary script, again like Phonetic Symbols, to aid literacy in Chinese characters. To put it differently, Pinyin was essentially Phonetic Symbols dressed in latinized clothes. How did that happen?

The eventual convergence of Pinyin and Phonetic Symbols had its origins in the Second World War, the sharpest turning point in the history of Chinese script reforms. Apart from the catastrophe that ensued after the

Japanese invasion, the war also overlapped with the death of Soviet latinization. With Stalin's order in 1938 to cyrillize national scripts in the USSR, the Latin alphabet lost its global revolutionary status, which had an immediate impact on the aura of the CLA in China. As explained in chapter 6, by the late 1930s, the most dedicated supporters of latinization who once imagined a multilingual nation were questioning the supposed value of the Latin alphabet. Even Xiao San, the staunch defender and leader of the CLA, lost faith both in multilingualism and in the will to annihilate the Chinese characters. As internationalist latinization failed and the Second World War raged on Chinese soil, the priorities of reformers and revolutionaries changed drastically. During the war, the CLA was still employed by left-wing intellectuals to print primers for non-Mandarin languages in China, but the CCP was no longer interested in defending a multilingual nation. Instead, the language politics of the CCP and the GMD converged to carry out a similar national and linguistic project, i.e., the spread of Mandarin as the one and only national language. When the CCP ceased to support the multilingual politics of the project, the Chinese latinists lost their institutional pillar and never recovered from it.

Diverging from the extant literature that draws a direct link between the CLA/Sin Wenz and Pinyin, this chapter demonstrates that the invention of Pinyin owed more to the GMD's institutionalization of wartime social communication engineering than to the internationalism of the Chinese Latin Alphabet. Phonetic Symbols played a critical role in this period as the party's weapon for information and propaganda warfare. The GMD had already been employing Phonetic Symbols in its propaganda war against the communists since 1930, but when the war turned propaganda into a matter of life and death in the hands of the Japanese, the GMD intensified its use of Phonetic Symbols to build national solidarity.

The main transformation in wartime communication engineering that I would like to underline was the inclusion of ethnic minorities into the GMD's—and later the CCP's—information network. Until 1937, Chinese script reforms were limited to the Chinese characters and to what constituted the ethno-national category of Han. Never did the reformers speak of non-Han languages, indicating a lack of interest to consider the non-Han in imagining a nation. Prominent Chinese intellectuals since the late Qing, some of whom worked with the GMD, did not even think about the non-Han, or did so only cursorily, while engineering the National Phonetic Alphabet or

Phonetic Symbols or Gwoyeu Romatzyh. Even the Chinese communists in Moscow avoided non-Han languages in their futuristic visions of the Latin alphabet—a notable omission given that the Latin alphabet in the Soviet Union was entirely about non-Russian nationalities. Until the war, Chinese script reforms were exclusively Han.

During the war, however, the geographical and ethnic dimensions of Chinese script reforms expanded to include people of different ethnic origins. This was more a necessary product of wartime conditions than a change of heart among Chinese reformers. The Japanese invasion forced the GMD to move the capital from Nanjing to Chongqing, close to the western frontiers. An academic relocation also followed. Coastal universities found new spots inland and the Institute of History and Philology (IHP), established in 1928 as a center for philological and linguistic research, relocated its headquarters to Kunming in southwestern China. As the ethnically diverse frontiers turned into geopolitically critical spaces for national security, the dimensions of communication engineering for propaganda purposes also went through a significant transformation. Phonetic Symbols thus became the medium to augment the GMD's propaganda network through increasing Mandarin literacy among the ethnic minorities.

From 1937 onward, Chinese script reforms were intricately bound to the linguistic and informational management of the non-Han, and mass literacy in Mandarin was inseparable from propaganda and national defense. Even institutional reorganization and shuffling of political figures between different ministries and bureaus were a testimony to this: Wang Shijie, the Minister of Education from 1933 to 1938, acted as the head of the Central Propaganda Bureau from 1939 to 1942; Chen Lifu 陳立夫 (1900–2001), the onetime chief of the Central Bureau of Statistics (CBS), the GMD's first intelligence department, acted as the minister of education from 1939 to 1944; Zhu Jiahua 朱家驊 (1893–1963), another chief of intelligence from the CBS, acted as the minister of education, the minister of communications, and the head of Academia Sinica during these two decades.[1] On a smaller scale, the National Language Commission brought together scholars with party officials. Leading Chinese script reformers such as Li Jinxi, Wei Jiangong, Lin Yutang, and Chen Lijiang were members of the commission's standing committee together with Pan Gongzhan 潘公展 (1895–1975), the vice minister of the Central Propaganda Bureau.[2] All these figures, and many others, were involved in the promotion of Phonetic Symbols. This propaganda origin of

Mandarin education in non-Han regions is significant to acknowledge, for it continued under the PRC immediately after the invention of Pinyin.[3]

Wartime communication engineering is thus essential in rethinking the paradoxical history of Pinyin. On the one hand, from the establishment of the PRC in 1949 to the invention of Pinyin in 1958, script reform was central to revolutionary endeavors. By the middle of the decade, there were hundreds of new script proposals for the new nation, and when Pinyin was devised, it was supposed to be the ultimate revolution. And yet, the same year, Zhou Enlai announced the party's decision to suspend the project to eliminate Chinese characters. Instead, the party officially simplified the characters and turned Pinyin into an auxiliary phonetic script for teaching and representing Mandarin. It seemed that decades of revolutionary thought had come to an abrupt end.

Ironically, however, complete pinyinization was suspended only for the Han. In the same year that Zhou Enlai made his announcement, the PRC launched an unexpectedly aggressive pinyinization campaign in its multiethnic frontiers—Inner Mongolia, Xinjiang, Tibet, and western and southwestern provinces. From 1958 until the start of the Cultural Revolution, PRC linguists, like those under the GMD, attempted to replace the existing minority scripts with Pinyin and turn Mandarin into an imperial lingua franca, not unlike English or Russian. The history of Pinyin thus illuminates the final contradiction in the long history of Chinese script reforms—the antiimperialist PRC aspiring to become an alphabetical empire.

Wartime Communication Engineering and Ethnic Minorities

Until the start of the war, the GMD's Phonetic Symbols reflected the party's reactionary tendencies to preserve the Chinese native culture while inventing one common national language that targeted predominantly Han communities. With the relocation of the capital to Chongqing and the universities to the southwest, however, the government's and linguists' perspective on language and script work radically shifted. From 1939–1940 onward, the politics of ethnic minorities' languages and scripts were inseparable from the politics of their Chinese counterparts. The government was no longer concerned with representing only Chinese languages with signs derived from Phonetic Symbols; it endeavored to create a permutation of Phonetic

Symbols as an all-inclusive writing system for all languages, including non-Han.

The ethnic minorities' inclusion into wartime propaganda had nominally started in 1930, with the official promulgation of Phonetic Symbols for Mandarin. That year, the GMD separately issued another order, decreeing that Phonetic Symbols be used for Mongolian and Tibetan languages in order to bring the diverse linguistic communities under the party's flag.[4] The order also resonated with the ideology of the founder of the republic, Sun Yat-sen. Since the last years of the Qing Empire, one of the building blocks of Sun Yat-sen's republican ideology had been the "unity of five races" (*wuzu gonghe* 五族共和), in which the five races represented the Han, Manchus, Tibetans, Mongolians, and Muslims (a vague construction that mostly referred to the Turco-Muslims in Xinjiang and the Chinese Muslims in the northwest). Although the place of the Manchus in this ideological framework diminished in the following decades, *wuzu gonghe* remained present in the GMD's effort to unite the nation under one party. The GMD entrusted the linguistic and informational leg of this project to the Mongolian and Tibetan Affairs Commission (Mengzang weiyuanhui 蒙藏委員會), which was institutionalized in 1928 for the specific purpose of managing the Mongolians and the Tibetans.[5] When the Ministry of Education issued the order to use Phonetic Symbols for Tibetan and Mongolian languages in 1930, the commission began working.

The GMD never sought to replace the Mongolian and Tibetan (and later the Turco-Muslim) writing systems with Phonetic Symbols. Instead, the party-state aimed to introduce the new phonetic script as an auxiliary script to teach Mandarin in the frontiers and bring the non-Han linguistic communities under the party's propaganda regime. But carrying out the order for frontier languages was even harder than phoneticizing Chinese. First of all, these ethnic populations had well-established writing systems that they had been using for centuries, which constituted an obstacle for the penetration of Phonetic Symbols into the ethnically diverse cultures of information. Secondly, there were linguistic differences among these communities, just like in Chinese. The transcription of these languages required linguistic standardization, which in turn required elaborate linguistic surveys and expertise that the central government found very difficult to acquire. Besides, during these two decades, the political situation in Tibet, Xinjiang, and Mongolia was uncertain at best, which made it even more difficult for both linguists and the party-state to carry out the plan for Phonetic Symbols in the frontiers. From 1930 until the start of the war in 1937, the use of Phonetic Symbols in the frontiers remained simply an order that was never carried out.

Languages of ethnic minorities remained marginal even for scholarly works until the war. Most of the philological and linguistic research during the war was undertaken by the Academia Sinica's Institute of History and Philology, established in 1928 to create a national scholarship that rivaled Western sinology. The IHP was at first composed of a handful of researchers: Fu Sinian 傅斯年 (1896–1950), Yuen Ren Chao, Luo Changpei 羅常培 (1899–1958), Li Fanggui 李方桂 (1902–1987), Chen Yinke 陳寅恪 (1890–1969), and Li Ji 李濟 (1896–1979), all of whom, except Luo Changpei, had received degrees in Europe or the United States.[6] Right after the IHP was established, Luo Changpei quickly devised an ambitious plan to undertake dialectological surveys and to complement linguistic studies with historical research on phonology. According to the original plan he drafted, five groups of linguists were going to be dispatched in February 1929 to Guangzhou, Siyi (southern Guangdong), Chaomei (eastern Guangdong), Minnan, and Hainan Island. Then, in the summer of 1929, Luo wanted to dispatch nine more groups to Fuzhou, Wenzhou, Ningbo, Jiangxi, Guilin, and Cangwu (Guangxi), and to the ethnic-minority regions of Zhuang, Yao, Lolo, and Miao.[7] When the surveys were first undertaken in 1929, however, they were much more modest in scope. Only two major surveys were completed—one by Yuen Ren Chao in Guangdong and Guangxi, and the other by Li Fanggui in Hainan. And only two non-Han languages were preliminarily studied by these linguists, that of the Yao and the Li.[8] The primary purpose of the IHP was the languages (and "dialects") of the Han, not the non-Han.

In 1939, however, linguistic work in the frontiers became an urgent matter of national security. The IHP moved to Kunming due to the war and encountered dozens of smaller ethnic populations with different languages and writing systems in Yunnan and the surrounding provinces in the southwest. During the 1940s, Li Fanggui, Luo Changpei, and others conducted linguistic surveys in non-Han regions on diverse languages such as Zhuang, Yi, Lolo, Sani, Lisu, Mexie, and Maru.[9] Of immediate concern in the 1940s was the GMD's desire to engineer a social communication network, and given the linguistic diversity combined with the lack of infrastructure in the frontiers, the project to implement Phonetic Symbols became even more complicated than before.

With the war raging, the exact language/script policy to be carried out in the frontiers was never well-defined. On the one hand, there were scholars like Fu Sinian, the head of the IHP, who unapologetically advocated sinicization (*hanhua* 漢化). In a letter to the historian Gu Jiegang 顧頡剛 (1893–1980), Fu voiced his anxieties about the future of the nation. In Siam, he noted, a strong Japanese propaganda was under way, disseminating the idea that Guizhou and Yunnan were the birthplaces of the Thai people. In Myanmar, the British were winning over the minds of *tusi* from the mainland and disseminating missionary propaganda among Chinese laborers recruited in large numbers. "All my life, I said that the Chinese nation [*zhonghua minzu*] is one," wrote Fu, "but in these circumstances, I secretly have worries; and when I came to western [China], my worries became even deeper." For him, the antidote to his worries was linguistic: "By prohibiting the Han people from invading the [lands of the] non-Han people by force, but [instead] making them accelerate sinicization, and putting an end to the use of all non-Han scripts, [we can] implement a Han ethnic consciousness [*hanzu zhi yishi*] in a short amount of time. This is the correct path."[10]

Fu Sinian's assimilationist doctrine did not resonate with everyone. Wu Zhihui and Li Jinxi, still the leading figures at the National Language Commission, were in favor of keeping the existing scripts while promoting Mandarin through Phonetic Symbols, although they were not quite sure about how to carry it out. Nevertheless, Wu Zhihui had more influence over party politics than Fu Sinian, given that he was the head of the National Language Commission. In April 1941, the Highest Commission of the Ministry of National Defense held a meeting, where Wu presented a report along with a large number of published materials in characters and Phonetic Symbols. The report was signed by eleven more people, including the minister of education and the earlier chief of CBS, Chen Lifu; another director of the CBS and the head of Academia Sinica, Zhu Jiahua; and other leading members of the Highest Commission of the Ministry of Defense and the party.[11]

The report proudly announced that the National Language Commission's work to represent all national languages and dialects with Phonetic Symbols was, once completed, going to aid the party to reach every linguistic community in China. Wu Zhihui had begun working on this project a year ago, in October 1940, when he brought together famous names to form the Commission for the Revision of Phonetic Symbols for Regional Sounds Across the Nation (Quanguo fangyin zhuyin fuhao xiuding weiyuanhui 全國方音注音符號修訂委員會). Composed of Wei Jiangong, Li Jinxi, Yuen Ren Chao, Lin Yutang, Wang Yi, Li Fanggui, Luo Changpei, Zhou Bianming, and Wang Li, the principal duty of the commission was to devise an all-inclusive alphabet for all languages and to engineer a communication network that encompassed all under one party.[12]

During the meeting of the Highest Commission in 1941, the report's signatories all believed that the publication of more materials with Phonetic Symbols would have an enormous propaganda effect. The report thus noted the need to order each propaganda office to add Phonetic Symbols to all booklets distributed to the people and soldiers, and each press to print Phonetic Symbols for all the daily newspapers and other publications. It also demanded that the periodicals that were specifically issued by the Ministry of Education must be published in high numbers so that they could reach every household; that popular publications and children's books issued by the Ministry of Education should also have Phonetic Symbols; that each education bureau in every province, city, and district should have the copper molds for Phonetic Symbols; and that these education bureaus should lend them to the print presses to expand their use.[13]

In 1942, Chen Lifu ordered each city to purchase a set of copper molds for Phonetic Symbols and noted that the Ministry of Education would provide the necessary matrices for those places that had special dialects, as listed in the National Phonetic Symbols Chart for Regional Sounds (*Quanguo fangyin zhuyin fuhao zongbiao*), which the National Language Commission was working on. All offices were ordered to publish their materials and slogans in Phonetic Symbols; and if they did not have the means to print, then they were ordered to handwrite them. Realizing the need to include the ethnic minorities within the party's network, the ministry also ordered all offices to change the phrase "Chinese characters with Phonetic Symbols" (*zhuyin hanzi* 注音漢字) to "national characters with Phonetic Symbols" (*zhuyin guozi* 注音國字), so as to downplay Han chauvinism, and ordered the National Language Commission to standardize Mandarin education in the frontiers as well.[14]

Even though the inclusion of the ethnic minorities into a propaganda regime governed by Phonetic Symbols was central to wartime party politics, progress was very slow. The National Phonetic Symbols Chart for Regional Sounds was a case in point. Devised in 1943, the chart was supposedly a revised set of Phonetic Symbols that could represent all the linguistic sounds of the nation. In theory, it was very similar to the USSR's All-Union Cyrillic Alphabet. When Stalin put a halt to latinization in the Soviet Union in 1938 and decided to cyrillize all the national alphabets, the result was an enlarged set of Cyrillic letters that included graphic derivatives of the Russian Cyrillic alphabet in order to correspond to non-Russian linguistic sounds, such as χ, ҡ, or ә. Much like the Soviet example, the GMD's enlarged set of Phonetic Symbols was supposed to become a sort of Chinese Intra-National Alphabet. In reality, however, the title of the National Phonetic Symbols Chart was highly deceptive. Even though the objective was to invent a more inclusive script for the sounds of the entire nation (*quanguo*), the chart represented very little beyond the main Han territories. The only non-Han "sounds" that the chart included came from Lhasa and Hakka (without a designation of locale). Xinjiang, Mongolian, and even Yunnanese languages were not part of the National Phonetic Symbols Chart.[15] It is surprising that the National Phonetic Symbols Chart by and large left out the non-Han territories, especially when most of the linguistic work was taking place in Yunnan, the most ethnically diverse region in China.

The reason, at least according to Li Jinxi, was the inability and/or unwillingness to translate expert knowledge to applied linguistic policy. When the list of the National Phonetic Symbols Chart was devised, the members of the Commission for the Revision of Phonetic Symbols came together with representatives from the Phonetic Literacy Commission in Chongqing to discuss the steps to be taken for the unification of language, especially in the frontiers. In this meeting, when linguists such as Wu Zhihui, Li Jinxi, Li Fanggui, and Fu Sinian discussed the future of education with government officials, Li Jinxi took the floor to talk about the accomplishments thus far.[16] Although the literacy movement was successful in the past years, claimed Li, no advance was made in the frontiers. They were receiving petitions from distant officials who reported that they had neither enough materials nor enough manpower to promote literacy.[17] The governmental support and linguistic expertise notwithstanding, the movement was extremely weak in the frontiers, especially in the ethnic-minority regions. Li Jinxi put the blame on experts (*zhuanjia* 專家), whose works focused so much on academic scholarship that they did not come up with real solutions to the language/script problems at hand.[18]

Li Jinxi was partially correct, but there were greater problems that inhibited the linguists from representing the sounds of the entire nation. While linguists were cooperating with the government in the southwest, neither the party-state nor the linguists could penetrate other parts of the country, especially Tibet, Inner Mongolia, and Xinjiang, mostly due to infrastructural and political problems. Tibet was almost out of reach, both geographically and politically, and Inner Mongolia was under Japanese influence since the 1930s.[19] Only in Xinjiang, despite the heavy Soviet influence, did the GMD still have nominal control, and in 1938, the government subsidized a project to use Phonetic Symbols for Uyghur. Zhengzhong Press, one of GMD's wartime publishing allies, published Xu Xihua's *List of Frequently Used Uyghur Words with Phonetic Symbols*. Xu's work was one of the peculiar specimens in Turkic linguistics under the GMD, and its goal was "to unify the nations, make the republic, strengthen national defense, and revive the nation."[20] He had prepared a draft of an Uyghur-Mandarin dictionary a year earlier, and in writing his book, he consulted with Yuen Ren Chao as well as Masud Sabri (1886–1952) and Isa Yusuf Alptekin (1901–1995), anti-communist Uyghur politicians who allied with the GMD, to represent the Ili and Altishahr dialects in Phonetic Symbols. Not surprisingly, Xu undertook his work with the support of Chen Lifu and Shao Lizi 邵力子 (1882–1967), then the minister of the Central Propaganda Bureau.

As the example of Uyghur Phonetic Symbols indicates, the party was keen to permeate into the society in Xinjiang, but its reach was, again, not as deep as it strived for. The educational infrastructure—schools, teachers, and printed materials—was not strong enough to expedite the transmission of party-endorsed information to the frontiers. Moreover, the Uyghur Phonetic Symbols were technically insufficient and phonetically wrong. Even though Xu claimed to have consulted Yuen Ren Chao and prominent Uyghur leaders, his Uyghur Phonetic Symbols were an exact copy of the Mandarin Phonetic Symbols, hence the incompatibility.

With the illusory success of Uyghur Phonetic Symbols, Li Jinxi designed a new plan for textbooks, which would be written in two languages (Mandarin and the local language) and three scripts (Chinese characters, Phonetic Symbols, and the local script). A prototype for Uyghur was published in 1941 in *Mongolian and Tibetan Monthly Journal*, but it remained only a prototype, and not a particularly successful one.[21] Prospects were even worse for other regions. Phonetic Symbols for Tibetan and Mongolian did not even exist, and neither was there a serious progress in the southwest. Speaking at a meeting in 1943, the ethnologist Ma Xueliang 馬學良 (1913–1999) noted the physical difficulties of working in the southwest. The geographical terrain posed hardships, and overcoming linguistic differences to communicate with local people proved to be more laborious than imagined.[22] As the war was drawing to an end, there were no Phonetic Symbols textbooks for any of the languages.[23] Writing in as late as 1947, Li Jinxi noted that textbooks were still not published for the ethnic frontiers. The Chinese-Uyghur textbook prototype, just like the Uyghur Phonetic Symbols, remained an isolated example that demonstrated the government's willingness as well as its failure to incorporate ethnic minority languages into a party-governed information circuit.[24] Since the party had minimal knowledge of ethnic minority languages, it was perhaps not surprising to have a National Phonetic Symbols Chart that covered only half of the national geography.

Even with the National Language Commission's relentless efforts to create an accurate linguistic map of China, the Ministry of Education's constant work to expand literacy in Mandarin, and the Ministry of National Defense's recognition of the value of this linguistic work for propaganda and national security, Phonetic Symbols never helped conquer the hearts and minds of the ethnic minorities. Given that even publications in Mandarin Phonetic Symbols were limited in number and circulation, the state reached neither the non-Mandarin nor the non-Han communities to the extent it had hoped for. When the GMD lost the civil war and relocated to Taiwan, taking Phonetic Symbols with it, communication engineering on the mainland was still unresolved. In 1949, the People's Republic of China inherited that complexity.

Pinyin

Zhou Youguang, the "father of Pinyin," is often regarded as an exceptional figure who revolutionized Chinese writing in 1958 with his alphabetic invention. Pinyin, some eulogies noted after Zhou's death in 2017, not only boosted literacy rates in the PRC, but also brought China and the West ever closer, as it bridged the two civilizations of the world. Today, billions of people use Pinyin on a daily basis while typing on their computers and smartphones, as Zhou's design offers an easy alphabetic interface to input Chinese characters. Pinyin does indeed look like a wonderful end to bitter decades of struggle, a final compromise for the technological incongruence between the alphabet and Chinese characters, and a story of revolutionary success.

However, when one examines the debates around script reforms in the early years of the PRC, a different story emerges. Many of the contradictions that script reformers had been confronting since the late Qing were still unresolved by the time the PRC was founded. Telegraphic communications based on four-digit numbers still posed hardships; the politics of linguistic representation were still an area of contestation; and the technological problems that would inevitably follow a potential transformation of the script—such as the overhaul of an entire print industry—were likely distressing to the reformers and revolutionaries. Viewed from such a perspective, the invention of Pinyin as an auxiliary script in 1958 was not a revolution at all; it was merely a temporary solution, one that distinctly resembled the GMD's employment of Phonetic Symbols.

The birth of Pinyin followed the growing power of Phonetic Symbols and the slow death of the Chinese Latin Alphabet. By the time the war had started, the original promises of the Chinese Latin Alphabet had already undergone a major shift in the minds of the Chinese communists. In 1940, as I quoted in chapter 6, the leading latinists Xiao San and Wu Yuzhang, who had both relocated to Yan'an, announced that "[they did] not at all propose to immediately replace Chinese characters with Sin Wenz, nor to call a halt toward continued modification of the latter." During the war, in other words, both the CCP and the GMD almost converged in their politics of language and script. The communist party members had almost entirely abandoned their former dedication to multilingualism, thus moving closer to the GMD's policies to unify language under Mandarin, and they turned the CLA into an auxiliary script to aid literacy in characters, again not unlike the GMD's use of Phonetic Symbols. The primary difference between the two parties, however, was that, for the CCP, the elimination of characters was still the ultimate revolutionary goal.

Despite the CCP's propensity to favor monolingualism over multilingualism, the CLA's original agenda was still fresh in the minds of the people when the PRC was founded in 1949. Starting early in 1950, reformers once again began publishing proposals for writing different vernacular languages in the Latin alphabet. In January 1950, a certain Li Yuanbu drafted a proposal for the Changshu vernacular language; the Zhejiang University New Language Research Committee wrote one for Zhejiang; and in February, the main publication for promoting the CLA, *Sin Wenz Weekly* (*Sin wenz zhoukan*), collated Latin alphabets concocted for seven different vernacular languages. The same month, a Sin Wenz version for Xiamen was prepared and published in May.[25] In March, a primer for workers was published for "Jiangnan" vernacular languages, the content of which is not very clear. The following month, booklets for Northern, Jiangnan, and Cantonese languages were printed by the Eastern Bookstore Press (Dongfang shudian).[26] In 1952, a primer for Shanghainese was also prepared by Ni Haishu, the chronicler of the Chinese Latinization Movement.[27] It was a moment of unexpected—but, as later years would prove, ephemeral—energy that brought back the memories of not only the 1930s but even the late-Qing multilingual reformers. By the mid-1950s, according to Ni's count, there were around 1,200 different script proposals from all around China, based on Latin and non-Latin alphabets.[28] Luo Changpei, for instance, endorsed the late-Qing polymath Lao Naixuan's project to represent each regional language in China, while noting that his own opinions about the issue were not "ripe yet."[29]

The excitement of the people did not easily map onto state policies. In February 1952, the Chinese Script Reform Research Commission (Zhongguo wenzi gaige yanjiu weiyuanhui 中國文字改革研究委員會) was officially established in Beijing under the State Council, comprised of a complicated mix of reformers. Wu Yuzhang, once a steadfast latinist, was now working with former linguists who worked under the GMD, such as Luo Changpei, Li Jinxi, and Wei Jiangong, among others. None of these ex-GMD figures had ever wanted to uproot Chinese characters in the past decades.[30] In the following years, the team of reformers even included erstwhile enemies. In December 1954, for instance, the State Council ordered Ye Laishi 葉籟士 (1911–1994) and Nie Gannu 聶紺弩 (1903–1986) to become members of the commission and work with Li Jinxi.[31] During the 1930s, Ye Laishi was a famed Esperantist and latinist whom Li Jinxi abhorred. Li had commented on the latinization movement with the following words: "Recently, also in Shanghai, people are often eating 'pudding,' bought with rubles and given to Manager Leprous [*laitou jingli* 癩頭經理]." The "pudding" bought with Russian rubles was written in latinized letters by Li as a demeaning remark about the CLA; and "Manager Leprous" was a pun on the Chinese character *lai* 籟, which referred to Ye Laishi 葉籟士 himself.³² Li Jinxi also had a hostile relationship with Nie Gannu. Nie, also a latinist in the 1930s, had written a severe critique of Li's *A Brief History of the National Language Movement* (1934). According to Li's narrative, the problem of the script was a technical one that the Phonetic Symbols and Gwoyeu Romatzyh succeeded in overcoming, as opposed to the CLA, which was a technically insufficient "political" project. Nie, in response, had pointed out Li's hypocrisy in emphasizing the technical merits of one script, while consciously and cleverly concealing its politics. Nie correctly noted that every script was political.³³ I could not agree more. But despite their former quarrels, all of these reformers were brought together by the State Council to come up with a plan for the PRC.

In the following years, the Chinese Script Reform Research Commission laid out a definitive plan for the future of the PRC's scripts and languages. Wu Yuzhang, who was appointed the head of the commission (renamed Chinese Script Reform Commission) in 1954 by the State Council, announced that Northern Mandarin (*beifanghua*) would be the unifying language of the nation, and even if local people could still use the CLA/Sin Wenz to write their own tongues, they would not be supported by the state.³⁴ Wu's announcement was indeed not surprising, as it echoed Xiao San's thoughts on the subject. When Xiao came together with Soviet Sinologists and latinists in Moscow in 1936, his ideas about the future of Chinese latinization had already become entirely different from those he had several years earlier. As Soviet latinization was falling apart, Xiao noted that the Chinese latinists had made a grave mistake by trying to use the CLA for multiple regional languages. The unifying language, as he put it, was that of the north. Less than two decades after he made that statement, his comrade Wu Yuzhang was officially announcing it as the party line. It was a significant statement, for it showed that the government was not willing to allocate resources for the teaching of regional languages—decades of work in linguistic pluralism was clearly coming to an end. In 1955, the Shanghai Script Reform Society, the center that still carried out the ideals cherished by Sin Wenz, was officially closed down, and its archives were transferred to Beijing, which became the sole center of script and language reform from then on. With the only place devoted to multilingualism shut down and no official support for regional languages, the fate of multilingual national imagination was most definitely sealed. The same year, the Chinese Script Reform

Commission also made it clear that complete alphabetization was almost indefinitely postponed. Instead, its yearly plan included the invention of Pinyin and the simplification of characters, which was curtailed by the GMD in 1936. The Chinese Script Reform Commission thus established two research labs for this purpose: the Research Lab for the Simplification of Chinese Characters (Hanzi jianhua yanjiushi), run by Cao Bohan, and the Research Lab for Pinyinization (Pinyinhua yanjiushi), run by Zhou Youguang.[35]

Zhou Youguang, the leading name in the invention of Pinyin, was formerly a banker in New York and London. In 1949, following the optimistic wave of liberation, he returned to Shanghai, and started working at Xinhua Bank and teaching at the Shanghai University of Finance and Economics. According to his memoirs, he had been interested in script reforms since the 1930s and had made acquaintances in the reform community with people like Ye Laishi and Ni Haishu. In the 1950s, he immediately got involved in the debates, and was working closely with Ni Haishu, who ran the Shanghai Script Reform Society. Initially, Zhou was also interested in representing all the languages in China, but he considered the alphabets invented for different languages to be too confusing, because the same letters had completely different phonetic values. At first, he wanted to invent a common alphabet for all, but following the change of national policy, he embarked on the project to invent Pinyin for Mandarin.[36]

In 2015, I had a very brief encounter with Zhou Youguang, who was then 109 years old. When I asked him what the purpose of Pinyin was, he told me that it was never meant to replace Chinese characters.[37] His writings in the 1950s were partially a testimony to this statement. Chinese characters, Zhou noted then, gave a conceptual unity to China. The characters for Marx (*makesi* 馬克思), for instance, were *visually* intelligible to anyone in the south, but when a northern speaker went down and *spoke* of Marx in the 1950s, people kept asking who this mysterious Ma-ke-si was, since the pronunciation of the characters 馬克思 could have great variances across linguistic regions. For the time being, Pinyin as an auxiliary script was the only solution—at least that was the new party line.[38]

It is hard to determine what went on behind closed doors in the creation of Pinyin, which turned out to be different from the CLA. When the PRC was founded in 1949, one of the big debates that took place was about the "national form" (*minzu xingshi* 民族形式) that the Chinese phonetic script was supposed to represent. Purportedly, when Mao visited Moscow and inquired into Stalin's views about Chinese phoneticization, Stalin told him that China must have a script that is nationalist in form. Partly due to Mao's demands and partly because of a greater nationalist sentiment in the age of decolonization, the Chinese Script Reform Commission received dozens of script proposals that claimed to be "national in form." Under the influence of Soviet experts, some even argued for the adoption of a Cyrillic alphabet, although it is hard to see how that could have possibly been the "national form" for a recently decolonized China. When Zhou Youguang started working in the commission in 1955, the proliferation of scripts had already resulted in the Latin alphabet being favored over other proposals. Still, the final product differed from the CLA. Some letters were assigned new phonetic values, such as the letters *x* or *j*, and new letters were added to replace the CLA's predominance, such as *q* and *ü*. Zhou Youguang and his pinyinist comrades most likely wanted to put distance between the internationalism of the 1930s and the national liberation of the 1950s.[39]

While inventing Pinyin, Zhou was directly involved in the effort to use it for telegraphic communications, not unlike the previous script reformers who were all concerned with the characters' incompatibility with Morse code. As discussed earlier, the invention of the National Phonetic Alphabet was partially a response to this issue. Later in the 1920s and 1930s, GMD engineers had tried to use the NPA and Phonetic Symbols for the telegraph, but given the lack of national linguistic unity and the technical problems caused by the four tones of Mandarin, the project had never come to fruition.[40] In the 1950s, Zhou Youguang picked up where the GMD had left off and tried to use Pinyin as the main medium of transmission.[41] Even though his project also failed in the end due to similar reasons, his involvement in telegraphic code engineering should be recognized as an important component in the invention of Pinyin. As a matter of fact, one of the main reasons that Pinyin took the shape it did was the Ministry of Postal Service and Telecommunications' resistance to an earlier draft that had letters such as ᴢ, ŋ, ş, ƶ, ɥ, and others.[42] These stand-alone letters were created at the insistence of the Institute of Linguistics at the Chinese Academy of Sciences, which demanded that each sound should be represented with one letter only—a demand that is reminiscent of the debates surrounding the UNTA. Yet, the Ministry of Postal Service and Telecommunications refused to accept them, since these letters did not lend themselves easily to Morse code, and neither were they part of the common Latin typewriters. When Pinyin was finalized in 1958, stand-alone letters were replaced by digraphs, not unlike in the CLA.

Zhou's work with machines and scripts was conducive to his thoughts about mental labor as well. Echoing late-Qing and republican efforts to optimize mental labor, Zhou preliminarily outlined a Marxist theory that fused machines, scripts, and labor into one another. During the "second industrial revolution," wrote Zhou, referring to the early phases of computerization, mental labor's (*naoli laodong*) mechanization, automation, and acceleration were reaching unprecedented levels. Electronic calculators had not only become the scientists' instrument for research, but also started to enter industrial, agricultural, and administrative institutions, as well as automatically controlled production, management, accounting, statistics, books, archives, and all related work. "If script work is at the center of the mechanization, automation, and acceleration of mental labor," noted Zhou, "it will have great meaning for the development of society's productive forces."[43]

Zhou's foray into theories of writing, technology, and mental labor are potent reminders of the political economy of information that I have underlined throughout this book as the main impetus behind script reform. The industrialist value of efficiency and productivity was strongly embedded in Pinyin as well, like all the other scripts designed prior to it. But the celebration of Pinyin concealed its own hegemonic power, for it eclipsed and rendered invisible the decades of struggle for multilingual representation. From the late Qing onwards, the place of mutually incomprehensible languages had constituted a major obstacle to the invention of a common phonetic script, and latinization's power had stemmed from its commitment to linguistic pluralism. Pinyin was in fact a betrayal to latinization, as it stood ideologically closer to the GMD's Phonetic Symbols or Yuen Ren Chao's Gwoyeu Romatzyh than the CLA. Mandarin was finally the sovereign language of the nation, enshrined in the letters of Pinyin. The rest had to obey its supremacy.

What was further absent in Zhou's narrative of Pinyin was its employment as a colonial technology in the PRC's domestic frontiers. In the late 1950s, as the invention and recognition of nationalities became one of the defining features of the PRC, "pinyinization" turned into a supranational imperial project of communication engineering. Reminiscent of the GMD's frontier script-engineering projects that had failed, the PRC scientists, most of whom were trained in the 1930s and 1940s under the auspices of the Institute of History and Philology, were dispatched to the ethnic-minority regions to pinyinize the non-Han languages. Contrary to the anti-imperial agenda of the CLA, Pinyin ironically turned out to be a weapon of imperial destruction.

Revolutionary Colonization: Pinyin in the Ethnic Frontiers

In 1958, the PRC embarked on a project to pinyinize the non-Han scripts of the ethnically diverse frontiers. On the surface, the PRC's frontier pinyinization was similar to the USSR's in the sense that it was intimately linked to the invention of ethnically defined nationalities, but the historical contexts of Soviet latinization and PRC pinyinization were very different. In the USSR of the 1920s and 1930s, latinization had started as a Turkic project, and while it did not receive the support of all Turkic intellectuals, it was clear that the Latin alphabet was not simply imposed on them from Moscow. In contrast, Pinyin was an alien technology for the nationalities inhabiting the PRC's frontiers, and it was directly imposed from Beijing. Moreover, again in contrast to the internationalism of the 1920s and 1930s, the PRC's investment in Pinyin followed the GMD's penchant for turning Mandarin into the main token of exchange among Han and non-Han communities. Teaching Mandarin to non-Han came prior to advancing the cultural technologies of the nationalities, which used to be, for better or for worse, the purpose of Soviet latinization. A comparison between the PRC and the Soviet Union makes it clear that the PRC's pinyinization was in many respects closer to the USSR's cyrillization project under Stalin, which had stepped away from alternative visions of internationalism and turned Russian into an imperial lingua franca.

Pinyinization incorporated more elements from the GMD's propaganda regime under Phonetic Symbols than the Soviet Union's latinization. The continuity from the GMD era into the PRC is detectable even at the level of experts involved in minority script reforms. Luo Changpei from the IHP, who conducted surveys on ethnic languages in the 1940s, acted as the director of the Institute of Linguistics at the Chinese Academy of Sciences and oversaw the minority script reforms until his death in 1958.[44] Another linguist, Fu Maoji 傅懋勣 (1911–1988), who was trained by the IHP's Li Fanggui in the southwest, was the chair of the Department of Minority Languages of the Institute of Linguistics and led minority script reforms after Luo's death.[45] Right after the invention of Pinyin in 1958, frontier pinyinization followed the logic of empire, as efficiency in the instruments of literacy turned out to be the weapon of precision in imperial domination. The implementation of Pinyin and Mandarin in the ethnic frontiers was not unlike Churchill's intention to use Basic English to build "an empire of the mind."[46]

It had not started as such, however. From 1949 to 1957, script and language reform in the ethnic-minority regions enjoyed a degree of freedom, where the minorities were encouraged to determine the future of their own writing systems and cultural technologies. This was a deliberate plan. As Benno Weiner demonstrated in his study of the Tibetan communities in Amdo in the 1950s, the CCP's goal in the region was not simply to build a state through brute domination, but to build a nation through persuasion. The party's goal in Amdo was to encourage active participation from the Tibetans in building a larger political community and to convince them that they indeed belonged to it.[47] Weiner's observation, I believe, was generally true for other regions as well. In the ethnically diverse frontiers, the CCP followed affirmative-action policies reminiscent of the early years of the USSR and chose to implement measures that would not alienate the ethnic minorities. During the First National Conference on Minority Education in 1951, the Ministry of Education of the State Council carefully outlined the non-assimilationist script and language reform policies, noting that "in minority communities with regularly used writing systems, such as Mongol, Korean, Tibetan, Uyghur, Kazakh, etc., native languages must be used as the medium of instruction."[48]

In regions where the Chinese Academy of Sciences (CAS) did not possess much linguistic expertise, such as Xinjiang and Inner Mongolia, national self-determination and the place of scripts in it were even more pronounced, sometimes with aid from the Soviet Union. As part of the Sino-Soviet Treaty of Friendship, signed in 1950, Soviet experts were assisting socialist state building in China in a variety of enterprises, including script reforms. With an added layer of optimism after Khrushchev's secret attack on Stalinism in 1956, the CAS invited experts from the Soviet Union to devise scripts for Turkic nationalities.[49]

In 1956, Edkhiam R. Tenishev (1921–2000) was dispatched to China by the USSR Academy of Sciences. Born in Penza to a Tatar family, Tenishev spent his childhood in Kyrgyzstan and studied at the Oriental Institute of Leningrad State University before writing his dissertation on the *Golden Light Sutra* composed in Old Uyghur. After receiving the invitation from the Chinese Academy of Sciences, he took a quick trip to Leningrad to visit his mentor Sergei E. Malov (1880–1957), the Russian Turcologist who had taken two separate trips to Xinjiang earlier. Soon afterward, Tenishev flew to Beijing, whence his journey into Xinjiang began. Tenishev arrived in Xinjiang in August 1956, and there he met with Chinese Turcologists and Uyghur intellectuals and politicians, such as Burhan Shahidi and Seypidin Azizi. He immediately started devising Cyrillic alphabets for the Uyghurs, Kazakhs, and Kyrgyz living in the region. During a conference on August 22, the Cyrillic proposals for these three languages were accepted unanimously, to Tenishev's surprise.[50] The new Cyrillic script for the Uyghurs was composed of thirty-three letters, for the Kazakhs of forty-two letters, and for the Kyrgyz of thirty-six letters.

A similar development took place in Inner Mongolia, also with involvement from the Soviet experts Georgii P. Serdiuchenko (1904–1965) and his wife, Buliash K. Todaeva (1915–2014).[51] In an effort to allow an informational unity between the Mongolian People's Republic and Inner Mongolia, cyrillization of Mongolian was a highly debated issue in Inner Mongolia. In 1955, linguists in Mongolia started comparing the advantages and disadvantages of cyrillization and a reformed writing system in the Mongolian script. In May 1956, representatives from various Mongolic nationalities—Mongolians, Daur, Dongxiang, Tu, and Bao'an—convened for a conference on script reforms, but there were disparate voices. Some proposed the adoption of the New Mongolian Script (*xin mengwen* 新蒙文), promulgated earlier that year as their main method of inscription, rather than Cyrillic or Latin alphabets. During the conference, some further claimed that a separate script, either Cyrillic or New Mongolian, should be devised for Daur, Dongxiang, Tu, and Bao'an nationalities.[52] But the conference ended with the acceptance of a Cyrillic writing system for Mongolian, which became the official script, until the predominance of Pinyin in 1958 challenged the newly established order.[53]

Tenishev's involvement in the cyrillization of Turkic languages and the Mongolic nationalities' debates around the New Mongolian Script and the Cyrillic alphabet reflected the political atmosphere in 1955–1956. Script and language reforms followed diverse paths that depended on regional politics and geopolitics. For Uyghurs, Kazakhs, and Kyrgyz in Xinjiang, sharing the same script with their ethnic kin who lived in the USSR was a justified request, hence the unanimity of votes. In Inner Mongolia as well, the adoption of either a Cyrillic alphabet or the New Mongolian Script mirrored the communication politics that the reformers sought to establish between the Mongolian People's Republic and Inner Mongolia. The acceptance of both requests by the State Council displayed the new government's willingness to give voice to the nationalities themselves.

The creation of native lexicons followed a similar path during this early period. Until 1958, Han linguists and scientists working in the borderlands were self-conscious about their status in the ethnic frontiers. As part of the nationalization policy, invention of national vocabularies was a particularly thorny issue, especially since the linguists were cautious about the import of Mandarin loanwords, which they believed projected Han chauvinism—a taboo subject that even Mao had cautioned against.[54] Abandoning the use of Mandarin loanwords seemed the natural way to break out of Han chauvinism while linguistically defining and inventing the borders of native languages. Strange as it may seem, however, de-sinification of national vocabularies was not always welcomed by native scholars. In Inner Mongolia, a debate about the term "cadre" (Ch. *ganbu*) helps to explain this point. Since 1949, *ganbu* had become commonplace for Mongolian speakers when referring to cadres. Chinese linguists who were not fluent in Mongolian and thus did not know much about Mongolians' daily use of language, however, argued that the term *ganbu* was in Mandarin, and should thus be changed into a Mongolian word that translated as "mature strength" (*chengshu liliang*) in order to avoid Han chauvinism. Observing that the new word did not make sense to anyone, they at last decided to borrow from Russian, and started using *kadr*, assuming that *kadr* would be more welcomed by the Mongolians than *ganbu*. Despite their rather benign intentions, however, many Mongolians were not fond of this change. A prominent Inner Mongolian linguist, Chinggeltei (1924–2013), who wrote the first modern Mongolian grammar book in China, argued against it. *Ganbu*, he claimed, was already used by Mongolians in daily life; what was the point of changing it? Speaking at the Scientific Conference on Minority Nationalities' Languages and Scripts in 1958, he noted that, to Mongolian ears, *kadr* sounded like a domestic-animal disease, which was arguably worse than saying *ganbu*.[55]

Unexpectedly problematic as they could be, the intentions of the Han linguists during this early period were more inclusive and progressive than what ensued in the next few years. In late 1957, as relations with the Soviet Union were deteriorating and ethnic tensions were increasing in the frontier provinces, Premier Zhou Enlai informally asked the Chinese Script Reform Commission to draft a plan for directly overseeing minority script reforms, which was a clear break from allowing the minorities to determine their own futures. The Chinese Script Reform Commission convened in October to pinyinize the Chinese-derived writing system of the Zhuang, the largest ethnic minority group living in the southwest. The report that the commission subsequently drafted suggested the adoption of Pinyin for all the minority scripts in China. In December, the principles of all-nation pinyinization were approved by the State Council, and immediately afterward, the Scientific Conference on Minority Nationalities' Languages and Scripts was convened from March 28 to April 16, 1958. Coinciding with the Great Leap Forward, the State Council sought a leap in the linguistic and informational unification of all nationalities.[56]

In Zhou Youguang's words, pinyinization of all scripts would be "beneficial for all nationalities in studying each other's languages and scripts, exchanging new terminologies, and jointly making use of technological apparatuses, such as print, typewriters, and telegraphy, to progress toward cultural unity."[57] In reality, however, frontier pinyinization after 1958 closely resembled the GMD's propaganda warfare and the USSR's union-wide cyrillization. During the Scientific Conference on Minority Nationalities' Languages and Scripts, Fu Maoji, who had just returned from a trip to the Soviet Union, took the stage to expound on the experiences of the USSR and endorsed the developments that were central to linguistic planning after the demise of latinization. The cyrillization of all scripts and the predominance of Russian language were the new model for the PRC, as the goal was to make Mandarin the lingua franca for all nationalities and engineer national lexicons accordingly.[58]

During the conference, Han and non-Han linguists and reformers coming from different minority regions had disparate visions for the road ahead. Pinyinization of Daur, for instance, was a major subject of debate. According to the resolutions of the Conference on Mongolic Languages in 1956, Daurs were supposed to have either a Cyrillic or a New Mongolian script, but with the new pinyinization wave, both proposals were shelved, and even its pinyinization raised issues that had not been discussed earlier.

Some linguists claimed that the Daurs themselves were demanding a script, hence the need to invent one. Others, however, claimed that 80 percent of more than ten thousand Daurs coming from Qiqihaer could already speak Mandarin. What was the purpose of pinyinizing Daur script, when the majority of the people could speak Mandarin?[59] Similar claims were made for other nationalities as well. Among the Qiang nationality in the southwest, one linguist claimed that 70-80 percent of the population could already speak Mandarin, so there was no need to pinyinize the Qiang language. Among the Tu nationality in Hunan, some pointed out that more than 51 percent could speak Mandarin, hence the futility of pinyinizing it. Others further claimed that most of the Wen people in Hainan (*wenzu* 芝族, who were not even recognized as a nationality in the end) did not even speak their own language (!). A certain part of the Miao people, known to speak "sour-soup language" (*suantanghua* 酸湯話), were also denied a script, since it sounded similar to the Mandarin spoken in Hunan.[60] These claims about the number of Mandarin speakers among ethnic minority populations obviously relied more on hearsay and arbitrary observation than actual statistical work. But even so, it highlighted one of the main purposes behind pinyiniziation, i.e., spreading Mandarin among minority nationalities, as opposed to helping them develop their own cultural technologies.

In 1959, the draft of a Pinyin dictionary was printed by the Institute of Linguistics for Minority Nationalities, supposedly as a model for imposing Mandarin terminologies to all nationalities, but the success of the project was dubious.[61] The Zhuang writing system was immediately pinyinized in 1958. In some cases, as in the Gelao languages in the southwest, certain terms were inserted with slight phonological differences.[62] But in places where the central government had less control over the population and faced more resistance, terminologies did not give way to Mandarin renderings, and Pinyin never became the main script in use. For example, Yu Xixian, a Han scholar conducting linguistic and literary work in Tibet, claimed that pinyinized Mandarin was certainly the correct approach for inventing new Tibetan terminologies, but Tibetan was never pinyinized.[63] Similarly, pinyinization was never carried out for some minority writing systems, like Sibe and Korean. For others, such as Yi and Dai nationalities, pinyinization officially started in 1958, but failed in the end, as the nationalities in question continued to use their own scripts.[64] Linguists also attempted to pinyinize Mongolian from

1958 to 1966, and the number of Mandarin loanwords in Mongolian gradually increased in tandem with propaganda work.[65] But even though the debates about Mongolian pinyinization continued until the end of the Cultural Revolution, Pinyin was never implemented for Mongolian.[66] The prospects of pinyinization in Xinjiang were similarly uncertain. The project started in 1958, but Pinyin alphabets for Kazakh and Uyghur were not developed until 1964, and the extent of their popularization remains unclear.[67]

Pinyinists after 1958 made constant references to printing, typewriters, and cultural advancement to justify the efficiency and progress they sought, but, as opposed to the latinists in the Soviet Union who ventured into engineering new machinery for nationalities, such as Morse codes and typewriters, the available evidence suggests that the PRC never built typewriter factories for advancing bureaucratic and literary efficiency in the pinyinized frontiers, nor did they engineer codes for telegraphic communications among nationalities. As a matter of fact, neither the Uyghurs nor the Mongols were given the right to use the telegraph in their own scripts until the 1980s. The information infrastructure in China was exclusively in Chinese, dominated by the Han.[68] The PRC engineers and linguists were invested in frontier pinyinization as an instrument of governance, information management, and linguistic assimilation.

The imperial hubris of the PRC linguists was curtailed by the same political, technological, and infrastructural limitations that their GMD predecessors had encountered earlier. From 1958 onward, despite the central government's assimilationist will, frontier pinyinization followed an uneven path, and complete pinyinization of all nationality scripts never crystallized. What frontier pinyinization instead signified was a bifurcated revolution. The meaning and the unfolding of script revolutions in the Han and non-Han regions were utterly different, for the PRC had to come to terms with its own quasi-colonial present while drawing legitimacy from an anticolonial discourse and upholding the revolutionary promises of liberation and progress. The outcome was what one may call "revolutionary colonization"—a paradox that was constitutive of the PRC's effort to build a socialist civilization that encompassed all nationalities, Han and non-Han. Pinyin—the simultaneously suspended and implemented technology of socialist modernization—encoded that paradox.

* * *

The future of pinyinization was already unclear by the time the Cultural Revolution started in 1966, but during the political turmoil that ensued, pinyinization also lost its brain power and institutional support as the leading pinyinists were either sent to labor camps or put in jail. With the sudden change in the political atmosphere that turned everything upside down, Pinyin was regarded as an instrument of foreign imperialism, and pinyinists as imperialist running dogs. Ni Haishu, the chronicler of latinization whose alleged last words were "Long live script reform [*wengai wansui* 文改萬歲]," was beaten up severely by the rebel faction before being sent to a labor camp.[69] Zhou Youguang and Ye Laishi also suffered a similar fate, spending two to three years in Pingluo, Ningxia, where the State Council's May 7 cadre school, i.e. reeducation camp, was located.[70] Even Xiao San, certainly the most prominent figure in the history of Chinese latinization, was jailed for seven years (1967–1974).[71]

But while it was vilified as a tool of imperialism in Beijing, frontier pinyinization was still an ongoing project throughout the Cultural Revolution. Rejection of foreign imperialism, it seemed, did not preclude the implementation of a domestic one, even if it was carried out on an ad hoc basis and encountered resistance in many of the ethnic-minority regions. This split revolutionary consciousness may indeed be conceptualized as an extension of Han-centrism coupled with the aftermath of wartime geopolitics when ethnic minorities first entered the political consciousness of Han scientists and statesmen as indispensable components of national security and state building. Pinyin, like its predecessor Phonetic Symbols, never conquered the minds of the non-Han, but the bifurcation of communication engineering into Han and non-Han reflected deeper ethnic, racial, and political problems that continued to haunt national unity in the PRC in the decades ahead.

By the early 1970s, the ideology of Pinyin as the anticipated telos of a robust knowledge economy was under serious doubt. The pinyinization of Chinese characters was already suspended in 1958, and pinyinization in the frontiers turned out to be a massive failure. But even so, it took another decade for pinyinization to be officially canceled as a governmental project. It was only in 1986 that the State Council of the PRC announced that Pinyin was never going to replace Chinese characters. This colossal shift not only put an end to a century of script reforms but also heralded the dawn of a new age in the PRC's information politics.

Epilogue

A New Age of Codes

IN JANUARY 1986, THE National Conference on Language Work was convened in Beijing under the auspices of the Central Committee of CCP and the State Council, with over 280 attendees. It was a milestone in the history of script reforms. After almost a century of debates, the participants of the national conference decided that pinyinization was not going to be a separate project, and that Pinyin was going to be used only as an auxiliary method to teach and write in Chinese characters. On the surface, the decision seemed to be a natural outcome of the discussions surrounding the annihilation of Chinese characters since the 1950s. After all, when Pinyin was ratified as an auxiliary script in 1958 and Zhou Enlai "suspended" complete pinyinization, the script's chances of becoming a stand-alone alphabet were already slim. During the Cultural Revolution, pinyinists were disparaged, ridiculed, and penalized as pawns of Western imperialism; and after the Cultural Revolution, even though Pinyin enjoyed a revival, it did not possess the institutional power to replace the Chinese characters. As a matter of fact, the main debate about script reform in the aftermath of the Cultural Revolution was taking place around the issue of character simplification, not pinyinization.[1]

This narrative, however, raises more questions than it answers. If the replacement of Chinese characters with Pinyin was already a failed project—and it certainly was—why did the verdict come as late as 1986? Was there simply a bureaucratic delay in putting an end to pinyinization due to post–Cultural Revolution political turmoil? Or were there forces at play that are

EPILOGUE

not immediately visible to an outside observer? Since the documents related to the conference are still not accessible, the aura of secrecy around the end of pinyinization invites speculation.

Throughout this book, I have explored Chinese scripts as critical technologies in the making of an information age. Script reform started at the turn of the twentieth century as a response to the political economy of information that transformed clerical and mental labor practices, and from that moment on, scripts possessed distinct technological and ideological powers to shape the Chinese society. The limitations and possibilities of such power were infrastructurally, economically, and politically shaped by the historical conditions of an era that spanned almost a century, from the late nineteenth to the late twentieth century. The end of that era, marked by the decision to cancel script reforms, should be understood as the beginning of a new information age that obviated previous desires and installed new ones.

To bookend the history of Chinese script reforms, I would like to once again focus on the ideological dimensions of information technologies. The end of pinyinization in the PRC in 1986 was a pivotal historical event that took place within a new economic and infrastructural environment shaped by growing computerization, which began to change the social and political patterns of information processing in the PRC. The impact that computerization had on the PRC in the 1980s was as critical as the impact that the telegraph had on the Qing in the 1890s. In fact, popular culture surrounding the use of mental power and brain energy in the 1980s was strikingly similar to that of the late Qing. The final years of the Qing, as I explored in chapter 1, saw an emergent discourse of the brain, which indexed the problem of mental labor in a rapidly modernizing knowledge economy. Almost a century later, the 1980s also saw a proliferation of brain-centered discourses that permeated the society at large. Sci-fi stories interrogated the meaning of labor in a postrevolutionary society through robots; avant-garde movies, like Huang Jianxin's *Dislocation* (*Cuowei* 错位), commented on bureaucracy, technology, and post-socialist subjectivity through cyborgs; and Qigong practitioners started wearing cooking pots, known as "information pots," to facilitate communication between their bodies and outer space.[2] While standing a hundred years apart, these similarities between late-Qing and post-socialist China demonstrate two separate periods of global capitalism in which information and cognition were valorized in distinct ways. The former was the product of a global information age that emerged out of an industrializing knowledge economy, and the latter was the product of an emergent (post)industrial one governed by computers.

Like the history of scripts, the history of computerization in the PRC was also part of a global history of computers. It began in Moscow, Harbin, and Beijing in the 1950s, when Soviet and Chinese engineers launched the first efforts to bring automation to Chinese language and writing. The same years witnessed the introduction of cybernetics to the PRC with the return of Qian Xuesen 錢學森 (1911–2009) from the United States—the first Chinese cybernetician, chief engineer of rocket sciences, and the leader of the space program. As Japan, Korea, and Taiwan also took part in the Cold War "code race" in the 1960s and 1970s, the PRC started to develop more advanced information-processing technologies.[3] And as the PRC emerged out of the turbulent years of the Cultural Revolution, information-processing technologies promised new means of organizing knowledge in a post-socialist economy. The following decade saw an anarchy of codes, as dozens of engineers started developing new input and retrieval technologies for Chinese characters. By 1989, according to one count, there were more than five hundred input methods for Chinese.[4] The sudden increase in the number of input-output technologies for computers mirrored the emergence of new indexing technologies in the 1920s and 1930s—they marked two critical eras in the global history of Chinese information processing.

Computerization of Chinese characters brought a concomitant endeavor to computerize non-Han scripts as well, in contrast to the earlier pinyinization efforts. As already discussed, information and linguistic management of the ethnic frontiers was an integral part of script reforms since the Second World War. Especially during the Great Leap Forward and the Cultural Revolution, Pinyin led a double life—it was abandoned by the Han but imposed on the non-Han as a form of revolutionary colonization. But by the 1970s, frontier pinyinization itself had turned into a fiasco, not unlike what happened in the 1930s in the Soviet Union. Using new methods to technologize non-Han languages started just around then. In 1973, the acclaimed Tibetologist Yu Daoquan 于道泉, who was one of the proponents of machine translation in the 1950s, began working on a numerical method to process Tibetan syllabaries, which he completed in 1977, and it became the basis on which Tibetan information processing was managed from the 1980s onward.[5] Mongolian script underwent a similar transformation during the same years, and by 1986, developments in Mongolian information-processing systems

EPILOGUE

had grown to include input methods for typing in Mongolian.[6] During the same decade, Uyghur computer scientists developed information-processing technologies for the Uyghur Arabic script.[7] Other minority scripts followed suit in the ensuing years.[8] By the 1980s, with an already suspended Han pinyinization, the debacle of frontier pinyinization, and amid an ongoing multilingual computerization, the technopolitical grounds under full pinyinization were already evaporating.

The PRC's transition into the computer age was not merely the product of new technologies. After all, technologies, as this book has demonstrated in detail, are political artifacts. Just as important as the technologies of computing was the transition of the CCP from a revolutionary party to a technocratic one soon after the death of Mao in 1976. From the late 1970s onward, computers and cybernetics turned into new political technologies to redesign the Chinese society and economy—ones distinctly unlike the Maoist technologies of governance. The one-child policy, for instance, was the brainchild of Chinese cyberneticians whose foray into demographic planning was an immediate outcome of their studies in rocket science, as Susan Greenhalgh has shown.[9] Computerized information processing was thus taking place within a new technocratic regime that abandoned earlier revolutionary promises. Pinyinization, with all its internal contradictions, was one of those promises that was no longer meaningful in a postrevolutionary order.

The year 1986 was indeed a critical turning point. As the National Conference on Language Work was issuing the final decree for the end of pinyinization, Deng Xiaoping was busy initiating the second phase of computerization. In March 1986, only two months after the conference, Deng announced the "863 Plan," which instituted a countrywide project to develop new computing technologies both for the Han and the non-Han.[10] The overlap between the two announcements was not a coincidence. It instead signaled the end of an imperial era and the beginning of a new one in which a socialist multinational polity was turning into a computerized network of nationalities under a new economic and governmental order.

Deng's technocratic reforms promised a society free of revolutionary ills, but what it instead brought were new contradictions that are at least as difficult to resolve as the earlier ones. Reminiscent of a century of script engineering that triggered excitement, amusement, despair, and frustration worldwide, the computer regime induces conflicting emotions. Hopes for a better society are entangled with anxieties about the future of corporate capitalism, artificial intelligence, disinformation, state surveillance, and the fate of millions in the PRC's multiethnic frontiers. Just like the scripts of the past, the codes of today continue to generate new contradictions for China and the world. And if a hundred years of script reforms in China are any indication, those contradictions are here to stay.

Notes

Introduction

1. Shen originally wrote the text in English under the title *Universal Script*, but a copy of it has not survived. He translated his work into Chinese with the title *Primordial Sounds for a Prosperous Age* (*Shengshi yuanyin* 盛世元音). Shen Xue, *Shengshi yuanyin* (Beijing: Wenzi gaige chubanshe, 1956 [1896]).
2. Elisabeth Kaske, *The Politics of Language in Chinese Education* (Leiden: Brill, 2008); Gina Tam, *Dialect and Nationalism in China, 1860-1960* (Cambridge: Cambridge University Press, 2020).
3. Yurou Zhong, *Chinese Grammatology: Script Revolution and Literary Modernity, 1916-1958* (New York: Columbia University Press, 2019). For a similar focus on phonocentrism in the Turkish context, see, Nergis Ertürk, *Grammatology and Literary Modernity in Turkey* (New York: Columbia University Press, 2011).
4. Scott Pacey, "Tan Sitong's 'Great Unity': Mental Processes and Yogācāra in *An Exposition of Benevolence*," in *Transforming Consciousness: Yogacara Thought in Modern China*, ed. John Makeham (Oxford: Oxford University Press, 2014), 103–122.
5. Tan Sitong, "Huang Yingchu 'Chuanyin kuaizi jianfa' xu," in *Tan Sitong Quanji*, ed. Cai Shangsi and Fang Xing (Beijing: Zhonghua shuju, 1981), 254–255.
6. Tan Sitong, "Renxue," in *Tan Sitong Quanji*, 329.
7. Lufei Kui, "Putong jiaoyu dang caiyong sutizi," *Jiaoyu zazhi* 1, no. 1 (1909): 1.
8. Qian Xuantong et al., "Guoyu tongyi choubei hui di si ci da hui, liang ge zhongyao de yi'an: Feichu hanzi caiyong xin pinyin wenzi an, jiansheng xianxing hanzi de bihua an," *Guoyu yuekan*, no. 1 (1922): 159.
9. Alfred D. Chandler Jr., "The Information Age in Historical Perspective: Introduction," in *A Nation Transformed by Information: How Information Has Shaped the United States from Colonial Times to the Present*, ed. Alfred D. Chandler Jr. and James W. Cortada (Oxford: Oxford University Press, 2000), 4.

INTRODUCTION

10. Benedict Anderson, *Imagined Communities: Reflections on the Origin and Spread of Nationalism* (New York: Verso, 1984).
11. Kenneth Cmiel and John Durham Peters, *Promiscuous Knowledge: Information, Image, and Other Truth Games in History* (Chicago: University of Chicago Press, 2020), 57.
12. James Beniger, *Control Revolution: Technological and Economic Origins of the Information Society* (Cambridge, Mass.: Harvard University Press, 1986).
13. John Durham Peters, "The Control of Information," *Critical Review* (Fall 1987): 5–23.
14. Wendy Hui Kyong Chun, *Control and Freedom: Power and Paranoia in the Age of Fiber Optics* (Cambridge, Mass.: MIT Press, 2008).
15. Christopher A. Reed, *Gutenberg in Shanghai: Chinese Print Capitalism, 1876–1937* (Vancouver: University of British Columbia Press, 2004); Robert Culp, *The Power of Print in Modern China: Intellectuals and Industrial Publishing from the End of Empire to Maoist State Socialism* (New York: Columbia University Press, 2019).
16. Erik Baark, *Lightning Wires: The Telegraph and China's Technological Modernization, 1860–1890* (Westport, Conn.: Greenwood Press, 1997); Zhou Yongming, *Zhongguo wangluo zhengzhide lishi kaocha: Dianbao yu qingmo shizheng* (Beijing: Shangwu yinshuguan, 2013).
17. Chu Chia-hua (Zhu Jiahua), *China's Postal and Other Communications Services* (London: Kegan Paul, Trench, Trubner, 1937), 166.
18. Gilles Deleuze and Felix Guattari, *Anti-Oedipus: Capitalism and Schizophrenia*, trans. Robert Hurley, Mark Seem, and Helen R. Lane (Minneapolis: University of Minnesota Press, 1983).
19. Jerrold S. Cooper, "Babylonian Beginnings: The Origin of the Cuneiform Writing System in Comparative Perspective," in *The First Writing: Script Invention as History and Process*, ed. Stephen D. Houston (Cambridge: Cambridge University Press, 2004), 71–99.
20. Zev Handel, *Sinograph: The Borrowing and Adaptation of the Chinese Script* (Leiden: Brill, 2019).
21. Ruth Rogaski, *Hygienic Modernity: Meanings of Health and Disease in Treaty-Port China* (Berkeley: University of California Press, 2004).
22. For a discussion of "historical presuppositions" and formal subsumption of labor, see Harry Harootunian, *Marx After Marx: History and Time in the Expansion of Capitalism* (New York: Columbia University Press, 2015); Raymond Williams, *Marxism and Literature* (Oxford: Oxford University Press, 1977), 121–127.
23. Andrew Liu, *Tea War: A History of Capitalism in China and India* (New Haven, Conn.: Yale University Press, 2020).
24. Sean Hsiang-lin Lei, *Neither Donkey nor Horse: Medicine in the Struggle Over China's Modernity* (Chicago: University of Chicago Press, 2014).
25. Langdon Winner, "Do Artifacts Have Politics?," *Daedalus* 109, no. 1 (1980): 121–136.
26. David Damrosch, "Scriptworlds: Writing Systems and the Formation of World Literature," *Modern Language Quarterly* 68, no. 2 (June 2007): 200.
27. Lydia Liu, "Scripts in Motion: Writing as Imperial Technology, Past and Present," *PMLA* 130, no. 2 (2015): 379 (emphasis mine).
28. John D. Peters, *Marvelous Clouds: Toward a Philosophy of Elemental Media* (Chicago: University of Chicago Press, 2015), 25.

29. Brian Larkin, "The Politics and Poetics of Infrastructure," *Annual Review of Anthropology* 42, no. 1 (2013): 327–343.
30. Donna Haraway, "Manifesto for Cyborgs: Science, Technology, and Socialist Feminism in the 1980s," *Socialist Review* 80 (1985): 65–108; Gregory Bateson, *Steps to an Ecology of Mind: A Revolutionary Approach to Man's Understanding of Himself* (San Francisco: Chandler, 1972).
31. Katherine Hayles, *How We Became Posthuman: Virtual Bodies in Cybernetics, Literature, and Informatics* (Chicago: University of Chicago Press, 1999).
32. Jennifer Light, "When Computers Were Women," *Technology and Culture* 40, no. 3 (1999): 455–483; Ruha Benjamin, *Race After Technology: Abolitionist Tools for the New Jim Code* (Medford, Mass.: Polity, 2019); Safiya Umoja Noble, *Algorithms of Oppression: How Search Engines Reinforce Racism* (New York: New York University Press, 2018).
33. Ann Blair, *Too Much to Know: Managing Scholarly Information Before the Modern Age* (New Haven, Conn.: Yale University Press, 2010); Ann Blair et al., eds., *Information: A Historical Companion* (Princeton, N.J.: Princeton University Press, 2021).
34. Jack Chen et al., eds., *Literary Information in China: A History* (New York: Columbia University Press, 2021).
35. Thomas Mullaney, *The Chinese Typewriter: A History* (Cambridge, Mass.: MIT Press, 2017).
36. Arif Dirlik, "Reversals, Ironies, Hegemonies: Notes on the Contemporary Historiography of Modern China," in *History After the Three Worlds: Post-Eurocentric Historiographies*, ed. Arif Dirlik, Vinay Bahl, and Peter Gran (Lanham, Md.: Rowman and Littlefield, 2000), 150–151.
37. Robeson Taj Frazier, *The East Is Black: Cold War China in Black Radical Imagination* (Durham, N.C.: Duke University Press, 2015); Alexander C. Cook, ed., *Mao's Little Red Book: A Global History* (Cambridge: Cambridge University Press, 2013).
38. Walter Benjamin, *Illuminations*, trans. Harry Zohn (New York: Harcourt, Brace, and World, 1968), 255–266.

1. Alphabetic Labor Time: Scripts, Wires, and Brains in the Late Qing

1. There were also overseas Chinese works on phoneticization that preceded Lu Zhuangzhang. See Jing Tsu, "Chinese Scripts, Codes, and Typewriting Machines," in *Science and Technology in Modern China*, ed. Jing Tsu and Benjamin Elman (Leiden: Brill, 2014), 125–131.
2. Xing Dao, "Duyin tongyi hui gongding guoyin zimu zhi gaishuo," *Dongfang zazhi* 10, no. 8 (1914): 11.
3. *Yellow Emperor's Inner Canon* was a collection of different works that were compiled around the first century BCE. The two books that are claimed to be extant parts of the *Inner Canon* did not exist before the eighth century. Nathan Sivin, *Traditional Medicine in Contemporary China: A Partial Translation of Revised Outline of*

1. ALPHABETIC LABOR TIME

Chinese Medicine (1972) (Ann Arbor: Center for Chinese Studies, University of Michigan, 1987), 5.
4. There were exceptions to this dominant paradigm. Jesuits translated Western anatomical knowledge in the seventeenth century, but the circulation of these translations was not wide. Hugh Shapiro, "Chinese and Western Medicine," in *Medicine Across Cultures: History and Practice of Medicine in Non-Western Cultures*, ed. Helaine Selin and Hugh Shapiro (Dordrecht: Kluwer Academic Publishers, 2003), 363; Daniel Asen, "'Manchu Anatomy': Anatomical Knowledge and the Jesuits in Seventeenth- and Eighteenth-Century China," *Social History of Medicine* 22, no. 1 (2009): 23–44.
5. Thomas Mullaney, "Semiotic Sovereignty: 1871 Chinese Telegraph Code in Historical Perspective," in *Science and Technology in Modern China*, ed. Jing Tsu and Benjamin Elman (Leiden: Brill, 2014), 164–165.
6. Ya Weitang, Zheng Wang, and Ju Zhengxiu, eds., *Zhongguo suji bainian shi* (Beijing: Xueyuan chubanshe, 2000), 17–23; Cai Xiyong, *Chuanyin kuaizi* (Hubei: Guanshu ju, 1905), 1.
7. Meng Yue, "Hybrid Science Versus Modernity: The Practice of the Jiangnan Arsenal, 1864–1897," *EASTM* 16 (1999): 13–52; Benjamin Elman, *On Their Own Terms: Science in China, 1550–1900* (Cambridge, Mass.: Harvard University Press, 2005), 355–395.
8. William Ayers, *Chang Chih-tung and Educational Reform in China* (Cambridge, Mass.: Harvard University Press, 1971), 100–136.
9. Cai Xiyong's book did not have the impact that his shorthand had. Ya, Zheng, and Ju, *Zhongguo suji bainian shi*, 19. For a history of accounting in China, see Robert Gardella, "Squaring Accounts: Commercial Bookkeeping Methods and Capitalist Rationalism in Late Qing and Republican China," *Journal of Asian Studies* 51, no. 2 (1992): 317–339.
10. Zhang Yonggang and Fan Xiaodong, "Cai Xiyong—Zhang Zhidong mufu qianqi shiye zongguan," *Hebei daxue xuebao* 31, no. 6 (2006): 115.
11. In the introduction to his *Chuanyin kuaizi*, Cai mentions that he inquired into the workings of government affairs and court disputes in the United States.
12. Cai, *Chuanyin kuaizi*, 2.
13. David Philip Lindsley, *The Compendium of Tachygraphy: Or Lindsley's Phonetic Shorthand* (Boston: Otis Clapp, 1864), 3. The edition that Cai used was published in 1882. See David P. Lindsley, *The Hand Book of Takigrafy* (New York: D. P. Lindsley, 1882), mentioned in Cai Xiyong and Cai Zhang, *Zhongguo suji xue* ([Beijing]: Suji chuanxi suo, 1913), no page number.
14. Lindsley, *The Compendium*, 10. In the 1882 edition, the number of consonants was twenty-eight. See Lindsley, *The Hand Book of Takigrafy*, 15.
15. Cai and Cai, *Zhongguo suji xue*. Kumasaki published *Shinago sokki jutsu* in 1908, and he was invited to Beijing in 1909 to teach shorthand, but he resigned shortly after. Ya, Zheng, and Ju, *Zhongguo suji bainian shi*, 29.
16. First Historical Archives, archive no. 03-7574-026, 3rd year, 5th month, 20th day of Xuantong Emperor (1911).
17. Cai and Cai, *Zhongguo suji xue*. Cai Zhang also received a medal of fourth degree from Yuan Shikai for his contribution.

1. ALPHABETIC LABOR TIME

18. Cai, *Chuanyin kuaizi*, 1.
19. Li Jiesan, *Minqiang kuaizi* (Beijing: Wenzi gaige chubanshe, 1956 [1896]).
20. Cai and Cai, *Zhongguo suji xue*.
21. Mullaney, "Semiotic Sovereignty," 153–183.
22. David Wright, *Translating Science: The Transmission of Western Chemistry Into Late Imperial China, 1840–1900* (Leiden: Brill, 2000), 86–87.
23. Daniel Jerome Macgowan, *Bowu tongshu* (Ningbo, 1851), 1. In this early stage, missionaries consciously appropriated Western medical terminology into Chinese in order to conform with local practices and facilitate the diffusion of Western scientific knowledge. See Bridie Andrews, "Tuberculosis and the Assimilation of Germ Theory in China, 1895–1937," *Journal of the History of Medicine* 52 (1997): 123.
24. Macgowan, *Bowu tongshu*, no page number.
25. See chapter 2.
26. Macgowan, *Bowu tongshu*.
27. Russel W. Burns, *Communications: An International History of the Formative Years* (Stevenage: Institution of Electrical Engineers, 2004); Ken Beauchamp, *History of Telegraphy* (London: Institution of Electrical Engineers, 2001); Brian Bowers, *Sir Charles Wheatstone FRS: 1802–1875* (Stevenage: Institution of Electrical Engineers in Association with the Science Museum, 2001).
28. Macgowan, *Bowu tongshu*, 22–23. The first Chinese-language newspaper that brought in news about European telegraphy was *Chinese Serial* (*Xiaer guanzhen* 遐爾貫珍). See Shi Bin, *Dianbao tongxin yu qingmo minchu de zhengzhi bianju* (Beijing: Zhongguo shehui kexue chubanshe, 2012), 41.
29. Erik Baark, *Lightning Wires: The Telegraph and China's Technological Modernization* (Westport, Conn.: Greenwood Press, 1997), 84; Mullaney, "Semiotic Sovereignty," 161.
30. I have taken the example from S. A. Viguier (Waijiye), *Dianbao xinshu* (Shanghai, 1872). The telegraph codebooks underwent serious changes in the following decades, including changes in the 214 radicals. The numbers in Viguier's codebook do not correspond to later codebooks, although the principles stayed the same. *Lai* 來, for instance, was designated under the radical *ren* 人 in the *Kangxi Dictionary* and Viguier's codebook, because the old character for *lai* was 徠. In later dictionaries and codebooks, however, the radical was changed to *mu* 木.
31. Chu Chia-hua (Zhu Jiahua), *China's Postal and Other Communications Services* (London: Kegan Paul, Trench, Trubner, 1937), 166. In February 1933, the Ministry of Communications started offering the plaintext-ciphertext-plaintext translation service free of charge.
32. For a more detailed explanation of the economy of signs in Morse code, and the methods Chinese technicians invented for the sake of a more economic interface between alphabetical letters and Chinese characters, see Mullaney, "Semiotic Sovereignty," 161–165.
33. Timothy Richard, "Non-Phonetic and Phonetic Systems of Writing Chinese," *Chinese Recorder* 29 (November 1898): 542.
34. Wang Bingyao, *Pinyin zipu* (Beijing: Wenzi gaige chubanshe, 1956 [1896]), 11–12.
35. Wang Bingyao, "Xu," in *Pinyin zipu*, unidentified page number.
36. Wang Bingyao, *Pinyin zipu*, unidentified page number.

37. Wang Bingyao, *Pinyin zipu*, 5.
38. Wang Bingyao, *Pinyin zipu*, 12.
39. Zhou Youguang, *Dianbao pinyinhua* (Beijing: Wenzi gaige chubanshe, 1965).
40. Macgowan did not make note of the brain in his translation of galvanism. On the history of galvanism, electricity, and communication in Europe, see Laura Otis, *Networking: Communicating with Bodies and Machines in the Nineteenth Century* (Ann Arbor: University of Michigan Press, 2011).
41. Benjamin Hobson, *Quanti xinlun* (Beijing: Zhonghua shuju, 1991), 75–76. One exception to Chinese medical tradition that did not centralize the brain was Wang Qingren, who wrote *Correcting the Errors in the Forest of Medicine* (*Yilin gaicuo* 醫林改錯) in 1832, and, quoting from late-Ming and early-Qing scholars who were exposed to Jesuit translations, argued that the brain was the center of the body. See Bridie Andrews, "An Introduction to the Yilin Gaicuo," in Wang Qingren, *Correcting the Errors in the Forest of Medicine*, trans. Yuhsing Chung, Herman Oving, and Simon Becker (Boulder, Colo.: Blue Poppy Press, 2007), vi.
42. Hobson, *Quanti xinlun*, 77.
43. Bridie Andrews, "The Making of Modern Chinese Medicine" (PhD diss., University of Cambridge, 1996), 31, quoted in Larissa Heinrich, *Afterlife of Images: Translating the Pathological Body Between China and the West* (Durham, N.C.: Duke University Press, 2008), 123–124.
44. Shuji Matsumoto, "Shinsue kankō no chūgoku bun jintai kaibō gaku sho," *Nihon yisshigaku zasshi* 53, no. 4 (2007): 548–552.
45. Matsumoto, "Shinsue kankō," 549.
46. "Dr. Porter of Pangchwang," *Missionary Herald* 112, no. 12 (December 1916): 542–543.
47. Henry Porter, *Shengshen zhizhang* (Beijing: Tongwen Guan Press, 1886), 45. Porter in another place gives the translation of *naozhu* as "ganglionic corpuscle," which was thought to be a part of the nerve substance.
48. Porter, *Shengshen zhizhang*, 45.
49. Heinrich, *Afterlife of Images*, 125.
50. For an early reception of Hobson and Chen's work, see Elman, *On Their Own Terms*, 292–295.
51. Shen Xue, *Shengshi yuanyin* (Beijing: Wenzi gaige chubanshe, 1956 [1896]), 19–20.
52. Shen Xue, *Shengshi yuanyin*, 20.
53. Andrew Liu, *Tea War: A History of Capitalism in China and India* (New Haven, Conn.: Yale University Press, 2020), 166–167.
54. Zheng Guanying, *Shengshi weiyan zengding xinbian* (Taipei: Taiwan xuesheng shuju, 1965), 1191–1197.
55. It is unclear what Shen Xue meant by the "pearl-bone" since the term was neither in Western anatomical treatises nor in their Chinese translations.
56. Shen Xue, *Shengshi yuanyin*, 11–13.
57. Shen Xue took the "dead words [*sizi*]" out of the equation.
58. Shen Xue, *Shengshi yuanyin*, 14. There were many translations of the terms "psychology" and "psyche" into Chinese in the nineteenth century. See Yan Shuchang, *Zhongguo jindai xinlixue shi* (Shanghai: Shanghai jiaoyu chubanshe, 2015).

59. Shen Xue, *Shengshi yuanyin*, 14.
60. James Ross, *On Aphasia: Being a Contribution to the Subject of the Dissolution of Speech from Cerebral Disease* (London: J. & A. Churchill, 1887), 112–113. The debates about the order of the loss of nouns, verbs, and adjectives started in the 1850s at the latest. See Frederic Bateman, *On Aphasia, or Loss of Speech, and the Localization of the Faculty of Articulate Language*, 2nd ed. (London: J. & A. Churchill, 1890), 50. Neuropathology and theories about aphasia have been an important part of nineteenth-century neurological debates, and they were closely connected to colonial anthropology. An overview of theories about aphasia can be found in Juergen Tesak and Chris Code, *Milestones in the History of Aphasia: Theories and Protagonists* (New York: Psychology Press, 2008).
61. Shen Xue, *Shengshi yuanyin*, 23.
62. Shen Xue, *Shengshi yuanyin*, 22.
63. Shen Xue, *Shengshi yuanyin*, 14.
64. Shen Xue, *Shengshi yuanyin*, 22.
65. Shen Xue, *Shengshi yuanyin*, 22.
66. The historical records suggest that Shen published a second edition with illustrations, *Pinyin xinzi* 拼音新字, but a copy has not survived the twentieth century.
67. Liang Qichao, "Lun youxue," in *Yinbingshi wenji, di yi ce*, ed. Liang Qichao (Taipei: Taiwan zhonghua shuju, 1960), 46–47. Murao Susumu argued that Liang's use of *danao* and *xiaonao* referred to the Yogacaric seventh consciousness (*manas*) and sixth consciousness (*manovijnana*). John Jorgensen referenced Murao to claim that Liang's thoughts on education were influenced by Yogacara thought, although he indicated in a footnote his hesitation to accept this position. Based on Liang's piece, I do not think it is possible to suggest that he was drawing on Yogacara theory. See Murao Susumu, "'Banki sen-sen': Jimu hō jiki no Ryō Keichō," in *Kyōdō kenkyū Ryō Keichō: Seiyō kindaishisō juyō to Meiji Nihon*, comp. Hazama Naoki (Tokyo: Misuzu, 1999), 44; John Jorgensen, "Indra's Network: Zhang Taiyan's Sino-Japanese Personal Networks and the Rise of Yogacara in Modern China," in *Transforming Consciousness: Yogacara Thought in Modern China*, ed. John Makeham (Oxford: Oxford University Press, 2014), 79.
68. Liang Qichao, "Lun xiaoshuoyu qunzhi zhi guanxi [1902]," in *Liang Qichao Quanji*, comp. Yang Gang and Wang Xiangyi (Beijing: Beijing chubanshe, 1999), 2:884–886. The terms Liang selected for his theory of the novel have significance. "Stimulation" (*ciji* 刺激) and "nerve" (*shenjing* 神經) were both Japanese neologisms—*shigeki* and *shinkei*, respectively. Liang's use of these terms shows his affinity with Japanese publications, signaling a greater history that demands a new exploration of the interconnection between neurophysiology and the birth of the modern novel. For a similar history, but in the case of Victorian England, see Nicholas Dames, *Physiology of the Novel: Reading, Neural Science, and the Form of Victorian Fiction* (Oxford: Oxford University Press, 2007); Richard Menke, *Telegraphic Realism: Victorian Fiction and Other Information Systems* (Stanford, Calif.: Stanford University Press, 2008).
69. *Gezhi jiaokeshu jiaoshou fa* (Shanghai: Commercial Press, 1906).

70. Zhang Zhongmin, "Bunaode zhengzhixue: 'Ailuo bunaozhi' yu wanqing xiaofei wenhua de jiangou," *Xeshu yuekan* 43, no. 9 (September 2011): 145–154; Zhang Ning, "Nao wei yishen zhi zhu: Cong 'ailuo bunaozhi' kan jindai zhongguo shentiguande bianhua," *Zhongyang yanjiuyuan jindaishi yanjiusuo jikan*, no. 74 (December 2011): 1–40; Sherman Cochran, *Chinese Medicine Men: Consumer Culture in China and Southeast Asia* (Cambridge, Mass.: Harvard University Press, 2006), 38–63.
71. Shaoling Ma, "'A Tale of New Mr. Braggadocio': Narrative Subjectivity and Brain Electricity in Late Qing Science Fiction," *Science Fiction Studies* 40, no. 1 (March 2013): 55–72.
72. Lufei Kui, "Putong jiaoyu dang caiyong sutizi," *Jiaoyu zazhi* 1, no. 1 (1909): 1. See chapter 4 for the history of Chinese simplification.
73. Xing Dao, "Duyin tongyi hui gongding guoyin zimu zhi gaishuo," 11.
74. E. P. Thompson, "Time, Work-Discipline, and Industrial Capitalism," *Past and Present*, no. 38 (December 1967): 56–97.
75. Vanessa Ogle, "Time, Temporality and the History of Capitalism," *Past and Present*, no. 243 (May 2019): 317.

2. The National Phonetic Alphabet: Scripts and the Birth of Language Politics

1. Victor Mair, "What Is a Chinese 'Dialect/Topolect'? Reflections on Some Key Sino-English Linguistic Terms," *Sino-Platonic Papers*, no. 29 (September 1991).
2. Gina Tam, *Dialect and Nationalism in China, 1860–1960* (Cambridge: Cambridge University Press, 2020). For a shorter book on the subject, see David Moser, *A Billion Voices: China's Search for a Common Language* (Scorsby: Penguin Books, 2016).
3. Langdon Winner, "Do Artifacts Have Politics?," *Daedalus* 109, no. 1 (1980): 123–124. While this history is still disputed, one does not need to look far to find similar examples of technologies and infrastructures that embody racial biases. As Safiya Noble notes, search engines offer another powerful example of racialized technologies. Safiya Umoja Noble, *Algorithms of Oppression: How Search Engines Reinforce Racism* (New York: New York University Press, 2018).
4. For a detailed analysis of the 1913 conference, see Elisabeth Kaske, *The Politics of Language in Chinese Education* (Leiden: Brill, 2008).
5. John DeFrancis, *Nationalism and Language Reform in China* (Princeton, N.J.: Princeton University Press, 1950), 14–28.
6. Lydia Liu, *The Clash of Empires: The Invention of China in Modern World Making* (Cambridge, Mass.: Harvard University Press, 2004); Tam, *Dialect and Nationalism*, 35–71.
7. For a lengthy discussion of nineteenth-century romanization in China, see Uluğ Kuzuoğlu, "Capital, Letter, Empire: Romanization in the Late Qing," *Twentieth-Century China* 46, no. 3 (October 2021): 223–246.
8. Nile Green, "Persian Print and the Stanhope Revolution: Industrialization, Evangelicalism, and the Birth of Printing in Early Qajar Iran," *Comparative Studies of South Asia, Africa and the Middle East* 30, no. 3 (2010): 477.

2. THE NATIONAL PHONETIC ALPHABET

9. Christopher A. Reed, *Gutenberg in Shanghai: Chinese Print Capitalism, 1876–1937* (Vancouver: University of British Columbia Press, 2004), 42.
10. "Advertisement," in *Specimen of Printing Types in Use at the Baptist Mission Press* (Calcutta: Baptist Mission Press, 1826).
11. Reed, *Gutenberg in Shanghai*, 36. The two other dictionaries were Water Henry Medhurst, *Dictionary of the Hok-këèn Dialect of the Chinese Language* (Macao: Printed at the Honorable East India Company's Press, 1832); and Samuel Wells Williams, *A Tonic Dictionary of the Chinese Language in the Canton Dialect* (Canton: Printed at the Office of the Chinese Repository, 1856).
12. Robert A. Yelle, *Language of Disenchantment: Protestant Literalism and Colonial Discourse in British India* (New York: Oxford University Press, 2013), 33–70.
13. Max Müller, *Proposals for a Missionary Alphabet* (London: Printed by A. and G. A. Spottiswoode, 1854), 26.
14. Robert Morrison, *A Dictionary of the Chinese Language*, vol. 1, part 1 (Macao: Printed at the Honorable East India Company Press, 1815), xi.
15. Marshall Broomhall, *The Chinese Empire: A General and Missionary Survey* (London: Morgan and Scott, China Inland Mission, 1907); John R. Hykes, *Translations of the Scriptures Into the Languages of China and Her Dependencies* (New York: American Bible Society, 1916).
16. Thomas Francis Wade, *The Peking Syllabary, Being a Collection of the Characters Representing the Dialect of Peking; Arranged After a New Orthography in Syllabic Classes, According to the Four Tones; Designed to Accompany the Hsin Ching Lu, or Book of Experiments* (Hongkong, 1859), 55.
17. Frederick W. Baller, *Mandarin Primer* (Shanghai: China Inland Mission and American Presbyterian Mission Press, 1894), v.
18. J. A. Silsby, "Reform in Etiquette Called For," *Chinese Recorder* 36 (March 1905): 144–145.
19. "Our Most Popular Books," *Chinese Recorder* 38 (August 1907): 437.
20. DeFrancis, *Nationalism and Language Reform in China*, 33.
21. Lu Zhuangzhang, *Yimu liaoran chujie* (Beijing: Wenzi gaige chubanshe, 1957 [1892]); Lu Zhuangzhang, *Beijing qieyin jiaokeshu* (Beijing: Wenzi gaige chubanshe, 1957 [1906]); Lu Zhuangzhang, *Zhongguo zimu beijing qieyin heding* (Beijing: Wenzi gaige chubanshe, 1957 [1906]).
22. Wang Bingyao, *Pinyin zipu* (Beijing: Wenzi gaige chubanshe, 1956 [1896]), 2.
23. Li Jiesan, *Minqiang kuaizi* (Beijing: Wenzi gaige chubanshe, 1956 [1896]).
24. Wang Zhao, *Guanhua zimu duwu ba zhong* (Beijing: Wenzi gaige chubanshe, 1957 [1906]).
25. Lao Naixuan, *Jianzi wuzhong* (Jinling, Guangxu dingwei [1907]), 2:1–6, 2:16. Lao's Simple Script was a derivative of Wang Zhao's.
26. Li Jinxi, *Gwoyeu yunndonq shyy gang [Guoyu yundong shigang], juan er* (Shanghai: Commercial Press, 1934), 51–52.
27. GMD Party History Archives, *Zhi* 稚 11546 and 11509; Wu Jingheng (Zhihui), "Sanshi wunian lai zhi yinfu yundong," in *Wanqing sanshiwu nian lai (1897–1931) zhi zhongguo jiaoyu*, ed. Cai Yuanpei (Longmen shudian, 1969 [1931]), 304.
28. Shō Konishi, "Translingual World Order: Language Without Culture in Post-Russo-Japanese War Japan," *Journal of Asian Studies* 72, no. 1 (February 2013): 92.

2. THE NATIONAL PHONETIC ALPHABET

29. Gregor Benton, *Chinese Migrants and Internationalism: Forgotten Histories, 1917–1945* (London: Routledge, 2007), 93–94.
30. Michael Gordin, *Scientific Babel: How Science Was Done Before and After Global English* (Chicago: University of Chicago Press, 2015), 105–131.
31. Wu Rulun, "Shang Zhang guanxue shu," in *Qingmo wenzi gaige wenji* (Beijing: Wenzi gaige chubanshe, 1958), 29; Jing Tsu, *The Kingdom of Characters* (New York: Riverhead Books, 2022), 1–42; DeFrancis, *Nationalism and Language Reform in China*, 40–47; Kaske, *The Politics of Language*, 133–135.
32. Wu Jingheng, "Sanshi wunian lai zhi yinfu yundong," 308–309; Kaske, *The Politics of Language*, 138–141.
33. Kaske, *The Politics of Language*, 136.
34. Kaske, *The Politics of Language*, 408.
35. Xing Dao, "Duyin tongyi hui gongding guoyin zimu zhi gaishuo," *Dongfang zazhi* 10, no. 8 (1914): 11.
36. Benton, *Chinese Migrants and Internationalism*, 96–97; Kaske, *The Politics of Language*, 380–386.
37. Zhang Taiyan, "Bo zhongguo yong wanguo xinyu shuo," *Minbao*, no. 21 (1908): 62–68.
38. Zhang Taiyan, "Aimie shu," *Zhang Taiyan quanji* (Shanghai: Shanghai renmin chubanshe, 1982), 3:324, quoted in Huang Jinshu, *Zhang Taiyan yuyan wenzi zhi xue de zhishi (jingshen) xipu* (Huamulan wenhua, 2012), 70.
39. Zhang Taiyan, "Wode pingsheng yu banshi fangfa," in *Zhang Taiyan de baihuawen* (Taipei: Yiwen yinshuguan, 1972), 69.
40. Li Chin-Shi, *Chinese Phonetic System and Language*, trans. Alex Mackenzie (Shanghai: Commercial Press, 1922), 34.
41. Kaske, *The Politics of Language*, 409.
42. Li Jinxi, *Gwoyeu yunndonq shyy gang*, 59.
43. Li Jinxi, *Gwoyeu yunndonq shyy gang*, 60.
44. Kaske, *The Politics of Language*, 413–416.
45. Li Chin-Shi, *Chinese Phonetic System and Language*, 39.
46. Li Chin-Shi, *Chinese Phonetic System and Language*, 40. For the original, see Li Jinxi, *Guoyuxue jiangyi* (Shanghai: Commercial Press, 1919), 28.
47. "Jiaoyu bu gongbu zhuyin zimu shufa tishi," *Shaoxing jiaoyujie* 1, no. 3 (1922): 1–3.
48. "Typewriting Machine." United States Patent Office, Burnham C. Stickney, of Elizabeth, New Jersey, Assignor to Underwood Typewriter Company of New York, NY, A Corporation of Delaware. Application Filed March 28, 1922. Serial no. 547,450. Patented April 9, 1924. The Burke Library Archives, Columbia University Libraries, Union Theological Seminary, New York Missionary Research Library Archives: Section 6 (hereafter MRL: 6), Phonetic Promotion Committee Records, 1919–1930 (hereafter PPCR), 1-1-14. It is likely that Underwood Typewriter Company solicited the help of Dr. Tewksbury, the typeface designer from the Phonetic Promotion Committee who was personally involved in keyboard designs.
49. Letter from Qian Xuantong to Wu Zhihui, May 26, 1919, GMD Archives, *Zhi* 稚 09995. It is likely the case, however, that they were not able to understand each other. In the letters I perused, the signs of the NPA were accompanied by Chinese characters below them. Both Wu and Qian were likely retranscribing the

2. THE NATIONAL PHONETIC ALPHABET

alphabet into characters in order to understand the text. The irony was clearly lost on them.

50. According to what seems to be an impossibly bloated missionary account, Yan printed two million textbooks in Shaanxi. Letter to American Board of Commissioners for Foreign Missions, in MRL: 6, China Continuation Committee Records, 1912–1922 (hereafter CCCR), 1-1-8.
51. L. H. Gaunt, ed., *The Chronicle of the London Missionary Society*, vol. 15, New Series (London: London Missionary Society, 1906), 45; Sidney G. Peill, "'Open Vision' in China," in *The Beloved Physician—and Others*, ed. J. Peill (London: London Missionary Society, 1922), 150–151.
52. Sidney G. Peill, "Scriptures in Phonetic for North China," *Chinese Recorder* 47 (1916): 330–335.
53. Sir Walter Hillier, *Memorandum Upon an Alphabetical System for Writing Chinese, the Application of This System to the Typewriter and to the Linotype or Other Typecasting and Composing Machines and Its Application to the Braille System for the Blind* (London: William Cloves and Sons, [1915]). Reprinted in *China and the Chinese: A Collection of Pamphlets Relating Thereto*, vol. 70, Wason Collection, Cornell University.
54. The missionaries unanimously voted for the NPA (*zhuyin zimui*) in the sixth annual meeting on September 24–25, 1918. *Proceedings of the Seventh Annual Meeting of the China Continuation Committee, Shanghai April 25–30, 1919* (Shanghai: Offices of the China Continuation Committee, 1919), 58. The proceedings of annual meetings are all preserved in CCCR, 1912–1922
55. L. S. Foster, *Fifty Years in China: An Eventful Memoir of Tarleton Perry Crawford* (Nashville, Tenn.: Bayless-Pullen Company, 1909), 354–361.
56. *Records of the General Conference of the Protestant Missionaries of China* (Shanghai: American Presbyterian Mission Press, 1890), 371.
57. John R. Mott, *The Continuation Committee* (Edinburgh: Continuation Committee of the World Missionary Conference, 1910), 17.
58. "Shanghai Missionary Conference," CCCR, 1-2-10; CCCR, 1-2-4. There were 105 missions in China, but only 65 members of the CCC. By rule, a third of the members had to be Chinese. There were twenty-two Chinese, nineteen British, nineteen American, and five continental European members.
59. "Shanghai Conference—Christian Education," CCCR, 1-2-10.
60. Letter from Warnshuis to C. H. Patton, CCCR, 1-1-11; "Minutes of the Meeting of the Phonetic Promotion Committee, November 19, 1920," CCCR, 1-1-9; *Proceedings of the Eighth Annual Meeting, Shanghai May 3–7, 1920* (Shanghai: Offices of the China Continuation Committee, 1920), 58; *Proceedings of the Seventh Annual Meeting*, 58.
61. "Attacking Illiteracy with the National Phonetic System," *China Sunday School Journal* 7, no. 12 (1918): 1101.
62. Letter from Sidney G. Peill to Susie J. Garland, April 8, 1920, CCCR, 1-1-8.
63. Sidney G. Peill, "'Open Vision' in China," 157–159.
64. Bulletin no. 4 (June 1920), 6, PPCR, 1-1-1; Bulletin no. 6 (April 1921), 4, PPCR, 1-1-2.
65. "Report of the Official Committee on the Promotion of Phonetic Script (1919)," 5, CCCR, 1-1-9.
66. Bulletin no. 5 (January 1921), 7, PPCR, 1-1-1.
67. Bulletin no. 7 (July 1921), 4, PPCR, 1-1-1.

68. Sidney G. Peill, "Rural Medical Evangelism," *Chinese Recorder* 56 (January 1925), 32.
69. "Minutes of the Meeting of the Phonetic Promotion Committee, November 19, 1920," CCCR, 1-1-9.
70. Ping Chen, *Modern Chinese: History and Sociolinguistics* (Cambridge: Cambridge University Press, 1999), 20.
71. Thomas Mullaney, *The Chinese Typewriter: A History* (Cambridge, Mass.: MIT Press, 2017).

3. Basic Chinese: Cognitive Management and Mass Literacy

1. Evelyn S. Rawski, *Education and Popular Literacy in Ch'ing China* (Ann Arbor: University of Michigan Press, 1979).
2. Charles W. Hayford, *To the People: James Yen and Village China* (New York: Columbia University Press, 1990); Kate Merkel-Hess, *The Rural Modern: Reconstructing the Self and State in Republican China* (Chicago: University of Chicago Press, 2016).
3. Zhou Xingsi, *Ch'ien tzu wen, The Thousand Character Classic: A Chinese Primer*, ed. Francis W. Paar (New York: F. Ungar, 1963).
4. Frank Bunker Gilbreth, *Applied Motion Study: A Collection of Papers on the Efficient Method to Industrial Preparedness* (New York: Sturgis and Walton, 1917), 17.
5. Gilbreth, *Applied Motion Study*, 52.
6. Frank Bunker Gilbreth, *Fatigue Study: The Elimination of Humanity's Greatest Unnecessary Waste, A First Step in Motion Study* (New York: MacMillan, 1919), 104–108.
7. *Proceedings of the Board of Aldermen of the City of New York from April 3 to June 26, 1917* (New York: Board of Aldermen, 1917), 2:716.
8. Charles H. Judd, *Genetic Psychology for Teachers* (New York: D. Appleton, 1909 [1903]), 161–196; Frank N. Freeman, *The Teaching of Handwriting* (Boston: Houghton, Mifflin, 1914), 11.
9. Edmund B. Huey, "Preliminary Experiments in the Physiology and Psychology of Reading," *American Journal of Psychology* 9, no. 4 (1898): 575–586.
10. Edmund B. Huey, *Psychology and Pedagogy of Reading* (New York: Macmillan, 1908).
11. Eugene Shen [Shen Youqian], "An Analysis of Eye Movements in Reading Chinese," *Journal of Experimental Psychology* 10, no. 2 (1927): 158–183.
12. Edward L. Thorndike, *Handwriting* (New York City: Teachers College, Columbia University, 1912), 36–39.
13. William J. Breen, "Foundations, Statistics, and State-Building: Leonard P. Ayres, the Russell Sage Foundation, and U.S. Government Statistics in the First World War," *Business History Review* 68, no. 4 (Winter 1994): 451–482.
14. Leonard P. Ayres, *A Scale for Measuring the Quality of Handwriting of School Children* (New York: Russell Sage Foundation, Department of Child Hygiene, 1912).
15. Leonard P. Ayres, *A Measuring Scale for Ability in Spelling* (New York: Russell Sage Foundation, Division of Education, 1915), 5.
16. Charles K. A. Wang, *An Annotated Bibliography of Mental Tests and Scales*, vol. 2 (Beijing: Catholic University Press, 1940).

17. Tamara P. Thornton, *Handwriting in America: A Cultural History* (New Haven, Conn.: Yale University Press, 1996).
18. Ying Kao Lin, "Academic and Professional Attainments of Native Chinese Students Graduating from Teachers College, Columbia University (1909–1950)" (PhD diss., Teachers College, Columbia University, 1951).
19. Stephen Jay Gould, *The Mismeasure of Man* (New York: Norton, 1981); John Carson, *The Measure of Merit: Talents, Intelligence, and Inequality in the French and American Republics, 1750–1940* (Princeton, N.J.: Princeton University Press, 2007).
20. Alfred Binet and N. Vaschide, "Influence du travail intellectuel, des émotions et du travail physique sur la pression du sang," *L'année Psychologique* 3 (1896): 127–183; Alfred Binet, "Note relative à l'influence du travail intellectuel sur la consommation du pain dans les écoles," *L'année psychologique* 5 (1898): 332–336.
21. Michael M. Sokal, "James McKeen Cattell and Mental Anthropometry: Nineteenth-Century Science and Reform and the Origins of Psychological Testing," in *Psychological Testing and American Society, 1890–1930*, ed. Michael M. Sokal (New Brunswick, N.J.: Rutgers University Press, 1987), 21–45.
22. Henry L. Milton, "Lewis M. Terman and Mental Testing: In Search of the Democratic Ideal," in Sokal, *Psychological Testing and American Society*, 95–112.
23. Robert M. Yerkes, "Report of the Psychology Committee of the National Research Council," *Psychological Review* 26, no. 2 (1919): 83–149; James Reed, "Robert M. Yerkes and the Mental Testing Movement," in Sokal, *Psychological Testing and American Society*, 75–94.
24. Yerkes, "Report of the Psychology Committee," 92.
25. Guy M. Whipple, "The National Intelligence Tests," *Journal of Educational Research* 4, no. 1 (1921): 16–31.
26. Liao Shicheng, "Zhili ceyan de lishi," *Xinli* 1, no. 1 (1922): 94.
27. H. H. Hsiao, "The Mentality of Chinese and Japanese," *Journal of Applied Psychology* 13 (1929): 9–31.
28. James McKeen Cattell, "A Statistical Study of Eminent Men," *Popular Science Monthly* 62 (1903): 359–377.
29. Lu Zhiwei, *Dingzheng bina-ximeng zhili ceyan shuomingshu* (Shanghai: Commercial Press, 1924).
30. Chen Heqin and Liao Shicheng, *Zhili ceyan fa* (Shanghai: Commercial Press, 1921), 6.
31. Chen and Liao, *Zhili ceyan fa*, 60–61, 93–94.
32. Herman Chan'en Liu, *Non-Verbal Intelligence Tests for Use in China* (New York: Teachers College, Columbia University, 1922).
33. William McCall, *How to Measure in Education* (New York: Macmillan, 1922), 4–5.
34. Lu Zhiwei, *Dingzheng bina-ximeng zhili ceyan shuomingshu* (Shanghai: Commercial Press, 1924).
35. *Shanghai tebie shili xiaoxue gebie zhili ceyan baogaoshu* (Shanghai: Shanghai tebieshi zhengfu jiaoyuju, 1928); Shanghai Municipal Archives, R48-1-775; Neizheng bu, *Putong jingcha zhili ceyan zhidao lu* (Neizheng bu, 1939); Xiao Xiaorong and Ding Zuyin, *Jingguan zhihui ceyan* (Neizheng bu, 1940).
36. Zhonghua pingmin jiaoyu cujin hui, *Pingmin xuexiao jiaoyu ceyan fa* (Shanghai: Commercial Press, 1928), 206–231; Zhonghua pingmin jiaoyu cujin hui, *Dingxian shiyan gongzuo tiyao* (Beijing: Zhonghua pingmin jiaoyu cujin hui, 1934), 53–58.

3. BASIC CHINESE

37. "Mass Education in China," *Pacific Affairs* 1, no. 2 (1928): 24.
38. Letter from Y. C. James Yen to John D. Rockefeller III, May 22, 1944, Rockefeller Archive Center, Office of the Messrs. Rockefeller Records, series G, box 3, folder 16.
39. Wu Xiangxiang, *Yan Yangchu Zhuan: Wei quanqiu xiangcun gaizao fendou liushi nian* (Taipei: Shibao wenhua chuban, 1981), 12–13.
40. Yurou Zhong, *Chinese Grammatology: Script Revolution and Chinese Literary Modernity, 1916-1958* (New York: Columbia University Press, 2019), 100–125.
41. Chen Heqin, "Yutiwen yingyong zihui," in *Chen Heqin quanji*, ed. Beijingshi jiaoyu kexue yanjiusuo (Nanjing: Jiangsu jiaoyu chubanshe, 1987), 6:78.
42. Ao Hongde, "Yutiwen yingyong zihui yanjiu baogao—Chen Heqin shi yutiwen yingyong zihui zhi xu," *Jiaoyu zazhi* 21, no. 2 (1929): 77–101; Ao Hongde, "Yutiwen yinyong zihui yanjiu baogao (xu)—Chen Heqin shi yutiwen yingyong zihui zhi xu," *Jiaoyu zazhi* 21, no. 3 (1929): 97–113.
43. Wang Wenxin, *Xiaoxue fenji zihui yanjiu* (Hankou: Minzhi shuju, 1930), 10–14.
44. Zhonghua pingmin jiaoyu cujin hui, *Shibing qianzi ke* (Beiping: Zhonghua pingmin jiaoyu cujin hui, 1929 [1928]), 15; Zhonghua pingmin jiaoyu cujin hui, *Nongmin qianzi ke* ([Beiping]: Zhonghua pingmin jiaoyu cujin hui, 1931), 8.
45. *Proceedings of the Board of Aldermen of the City of New York*, 716.
46. "Memorandum Regarding the Political Trends in China and the Progress of the Mass Education Movement in China," January 14, 1949, Rockefeller Archive Center, Office of the Messrs. Rockefeller Records, series G, box 3, folder 17.
47. I. A. Richards, "Basic English and Its Applications," *Journal of the Royal Society of Arts* (June 1939): 737.
48. C. K. Ogden, *Basic English: A General Introduction with Rules and Grammar* (London: Kegan Paul, Trench and Trubner, 1930); C. K. Ogden, *The System of Basic English* (New York: Harcourt, Brace, 1934).
49. C. K. Ogden, *C. K. Ogden and Linguistics* (London: Routledge/Thoemmes Press, 1994), 229.
50. C. K. Ogden, *Basic English: International Second Language* (New York: Harcourt, Brace & World, 1968), 55.
51. C. K. Ogden and I. A. Richards, *The Meaning of Meaning: A Study of the Influence of Language Upon Thought and of the Science of Symbolism* (New York: Harcourt, Brace, 1923).
52. I. A. Richards, "Basic English and Its Applications," 737–738.
53. Michael Gordin, *Scientific Babel: How Science Was Done Before and After Global English* (Chicago: University of Chicago Press, 2015), 297.
54. Rodney Koeneke, *Empires of the Mind: I. A. Richards and Basic English in China, 1929-1979* (Stanford, Calif.: Stanford University Press, 2004), 187.
55. John Durham Peters, *Speaking Into the Air: A History of the Idea of Communication* (Chicago: University of Chicago Press, 1999), 13.
56. Ogden, *The System of Basic English*, 21–22.
57. I. A. Richards, "Basic English and Its Applications," 744–745.
58. Hong Shen, "1100 ge jiben hanzi shiyongfa," *Dongfang zazhi* 32, no. 14 (1935): 6.
59. Hong, "1100 ge jiben hanzi shiyongfa," 6.

60. Hong, "1100 ge jiben hanzi shiyongfa," 9–11.
61. Hong Shen, *Yi qian yi bai ge jiben hanzi shiyong jiaoxue fa* (Shanghai: Shenghuo shudian, 1936), 38.
62. Hong, "1100 ge jiben hanzi shiyongfa," 6–8.
63. Hong, "1100 ge jiben hanzi shiyongfa," 9–10.
64. Peters, *Speaking Into the Air*, 12; Ogden and Richards, *The Meaning of Meaning*, 205–206.
65. Yuen Ren Chao, *Mandarin Primer: An Intensive Course in Spoken Chinese* (Cambridge, Mass.: Harvard University Press, 1964 [1948]), 14–16.
66. Shen Youqian [Eugene Shen], "Hanzi de jianglai," *Jiaoyu zazhi* 27, no. 5 (1937): 410.
67. Andrew Liu, *Tea War: A History of Capitalism in China and India* (New Haven, Conn.: Yale University Press, 2020), 48 (emphasis mine).

4. Simplification of Chinese Characters: Mining, Counting, Seeing

1. Yao-Chiang Chang (Zhang Yaoxiang), "Factors Affecting the Speed and Clearness of Reading Chinese" (master's thesis, Columbia University, 1919), 1.
2. Qian Xuantong et al., "Guoyu tongyi choubei hui di si ci da hui, liang ge zhongyao de yi'an: feichu hanzi caiyong xin pinyin wenzi an, Jiansheng xianxing hanzi de bihua an," *Guoyu yuekan* 1 (1922): 160. Qian Xuantong's article was published earlier, in 1920. See Qian Xuantong, "Jiansheng hanzi bihua de tiyi," *Xin qingnian* 7, no. 3 (1920).
3. Lufei Kui, "Putong jiaoyu dang caiyong sutizi," *Jiaoyu zazhi* 1, no. 1 (1909): 1.
4. Lufei Kui, "Zhengli hanzi de yijian," *Guoyu yuekan* 1, no. 1 (1922): 7.
5. Qian Xuantong et al., "Guoyu tongyi choubei hui di si ci da hui," 162.
6. Hu Huaichen, *Jianyizi shuo* (Shanghai: Commercial Press, 1928), 34.
7. Liu Fu and Li Jiarui, *Song yuan yilai suzi pu* (Guoli zhongyang yanjiuyuan lishi yuyan yanjiusuo, 1930).
8. This was *huiyi*, one of the six principles (*liushu* 六書) proposed by Xu Shen to categorize Chinese characters. The explanation of each character can be found in Chen Guangyao, "Jianxie zongli yizhu jie," in Lin Yutang, "Wode hua—tichang suzi," *Lun yu* 29 (November 1933): 215–217; Chen Guangyao, *Jianzi lunji* (Shanghai: Commercial Press, 1931).
9. Jing Tsu, "Chinese Scripts, Codes, and Typewriting Machines," in *Science and Technology in Modern China*, ed. Jing Tsu and Benjamin Elman (Leiden: Brill, 2014), 135–137; Thomas Mullaney, *The Chinese Typewriter: A History* (Cambridge, Mass.: MIT Press, 2017), 237–282.
10. Lin Yutang, "Wo de hua—tichang suzi," *Lun yu* 29 (November 1933): 216.
11. Lin Yutang, "Wo de hua—tichang suzi," 217.
12. Timothy Tingfang Lew, *The Psychology of Learning Chinese: A Preliminary Analysis by Means of Experimental Psychology of Some of the Factors Involved in the Process of Learning Chinese Characters* (Peking, 1924?), 3–4.

13. Timothy Ting-fang Lew, "The Psychology of Learning Chinese, Part IV: Interpretations and Conclusions," *Chinese Social and Political Science Review* (1924): 145.
14. Lew, *The Psychology of Learning Chinese*, 23.
15. Lew, *The Psychology of Learning* Chinese, 17–20.
16. Lew, "The Psychology of Learning Chinese, Part IV," 144–189.
17. Lew, "The Psychology of Learning Chinese, Part IV," 34–105.
18. Loh Seng Tsai (Cai Lesheng) and Ethel Abernethy, "The Psychology of Chinese Characters," *Journal of Experimental Psychology* 11, no. 6 (December 1928): 430–442.
19. Ai Wei, "Hanzi zhi xinli yanjiu (wei wan)," *Jiaoyu zazhi* 20, no. 4 (1928): 13–15.
20. Ai Wei, "Hanzi zhi xinli yanjiu (xu)," *Jiaoyu zazhi* 20, no. 5 (1928): 1.
21. Ai, "Hanzi zhi xinli yanjiu (xu)," 7.
22. Xu Zemin, "Hanzi bihua tongji baogao," *Zhonghua jiaoyujie* 18, no. 12 (1930): 44.
23. Xu Zemin, "Hanzi bihua tongji baogao," 46.
24. Xu Zemin, "550 suzi biao," *Lun yu* 45 (1934): 40–42.
25. Uluğ Kuzuoğlu, "Codebooks for the Mind: Dictionary Index Reforms in Republican China, 1912–1937," *Information and Culture* 53, no. 3/4 (2018): 337–366.
26. Du Dingyou, *Xin shifan xinli* (Zhonghua Press, 1931 [1925]).
27. Du Dingyou, "[Tushuguan] xin zi zhi shangque (di san ci)," *Tushuguanxue jikan* 6, no. 2 (1932): 292–293.
28. Du Dingyou, "[Tushuguan] xin zi zhi shangque (di er ci)," *Tushuguanxue jikan* 3, no. 4 (1929): 625–627.
29. Eugene Shen, "An Analysis of Eye Movements in Reading Chinese," *Journal of Experimental Psychology* 10, no. 2 (1927): 179; Yao-Chiang Chang, "Factors Affecting the Speed and Clearness"; Horace Tu, "The Effects of Different Arrangements of the Chinese Characters Upon Speed and Comprehension in Silent Reading," *Chinese Social and Political Science Review*, no. 2 (April 1926): 278–301; Li Kiang Chen and H. A. Carr, "The Ability of Chinese Students to Read in Vertical and Horizontal Directions," *Experimental Psychology* 9 (1926): 110–117; W. R. Miles and Eugene Shen, "Photographic Recording of Eye Movements in the Reading of Chinese in Vertical and Horizontal Axes: Method and Preliminary Results," *Journal of Experimental Psychology* 10 (1925): 344–362.
30. Siegen K. Chou (Zhou Xiangeng), "*Gestalt* in Reading Chinese Characters," *Psychological Review* 37, no. 1 (January 1930): 54–70.
31. Chou, "*Gestalt* in Reading Chinese Characters," 64.
32. Chou, "*Gestalt* in Reading Chinese Characters," 65.
33. Chou, "*Gestalt* in Reading Chinese Characters," 65–68 (emphasis mine).
34. Du Dingyou, *Zhongguo jianzi wenti* (Unidentified publisher, 1931), 53.
35. Du Dingyou, *Hanzi xingwei pai jian fa* (Shanghai: Zhonghua Press, 1932), 2.
36. Du Dingyou, *Tushuguan bian muyong jianzi biaozhun zibiao* (Shanghai: Zhongguo tushuguan fuwushe, 1934), 1.
37. Frederick Wakeman, "A Revisionist View of the Nanjing Decade: Confucian Fascism," *China Quarterly* 150 (1997): 396.
38. Arif Dirlik, "The Ideological Foundations of the New Life Movement: A Study in Counterrevolution," *Journal of Asian Studies* 34, no. 4 (August 1975): 955–956; Federica Ferlanti, "The New Life Movement in Jiangxi Province, 1934–1938," *Modern Asian Studies* 44, no. 5 (2010): 963.

5. THE NEW DUNGANESE ALPHABET

39. Academia Historica (Guoshi guan, hereafter AH), 148000000001A; Guofangbu junshi qingbaoju [Ministry of Defense Intelligence Bureau], "Tewu chu zuzhi gongzuo kaizhan" [Developing the organizational tasks of the Special Services Unit], 1934, 10: 015a.
40. Qian Xuantong, "Soucai guyou er jiao shiyong de jiantizi an," *Guoyu zhoukan* 23 (1934): 1 (emphasis mine).
41. AH, 200000000A; Guomin zhengfu [Nationalist Government], "Jiantizi tuixing faling an" [The file on the laws and decrees (related to) the promotion of simplified characters], June 7, 1935–May 30, 1947; 001090002008010a-15a.
42. AH, 200000000A.
43. Lu Xun famously dubbed the Chinese characters as "tubercles" and "microbes" on the bodies of the masses, devouring the people. Lu Xun, "Guanyu xin wenzi" [1934], in *Lu Xun lun wenzi gaige* (Shandong renmin chubanshe, 1979), 73. See also Ping, "'Dazhongyu' gen 'shoutouzi,'" *Qinghua zhoukan* 43, no. 1 (1935): 54–55. For some, "handy characters" were even the path to Esperanto; see Yang Jinhao, "Cong shoutouzi dao shijieyu," *Qingnian jie* 8, no. 2 (1935): 5–6.
44. Zhang Shuyan, *Jianhua zi suyuan* (Beijing: Yuwen chubanshe, 2005 [1997]), 13.
45. Pan Guangrong, "Jianbizi yu shoutouzi," *Wenyuan* 1, no. 1 (1935): 1.
46. Pan, "Jianbizi yu shoutouzi," 3–4.
47. "Tuixing shoutouzi yuanqi," *Xinsheng zhoukan* 2, no. 6 (1935): 22.
48. Shu (Zhang Shuhuang), "Zisha minzu de shoutouzi," *Guoguang zazhi* 6 (1935): 12.
49. Jiaoyu bu, *Jianti zibiao, di yi pi* (Jiaoyu bu, 1935).
50. Zhang Shuyan, *Jianhua zi suyuan*, 16.
51. AH, Jiang Zhongzheng zongtong wenwu [Chiang Kaishek Presidential Records and Artifacts]; Yiban ziliao [General materials], 1935 (57), 1935/10/09 (002-080200-00255-025).
52. "Hunan sheng zhuxi he jian fandui tuixing jiantizi yuanwen," *Lun yu* 77 (1935): 44.
53. Zhang Shuyan, *Jianhua zi suyuan*, 17.
54. Jeffrey Weng, "Stop the Presses! Character Simplification and the Publishing Industry in China Under the Nationalists, 1935–36," *Harvard Journal of Asiatic Studies* (forthcoming).
55. AH, 200000000A; 8081a–82a, and 8084a.
56. Joseph Schumpeter, *Capitalism, Socialism and Democracy* (London: Routledge, 2003 [1944]), 83 (emphasis in the original).
57. On the "spirit of informationalism," see Manuel Castells, *Information Age: Economy, Society, and Culture* (Malden, Mass.: Blackwell, 1996), 1:199.

5. The New Dunganese Alphabet: Latinization Across Eurasia

1. John DeFrancis, *Nationalism and Language Reform in China* (Princeton, N.J.: Princeton University Press, 1950), 87–108; Yurou Zhong, *Chinese Grammatology: Script Revolution and Literary Modernity, 1916–1958* (New York: Columbia University Press, 2019), 67–99.

5. THE NEW DUNGANESE ALPHABET

2. Uluğ Kuzuoğlu, "Telegraphy, Typography, and the Alphabet: The Origins of Alphabet Revolutions in the Russo-Ottoman Space," *International Journal of Middle East Studies* 52 (2020): 413–431.
3. Terry Martin, *The Affirmative Action Empire: Nations and Nationalism in the Soviet Union, 1923-1939* (Ithaca, N.Y.: Cornell University Press, 2001), 187.
4. John Riddell, ed., *To See the Dawn: Baku, 1920—First Congress of the Peoples of the East* (New York: Pathfinder, 2010); Nergis Ertürk, "Toward a Literary Communism: The 1926 Baku Turcological Congress," *Boundary 2* 40, no. 2 (Summer 2013): 183–213.
5. Raja Adal, *Beauty in the Age of Empire: Japan, Egypt, and the Global History of Aesthetic Education* (New York: Columbia University Press, 2019), 74–85.
6. Kendall E. Bailes, "Alexei Gastev and the Soviet Controversy Over Taylorism, 1918-1924," *Soviet Studies* 29, no. 3 (July 1977): 373; Marshall McLuhan, *Understanding Media: The Extensions of Man* (New York: McGraw-Hill, 1964).
7. Mark R. Beissinger, *Scientific Management, Socialist Discipline, and Soviet Power* (Cambridge, Mass.: Harvard University Press, 1988), 51.
8. Aleksei K. Gastev, *Kak nado rabotat': Prakticheskoe vvedenie v nauku organizatsii truda*, 2nd ed. (Moscow: Ekonomika, 1972), 28 (emphasis in original).
9. Gastev, *Kak nado rabotat'*, 198.
10. Devin Fore, "The Operative Word in Soviet Factography," *October* 118 (2006): 118–119.
11. Gastev, *Kak nado rabotat'*, 97–98.
12. Ana Olenina, "Engineering Performance: Lev Kuleshov, Soviet Reflexology, and Labor Efficiency Studies," *Discourse* 35, no. 3 (2013): 297–336; Julia Kursell, "*Piano Mecanique* and *Piano Biologique*: Nikolai Bernstein's Neurophysiological Study of Piano Touch," *Configurations* 14, no. 3 (Fall 2006): 245–273; Beissinger, *Scientific Management*, 50–58; Fore, "The Operative Word in Soviet Factography."
13. Nikolai Iakovlev, "Problemy natsional'noi pis'mennosti vostochnykh narodov SSSR," *Novyi Vostok*, no. 10–11 (1925): 237; Nikolai Iakovlev, "Matematicheskaia formula postroeniia alfavita," *Kul'tura i pis'mennost' vostoka*, no. 1 (1928): 49–64. Iakovlev's theories did not go unchallenged: R. O. Shor, "K voprosu o sokrashchenii alfavita (kriticheskie zamechaniia na stat'iu prof. N. F. Iakovleva 'Matematicheskaia formula postroeniia alfavita,' *Kul'tura i pis'mennost' vostoka*, no. 1 [1928])," *Kul'tura i pis'mennost' vostoka*, no. 2 (1928): 62–75.
14. Nikolai Iakovlev, "Za latinizatsiiu russkogo alfavita," *Kul'tura i pis'mennost' vostoka*, no. 6 (1930): 37.
15. A. Lunacharskii, "Latinizatsiia russkoi pis'mennosti," *Kul'tura i pis'mennost' vostoka*, no. 6 (1930): 22.
16. Lev Zhirkov, "K reforme alfavitov vostochnikh narodnostei," *Novyi Vostok*, no. 10–11 (1925): 223–235; *Pervyi Vsesoiuznyi Tiurkologicheskii S"ezd (26 Fevralia—6 Marta), Stenograficheskii otchet* (Baku: Obshchestvo Obsledovaniia i Izucheniia Azerbaidzhana, 1926), 232–233.
17. *Pervyi Vsesoiuznyi Tiurkologicheskii S"ezd*, 243 (emphasis mine).
18. *Pervyi Vsesoiuznyi Tiurkologicheskii S"ezd*, 244.
19. *Pervyi Vsesoiuznyi Tiurkologicheskii S"ezd*, 245–264.
20. *Pervyi Vsesoiuznyi Tiurkologicheskii S"ezd*, 264–265, 313–316.

5. THE NEW DUNGANESE ALPHABET

21. *Pervyi Vsesoiuznyi Tiurkologicheskii S"ezd*, 165.
22. There is no historical source that traces this dictum to Lenin himself. It was S. A. Agamalyogly, the leader of the latinization movement in Azerbaijan, who narrated the following story in a book he published in 1925. According to Agamalyogly's account, in 1922, right after the latinized New Turkic Alphabet made its debut in Azerbaijan, Agamalyogly visited Lenin in his dacha Gorki, and Lenin asked him what the peasants thought about latinization. Agamalyogly responded that the feedback was positive, and Lenin said, "That is the revolution in the East." In 1928, Agamalyogly changed his recollections and claimed that what Lenin really said was, "That is the great revolution in the East," which later became the slogan for the movement. S. Agamalyogly, *Neotlozhnye kul'turnye nuzhdy tiurko-tatarskikh narodov* (Baku: Izdanie Komiteta Novogo Tiurkskogo Alfavita, 1925), 3; Martin, *The Affirmative Action Empire*, 187.
23. S. Agamalyogly, *V zashchitu novogo tiurkskogo alfavita* (Baku: AZGIZ, 1927), 15, 64.
24. Agamalyogly, *V zashchitu novogo tiurkskogo alfavita*, 66.
25. Agamalyogly, *Neotlozhnye kul'turnye nuzhdy tiurko-tatarskikh narodov*, 8.
26. Jacob M. Landau, *Pan-Turkism: From Irredentism to Cooperation* (Indianapolis: Indiana University Press, 1995); Selçuk Esenbel, "Japan's Global Claim to Asia and the World of Islam: Transnational Nationalism and World Power, 1900–1945," *American Historical Review* 109, no. 4 (2004): 140–170.
27. The quotation comes from Pedersen's study on infrastructure building in northern Mongolia: Morten A. Pedersen, *Not Quite Shamans: Spirit Worlds and Political Lives in Northern Mongolia* (Ithaca, N.Y.: Cornell University Press, 2011), 45.
28. A. Frings, "Sorevnovanie modelei: Tatarskaia delegatsiia na tiurkologicheskom s"ezde v Baku v 1926 g.," *Etnograficheskoe obozrenie* 6 (2005): 47.
29. *Stenograficheskii otchet pervogo plenuma vsesoiuznogo tsentral'nogo komiteta novogo tiurkskogo alfavita zasedavshego v Baku ot 3-go do 7-go iiunia 1927 goda* (Moscow: Izdanie VTsK NTA, 1927), 1.
30. F. Agazade and K. Karakashly, *Ocherk po istorii razvitiia dvizheniia novogo alfavita i ego dostizheniia* (Kazan: VTsK NTA, 1928), 87.
31. *Stenograficheskii otchet pervogo plenuma*, 159–162.
32. *Stenograficheskii otchet tret'ego plenuma vsesoiuznogo tsentral'nogo komiteta novogo tiurkskogo alfavita zasedavshego v g. Kazani ot 18-go po 23-e dekabriia 1928 g.* (Baku: Gos. Publichin., 1929), 68–73.
33. *Stenograficheskii otchet tret'ego plenuma*, 83.
34. I. Khansurov, *Latinizatsiia—orudie leninskoi natsional'noi politiki* (Moscow: Politizdat, 1932), 29.
35. Even though the name of the alphabet changed from the Unified New Turkic Alphabet to New Alphabet for All, I will keep using the acronym UNTA to refer to it.
36. Jing Tsu, "Romanization Without Rome: China's Latin New Script and Soviet Central Asia," in *Asia Inside Out: Connected Places*, ed. Eric Tagliocozzo, Helen F. Siu, and Peter C. Perdue (Cambridge, Mass.: Harvard University Press, 2015), 342–348; Svetlana Rimsky-Korsakoff Dyer, *Soviet Dungan Kolkhozes in the Kirghiz SSR and the Kazakh SSR* (Canberra: Faculty of Asian Studies, ANU, 1979); Svetlana

Rimsky-Korsakoff Dyer, "The Superstitions and Beliefs of the Early Chinese Muslims in Russian Central Asia," *Monumenta Serica* 48 (2000): 429–510.
37. B. A. Vasil'ev, "Dungane," *Kul'tura i pis'mennost' vostoka*, no. 7-8 (1931): 141–144.
38. *Stenograficheskii otchet tret'ego plenuma*, 82.
39. Zvi Ben-Dor Benite, *The Dao of Muhammad: A Cultural History of Muslims in Late Imperial China* (Cambridge, Mass.: Harvard University Press, 2005).
40. Jonathan N. Lipman, *Familial Strangers: A History of Muslims in Northwest China* (Seattle: University of Washington Press, 1997), 50–51.
41. O. I. Zavyalova, "Sino-Islamic Language Contacts Along the Great Silk Road: Chinese Texts Written in Arabic Script," *Hanxue yanjiu* 17, no. 1 (June 1988): 293.
42. I. I. Iusupov, *Sovietskie Dungane v period stroitel'stva sotsializma* (Frunze: Ilim, 1977), 149.
43. B. Chobanzade, "Itogi unifikatsii alfavitov tiurko-tatarskikh narodov," *Kul'tura i pis'mennost' vostoka*, no. 3 (1928): 24–26.
44. Svetlana Rimsky-Korsakoff Dyer, *Iasyr Shivaza: The Life and Works of a Soviet Dungan Poet* (Frankfurt: Peter Lang, 1991), 241.
45. Saime Göksu and Edward Timms, *Romantic Communist: The Life and Work of Nazım Hikmet* (London: Hurst, 1999).
46. Nergis Ertürk, *Grammatology and Literary Modernity in Turkey* (New York: Columbia University Press, 2011), 159–181.
47. Nazım Hikmet, *835 Satır* (Istanbul: İstanbul Milliyet Matbaası, 1929), 15–16. I tried to remain faithful to the typographical form of the poem, in which the lines "trrrrum, / trrrrum, / trrrrum, / trak tiki tak / I want to be / Mechanized!" were printed in a larger typeface. The translation is mine.
48. Donna Haraway, "A Cyborg Manifesto: Science, Technology, and Socialist-Feminism in the Late Twentieth Century," in *Simians, Cyborgs and Women: The Reinvention of Nature* (New York: Routledge, 1991), 149.
49. B. Arbatov, "Aleksei Gastev, 'Pachka Orderov,' Riga 1921 g.," *Lef* 1 (1923): 243–245; Fore, "The Operative Word in Soviet Factography."
50. On the development of Russian Futurism and the divide between the transrationalists and LEF, see Anna Lawton, *Russian Futurism Through Its Manifestoes, 1912–1928* (Ithaca, N.Y.: Cornell University Press, 1988).
51. Zafer Toprak, "Nazım Hikmet'in Putları Kırıyoruz Kampanyası ve Yeni Edebiyat," *Toplumsal Tarih* 261 (2015): 36.
52. Nazım Hikmet, *Jokond ile Si-Ya-U, Taranta Babu'ya Mektuplar, Benerci Kendini Niçin Öldürdü?* (Ankara: Dost Yayınları, 1965), 5–30. All translations are mine.
53. Katerina Clark refers to this very poem in coining the term "red cosmopolitanism." See Katerina Clark, "European and Russian Cultural Interactions with Turkey: 1910–1930s," *Comparative Studies of South Asia, Africa and the Middle East* 33, no. 2 (2013): 201–213. Nazım Hikmet wrote two more poems that spoke to his internationalist vision: "Why Did Banerjee Kill Himself?" ("Benerci Kendini Niçin Öldürdü?") and "Letters to Taranta Babu" ("Taranta Babu'ya Mektuplar").
54. Göksu and Timms, *Romantic Communist*.
55. "Tuerqi daibiao xi-ke-mei-te de fayan," *Yazhou ji taipingyang quyu heping huiyi gongbao* 5 (October 1952): 70–71.

56. [Nazım Hikmet], *Xikemeite shi xuan* (Beijing: Renmin wenxue chubanshe, 1952); Nazım Hikmet (Xikemeite), *Tuerqi de gushi*, trans. Wu Meng (Shanghai: Pingmin chubanshe, 1953); Nazım Hikmet (Xikemeite), *Aiqing de chuanshuo: Xiju shi*, trans. Chen Yansheng and Wu Chunqiu (Shanghai: Pingmin chubanshe, 1955); Nazım Hikmet (Xikemeite) and Anna Begicheva (Biejiqiewa), *Ta yongyuan huozhe*, trans. Lei Nan (Beijing: Zhongguo dianying chubanshe, 1957). In 1960, a selection of Turkish poetry was translated into Chinese, including the poems of Nazım Hikmet, Oktay Rifat, and Melih Cevdet Anday; see [Nazım Hikmet] Xikemeite, *Tuerqi shi xuan* (Shanghai: Shanghai wenyi chubanshe, 1960). Also, a selection of poems from socialist writers of the world was published in 1954, in which Nazım Hikmet's "Alioğlu Ahmet" (a poem written to an imagined Turkish soldier fighting on the American side against China in the Korean War) was printed as the first poem. Xikemeite, *Wushi duo fan honghua*, trans. Yuan Shuipai (Shanghai: Pingmin chubanshe, 1954).
57. Ertürk, "Toward a Literary Communism," 186–187.

6. The Chinese Latin Alphabet: A Revolutionary Script

1. Manuel Castells, *Communication Power* (Oxford: Oxford University Press, 2009), 430–431. Writing for the network society of the 1990s, Castells noted the following: "If power is exercised by programming and switching networks, counter power, the deliberate attempt to change power relationships, is enacted by reprogramming networks around alternative interests and values, and/or disrupting the dominant switches while switching networks of resistance and social change."
2. The latinization of Dunganese was run by Vasilii M. Alekseev at the Institute of Oriental Studies of the Academy of Sciences, aided by Lev Shcherba, Evgenii Polivanov, and Aleksandr Dragunov; and the latinization of Chinese started at the end of 1928 at the Institute for Scientific Research on China (Nauchno-issledovatel'skii institut po Kitaiu) under the Comintern.
3. Yurou Zhong, *Chinese Grammatology: Script Revolution and Literary Modernity, 1916–1958* (New York: Columbia University Press, 2019), 27–63, 81–88.
4. "Guoyu luomazi pinyin fashi—guoyin zimu di er shi," *Guoyu yuebao* 1 (1927): 1–2.
5. Zhong, *Chinese Grammatology*, 70.
6. I. Laikhter, "O latinizatsii kitaiskoi pis'mennosti," *Kul'tura i pis'mennost' vostoka* 9 (1931): 28–29.
7. Yuen Ren Chao, "Languages and Dialects in China," *Geographical Journal* 102, no. 2 (August 1943): 66.
8. Jing Tsu, "Romanization Without Rome: China's Latin New Script and Soviet Central Asia," in *Asia Inside Out: Connected Places*, ed. Eric Tagliocozzo, Helen F. Siu, and Peter C. Perdue (Cambridge, Mass.: Harvard University Press, 2015), 335–336.
9. [Qu Qiubai] Tsiui Tsiubo (Strakhov), *Kitaiskaia latinizirovannaia azbuka* (Moscow: KUTK, 1930), 31–33; [Qu Qiubai] Tsiui Vei-To, "Kitaiskaia latinizirovannaia azbuka," *Problemy Kitaia* 2 (1930), 136–139.
10. [Qu Qiubai] Tsiui Tsiubo, *Kitaiskaia latinizirovannaia azbuka*, 7–9.

6. THE CHINESE LATIN ALPHABET

11. [Qu Qiubai] Tsiui Tsiubo, *Kitaiskaia latinizirovannaia azbuka*, 11.
12. [Qu Qiubai] Tsiui Tsiubo, *Kitaiskaia latinizirovannaia azbuka*, 70.
13. Ni Haishu, *Ladinghua xin wenzi yundong biannian jishi* (Beijing: Zhongguo renmin daxue yuyan wenzi yanjiusuo, 1978), 1:25–26.
14. AH, Guomin zhengfu [National Government], Guoyu zhuyin fuhao tuixing faling an [The file on the laws and decrees promoting the National Language Phonetic Symbols], "Zhongzhihui jueyi gai zhuyin zimu mingcheng wei zhuyin fuhao ji tuixing banfa" [Central Executive Committee's resolution on changing the name of the National Phonetic Alphabet to Phonetic Symbols and methods to promote it] (April 1930), 2004010a.
15. AH, Guomin zhengfu, 2004010a.
16. AH, Guomin zhengfu, 2004011a-12a.
17. AH, Guomin zhengfu, 1922–1923.
18. Arkhivy Rossiiskoi Akademii Nauk (hereafter ARAN), f. 676, op. 1, d. 245, l. 57–59.
19. Sh Pingcing, *Latinxuadi zhungwen gungrhen duben (beifang koujin)*, ed. Emi Siao (Vladivostok: Guogia lienxo chubanhu juandung fenbu Chuban, 1931), in ARAN, f. 676, op. 1, d. 245, l. 27–38.
20. ARAN, f. 676, op. 1, d. 245, l. 57–58.
21. ARAN, f. 676, op. 1, d. 245, l. 48.
22. The particularity of China in implementing Leninist and Stalinist policies of language and nationality was addressed by one of the Russian latinists of Chinese, Shprintsin. See "G. Shprintsin, 'O t.n. kitaiskikh dialektakh i obshcheliteraturnom kitaiskom iazyke' " [On Chinese dialects and general literature in Chinese language], Arkhiv Vostokovedov Instituta Vostochnykh Rukopisei Rossiiskoi Akademii Nauk (hereafter AV IVR RAN), r. 1, op. 1, d. 267.
23. For the original Chinese, see ARAN, f. 676, op. 1, d. 245, l. 59; the Russian draft is on l. 48.
24. "Shprintsin, 'Kitaiskii iazyk v DV Krae,' " AV IVR RAN, r. 1, op. 1, d. 268, l. 2–3.
25. ARAN, f. 676, op. 1, d. 326, l. 30.
26. I have not been able to find Vasilii Sergeevich Pukhov's Chinese name. If the Palladian spelling is correct, the Pinyin for his name would be Huang Zhongzhe (Хуан Чжун-Чжэ). In May–June 1932, the preliminary list of books to be published in the Chinese Latin Alphabet included a political brochure in Cantonese and a short Cantonese dictionary, both of which were to be authored by Pukhov. Later, Pukhov's books were taken off the final list. ARAN, f. 676, op. 1, d. 310, l. 2–3 and 20–21.
27. One of those plans was made for 1933–1934, but it was never implemented. See ARAN, f. 676, op. 1, d. 328, l. 55.
28. Vladimir G. Datsyshen. "Kitaiskii iazyk i kul'turnaia revoliutsiia v Sovetskoi Rossii," in *Rossiia i Kitai: Istoricheskii opyt vzaimodeistviia i novye grani cotrudnichestva—Materialy nauch.-prakt. konf., Ekaterinburg, 25-26 noiabria 2008* (Ekaterinburg: Izd-vo Ural. Un-ta, 2009), 15–16; Vladimir G. Datsyshen, "Dvizhenie za latinizatsiiu kitaiskok pis'mennosti i razvitie kitaiskoi shkoly na sovetskom dal'nem vostoke," *Rossiia i ATR* 3 (2008): 160–169. The DVKNA was chaired by Wang Xiangbao (Liu Changsheng), who was aided by Xiao San, Wang Changxi, Li Tangbin, Lin Boqu, Wu Yuzhang, Zhang Chenggong, and Zhou Songyuan.

29. ARAN, f. 676, op. 1, d. 326, l. 86.
30. Letter from the Executive Secretary of VTsK NA Iumankulov to the Presidium of the Soviet of Nationalities of the Central Executive Committee of the USSR (July 21, 1932), ARAN, f. 676, op. 1, d. 327, l. 21.
31. Letter from the Secretary of the VTsK NA Iunusov to Gosplan SSSR (March 22, 1932), ARAN, f. 676, op. 1, d. 327, l. 2 and 7. DVKNA requested tons of typesets to be delivered to Khabarovsk, Vladivostok, Blagoshchevensk, Nikolsk, Posyet, Artom, Suchan, and Verkhneudinsk. ARAN, f. 676, op. 1, d. 326, l. 18.
32. ARAN, f. 676, op. 1, d. 286, l. 20.
33. In fact, the very first typewriter in the USSR, before Janalif, was also invented in Kazan in 1924 for the Arabic script then in use. After latinization, it was again the Tatar engineers who spearheaded typewriter production in Kazan, this time for latinized letters. The Tatars played a crucial, yet unrecognized, role in the history of early Soviet typewriters. ARAN, f. 676, op. 1, d. 147.
34. ARAN, f. 676, op. 1, d. 1314, l. 46–90. Idrisov et al. did not invent a keyboard for every nationality in the Soviet Union. In total, there were about twenty keyboards. See ARAN, f. 676, op. 1, d. 1055, l. 40.
35. ARAN, f. 676, op. 1, d. 520, l. 5–12.
36. ARAN, f. 676, op. 1, d. 813, l. 1.
37. ARAN, f. 676, op. 1, d. 1055, l. 13 and 28.
38. ARAN, f. 676, op. 1, d. 813, l. 1.
39. ARAN, f. 676, op. 1, d. 327, l. 45–53.
40. Terry Martin, *The Affirmative Action Empire: Nations and Nationalism in the Soviet Union, 1923-1939* (Ithaca, N.Y.: Cornell University Press, 2001), 204–207.
41. Martin, *The Affirmative Action Empire*, 202.
42. ARAN, f. 676, op. 1, d. 1050, l. 6–15.
43. ARAN, f. 676, op. 1., d. 874, l. 15. For the stenographic records of the conference, see ARAN, f. 676, op. 1, d. 810 and 811.
44. V. M. Alekseev, "Voprosy napisaniia i orfografii v kitaiskoi latinizirovannoi pis'mennosti" [Questions of writing and orthography in Chinese latinized script], ARAN, f. 676, op. 1, d. 1095, l. 3, 23, and 29.
45. ARAN, f. 656, op. 1, d. 810, l. 79.
46. ARAN, f. 967, op. 1, d. 989, l. 14.
47. ARAN, f. 967, op. 1, d. 990, l. 18–19.
48. ARAN, f. 967, op. 1, d. 990, l. 13.
49. Ni, *Ladinghua xin wenzi yundong biannian jishi*, 1:34–60.
50. Ni, *Ladinghua xin wenzi yundong biannian jishi*, 1:62–83.
51. "Xunlian zongjianbu guanyu chakou ladinghua keben shi zhi shanghai fazheng xueyuan de miling" [Secret order from the Military Training Inspection Bureau to the Shanghai Institute of Law and Politics on seizing the latinized primers], 1935.2.12, Shanghai Municipal Archives, Q248-1-385-135.
52. "Xunlian zongjianbu."
53. Ni, *Ladinghua xin wenzi yundong biannian jishi*, vol. 1.
54. "Women duiyu tuixing xin wenzi de yijian," *Zhongguo yuyan* 1 (1936): 19. I have built on DeFrancis's translation. See John DeFrancis, *Nationalism and Language Reform in China* (Princeton, N.J.: Princeton University Press, 1950), 118–119.

6. THE CHINESE LATIN ALPHABET

55. "Women duiyu tuixing xin wenzi de yijian," 19. The Chinese stenography project was also a part of the Chinese Latinization Movement in the Soviet Union, spearheaded by Shchutskii. AV IVR RAN, r. 1, op. 1, d. 264.
56. ARAN, f. 676, op. 1, d. 810, l. 50.
57. "Shanghai hua xin wenzi duwu," *Zhongguo yuyan* 1 (1936): 16.
58. "Z. S. V. N. jiji gongzuo," *Zhongguo yuyan* 4 (1936): 22.
59. "Minnan xin wenzi xiehui chengli: Caiqu yizhi de bufa, maibu qianjin!," *Zhongguo yuyan* 4 (1936): 23; "Xinshu liuben jiang zai benyue zhong chuban: Xin wenzi shudian ba yue fen jihua," *Zhongguo yuyan* 4 (1936): 22–23; Ni, *Ladinghua xin wenzi yundong biannian jishi*, 1:84.
60. For a brief discussion of the technical problems in printing, see Li Jinxi, *Guoyu xin wenzi lun* ([unidentified publisher], 1949), 22.
61. GMD Party History Archives, "Qudi zuoqing fenzi suo tichang lading xin wenzi yundong zhi shukan" [Prohibiting the publications of the latinization movement that is promoted by left-leaning intellectuals], huiyi jilu, hui5.3/10.23 (1936/4/7). The final order to ban all publications in Sin Wenz came in 1936, although the exact date is not clear.
62. Shanghai Municipal Archives, Q6-18-368 (1937).
63. DeFrancis, *Nationalism and Language Reform in China*, 120–129.
64. Chen Heqin, "Xin wenzi yu nanmin jiaoyu" and "Minzhong keben," in *Chen Heqin quanji*, vol. 6, ed. Beijingshi jiaoyu kexue yanjiusuo (Nanjing: Jiangsu jiaoyu chubanshe, 1991), 174–179, 187–212. Chen also latinized Lou Shiyi's Chinese translation of "A Dog of Flanders" by Marie Louis de la Ramée. See Chen, "Kyngr kugou," in *Chen Heqin quanji*, 6:213–230.
65. DeFrancis, *Nationalism and Language Reform in China*, 130.
66. Akademiia Nauk SSSR Institut Iazykovaniia, *Voprosy sovershenstvovaniia alfavitov tiurkshikh iazykov SSSR* (Moscow: Izdatel'stvo Nauka, 1972), 40 and 155.
67. F. D. Ashnin, V. M. Allatov, and D. M. Nasilov, *Repressirovannaia Tiurkologiia* (Moscow: Izdatel'skaia firma "Vostochnaia Literatura" RAN, 2002).
68. Eva Siao, *Women yijian zhongqing—wo yu Xiao San*, trans. Zhu Yandong (Beijing: Zhongguo qingnian chubanshe, 2011), 59–65.
69. Ni Haishu, *Zhongguo pinyin wenzi yundong shi [jianbian]* (Shanghai: Shidai shubao chubanshe, 1948), 165–166.
70. Rebecca Karl, *Mao Zedong and China in the Twentieth-Century World: A Concise History* (Durham, N.C.: Duke University Press, 2010), 62–63.
71. ARAN, f. 656, op. 1, d. 810, l. 78–81.
72. ARAN, f. 656, op. 1, d. 810, l. 81 (emphasis mine).

7. The Empire of Pinyin

1. Zhang Pengyuan and Shen Huaiyu, eds., *Guomin zhengfu zhiguan nianbiao (1925-1949), di yi ce* (Taibei: Academia Sinica, 1987), 186–194.
2. Other members included linguists, folklorists, and literary figures such as Yuen Ren Chao, Wang Yi, Xiao Jialin, Gu Jiegang, Fu Sinian, Hu Shi, Xu Dishan, and the

7. THE EMPIRE OF PINYIN

psychologists Chen Heqin and Liao Shicheng. See Wang Ju, *Guoyu yundong de lilun yu shiji* (Taipei: Guoyu ribao she, 1941), 103–105.
3. One wonders whether the birth of Confucian institutes can be traced back to this wartime era.
4. Ma Fuxiang, "Zhunhan song mengzang gedi tuixing zhuyin fuhao banfa," *Mengzang weiyuanhui gongbao* 13 (1931): 139.
5. The Qing Empire's Lifanyuan was reorganized as the Mongolian and Tibetan Affairs Department (Mengzang shiwu chu 蒙藏事务处) under the Beiyang government in 1913. For more information, see Liping Wang, "Ethnicizing the Frontier: Imperial Transformation and Ethnic Confrontations in China–Inner Mongolia, 1890s–1930s" (PhD diss., University of Chicago, 2013).
6. Fang-Kuei Li, *Linguistics East and West: American Indian, Sino-Tibetan, and Thai*, interviews conducted by Ning-Ping Chan and Randy LaPolla (Berkeley: University of California, 1988), 43.
7. Academia Sinica Institute of History and Philology Archives (Lishi yuyan yanjiusuo cangpin [LYSCP]), *Yuan* 元 122-2: Luo Changpei to Fu Mengzhen, November 6, 1928.
8. Yuen Ren Chao, *Linguistic Essays by Yuenren Chao* (Beijing: Commercial Press, 2006), 975; Yang Shifeng, "Yuyan diaocha yu yuyin shiyan," in *Fu suozhang jinian tekan* (Taipei: Academia Sinica Institute of History and Philology, 1951), 27–28.
9. Luo Changpei, "Yuyanxue zai yunnan," in *Yuyan yu wenhua* (Beijing: Beijing chubanshe, 2004), 200–220.
10. Fu Sinian, "Zhi Gu Jiegang (1939)," in *Fu Sinian Quanji*, vol. 7, ed. Ouyang Zhesheng (Changsha: Hunan jiaoyu chubanshe, 2003), 205.
11. The other signatories were Wang Chonghui 王寵惠, Zhang Daofan 張道藩, Liu Wendao 劉文島, Li Wenfan 李文範, Wang Zizhuang 王子壯, and Cheng Tianfang 程天放. AH 014000000267A, Xingzhengyuan: "Zhongguo Guomindang wujie bazhong quanhui huiyi an (5)" [The file on the GMD's Fifth Year Eighth Plenary Session Meeting], 014-000400-0036-012.
12. Second Historical Archives, Jiaoyu bu, 5-12295(3), 10/1941–11/1948. Not all of the commission members were in China at the time. Yuen Ren Chao and Lin Yutang were in the United States.
13. Second Historical Archives, Jiaoyu bu, 5-12295(3), 10/1941–11/1948. Since the capital moved to Chongqing in 1939, the Military Affairs Commission had already been working on publishing materials with Phonetic Symbols, some of which were printed *only* with Phonetic Symbols *without* Chinese characters. See GMD Archives, "Zhuyin fuhao congshu (kangzhan gushi)" [Phonetic Symbols Series (Stories from the war against Japan)], *Yiban dang'an, yiban* 537/46. A particular book in this collection printed solely in Phonetic Symbols is *Kangzhan liangnian shouhuo (zhuyin fuhao congshu di sishi zhong)* [What we gained in two years during the war against Japan (Phonetic Symbols Series, no. 40)], published by Junshi weiyuanhui houfang qinwubu zhenzhibu bianyin. Also see Yu Jin'en, *Minguo zhuyin zimu zhengce shilun* (Beijing: Zhonghua shuju, 2007), 261.
14. AH, 014000000267A, Xingzhengyuan, "Zhongguo Guomindang," 014-000400-0036-015 to 020, and 025. The same year, under the leadership of Chen Lifu, a new commission was formed: Central Phonetic Literacy Movement Commission

7. THE EMPIRE OF PINYIN

(Zhongyang tuixing zhuyin shizi yundong weiyuanhui), whose duty was to prepare and carry out the plan for expanding phonetic literacy (*zhuyin shizi*). As opposed to the National Language Commission or the Cultural Movement Commission, which were under the administration of the Ministry of Education and the Central Propaganda Bureau, respectively, the new commission was formed through the participation of different bureaus: Central Propaganda Bureau, Central Overseas Bureau, Central Training Commission, Three Peoples Principles Youth Corps, Military Affairs Commission Political Bureau, Mongolian and Tibetan Affairs Commission, Overseas Chinese Commission, Ministry of Social Affairs, and Ministry of Education.

15. Second Historical Archives, Jiaoyu bu, 5-12300 (4). The list of the places mentioned in the chart is as follows: Suzhou, Songjiang, Changsha, Nantong, Xian, Xiamen, Guangzhou, Tengzhou, Taishan, Taixing, Beiping, Tianjin, Fuzhou, Nanjing, Chongqing, Nanzheng, Lhasa, Xianyang, Liling, Chengdu, Baoding, Hechuan, Linzi, Hakka, Ningbo, Wuchang, Yuyao, Changshu, Huangling, Guihua, Hefei, Wujiang, Changzhou, and Wenzhou.
16. Second Historical Archives, Jiaoyu bu, 5-134 (3/1941–5/1946).
17. Second Historical Archives, Jiaoyu bu, 5-12289 (12/1943–8/1948), 5–7.
18. Second Historical Archives, Jiaoyu bu, 5-134 (3/1941–5/1946), 114.
19. Hsiao-Ting Lin, *Modern China's Ethnic Frontiers: A Journey to the West* (New York: Routledge, 2011), 54–72.
20. Xu Xihua, *Zhuyin xinjiang huiwen changyong zibiao* (Kunming: Zhengzhong shuju, 1938), 10.
21. Li Jinxi, "Kaifa bianjiang de di yi jian shi," *Meng-zang yuebao* 13, no. 10 (1941): 10.
22. "Bianjiang zizhi yu wenhua: benkan bianjiang wenti zuotan hui jilu," *Bianzheng gonglun* 6, no. 2 (1947): 5–6. Despite the lack of Phonetic Symbols textbooks, Mandarin education continued in the frontiers. Fu Sinian's assimilationist doctrine was de facto carried out.
23. Li Jinxi, "Guoyu bianyu duizhao 'sihang keben' jianyi," *Wenyi yu shenghuo* 4, no. 1 (1947): 3. An even more isolated example was the Miao Phonetic Symbols, which was invented by an Australian missionary, Maurice Hutton, in the 1920s, but there is no evidence that suggests that Hutton's scheme was used by the government. See Wang Guisheng, "Qiandongnan lao miaowen de lishi ji xianzhuang de diaocha he yanjiu," *Kaili xueyuan xuebao* 28, no. 5 (October 2010): 53–59. For all the non-Han linguistic communities concerned, the biggest problem was the Chinese characters themselves, even though only a few Chinese intellectuals and government officials acknowledged the elephant in the room. Chen Guangyao, the famous name in the character simplification project discussed in chapter 4, was one of the few who recognized the difficulty posed by characters, and still defended their simplification in order to educate the frontier populations. Chen's proposal fell on deaf ears, however, for simplification was already off the GMD's agenda. See Chen Guangyao, "Jianshe xibei bi xian tongyi yuwen," *Sanmin zhuyi banyuekan* 2, no. 10 (1943): 16–17.
24. Xinjiang occupied a special place. According to the statistics from 1946, Xinjiang had the highest number of primary schools (2,850 in total) among all the

frontier provinces. The next was Guangxi with 752 primary schools, then Guizhou with 692. Then the numbers fell down to 162 in Taiwan, 141 in Gansu, and even fewer in other provinces. See Zhu Jiahua, *Bianjiang jiaoyu gaikuang* (Jiaoyu bu bianjiang jiaoyu si, 1947), 117, 130.

25. Ni Haishu, *Ladinghua xin wenzi yundong biannian jishi* (Beijing: Zhongguo renmin daxue yuyan wenzi yanjiusuo, 1979), 2:274–288.
26. Ni, *Ladinghua xin wenzi yundong biannian jishi*, 2:296.
27. Ni Haishu, *Shanghai yin pinyin shizi keben—shongxein pinyin seqsh ku ben* (Shanghai: Dongfang shudian chubanshe, 1952).
28. Ni, *Ladinghua xin wenzi yundong biannian jishi*, 2:396.
29. Luo Changpei, "Zhongguo yuyanxue de xin fangxiang," *Xin jianshe* 1, no. 12 (1950), quoted in Ni, *Ladinghua xin wenzi yundong biannian jishi*, 2:286–287.
30. Ni, *Ladinghua xin wenzi yundong biannian jishi*, 2:372.
31. "Zhongguo wenzi gaige weiyuanhui chengli," *Zhongguo yuwen* 31 (January 1955): 38.
32. (Nie) Gannu, "Zhongguo xin wenzi ne? Guoyu luomazi ne?," *Zhongguo yuyan* 1 (1936): 4.
33. (Nie) Gannu, "Zhongguo xin wenzi ne?," 4.
34. Wu Yuzhang, "Wu Yuzhang wei wusi jinian ladinghua xin wenzi yundong," *Guangming ribao*, May 4, 1950, quoted in Ni, *Ladinghua xin wenzi yundong biannian jishi*, 2:299–300.
35. Zhou Youguang, *Zhou Youguang baisui koushu*, transcr. Li Huaiyu (Guilin: Guangxi shifan daxue chubanshe, 2008), 111.
36. Zhou Youguang, *Zhou Youguang bainian koushu: Wo suo duguo de shiguang* (Hong Kong: Chinese University of Hong Kong, 2015), 297–303.
37. Interview with Zhou Youguang, July 4, 2015.
38. Zhou Youguang, "Ladinghua yundong de renwu he fangxiang," *Xin wenzi zhoukan* 3 (June 1950), quoted in Ni, *Ladinghua xin wenzi yundong biannian jishi*, 2:320.
39. Zhou Youguang, *Zhou Youguang bainian koushu*, 306–308.
40. *Jiaotong bu guiding guoyin dianbao huibian (fu guoyin dianbao fashi)* (May 1928).
41. Zhou Youguang, *Dianbao pinyinhua* (Beijing: Wenzi gaige chubanshe, 1965).
42. Zhou Youguang, *Zhou Youguang bainian koushu*, 309–311; Zhou Youguang, *Hanzi gaige gailun* (Beijing: Wenzi gaige chubanshe, 1961), 133–141.
43. Zhou Youguang, "Hanzi gaige gailun [1961]," in Zhou Youguang, *Zhou Youguang wenji* (Beijing: Zhongyang bianyi chubanshe, 2013), 1:255–256.
44. Luo, "Yuyanxue zai yunnan," 200–220.
45. Minglang Zhou, *Multilingualism in China: The Politics of Writing Reforms for Minority Languages, 1949-2002* (Berlin: Mouton de Gruyter, 2003), 158–159.
46. Rodney Koeneke, *Empires of the Mind: I. A. Richards and Basic English in China, 1929-1979* (Stanford, Calif.: Stanford University Press, 2004), 187. Pinyinization was concomitant with the resettlement of Han immigrants into the frontiers. See James Millward and Nabijan Tursun, "Political History and Strategies of Control," in *Xinjiang: China's Muslim Borderland*, ed. S. Frederick Starr (Armonk, N.Y.: M. E. Sharpe, 2004), 90; Gregory Rohlf, *Building New China, Colonizing Kokonor: Resettlement to Qinghai in the 1950s* (Lanham, Md.: Lexington Books, 2016), 69–100.

47. Benno Weiner, *The Chinese Revolution on the Tibetan Frontier* (Ithaca, N.Y.: Cornell University Press, 2020).
48. *Shaoshu minzu jiaoyu gongzuo wenjian xuanbian, 1949-1988* (Hohhot: Inner Mongolian Education Press, 1991), 28–39, quoted in Minglang Zhou, *Multilingualism in China*, 48.
49. Roderick MacFarquhar, *The Origins of the Cultural Revolution*, vol. 1, *Contradictions Among the People, 1956-1957* (New York: Columbia University Press, 1974), 48–51.
50. E. R. Tenishev, *U Tiurkskikh Narodov Kitaia (Dnevniki 1956-1958 gg.)* (Moscow: Nasledie, 1995), 5–18.
51. Todaeva was involved in these reform projects, but the extent of her involvement is unclear. See [Buliash K.] Tuodayewa, *Youguan zhongguo menggu yuzu yuyan he fangyande yanjiu wenti* (Minzu yuwen kexue taolunhui yin, December 1955, [Beijing?]).
52. *Menggu yuzu yuyan kexue taolunhui jueyi* (Menggu yuzu yuyan kexue taolun mishuchu yin, May 29, 1956), 1–3.
53. Minglang Zhou, *Multilingualism in China*, 290–299.
54. Minglang Zhou, *Multilingualism in China*, 46.
55. *Di er ci shaoshu minzu yuwen kexue taolunhui, dazibao huiji, di er ji, 3/30* (Di er ci shaoshu minzu yuwen kexue taolunhui jianbaozu yinfa, 1958), 10.
56. Minglang Zhou, *Multilingualism in China*, 58–59.
57. Zhou Youguang, "Hanzi gaige gailun [1961]," 257–261.
58. Fu Maoji, "Sulian minzu yuwen fazhande qingkuang he jiejue minzu wenzi wentide jingyan," in *Fu Maoji xiansheng minzu yuwen lunji* (Beijing: Zhongguo shehui kexue chubanshe, 1995), 237–256. The article was originally published in *Kexue tongbao* 11 (1958).
59. *Di er ci shaoshu minzu yuwen kexue taolunhui, dazibao huiji, di san ji, 3/31* (Di er ci shaoshu minzu yuwen kexue taolunhui jianbaozu yinfa, 1958), 1.
60. *Di er ci shaoshu minzu yuwen kexue taolunhui, dazibao huiji, di san ji, 3/31*, 10–11.
61. *Xinci shuyu cidian, hanyu gaoben, di yi ji* (Beijing: Zhongguo kexueyuan shaoshu minzu yuyan yanjiu suo, 1959).
62. Minglang Zhou, *Multilingualism in China*, 350–354.
63. *Di er ci shaoshu minzu yuwen kexue taolunhui, dazibao huiji, di er ji, 3/30*, 11.
64. *Zhongguo shaoshu minzu yuyan wenzi qingkuang jianbiao (neibu cankao)* (Zhonghua renmin gongheguo minzu shiwu weiyuanhui wenjiaosi bianzhi, February 1958); David Bradley, "Language Policy for China's Minorities: Orthography Development for the Yi," *Written Language and Literacy* 12, no. 2 (2009): 179.
65. Minglang Zhou, *Multilingualism in China*, 351; Caodaobateer, "The Use and Development of Mongol and Its Writing Systems in China," in *Language Policy in the People's Republic of China*, ed. Minglang Zhou and Hongkai Sun (Boston: Kluwer Academic Publishers, 2004), 297.
66. Minglang Zhou, *Multilingualism in China*, 116–119.
67. "Guowuyuan guanyu tuixing weiwuer, hasake liangge xin wenzi fangan wenti de pifu," *Wenzi gaige* 1 (1965): 1; Minglang Zhou, *Multilingualism in China*, 299–308.
68. Weng Shiwei, "Woguo shouchuangde weiwen dianbao," *Zhongguo minzu* (March 1986): 38–39; Ji Gendao'er, "Mengguwen biaozhun dianma," *Nei menggu minzu shiyuan xuebao (shehui kexue hanwen ban)* (July 1980): 55–60.

69. Interview with Su Peicheng, May 18, 2015.
70. Zhou Youguang, *Zhou Youguang bainian koushu*, 378–379, 422.
71. Eva Siao, *Women yijian zhongqing—wo yu Xiao San*, trans. Zhu Yandong (Beijing: Zhongguo qingnian chubanshe, 2011), 293–306.

Epilogue: A New Age of Codes

1. Shouhui Zhao and Richard B. Baldauf have meticulously pieced together the scattered information about this decision and the politicized environment that led to it. Shouhui Zhao and Richard B. Baldauf, *Planning Chinese Characters: Reaction, Evolution or Revolution?* (Dordrecht: Springer, 2008), 56–69.
2. Xiao Liu, *Information Fantasies: Precarious Mediation in Postsocialist China* (Minneapolis: University of Minnesota Press, 2019).
3. Jing Tsu, *The Kingdom of Characters* (New York: Riverhead Books, 2022), 211–248.
4. Feng Zhiwei, *Xiandai hanzi he jisuanji* (Beijing: Beijing daxue chubanshe, 1989), 43.
5. Yu Daoquan, "Zangwen shuma daizi," *Minzu yuwen* (1982): 1–7; Zhang Liansheng, "Zangwen haoma daizi jiqi jisuanji paisuo," *Yuyan yanjiu* 2 (1983): 35–40.
6. Ji Gendao'er, "Mengguwen biaozhun dianma," *Nei menggu minzu shiyuan xuebao (shehui kexue hanwen ban)* (July 1980): 55–60; Ga Ridi and Zhu Zhang, "Mengwen xinxi chuli yanjiu yu sheji," *Jisuanji yanjiu yu fazhan* 23, no. 12 (1986): 39–44; Qi Dehua, "Mengwen duyin shuru fangfa," *Nei menggu daxue xuebao (zhexue shehui kexueban)* 3 (1992): 104–110.
7. Weng Shiwei, "Woguo shouchuangde weiwen dianbao," *Zhongguo minzu* (March 1986): 38–39; Wu-shou-er Si-la-mu, "Dui weiwen xinxi chuli yong sanxiang biaozhunde tantao," *Zhongwen xinxi xuebao* 1, no. 4 (1988): 61–66.
8. Sha-ma-la-yi, "Jisuanji yiwen xinxi chuli yanjiu," *Xinan minzu xueyuan xuebao (zhexue shehui kexueban)* 21 (August 2000): 42–46.
9. Susan Greenhalgh, *Just One Child: Science and Policy in Deng's China* (Berkeley: University of California Press, 2008).
10. Yang Xiaofeng, "1986–2001 nian guojia 863 jihua chengguo tongji yu fenxi," *Xiandai qingbao* 5 (May 2007): 37–40.

Bibliography

Archives

Academia Historica (Guoshiguan 國史館). Taipei.
Academia Sinica, Institute of History and Philology Archives (Lishi yuyan yanjiusuo cangpin 歷史語言研究所藏品). Taipei.
Archive of the Institute of Oriental Manuscripts of the Russian Academy of Sciences (Arkhiv vostokovedov Instituta vostochnykh rukopisei Rossiiskoi Akademii Nauk [AV IVR RAN]). St. Petersburg.
Archives of the Russian Academy of Sciences (Arkhivy Rossiiskoi Akademii Nauk [ARAN]). Moscow.
Burke Library, Columbia University, Union Theological Seminary, Missionary Research. New York.
First Historical Archives of China (Zhongguo di yi lishi dang'anguan 中國第一歷史檔案館). Beijing.
GMD Party History Archives (Guomindang Dangshiguan 國民黨黨史館). Taipei.
Second Historical Archives of China (Zhongguo di er lishi dang'anguan 中國第二歷史檔案館). Nanjing.
Shanghai Municipal Archives (Shanghai shi dang'anguan 上海市檔案館). Shanghai.

Published Sources

1913 nian duyin tongyi hui ziliao huibian [Collection of sources on the unification of pronunciation conference in 1913]. In *Pinyin wenzi shiliao congshu* [Collection of historical materials on phonetic scripts]. Vol. 5, edited by Wenzi gaige chubanshe. Beijing: Guojia tushuguan chubanshe, 2015.

BIBLIOGRAPHY

Adal, Raja. *Beauty in the Age of Empire: Japan, Egypt, and the Global History of Aesthetic Education.* New York: Columbia University Press, 2019.

Agamalyogly, S. *Neotlozhnye kul'turnye nuzhdy tiurko-tatarskikh narodov* [Urgent cultural needs of the Turco-Tatar people]. Baku: Izdanie Komiteta Novogo Tiurkskogo Alfavita, 1925.

Agamalyogly, S. *V zashchitu novogo tiurkskogo* alfavita [In defense of the New Turkic Alphabet]. Baku: AZGIZ, 1927.

Agazade, F. *Istoriia vozniknoveniia novogo tiurkskogo alfavita v ASSR, s 1922 po 1925 god* [A history of the development of the New Turkic Alphabet in ASSR, from 1922 to 1925]. Baku: Komiteta po provedeniiu novogo tiurkskogo alfavita, 1926.

Agazade, F., and K. Karakashly. *Ocherk po istorii razvitiia dvizheniia novogo alfavita i ego dostizheniia* [A study on the history of the development of the new alphabet movement and its achievements]. Kazan: VTsK NTA, 1928.

Ai Wei. "Hanzi zhi xinli yanjiu (wei wan)" [A psychological study of Chinese characters (to be continued)]. *Jiaoyu zazhi* 20, no. 4 (1928): 1–21.

Ai Wei. "Hanzi zhi xinli yanjiu (xu)" [A psychological study of Chinese characters (continued)]. *Jiaoyu zazhi* 20, no. 5 (1928): 1–27.

Akademiia Nauk SSSR Institut Iazykovaniia. *Voprosy sovershenstvovaniia alfavitov tiurkshikh iazykov SSSR* [Questions regarding the improvement of the alphabets of Turkic languages of the USSR]. Moscow: Izdatel'stvo Nauka, 1972.

Anderson, Benedict. *Imagined Communities: Reflections on the Origin and Spread of Nationalism.* New York: Verso, 1984.

Andrews, Bridie. "An Introduction to the Yilin Gaicuo." In Wang Qingren, *Correcting the Errors in the Forest of Medicine*, translated by Yuhsing Chung, Herman Oving, and Simon Becker, v–xiv. Boulder, Colo.: Blue Poppy Press, 2007.

Andrews, Bridie. "Tuberculosis and the Assimilation of Germ Theory in China, 1895–1937." *Journal of the History of Medicine* 52 (1997): 114–157.

Ao Hongde. "Yutiwen yingyong zihui yanjiu baogao—Chen Heqin shi yutiwen yingyong zihui zhi xu" [A research report on the applied vocabulary of *yutiwen*—continuing Mr. Chen Heqin's applied vocabulary of *yutiwen*]. *Jiaoyu zazhi* 21, no. 2 (1929): 77–101.

Ao Hongde. "Yutiwen yingyong zihui yanjiu baogao (xu)—Chen Heqin shi yutiwen yingyong zihui zhi xu" [A research report on the applied vocabulary of *yutiwen* (continued)—continuing Mr. Chen Heqin's applied vocabulary of *yutiwen*]. *Jiaoyu zazhi* 21, no. 3 (1929): 97–113.

Arbatov, B. "Aleksei Gastev, 'Pachka Orderov,' Riga 1921 g." [Aleksei Gastev, Stack of orders, Riga 1921]. *Lef* 1 (1923): 243–245.

Asen, Daniel. "'Manchu Anatomy': Anatomical Knowledge and the Jesuits in Seventeenth- and Eighteenth-Century China." *Social History of Medicine* 22, no. 1 (2009): 23–44.

Ashnin, F. D., V. M. Allatov, and D. M. Nasilov. *Repressirovannaia Tiurkologiia* [Turcology Repressed]. Moscow: Izdatel'skaia firma "Vostochnaia Literatura" RAN, 2002.

"Attacking Illiteracy with the National Phonetic System." *China Sunday School Journal* 7, no. 12 (1918): 1099–1101.

Ayres, Leonard P. *A Measuring Scale for Ability in Spelling.* New York: New York: Russell Sage Foundation, Division of Education, 1915.

Ayres, Leonard P. *A Scale for Measuring the Quality of Handwriting of School Children.* New York: Russell Sage Foundation, Department of Child Hygiene, 1912.
Ayers, William. *Chang Chih-tung and Educational Reform in China.* Cambridge, Mass.: Harvard University Press, 1971.
Baark, Erik. *Lightning Wires: The Telegraph and China's Technological Modernization, 1860–1890.* Westport, Conn.: Greenwood Press, 1997.
Bai Shouyi, ed. *Huimin qiyi* [The Muslim uprising]. Vol. 3. Shanghai: Shenzhou guoguang she, 1953.
Bailes, Kendall E. "Alexei Gastev and the Soviet Controversy Over Taylorism, 1918–1924." *Soviet Studies* 29, no. 3 (July 1977): 373–394.
Baller, Frederick W. *Mandarin Primer.* Shanghai: China Inland Mission and American Presbyterian Mission Press, 1894.
Bateman, Frederic. *On Aphasia, or Loss of Speech, and the Localization of the Faculty of Articulate Language.* 2nd ed. London: J. & A. Churchill, 1890.
Bateson, Gregory. *Steps to an Ecology of Mind: A Revolutionary Approach to Man's Understanding of Himself.* San Francisco: Chandler, 1972.
Beauchamp, Ken. *History of Telegraphy.* London: Institution of Electrical Engineers, 2001.
Beissinger, Mark R. *Scientific Management, Socialist Discipline, and Soviet Power.* Cambridge, Mass.: Harvard University Press, 1988.
Beniger, James. *Control Revolution: Technological and Economic Origins of the Information Society.* Cambridge, Mass.: Harvard University Press, 1986.
Benite, Zvi Ben-Dor. *The Dao of Muhammad: A Cultural History of Muslims in Late Imperial China.* Cambridge, Mass.: Harvard University Press, 2005.
Benjamin, Ruha. *Race After Technology: Abolitionist Tools for the New Jim Code.* Medford, Mass.: Polity, 2019.
Benjamin, Walter. *Illuminations.* Translated by Harry Zohn. New York: Harcourt, Brace, and World, 1968.
Benton, Gregor. *Chinese Migrants and Internationalism: Forgotten Histories, 1917–1945.* London: Routledge, 2007.
"Bianjiang zizhi yu wenhua: Benkan bianjiang wenti zuotan hui jilu" [Frontier self-rule and culture: Records of this journal's discussion on frontier issues]. *Bianzheng gonglun* 6, no. 2 (1947): 5–6.
Binet, Alfred. "Note relative à l'influence du travail intellectuel sur la consommation du pain dans les écoles" [A note on the influence of intellectual work on the consumption of bread in schools]. *L'année psychologique* 5 (1898): 332–336.
Binet, Alfred, and N. Vaschide. "Influence du travail intellectuel, des émotions et du travail physique sur la pression du sang" [Influence of intellectual work, emotions, and physical work on blood pressure]. *L'année Psychologique* 3 (1896): 127–183.
Blair, Ann. *Too Much to Know: Managing Scholarly Information Before the Modern Age.* New Haven, Conn.: Yale University Press, 2010.
Blair, Ann, Paul Duguid, Anja-Silvia Goeing, and Anthony Grafton, eds. *Information: A Historical Companion.* Princeton, N.J.: Princeton University Press, 2021.
Bowers, Brian. *Sir Charles Wheatstone FRS: 1802–1875.* Stevenage: Institution of Electrical Engineers in Association with the Science Museum, 2001.

Bradley, David. "Language Policy for China's Minorities: Orthography Development for the Yi." *Written Language and Literacy* 12, no. 2 (2009): 170–187.
Breen, William J. "Foundations, Statistics, and State-Building: Leonard P. Ayres, the Russell Sage Foundation, and U.S. Government Statistics in the First World War." *Business History Review* 68, no. 4 (Winter 1994): 451–482.
Broomhall, Marshall. *The Chinese Empire: A General and Missionary Survey*. London: Morgan and Scott, China Inland Mission, 1907.
Burns, Russel W. *Communications: An International History of the Formative Years*. Stevenage: Institution of Electrical Engineers, 2004.
Cai Xiyong. *Chuanyin kuaizi* [Transmission of sounds and rapid writing]. Hubei: Guanshu ju, 1905.
Cai Xiyong and Cai Zhang. *Zhongguo suji xue* [Chinese stenography]. [Beijing]: Suji chuanxi suo, 1913.
Caodaobateer. "The Use and Development of Mongol and Its Writing Systems in China." In *Language Policy in the People's Republic of China*, edited by Minglang Zhou and Hongkai Sun. Boston: Kluwer Academic Publishers, 2004.
Carson, John. *The Measure of Merit: Talents, Intelligence, and Inequality in the French and American Republics, 1750–1940*. Princeton, N.J.: Princeton University Press, 2007.
Castells, Manuel. *Communication Power*. Oxford: Oxford University Press, 2009.
Castells, Manuel. *Information Age: Economy, Society, and Culture*. Vol. 1. Malden, Mass.: Blackwell, 1996.
Cattell, James McKeen. "A Statistical Study of Eminent Men." *Popular Science Monthly* 62 (1903): 359–377.
Chandler, Alfred D., Jr. "The Information Age in Historical Perspective: Introduction." In *A Nation Transformed by Information: How Information Has Shaped the United States from Colonial Times to the Present*, edited by Alfred D. Chandler Jr. and James W. Cortada, 3–38. Oxford: Oxford University Press, 2000.
Chang, Yao-Chiang (Zhang Yaoxiang). "Factor Affecting the Speed and Clearness of Reading Chinese." Master's thesis, Columbia University, 1919.
Chao, Yuen Ren. "Languages and Dialects in China." *Geographical Journal* 102, no. 2 (August 1943): 63–66.
Chao, Yuen Ren. *Linguistic Essays by Yuenren Chao*. Beijing: Commercial Press, 2006.
Chao, Yuen Ren. *Mandarin Primer: An Intensive Course in Spoken Chinese*. Cambridge, Mass.: Harvard University Press, 1964 [1948].
Chen Guangyao. "Jianshe xibei bi xian tongyi yuwen" [In order to build the northwest, we must first unite language and writing]. *Sanmin zhuyi banyuekan* 2, no. 10 (1943): 16–17.
Chen Guangyao. "Jianxie zongli yizhu jie" [An explanation for writing the President's Will in simplified characters]. In Lin Yutang, "Wode hua—tichang suzi" [My word—promote suzi], *Lun yu* 29 (November 1933): 215–217.
Chen Guangyao. *Jianzi lunji* [Collection of essays on simplified characters]. Shanghai: Commercial Press, 1931.
Chen Heqin. "Kyngr kugou" [The poor boy and the suffering dog]. In *Chen Heqin quanji*, vol. 6, edited by Beijingshi jiaoyu kexue yanjiusuo, 213–230. Nanjing: Jiangsu jiaoyu chubanshe, 1991.

BIBLIOGRAPHY

Chen Heqin. "Minzhong keben" [Textbook for the common people]. In *Chen Heqin quanji*, vol. 6, edited by Beijingshi jiaoyu kexue yanjiusuo, 187–212. Nanjing: Jiangsu jiaoyu chubanshe, 1991.

Chen Heqin. "Xin wenzi yu nanmin jiaoyu" [Sin Wenz and refugee education]. In *Chen Heqin quanji*, vol. 6, edited by Beijingshi jiaoyu kexue yanjiusuo, 174–179. Nanjing: Jiangsu jiaoyu chubanshe, 1991.

Chen Heqin. "Yutiwen yingyong zihui" [Applied vocabulary of *yutiwen*]. In *Chen Heqin quanji*, vol. 6, edited by Beijingshi jiaoyu kexue yanjiusuo. Nanjing: Jiangsu jiaoyu chubanshe, 1987.

Chen Heqin and Liao Shicheng. *Zhili ceyan fa* [The method for intelligence testing]. Shanghai: Commercial Press, 1921.

Chen, Jack, Anatoly Detwyler, Xiao Liu, Christopher M. B. Nugent, and Bruce Rusk, eds. *Literary Information in China: A History*. New York: Columbia University Press, 2021.

Chen, Li Kiang, and H. A. Carr. "The Ability of Chinese Students to Read in Vertical and Horizontal Directions." *Experimental Psychology* 9 (1926): 110–117.

Chen, Ping. *Modern Chinese: History and Sociolinguistics*. Cambridge: Cambridge University Press, 1999.

Chobanzade, B. "Itogi unifikatsii alfavitov tiurko-tatarskikh narodov" [The results of the unification of the alphabets of Turco-Tatar peoples]. *Kul'tura i pis'mennost' vostoka*, no. 3 (1928): 18–34.

Chou, Siegen K. (Zhou Xiangeng). "'Gestalt' in Reading Chinese Characters." *Psychological Review* 37, no. 1 (January 1930): 54–70.

Chu Chia-hua (Zhu Jiahua). *China's Postal and Other Communications Services*. London: Kegan Paul, Trench, Trubner, 1937.

Chun, Wendy Hui Kyong. *Control and Freedom: Power and Paranoia in the Age of Fiber Optics*. Cambridge, Mass.: MIT Press, 2008.

Clark, Katerina. "European and Russian Cultural Interactions with Turkey: 1910–1930s." *Comparative Studies of South Asia, Africa and the Middle East* 33, no. 2 (2013): 201–213.

Cmiel, Kenneth, and John Durham Peters. *Promiscuous Knowledge: Information, Image, and Other Truth Games in History*. Chicago: University of Chicago Press, 2020.

Cochran, Sherman. *Chinese Medicine Men: Consumer Culture in China and Southeast Asia*. Cambridge, Mass.: Harvard University Press, 2006.

Cook, Alexander C., ed. *Mao's Little Red Book: A Global History*. Cambridge: Cambridge University Press, 2013.

Cooper, Jerrold S. "Babylonian Beginnings: The Origin of the Cuneiform Writing System in Comparative Perspective." In *The First Writing: Script Invention as History and Process*, edited by Stephen D. Houston, 71–99. Cambridge: Cambridge University Press, 2004.

Culp, Robert. *The Power of Print in Modern China: Intellectuals and Industrial Publishing from the End of Empire to Maoist State Socialism*. New York: Columbia University Press, 2019.

Dames, Nicholas. *Physiology of the Novel: Reading, Neural Science, and the Form of Victorian Fiction*. Oxford: Oxford University Press, 2007.

BIBLIOGRAPHY

Damrosch, David. "Scriptworlds: Writing Systems and the Formation of World Literature." *Modern Language Quarterly* 68, no. 2 (June 2007): 195–219.

Datsyshen, Vladimir G. "Dvizhenie za latinizatsiiu kitaiskoi pis'mennosti i razvitie kitaiskoi shkoly na sovetskom dal'nem vostoke" [The movement for the latinization of Chinese writing and the development of the Chinese school in the Soviet Far East]. *Rossiia i ATR* 3 (2008): 160–169.

Datsyshen, Vladimir G. "Kitaiskii iazyk i kul'turnaia revoliutsiia v Sovetskoi Rossii" [Chinese language and the cultural revolution in Soviet Russia]. In *Rossiia i Kitai: Istoricheskii opyt vzaimodeistviia i novye grani cotrudnichestva—Materialy nauch.-prakt. konf., Ekaterinburg, 25–26 noiabria 2008*, 13–19. Ekaterinburg: Izd-vo Ural. Un-ta, 2009.

DeFrancis, John. *Nationalism and Language Reform in China*. Princeton, N.J.: Princeton University Press, 1950.

Deleuze, Gilles, and Felix Guattari. *Anti-Oedipus: Capitalism and Schizophrenia*. Translated by Robert Hurley, Mark Seem, and Helen R. Lane. Minneapolis: University of Minnesota Press, 1983.

Di er ci shaoshu minzu yuwen kexue taolunhui, dazibao huiji, di er ji, 3/30 [The second scientific symposium on ethnic-minority languages and scripts, the second meeting, 3/30]. Di er ci shaoshu minzu yuwen kexue taolunhui jianbaozu yinfa, 1958.

Di er ci shaoshu minzu yuwen kexue taolunhui, dazibao huiji, di san ji, 3/31 [The second scientific symposium on ethnic-minority languages and scripts, the third meeting, 3/31]. Di er ci shaoshu minzu yuwen kexue taolunhui jianbaozu yinfa, 1958.

Dirlik, Arif. "The Ideological Foundations of the New Life Movement: A Study in Counterrevolution." *Journal of Asian Studies* 34, no. 4 (August 1975): 945–980.

Dirlik, Arif. "Reversals, Ironies, Hegemonies: Notes on the Contemporary Historiography of Modern China." In *History After the Three Worlds: Post-Eurocentric Historiographies*, edited by Arif Dirlik, Vinay Bahl, and Peter Gran, 125–156. Lanham, Md.: Rowman and Littlefield, 2000.

"Dr. Porter of Pangchwang." *Missionary Herald* 112, no. 12 (December 1916): 542–543.

Du Dingyou. *Hanzi xingwei pai jian fa* [An arrangement method for Chinese character forms]. Shanghai: Zhonghua Press, 1932.

Du Dingyou. *Tushuguan bian muyong jianzi biaozhun zibiao* [A standardized list of simplified character for use in library catalogues]. Shanghai: Zhongguo tushuguan fuwushe, 1934.

Du Dingyou. "[Tushuguan] xin zi zhi shangque (di er ci)" [A discussion of the new character for *tushuguan* (no. 2)]. *Tushuguanxue jikan* 3, no. 4 (1929): 625–627.

Du Dingyou. "[Tushuguan] xin zi zhi shangque (di san ci)" [A discussion of the new character for *tushuguan* (no. 3)]. *Tushuguanxue jikan* 6, no. 2 (1932): 292–293.

Du Dingyou. *Xin shifan xinlixue* [New pedagogical psychology]. Zhonghua Press, 1931 [1925].

Du Dingyou. *Zhongguo jianzi wenti* [The issue of simplified characters in China]. Unidentified publisher, 1931.

Dyer, Svetlana Rimsky-Korsakoff. *Iasyr Shivaza: The Life and Works of a Soviet Dungan Poet*. Frankfurt: Peter Lang, 1991.

Dyer, Svetlana Rimsky-Korsakoff. *Soviet Dungan Kolkhozes in the Kirghiz SSR and the Kazakh SSR*. Canberra: Faculty of Asian Studies, ANU, 1979.

Dyer, Svetlana Rimsky-Korsakoff. "The Superstitions and Beliefs of the Early Chinese Muslims in Russian Central Asia." *Monumenta Serica* 48 (2000): 429–510.
Elman, Benjamin. *On Their Own Terms: Science in China, 1550–1900.* Cambridge, Mass.: Harvard University Press, 2005.
Ertürk, Nergis. *Grammatology and Literary Modernity in Turkey.* New York: Columbia University Press, 2011.
Ertürk, Nergis. "Toward a Literary Communism: The 1926 Baku Turcological Congress." *Boundary 2* 40, no. 2 (Summer 2013): 183–213.
Esenbel, Selçuk. "Japan's Global Claim to Asia and the World of Islam: Transnational Nationalism and World Power, 1900–1945." *American Historical Review* 109, no. 4 (2004): 140–170.
Feng, Zhiwei. *Xiandai hanzi he jisuanji* [Modern Chinese characters and computers]. Beijing: Beijing daxue chubanshe, 1989.
Ferlanti, Federica. "The New Life Movement in Jiangxi Province, 1934–1938." *Modern Asian Studies* 44, no. 5 (2010): 961–1000.
Fore, Devin. "The Operative Word in Soviet Factography." *October* 118 (2006): 95–131.
Foster, L. S. *Fifty Years in China: An Eventful Memoir of Tarleton Perry Crawford.* Nashville, Tenn.: Bayless-Pullen Company, 1909.
Frazier, Robeson Taj. *The East Is Black: Cold War China in Black Radical Imagination.* Durham, N.C.: Duke University Press, 2015.
Freeman, Frank N. *The Teaching of Handwriting.* Boston: Houghton, Mifflin, 1914.
Frings, A. "Sorevnovanie modelei: Tatarskaia delegatsiia na tiurkologicheskom s"ezde v Baku v 1926 g." [Competition of models: The Tatar delegation in the Turcology Congress in Baku in 1926]. *Etnograficheskoe obozrenie* 6 (2005): 44–47.
Fu Maoji. "Sulian minzu yuwen fazhande qingkuang he jiejue minzu wenzi wentide jingyan" [The state of the development of nationality languages and scripts and the experience of resolving nationality script problems in the Soviet Union]. In *Fu Maoji xiansheng minzu yuwen lunji*, 237–256. Beijing: Zhongguo shehui kexue chubanshe, 1995.
Fu Sinian. "Zhi Gu Jiegang (1939)" [To Gu Jiegang (1939)]. In *Fu Sinian Quanji*, vol. 7, edited by Ouyang Zhesheng, 205. Changsha: Hunan jiaoyu chubanshe, 2003.
Ga Ridi and Zhu Zhang. "Mengwen xinxi chuli yanjiu yu sheji" [Research and implementation of information processing in Mongolian script]. *Jisuanji yanjiu yu fazhan* 23, no. 12 (1986): 39–44.
Gardella, Robert. "Squaring Accounts: Commercial Bookkeeping Methods and Capitalist Rationalism in Late Qing and Republican China." *Journal of Asian Studies* 51, no. 2 (1992): 317–339.
Gastev, Aleksei K. *Kak nado rabotat': Prakticheskoe vvedenie v nauku organizatsii truda* [How to work: Practical introduction to the scientific organization of labor]. 2nd ed. Moscow: Ekonomika, 1972.
Gaunt, L. H., ed. *The Chronicle of the London Missionary Society.* Vol. 15, *New Series.* London: London Missionary Society, 1906.
Gezhi jiaokeshu jiaoshou fa [The teaching method for the textbook on science]. Shanghai: Commercial Press, 1906.

Gilbreth, Frank Bunker. *Applied Motion Study: A Collection of Papers on the Efficient Method to Industrial Preparedness.* New York: Sturgis and Walton, 1917.

Gilbreth, Frank Bunker. *Fatigue Study: The Elimination of Humanity's Greatest Unnecessary Waste, A First Step in Motion Study.* New York: MacMillan, 1919.

Göksu, Saime, and Edward Timms. *Romantic Communist: The Life and Work of Nazım Hikmet.* London: Hurst, 1999.

Gordin, Michael. *Scientific Babel: How Science Was Done Before and After Global English.* Chicago: University of Chicago Press, 2015.

Gould, Stephen Jay. *The Mismeasure of Man.* New York: Norton, 1981.

Green, Nile. "Persian Print and the Stanhope Revolution: Industrialization, Evangelicalism, and the Birth of Printing in Early Qajar Iran." *Comparative Studies of South Asia, Africa and the Middle East* 30, no. 3 (2010): 473–490.

Greenhalgh, Susan. *Just One Child: Science and Policy in Deng's China.* Berkeley: University of California Press, 2008.

"Guowuyuan guanyu tuixing weiwuer, hasake liangge xin wenzi fangan wenti de pifu" [The State Council's official response to questions regarding the implementation of the new Uyghur and Kazakh script proposals]. *Wenzi gaige* 1 (1965): 1.

"Guoyu luomazi pinyin fashi—guoyin zimu di er shi" [The transcription method for Gwoyeu Romatyzh—the second National Phonetic Alphabet]. *Guoyu yuebao* 1 (1927): 1–2.

Handel, Zev. *Sinograph: The Borrowing and Adaptation of the Chinese Script.* Leiden: Brill, 2019.

Haraway, Donna. "A Cyborg Manifesto: Science, Technology, and Socialist-Feminism in the Late Twentieth Century." In *Simians, Cyborgs and Women: The Reinvention of Nature,* 149–181. New York: Routledge, 1991.

Haraway, Donna. "Manifesto for Cyborgs: Science, Technology, and Socialist Feminism in the 1980s." *Socialist Review* 80 (1985): 65–108.

Harootunian, Harry. *Marx After Marx: History and Time in the Expansion of Capitalism.* New York: Columbia University Press, 2015.

Hayford, Charles W. *To the People: James Yen and Village China.* New York: Columbia University Press, 1990.

Hayles, Katherine. *How We Became Posthuman: Virtual Bodies in Cybernetics, Literature, and Informatics.* Chicago: University of Chicago Press, 1999.

Heinrich, Larissa. *Afterlife of Images: Translating the Pathological Body Between China and the West.* Durham, N.C.: Duke University Press, 2008.

Hillier, Sir Walter. *Memorandum Upon an Alphabetical System for Writing Chinese, the Application of This System to the Typewriter and to the Linotype or Other Typecasting and Composing Machines and Its Application to the Braille System for the Blind.* (London: William Cloves and Sons, [1915]). In *China and the Chinese: A Collection of Pamphlets Relating Thereto,* vol. 70, Wason Collection, Cornell University.

Hobson, Benjamin. *Quanti xinlun* [A new treatise on anatomy]. Beijing: Zhonghua shuju, 1991.

Hong Shen. "1100 ge jiben hanzi shiyongfa" [The method for using 1100 basic Chinese characters]. *Dongfang zazhi* 32, no. 14 (1935): 5–19.

Hong Shen. *Yi qian yi bai ge jiben hanzi shiyong jiaoxuefa* [The use and instruction of 1100 basic Chinese characters]. Shanghai: Shenghuo shudian, 1936.

Hsiao, H. H. "The Mentality of Chinese and Japanese." *Journal of Applied Psychology* 13 (1929): 9–31.

Hu Huaichen. *Jianyizi shuo* [On simplified characters]. Shanghai: Commercial Press, 1928.

Huang Jinshu. *Zhang Taiyan yuyan wenzi zhi xue de zhishi (jingshen) xipu* [An epistemological (and spiritual) genealogy of Zhang Taiyan's studies on language and writing]. Huamulan wenhua, 2012.

Huey, Edmund B. "Preliminary Experiments in the Physiology and Psychology of Reading." *American Journal of Psychology* 9, no. 4 (1898): 575–586.

Huey, Edmund B. *Psychology and Pedagogy of Reading*. New York: Macmillan, 1908.

"Hunan sheng zhuxi He Jian fandui tuixing jiantizi yuanwen" [The chairman of Hunan Province He Jian's original article for opposing the promotion of simplified characters]. *Lun yu* 77 (1935): 44.

Hykes, John R. *Translations of the Scriptures Into the Languages of China and Her Dependencies*. New York: American Bible Society, 1916.

Iakovlev, Nikolai. "Matematicheskaia formula postroeniia alfavita" [A mathematical formula of alphabet construction]. *Kul'tura i pis'mennost' vostoka*, no. 1 (1928): 41–64.

Iakovlev, Nikolai. "Problemy natsional'noi pis'mennosti vostochnykh narodov SSSR" [Problems of national writing among the eastern peoples of USSR]. *Novyi Vostok*, no. 10–11 (1925).

Iakovlev, Nikolai. "Za latinizatsiiu russkogo alfavita" [For the latinization of the Russian alphabet]. *Kul'tura i pis'mennost' vostoka*, no. 6 (1930): 27–43.

Iusupov, I. I. *Sovietskie Dungane v period stroitel'stva sotsializma* [Soviet Dungans during the building of socialism]. Frunze: Ilim, 1977.

Ji Gendao'er. "Mengguwen biaozhun dianma" [Standard coding for Mongolian script]. *Nei menggu minzu shiyuan xuebao (shehui kexue hanwen ban)* (July 1980): 55–60.

Jiaotong bu guiding guoyin dianbao huibian (fu guoyin dianbao fashi) [The collection of the Ministry of Communications regulations on the telegraph in National Phonetic Alphabet (the method of telegraphy in the NPA attached)]. May 1928.

Jiaoyu bu. *Jianti zibiao di yi pi* [A list of simplified characters, first batch]. Jiaoyu bu, 1935.

"Jiaoyu bu gongbu zhuyin zimu shufa tishi" [Ministry of Education announces the National Phonetic Alphabet typeface]. *Shaoxing jiaoyujie* 1, no. 3 (1922): 1–3.

Jorgensen, John. "Indra's Network: Zhang Taiyan's Sino-Japanese Personal Networks and the Rise of Yogacara in Modern China." In *Transforming Consciousness: Yogacara Thought in Modern China*, edited by John Makeham, 64–98. Oxford: Oxford University Press, 2014.

Judd, Charles H. *Genetic Psychology for Teachers*. New York: D. Appleton, 1909 [1903].

Karl, Rebecca. *Mao Zedong and China in the Twentieth-Century World: A Concise History*. Durham, N.C.: Duke University Press, 2010.

Kaske, Elisabeth. *The Politics of Language in Chinese Education*. Leiden: Brill, 2008.

Khansurov, I. *Latinizatsiia—orudie leninskoi natsional'noi politiki* [Latinization—the weapon of Leninist nationality policy]. Moscow: Politizdat, 1932.

Koeneke, Rodney. *Empires of the Mind: I. A. Richards and Basic English in China, 1929–1979.* Stanford, Calif.: Stanford University Press, 2004.

Konishi, Sho. "Translingual World Order: Language Without Culture in Post–Russo-Japanese War Japan." *Journal of Asian Studies* 72, no. 1 (February 2013): 91–114.

Kursell, Julia. "*Piano Mecanique* and *Piano Biologique*: Nikolai Bernstein's Neurophysiological Study of Piano Touch." *Configurations* 14, no. 3 (Fall 2006): 245–273.

Kuzuoğlu, Uluğ. "Capital, Letter, Empire: Romanization in the Late Qing." *Twentieth-Century China* 46, no. 3 (October 2021): 223–246.

Kuzuoğlu, Uluğ. "Codebooks for the Mind: Dictionary Index Reforms in Republican China, 1912–1937." *Information and Culture* 53, no. 3/4 (2018): 337–366.

Kuzuoğlu, Uluğ. "Telegraphy, Typography, and the Alphabet: The Origins of Alphabet Revolutions in the Russo-Ottoman Space." *International Journal of Middle East Studies* 52 (2020): 413–431.

Laikhter, I. "O latinizatsii kitaiskoi pis'mennosti" [On the latinization of Chinese writing]. *Kul'tura i pis'mennost' vostoka* 9 (1931): 22–32.

Landau, Jacob M. *Pan-Turkism: From Irredentism to Cooperation.* Indianapolis: Indiana University Press, 1995.

Lao Naixuan. *Jianzi wuzhong* [Simple script in five kinds]. Vol. 2. Jinling, Guangxu dingwei [1907].

Larkin, Brian. "The Politics and Poetics of Infrastructure." *Annual Review of Anthropology* 42, no. 1 (2013): 327–343.

Lawton, Anna. *Russian Futurism Through Its Manifestoes, 1912–1928.* Ithaca, N.Y.: Cornell University Press, 1988.

Lei, Sean Hsiang-lin. *Neither Donkey nor Horse: Medicine in the Struggle Over China's Modernity.* Chicago: University of Chicago Press, 2014.

Lew, Timothy Ting-fang. "The Psychology of Learning Chinese, Part IV: Interpretations and Conclusions." *Chinese Social and Political Science Review* (1924): 1–219.

Lew, Timothy Tingfang (Liu Tingfang). *The Psychology of Learning Chinese: A Preliminary Analysis by Means of Experimental Psychology of Some of the Factors Involved in the Process of Learning Chinese Characters.* Peking, 1924(?).

Li Chin-Shi (Li Jinxi). *Chinese Phonetic System and Language.* Translated by Alex Mackenzie. Shanghai: Commercial Press, 1922.

Li, Fang-Kuei. *Linguistics East and West: American Indian, Sino-Tibetan, and Thai.* Interviews conducted by Ning-Ping Chan and Randy LaPolla. Berkeley: University of California, 1988.

Li Jiesan. *Minqiang kuaizi* [Rapid writing in Min language]. Beijing: Wenzi gaige chubanshe, 1956 [1896].

Li Jinxi. "Guoyu bianyu duizhao 'sihang keben' jianyi" [A proposal for a "four-column textbook" that compares the national language and frontier languages]. *Wenyi yu shenghuo* 4, no. 1 (1947): 1–5.

Li Jinxi. *Guoyu xin wenzi lun* [On the national language Sin Wenz]. Unidentified publisher, 1949.

Li Jinxi. *Guoyuxue jiangyi* [Lectures for the study of national language]. Shanghai: Commercial Press, 1919.

BIBLIOGRAPHY

Li Jinxi. *Gwoyeu yunndonq shyy gang [Guoyu yundong shigang]* [A brief history of the National Language Movement]. Shanghai: Commercial Press, 1934.

Li Jinxi. "Kaifa bianjiang de di yi jian shi" [The first thing in opening and developing the frontiers]. *Meng-zang yuebao* 13, no. 10 (1941): 10.

Liang Qichao. "Lun xiaoshuo yu qunzhi zhi guanxi" [On the relationship between novels and government of the people] [1902]. In *Liang Qichao Quanji*, vol. 2, compiled by Yang Gang and Wang Xiangyi, 884–886. Beijing: Beijing chubanshe, 1999.

Liang Qichao. "Lun youxue" [On the study of children]. In *Yinbingshi wenji, di yi ce*, edited by Liang Qichao, 44–59. Taipei: Taiwan zhonghua shuju, 1960.

Liao Shicheng. "Zhili ceyan de lishi" [The history of intelligence tests]. *Xinli* 1, no. 1 (1922): 91–96.

Light, Jennifer. "When Computers Were Women." *Technology and Culture* 40, no. 3 (1999): 455–483.

Lin, Hsiao-Ting. *Modern China's Ethnic Frontiers: A Journey to the West*. New York: Routledge, 2011.

Lin, Ying Kao. "Academic and Professional Attainments of Native Chinese Students Graduating from Teachers College, Columbia University (1909–1950)." PhD diss., Teachers College, Columbia University, 1951.

Lindsley, David Philip. *The Compendium of Tachygraphy: Or Lindsley's Phonetic Shorthand*. Boston: Otis Clapp, 1864.

Lindsley, David P. *The Hand Book of Takigrafy*. New York: D. P. Lindsley, 1882.

Lipman, Jonathan N. *Familial Strangers: A History of Muslims in Northwest China*. Seattle: University of Washington Press, 1997.

Liu, Andrew. *Tea War: A History of Capitalism in China and India*. New Haven, Conn.: Yale University Press, 2020.

Liu Fu and Li Jiarui. *Song yuan yilai suzi pu* [A record of common Characters since the Song and Yuan dynasties]. Guoli zhongyang yanjiuyuan lishi yuyan yanjiusuo, 1930.

Liu, Herman Chan'en. *Non-Verbal Intelligence Tests for Use in China*. New York: Teachers College, Columbia University, 1922.

Liu, Lydia. *The Clash of Empires: The Invention of China in Modern World Making*. Cambridge, Mass.: Harvard University Press, 2004.

Liu, Lydia. "Scripts in Motion: Writing as Imperial Technology, Past and Present." *PMLA* 130, no. 2 (2015): 375–383.

Liu, Xiao. *Information Fantasies: Precarious Mediation in Postsocialist China*. Minneapolis: University of Minnesota Press, 2019.

Lu Xun. "Guanyu xin wenzi" [On the new script] [1934]. In *Lu Xun lun wenzi gaige*. Shandong renmin chubanshe, 1979.

Lu Zhiwei. *Dingzheng bina-ximeng zhili ceyan shuomingshu* [An explanation of correcting the Binet-Simon intelligence tests]. Shanghai: Commercial Press, 1924.

Lu Zhuangzhang. *Beijing qieyin jiaokeshu* [Textbook on Beijing phonetics]. Beijing: Wenzi gaige chubanshe, 1957 [1906].

Lu Zhuangzhang. *Yimu liaoran chujie* [First steps at being able to understand at a glance]. Beijing: Wenzi gaige chubanshe, 1957 [1892].

Lu Zhuangzhang. *Zhongguo zimu beijing qieyin heding* [A volume on Beijing phonetics using a Chinese alphabet]. Beijing: Wenzi gaige chubanshe, 1957 [1906].

Lufei Kui. "Putong jiaoyu dang caiyong sutizi" [Mass education must use common characters]. *Jiaoyu zazhi* 1, no. 1 (1909): 1–4.

Lufei Kui. "Zhengli hanzi de yijian" [A suggestion for managing Chinese characters]. *Guoyu yuekan* 1, no. 1 (1922): 5–7.

Lunacharskii, A. "Latinizatsiia russkoi pis'mennosti" [Latinization of Russian writing]. *Kul'tura i pis'mennost' vostoka*, no. 6 (1930): 20–26.

Luo Changpei. "Yuyanxue zai Yunnan" [Linguistics in Yunnan]. In *Yuyan yu wenhua*, 200–220. Beijing: Beijing chubanshe, 2004.

Ma Fuxiang. "Zhunhan song mengzang gedi tuixing zhuyin fuhao banfa" [Informing Mongolian and Tibetan regions on how to promote Phonetic Symbols]. *Mengzang weiyuanhui gongbao* 13 (1931): 139.

Ma, Shaoling. " 'A Tale of New Mr. Braggadocio': Narrative Subjectivity and Brain Electricity in Late Qing Science Fiction." *Science Fiction Studies* 40, no. 1 (March 2013): 55–72.

MacFarquhar, Roderick. *The Origins of the Cultural Revolution*. Vol. 1, *Contradictions Among the People, 1956-1957*. New York: Columbia University Press, 1974.

Macgowan, Daniel Jerome. *Bowu tongshu* [Philosophical almanac]. Ningbo, 1851.

Mair, Victor. "What Is a Chinese 'Dialect/Topolect'? Reflections on Some Key Sino-English Linguistic Terms." *Sino-Platonic Papers*, no. 29 (September 1991).

Martin, Terry. *The Affirmative Action Empire: Nations and Nationalism in the Soviet Union, 1923-1939*. Ithaca, N.Y.: Cornell University Press, 2001.

"Mass Education in China." *Pacific Affairs* 1, no. 2 (1928): 23–24.

Matsumoto, Shuji. "Shinsue kankō no chūgoku bun jintai kaibō gaku sho" [On the Chinese-language books on anatomical dissection published in late Qing]. *Nihon yisshigaku zasshi* 53, no. 4 (2007): 548–552.

McCall, William. *How to Measure in Education*. New York: Macmillan, 1922.

McLuhan, Marshall. *Understanding Media: The Extensions of Man*. New York: McGraw-Hill, 1964.

Medhurst, Water Henry. *Dictionary of the Hok-këèn Dialect of the Chinese Language*. Macao: Printed at the Honorable East India Company's Press, 1832.

Menggu yuzu yuyan kexue taolunhui jueyi [The resolution on the scientific meeting on Mongolian languages]. Menggu yuzu yuyan kexue taolun mishuchu yin, May 29, 1956.

Menke, Richard. *Telegraphic Realism: Victorian Fiction and Other Information Systems*. Stanford, Calif.: Stanford University Press, 2008.

Merkel-Hess, Kate. *The Rural Modern: Reconstructing the Self and State in Republican China*. Chicago: University of Chicago Press, 2016.

Miles, W. R., and Eugene Shen. "Photographic Recording of Eye Movements in the Reading of Chinese in Vertical and Horizontal Axes: Method and Preliminary Results." *Journal of Experimental Psychology* 10 (1925): 344–362.

Millward, James, and Nabijan Tursun. "Political History and Strategies of Control." In *Xinjiang: China's Muslim Borderland*, edited by S. Frederick Starr. Armonk, N.Y.: M. E. Sharpe, 2004.

Milton, Henry L. "Lewis M. Terman and Mental Testing: In Search of the Democratic Ideal." In *Psychological Testing and American Society, 1890-1930*, edited by Michael M. Sokal, 95–112. New Brunswick, N.J.: Rutgers University Press, 1987.

"Minnan xin wenzi xiehui chengli: Caiqu yizhi de bufa, maibu qianjin" [Minnan Sin Wenz Society established: Acting in unison, stepping forward and marching on]! *Zhongguo yuyan* 4 (1936): 23.

Morrison, Robert. *A Dictionary of the Chinese Language*. Vol. 1, Part 1. Macao: Printed at the Honorable East India Company Press, 1815.

Moser, David. *A Billion Voices: China's Search for a Common Language*. Scorsby: Penguin Books, 2016.

Mott, John R. *The Continuation Committee*. Edinburgh: Continuation Committee of the World Missionary Conference, 1910.

Mullaney, Thomas. *The Chinese Typewriter: A History*. Cambridge, Mass.: MIT Press, 2017.

Mullaney, Thomas. "Semiotic Sovereignty: 1871 Chinese Telegraph Code in Historical Perspective." In *Science and Technology in Modern China*, edited by Jing Tsu and Benjamin Elman, 153–183. Leiden: Brill, 2014.

Müller, Max. *Proposals for a Missionary Alphabet*. London: Printed by A. and G. A. Spottiswoode, 1854.

Murao Susumu. " 'Banki sen-sen': Jimu hō jiki no Ryō Keichō" ["The luxuriant forest": Liang Qichao and the *Shiwubao* period]. In *Kyōdō kenkyū Ryō Keichō: Seiyō kindaishisō juyō to Meiji Nihon*, compiled by Hazama Naoki. Tokyo: Misuzu, 1999.

Nazım Hikmet. *835 Satır* [835 lines]. Istanbul: İstanbul Milliyet Matbaası, 1929.

Nazım Hikmet (Xikemeite). *Aiqing de chuanshuo: Xiju shi* [Legend of love: Poem for a play]. Translated by Chen Yansheng and Wu Chunqiu. Shanghai: Pingmin chubanshe, 1955.

Nazım Hikmet. *Jokond ile Si-Ya-U, Taranta Babu'ya Mektuplar, Benerci Kendini Niçin Öldürdü?* [Gioconda and Si-Ya-U, Letters to Taranta Babu, Why did Banerjee kill himself?]. Ankara: Dost Yayınları, 1965.

Nazım Hikmet (Xikemeite). *Tuerqi de gushi* [Turkish stories]. Translated by Wu Meng. Shanghai: Pingmin chubanshe, 1953.

Nazım Hikmet (Xikemeite). *Tuerqi shi xuan* [A selection of Turkish poems]. Shanghai: Shanghai wenyi chubanshe, 1960.

Nazım Hikmet (Xikemeite). *Wushi duo fan honghua* [Fifty foreign red flowers]. Translated by Yuan Shuipai. Shanghai: Pingmin chubanshe, 1954.

[Nazım Hikmet]. *Xikemeite shixuan* [A selection of Nazım Hikmet's poems]. Beijing: Renmin wenxue chubanshe, 1952.

Nazım Hikmet (Xikemeite) and Anna Begicheva (Biejiqiewa). *Ta yongyuan huozhe* [He will live forever]. Translated by Lei Nan. Beijing: Zhongguo dianying chubanshe, 1957.

Neizheng bu. *Putong jingcha zhili ceyan zhidao lu* [A guide on the intelligence tests for the general police force]. Neizheng bu, 1939.

Ni Haishu. *Ladinghua xin wenzi yundong biannian jishi* [A chronological record of the latinized Sin Wenz movement]. Vol. 1. Beijing: Zhongguo renmin daxue yuyan wenzi yanjiusuo, 1978.

Ni Haishu. *Ladinghua xin wenzi yundong biannian jishi* [A chronological record of the latinized Sin Wenz movement]. Vol. 2. Beijing: Zhongguo renmin daxue yuyan wenzi yanjiusuo, 1979.

Ni Haishu. *Shanghai yin pinyin shizi keben—shongxein pinyin seqsh ku ben* [A literary primer for phonetically transcribing Shanghainese]. Shanghai: Dongfang shudian chubanshe, 1952.
Ni Haishu. *Zhongguo pinyin wenzi yundong shi [jianbian]* [A history of the phonetic writing movement in China (simplified edition)]. Shanghai: Shidai shubao chubanshe, 1948.
(Nie) Gannu. "Zhongguo xin wenzi ne? Guoyu luomazi ne?" [Chinese Sin Wenz? Or Gwoyeu Romatzyh?]. *Zhongguo yuyan* 1 (1936): 4–5.
Noble, Safiya Umoja. *Algorithms of Oppression: How Search Engines Reinforce Racism*. New York: New York University Press, 2018.
Ogden, C. K. *Basic English: A General Introduction with Rules and Grammar*. London: Kegan Paul, Trench and Trubner, 1930.
Ogden, C. K. *Basic English: International Second Language*. New York: Harcourt, Brace & World, 1968.
Ogden, C. K. *C. K. Ogden and Linguistics*. London: Routledge/Thoemmes Press, 1994.
Ogden, C. K. *The System of Basic English*. New York: Harcourt, Brace, 1934.
Ogden, C. K., and I. A. Richards. *The Meaning of Meaning: A Study of the Influence of Language Upon Thought and of the Science of Symbolism*. New York: Harcourt, Brace, 1923.
Ogle, Vanessa. "Time, Temporality and the History of Capitalism." *Past and Present*, no. 243 (May 2019): 312–327.
Olenina, Ana. "Engineering Performance: Lev Kuleshov, Soviet Reflexology, and Labor Efficiency Studies." *Discourse* 35, no. 3 (2013): 297–336.
Otis, Laura. *Networking: Communicating with Bodies and Machines in the Nineteenth Century*. Ann Arbor: University of Michigan Press, 2011.
"Our Most Popular Books." *Chinese Recorder* 38 (August 1907): 437.
Pacey, Scott. "Tan Sitong's 'Great Unity': Mental Processes and Yogācāra in *An Exposition of Benevolence*." In *Transforming Consciousness: Yogacara Thought in Modern China*, edited by John Makeham, 103–122. Oxford: Oxford University Press, 2014.
Pan, Guangrong. "Jianbizi yu shoutouzi" [Simplified characters and handy characters]. *Wenyuan* 1, no. 1 (1935): 1–5.
Pedersen, Morten A. *Not Quite Shamans: Spirit Worlds and Political Lives in Northern Mongolia*. Ithaca, N.Y.: Cornell University Press, 2011.
Peill, Sidney G. "'Open Vision' in China." In *The Beloved Physician—and Others*, edited by J. Peill, 150–151. London: London Missionary Society, 1922.
Peill, Sidney G. "Rural Medical Evangelism." *Chinese Recorder* 56 (January 1925): 26–32.
Peill, Sidney G. "Scriptures in Phonetic for North China." *Chinese Recorder* 47 (1916): 330–335.
Pervyi Vsesoiuznyi Tiurkologicheskii S"ezd (26 Fevralia—6 Marta), Stenograficheskii otchet [First All-Union Turcology Congress (February 26–March 6), stenographic records]. Baku: Obshchestvo Obsledovaniia i Izucheniia Azerbaidzhana, 1926.
Peters, John D. *Marvelous Clouds: Toward a Philosophy of Elemental Media*. Chicago: University of Chicago Press, 2015.
Peters, John Durham. "The Control of Information." *Critical Review* (Fall 1987): 5–23.

Peters, John Durham. *Speaking Into the Air: A History of the Idea of Communication*. Chicago: University of Chicago Press, 1999.

Ping. "'Dazhongyu' gen 'shoutouzi.'" ["Language of the masses" and "Handy characters"]. *Qinghua zhoukan* 43, no. 1 (1935): 54–55.

Porter, Henry. *Shengshen zhizhang* [Elementary physiology]. Beijing: Tongwen Guan Press, 1886.

Proceedings of the Board of Aldermen of the City of New York from April 3 to June 26, 1917. Vol. 2. New York: Board of Aldermen, 1917.

Proceedings of the Seventh Annual Meeting of the China Continuation Committee, Shanghai April 25-30, 1919. Shanghai: Offices of the China Continuation Committee, 1919.

Qi Dehua. "Mengwen duyin shuru fangfa" [Phonetic input method for the Mongolian script]. *Nei menggu daxue xuebao (zhexue shehui kexueban)* 3 (1992): 104–110.

Qian Xuantong. "Jiansheng hanzi bihua de tiyi" [A proposal to reduce stroke count in Chinese characters]. *Xin qingnian* 7, no. 3 (1920).

Qian Xuantong. "Soucai guyou er jiao shiyong de jiantizi an" [A proposal for mining the native and thus more appropriate simplified characters]. *Guoyu zhoukan* 23 (1934): 1.

Qian Xuantong, Lu Ji, Li Jinxi, and Yang Shuda. "Guoyu tongyi choubei hui di si ci da hui, liang ge zhongyao de yi'an: Feichu hanzi caiyong xin pinyin wenzi an, jiansheng xianxing hanzi de bihua an" [The Fourth Congress of the Preparatory Committee for the Unification of National Language, two important proposals: The proposal for eliminating Chinese characters and using a phonetic script, and the proposal for reducing the stroke counts of the Chinese characters currently in use]. *Guoyu yuekan*, no. 1 (1922): 157–168.

[Qu Qiubai] Tsiui Tsiubo (Strakhov). *Kitaiskaia latinizirovannaia azbuka* [Chinese latinized alphabet]. Moscow: KUTK, 1930.

[Qu Qiubai] Tsiui Vei-To. "Kitaiskaia latinizirovannaia azbuka" [Chinese latinized alphabet]. *Problemy Kitaia* 2 (1930): 136–139.

Rawski, Evelyn S. *Education and Popular Literacy in Ch'ing China*. Ann Arbor: University of Michigan Press, 1979.

Records of the General Conference of the Protestant Missionaries of China. Shanghai: American Presbyterian Mission Press, 1890.

Reed, Christopher A. *Gutenberg in Shanghai: Chinese Print Capitalism, 1876-1937*. Vancouver: University of British Columbia Press, 2004.

Reed, James. "Robert M. Yerkes and the Mental Testing Movement." In *Psychological Testing and American Society, 1890-1930*, edited by Michael M. Sokal, 75–94. New Brunswick, N.J.: Rutgers University Press, 1987.

Richard, Timothy. "Non-Phonetic and Phonetic Systems of Writing Chinese." *Chinese Recorder* 29 (November 1898): 540–545.

Richards, I. A. "Basic English and Its Applications." *Journal of the Royal Society of Arts* (June 1939): 735–737.

Riddell, John, ed. *To See the Dawn: Baku, 1920—First Congress of the Peoples of the East*. New York: Pathfinder, 2010.

Rogaski, Ruth. *Hygienic Modernity: Meanings of Health and Disease in Treaty-Port China*. Berkeley: University of California Press, 2004.

Rohlf, Gregory. *Building New China, Colonizing Kokonor: Resettlement to Qinghai in the 1950s.* Lanham, Md.: Lexington Books, 2016.

Ross, James. *On Aphasia: Being a Contribution to the Subject of the Dissolution of Speech from Cerebral Disease.* London: J. & A. Churchill, 1887.

Rossiia i Kitai: Istoricheskii opyt vzaimodeistviia i novye grani sotrudnichestva—Materialy nauch.-prakt. konf., Ekaterinburg, 25-26 noiabria 2008 [Russia and China: Historical experience of mutual interaction and new facets of cooperation—materials from the academic conference, Ekaterinburg, November 25-26, 2008]. Ekaterinburg: Izd-vo Ural. Un-ta, 2009.

Schumpeter, Joseph. *Capitalism, Socialism and Democracy.* London: Routledge, 2003 [1944].

Sh Pingcing. *Latinxuadi zhungwen gungrhen duben (beifang koujin)* [Latinized Chinese reader for workers (northern dialect)]. Edited by Emi Siao. Vladivostok: Guogia lienxo chubanhu juandung fenbu Chuban, 1931.

Sha-ma-la-yi. "Jisuanji yiwen xinxi chuli yanjiu" [A study on the computerized Yi script information processing]. *Xinan minzu xueyuan xuebao (zhexue shehui kexueban)* 21 (August 2000): 42–46.

"Shanghai hua xin wenzi duwu" [Texts for reading in Shanghainese Sin Wenz]. *Zhongguo yuyan* 1 (1936): 16.

Shanghai tebie shili xiaoxue gebie zhili ceyan baogaoshu [A report on the individual intelligence tests in Shanghai primary schools]. Shanghai: Shanghai tebieshi zhengfu jiaoyuju, 1928.

Shapiro, Hugh. "Chinese and Western Medicine." In *Medicine Across Cultures: History and Practice of Medicine in Non-Western Cultures*, edited by Helaine Selin and Hugh Shapiro, 351–372. Dordrecht: Kluwer Academic Publishers, 2003.

Shen, Eugene (Shen Youqian). "An Analysis of Eye Movements in Reading Chinese." *Journal of Experimental Psychology* 10, no. 2 (1927): 158–183.

Shen Xue. *Shengshi yuanyin* [Primordial sounds for a prosperous age]. Beijing: Wenzi gaige chubanshe, 1956 [1896].

Shen Youqian [Eugene Shen]. "Hanzi de jianglai" [The future of Chinese characters]. *Jiaoyu zazhi* 27, no. 5 (1937): 405–412.

Shi Bin. *Dianbao tongxin yu qingmo minchu de zhengzhi bianju* [The telegraph and political transformation in the late Qing and early republic]. Beijing: Zhongguo shehui kexue chubanshe, 2012.

Shor, R. O. "K voprosu o sokrashchenii alfavita (kriticheskie zamechaniia na stat'iu prof. N. F. Iakovleva 'Matematicheskaia formula postroeniia alfavita' *Kul'tura i pis'mennost' vostoka*, no. 1 [1928])" [To the question on the abbreviation of the alphabet (critical remarks on Prof. N. F. Iakovlev's article "A mathematical formula of alphabet construction" in *Kul'tura i pismennost' vostoka*, no. 1)]. *Kul'tura i pis'mennost' vostoka*, no. 2 (1928): 62–75.

Shu (Zhang Shuhuang). "Zisha minzu de shoutouzi" [The suicidal handy characters]. *Guoguang zazhi* 6 (1935): 12–15.

Si-la-mu, Wu-shou-er. "Dui weiwen xinxi chuli yong sanxiang biaozhunde tantao" [A discussion on using three standardizations for Uyghur information processing]. *Zhongwen xinxi xuebao* 1, no. 4 (1988): 61–66.

Siao, Eva. *Women yijian zhongqing—wo yu Xiao San* [We fell in love at first sight—Xiao San and I]. Translated by Zhu Yandong. Beijing: Zhongguo qingnian chubanshe, 2011.

Silsby, J. A. "Reform in Etiquette Called For." *Chinese Recorder* 36 (March 1905): 144–145.

Sivin, Nathan. *Traditional Medicine in Contemporary China: A Partial Translation of Revised Outline of Chinese Medicine (1972).* Ann Arbor: Center for Chinese Studies, University of Michigan, 1987.

Sokal, Michael M. "James McKeen Cattell and Mental Anthropometry: Nineteenth-Century Science and Reform and the Origins of Psychological Testing." In *Psychological Testing and American Society, 1890-1930*, edited by Michael M. Sokal, 21–45. New Brunswick, N.J.: Rutgers University Press, 1987.

Specimen of Printing Types in Use at the Baptist Mission Press. Calcutta: Baptist Mission Press, 1826.

Stenograficheskii otchet pervogo plenuma vsesoiuznogo tsentral'nogo komiteta novogo tiurkskogo alfavita zasedavshego v Baku ot 3-go do 7-go iiunia 1927 goda [Stenographic record of the first plenum of All-Union Central Committee of the New Turkic Alphabet, which met in Baku June 3–7, 1927]. Moscow: Izdanie VTsK NTA, 1927.

Stenograficheskii otchet tret'ego plenuma vsesoiuznogo tsentral'nogo komiteta novogo tiurkskogo alfavita zasedavshego v g. Kazani ot 18-go do 23-e dekabriia 1928 g [Stenographic record of the third plenum of All-Union Central Committee of the New Turkic Alphabet, which met in Kazan December 18–23, 1928]. Baku: Gos. Publichin., 1929.

Tam, Gina. *Dialect and Nationalism in China, 1860-1960.* Cambridge: Cambridge University Press, 2020.

Tan Sitong. "Huang Yingchu 'Chuanyin kuaizi jianfa' xu" [Introduction to Huang Yingchu's "A simple method for the transmission of sounds and rapid writing"]. In *Tan Sitong Quanji*, edited by Cai Shangsi and Fang Xing, 254–255. Beijing: Zhonghua shuju, 1981.

Tan Sitong. "Renxue" [An exposition of Ren]. In *Tan Sitong Quanji*, edited by Cai Shangsi and Fang Xing, 289–374. Beijing: Zhonghua shuju, 1981.

Tanksukname-i Ilhani der Ulum-u Funun-u Khatai [The book of rarities of the Ilkhanids on the arts and sciences of China]. Suleymaniye Manuscript Library, Ayasofya no. 3596.

Taylor, Frederick Winslow. *The Principles of Scientific Management.* New York: Harper & Brothers, 1911.

Tenishev, E. R. *U Tiurkskikh Narodov Kitaiia (Dnevniki 1956-1958 gg.)* [Among the Turkic peoples of China (Diaries, 1956–1958)]. Moscow: Nasledie, 1995.

Tesak, Juergen, and Chris Code. *Milestones in the History of Aphasia: Theories and Protagonists.* New York: Psychology Press, 2008.

Thompson, E. P. "Time, Work-Discipline, and Industrial Capitalism." *Past and Present*, no. 38 (December 1967): 56–97.

Thorndike, Edward L. *Handwriting.* New York City: Teachers College, Columbia University, 1912.

Thornton, Tamara P. *Handwriting in America: A Cultural History.* New Haven, Conn.: Yale University Press, 1996.

BIBLIOGRAPHY

Toprak, Zafer. "Nazım Hikmet'in Putları Kırıyoruz Kampanyası ve Yeni Edebiyat" [Nazım Hikmet's Down with the Icons campaign and new literature]. *Toplumsal Tarih* 261 (2015): 34–42.

Tsai, Loh Seng (Cai Lesheng), and Ethel Abernethy. "The Psychology of Chinese Characters." *Journal of Experimental Psychology* 11, no. 6 (December 1928): 430–442.

Tsu, Jing. "Chinese Scripts, Codes, and Typewriting Machines." In *Science and Technology in Modern China*, edited by Jing Tsu and Benjamin Elman, 115–151. Leiden: Brill, 2014.

Tsu, Jing. *The Kingdom of Characters.* New York: Riverhead Books, 2022.

Tsu, Jing. "Romanization Without Rome: China's Latin New Script and Soviet Central Asia." In *Asia Inside Out: Connected Places*, edited by Eric Tagliocozzo, Helen F. Siu, and Peter C. Perdue, 321–353. Cambridge, Mass.: Harvard University Press, 2015.

Tu, Horace. "The Effects of Different Arrangements of the Chinese Characters Upon Speed and Comprehension in Silent Reading." *Chinese Social and Political Science Review*, no. 2 (April 1926): 278–301.

"Tuerqi daibiao xi-ke-mei-te de fayan" [The speech of the Turkish representative Nazım Hikmet]. *Yazhou ji taipingyang quyu heping huiyi gongbao* 5 (October 1952): 70–71.

"Tuixing shoutouzi yuanqi" [The origins of carrying out handy characters]. *Xinsheng zhoukan* 2, no. 6 (1935): 22–23.

Tuodayewa (Todaeva), [Buliash K.]. *Youguan zhongguo menggu yuzu yuyan he fangyande yanjiu wenti* [Some research issues concerning the Mongolian languages and dialects of China]. Minzu yuwen kexue taolunhui yin, December, 1955 [Beijing?].

Vasil'ev, B. A. "Dungane" [Dungans]. *Kul'tura i pis'mennost' vostoka*, no. 7–8 (1931): 141–144.

Viguier, S. A. (Waijiye). *Dianbao xinshu* [New telegraph codebook]. Shanghai, 1872.

Wade, Thomas Francis. *The Peking Syllabary, Being a Collection of the Characters Representing the Dialect of Peking; Arranged After a New Orthography in Syllabic Classes, According to the Four Tones; Designed to Accompany the Hsin Ching Lu, or Book of Experiments.* Hongkong, 1859.

Wakeman, Frederick. "A Revisionist View of the Nanjing Decade: Confucian Fascism." *China Quarterly* 150 (1997): 395–432.

Wang Bingyao. *Pinyin zipu* [A record of phonetic letters]. Beijing: Wenzi gaige chubanshe, 1956 [1896].

Wang, Charles K. A. *An Annotated Bibliography of Mental Tests and Scales.* Vol. 2. Beijing: Catholic University Press, 1940.

Wang, Guisheng. "Qiandongnan lao miaowen de lishi ji xianzhuang de diaocha he yanjiu" [A survey and study of the history and contemporary state of the old Miao script in southeastern Guizhou]. *Kaili xueyuan xuebao* 28, no. 5 (October 2010): 53–59.

Wang Ju. *Guoyu yundong de lilun yu shiji* [Theory and practice in the National Language Movement]. Taipei: Guoyu ribao she, 1941.

Wang, Liping. "Ethnicizing the Frontier: Imperial Transformation and Ethnic Confrontations in China–Inner Mongolia, 1890s–1930s." PhD diss., University of Chicago, 2013.
Wang Wenxin. *Xiaoxue fenji zihui yanjiu* [A study on the vocabularies for primary school grades]. Hankou: Minzhi shuju, 1930.
Wang Zhao. *Guanhua zimu duwu ba zhong* [Eight kinds of reading materials in Mandarin Syllabary]. Beijing: Wenzi gaige chubanshe, 1957 [1906].
Weiner, Benno. *The Chinese Revolution on the Tibetan Frontier*. Ithaca, N.Y.: Cornell University Press, 2020.
Weng, Jeffrey. "Stop the Presses! Character Simplification and the Publishing Industry in China Under the Nationalists, 1935–36." *Harvard Journal of Asiatic Studies* (forthcoming).
Weng Shiwei. "Woguo shouchuangde weiwen dianbao" [The first telegraph in Uyghur]. *Zhongguo minzu* (March 1986): 38–39.
Whipple, Guy M. "The National Intelligence Tests." *Journal of Educational Research* 4, no. 1 (1921): 16–31.
Williams, Raymond. *Marxism and Literature*. Oxford: Oxford University Press, 1977.
Williams, Samuel Wells. *A Tonic Dictionary of the Chinese Language in the Canton Dialect*. Canton: Printed at the Office of the Chinese Repository, 1856.
Winner, Langdon. "Do Artifacts Have Politics?" *Daedalus* 109, no. 1 (1980): 121–136.
"Women duiyu tuixing xin wenzi de yijian" [Our views on promoting Sin Wenz]. *Zhongguo yuyan* 1 (1936): 18–19.
Wright, David. *Translating Science: The Transmission of Western Chemistry Into Late Imperial China, 1840–1900*. Leiden: Brill, 2000.
Wu Jingheng (Zhihui). "Sanshi wunian lai zhi yinfu yundong" [Thirty-five years of phoneticization movement]. In *Wanqing sanshiwu nian lai (1897–1931) zhi zhongguo jiaoyu*, edited by Cai Yuanpei. Longmen shudian, 1969 [1931].
Wu Rulun. "Shang Zhang guanxue shu" [A letter concerning the management of learning]. In *Qingmo wenzi gaige wenji*, 29. Beijing: Wenzi gaige chubanshe, 1958.
Wu Xiangxiang. *Yan Yangchu Zhuan: Wei quanqiu xiangcun gaizao fendou liushi nian* [Biography of James Yen: Sixty years of struggle for global rural reform]. Taipei: Shibao wenhua chuban, 1981.
Xiao Xiaorong and Ding Zuyin. *Jingguan zhihui ceyan* [Intelligence tests for police officers]. Neizheng bu, 1940.
Xinci shuyu cidian, hanyu gaoben, di yi ji [Dictionary for new terminologies, Mandarin edition, first edition]. Beijing: Zhongguo kexueyuan shaoshu minzu yuyan yanjiu suo, 1959.
Xing Dao. "Duyin tongyi hui gongding guoyin zimu zhi gaishuo" [A summary of how the conference for the unification of pronunciation decided the National Phonetic Alphabet]. *Dongfang zazhi* 10, no. 8 (1914): 11–15.
"Xinshu liuben jiang zai benyue zhong chuban: Xin wenzi shudian ba yue fen jihua" [Six new books will be published this month: Sin Wenz bookstore's August plan]. *Zhongguo yuyan* 4 (1936): 22–23.
Xu Xihua. *Zhuyin xinjiang huiwen changyong zibiao* [List of frequently used Uyghur words with phonetic symbols]. Kunming: Zhengzhong shuju, 1938.

BIBLIOGRAPHY

Xu Zemin. "550 suzi biao" [A list of 550 suzi]. *Lun yu* 45 (1934): 40–42.

Xu Zemin. "Hanzi bihua tongji baogao" [A statistical report on the stroke counts of Chinese characters]. *Zhonghua jiaoyujie* 18, no. 12 (1930): 39–47.

Ya Weitang, Zheng Wang, and Ju Zhengxiu, eds. *Zhongguo suji bainian shi* [A century-long history of Chinese stenography]. Beijing: Xueyuan chubanshe, 2000.

Yan Shuchang. *Zhongguo jindai xinlixue shi* [Modern Chinese history of psychology]. Shanghai: Shanghai jiaoyu chubanshe, 2015.

Yang Jinhao. "Cong shoutouzi dao shijieyu" [From handy characters to Esperanto]. *Qingnian jie* 8, no. 2 (1935): 5–6.

Yang Shifeng. "Yuyan diaocha yu yuyin shiyan" [Language surveys and experiments on pronunciation]. In *Fu suozhang jinian tekan*, 27–28. Taipei: Academia Sinica Institute of History and Philology, 1951.

Yang Xiaofeng. "1986–2001 nian guojia 863 jihua chengguo tongji yu fenxi" [Statistics and analysis of the results of the 863 Plan between 1986 and 2011]. *Xiandai qingbao* 5 (May 2007): 37–40.

Yelle, Robert A. *Language of Disenchantment: Protestant Literalism and Colonial Discourse in British India*. New York: Oxford University Press, 2013.

Yerkes, Robert M. "Report of the Psychology Committee of the National Research Council." *Psychological Review* 26, no. 2 (1919): 83–149.

Yu Daoquan. "Zangwen shuma daizi" [Coding Tibetan script]. *Minzu yuwen* (1982): 1–7.

Yu Jin'en. *Minguo zhuyin zimu zhengce shilun* [A historical work on the republican policies on the National Phonetic Alphabet]. Beijing: Zhonghua shuju, 2007.

Yue, Meng. "Hybrid Science Versus Modernity: The Practice of the Jiangnan Arsenal, 1864–1897." *EASTM* 16 (1999): 13–52.

"Z. S. V. N. jiji gongzuo" [The energetic work of Shanghai Sin Wenz Research Society]. *Zhongguo yuyan* 4 (1936): 22.

Zavyalova, O. I. "Sino-Islamic Language Contacts Along the Great Silk Road: Chinese Texts Written in Arabic Script." *Hanxue yanjiu* 17, no. 1 (June 1988): 285–303.

Zhang Liansheng. "Zangwen haoma daizi jiqi jisuanji paisuo" [Tibetan code and its arrangement for computers]. *Yuyan yanjiu* 2 (1983): 35–40.

Zhang Ning. "Nao wei yishen zhi zhu: Cong 'ailuo bunaozhi' kan jindai zhongguo shentiguande bianhua" [The brain as the sovereign of the body: Looking at modern Chinese transformation of the body through "ailuo brain tonic"]. *Zhongyang yanjiuyuan jindaishi yanjiusuo jikan*, no. 74 (Dec. 2011): 1–40.

Zhang Pengyuan and Shen Huaiyu, eds. *Guomin zhengfu zhiguan nianbiao (1925–1949), di yi ce* [A chronological order of republican government officials (1925–1949), vol. 1]. Taipei: Academia Sinica, 1987.

Zhang Shuyan. *Jianhua zi suyuan* [The source of simplified characters]. Beijing: Yuwen chubanshe, 2005 [1997].

Zhang Taiyan. "Bo zhongguo yong wanguo xinyu shuo" [Refuting the argument for China to use Esperanto]. *Minbao*, no. 21 (1908): 62–68.

Zhang Taiyan. "Wode pingsheng yu banshi fangfa" [My life and how I handled my affairs]. In *Zhang Taiyan de baihuawen*. Taipei: Yiwen yinshuguan, 1972.

Zhang Yonggang and Fan Xiaodong. "Cai Xiyong—Zhang Zhidong mufu qianqi shiye zongguan" [Cai Xiyong—the general manager of Zhang Zhidong's early facilities]. *Hebei daxue xuebao* 31, no. 6 (2006): 115–118.

Zhang Zhongmin. "Bunaode zhengzhixue: 'Ailuo bunaozhi' yu wanqing xiaofei wenhua de jiangou" [Politics of brain supplements: "Ailuo brain tonic" and the construction of late-Qing consumer culture]. *Xeshu yuekan* 43, no. 9 (September 2011): 145–154.

Zhao, Shouhui, and Richard B. Baldauf. *Planning Chinese Characters: Reaction, Evolution or Revolution?* Dordrecht: Springer, 2008.

Zheng Guanying. *Shengshi weiyan zengding xinbian* [New and revised edition of *Words of Warning for a Prosperous Age*]. Taipei: Taiwan xuesheng shuju, 1965.

Zhirkov, Lev. "K reforme alfavitov vostochnikh narodnostei" [For the reform of eastern peoples' alphabets]. *Novyi Vostok*, no. 10–11 (1925): 223–235.

Zhong, Yurou. *Chinese Grammatology: Script Revolution and Literary Modernity, 1916–1958*. New York: Columbia University Press, 2019.

Zhongguo shaoshu minzu yuyan wenzi qingkuang jianbiao (neibu cankao) [A table explaining the current state of China's ethnic-minority languages and scripts (for the Ministry of Interior's use)]. Zhonghua renmin gongheguo minzu shiwu weiyuanhui wenjiaosi bianzhi, February 1958.

"Zhongguo wenzi gaige weiyuanhui chengli" [The establishment of the Chinese Script Reform Commission]. *Zhongguo yuwen* 31 (January 1955): 38.

Zhonghua pingmin jiaoyu cujin hui. *Dingxian shiyan gongzuo tiyao* [A summary of the work on Ding County experiment]. Beiping: Zhonghua pingmin jiaoyu cujin hui, 1934.

Zhonghua pingmin jiaoyu cujin hui. *Nongmin qianzi ke* [Thousand-character primer for peasants]. [Beijing]: Zhonghua pingmin jiaoyu cujin hui, 1931.

Zhonghua pingmin jiaoyu cujin hui. *Pingmin xuexiao jiaoyu ceyan fa* [Educational testing method for common primary schools]. Shanghai: Commercial Press, 1928.

Zhonghua pingmin jiaoyu cujin hui. *Shibing qianzi ke* [Thousand-character primer for soldiers]. Beijing: Zhonghua pingmin jiaoyu cujin hui, 1929 [1928].

Zhou, Minglang. *Multilingualism in China: The Politics of Writing Reforms for Minority Languages, 1949–2002*. Berlin: Mouton de Gruyter, 2003.

Zhou Xingsi. *Ch'ien tzu wen, The Thousand Character Classic: A Chinese Primer*. Edited by Francis W. Paar. New York: F. Ungar, 1963.

Zhou Yongming. *Zhongguo wangluo zhengzhide lishi kaocha: Dianbao yu qingmo shizheng* [A historical investigation of the Chinese network politics: Telegraph and late-Qing politics]. Beijing: Shangwu yinshuguan, 2013.

Zhou Youguang. *Dianbao pinyinhua* [Pinyinization of the telegraph]. Beijing: Wenzi gaige chubanshe, 1965.

Zhou Youguang. *Hanzi gaige gailun* [An outline of the reform of Chinese characters]. Beijing: Wenzi gaige chubanshe, 1961.

Zhou Youguang. "Hanzi gaige gailun [1961]" [An outline of the reform of Chinese characters (1961)]. In *Zhou Youguang wenji*, vol. 1. Beijing: Zhongyang bianyi chubanshe, 2013.

Zhou Youguang. *Zhou Youguang baisui koushu* [Zhou Youguang gives an account of one hundred years]. Transcribed by Li Huaiyu. Guilin: Guangxi shifan daxue chubanshe, 2008.

Zhou Youguang. *Zhou Youguang bainian koushu: Wo suo duguo de shiguang* [Zhou Youguang gives an account of one hundred years: The times that I've been through]. Hong Kong: Chinese University of Hong Kong, 2015.

Zhu Jiahua. *Bianjiang jiaoyu gaikuang* [The situation of frontier education]. Jiaoyu bu bianjiang jiaoyu si, 1947.

Index

Page numbers in italics refer to figures.

Agamalyogly, S.: convening of the First Turcology Congress, 157; first plenum of the All-Union Central Committee of the New Turkic Alphabet attended by, 167; latinization promoted by, 165–167, 261n22

Ai Wei, about, 130

Ai Wei, and psychology of learning characters: character forms associated with reading efficiency, 130, 135; stroke count associated with learning speed, 130, *131*; Xu Zemin's proposal for simplification impacted by, 130–132; Yen's Thousand-Character Primer as the dataset for, 130

All-Union Central Committee of the New Turkic Alphabet. *See under* Unified New Turkic Alphabet (UNTA)

alphabetic order: alphabetization of Amoy (Xiamen), 24–25, 66; imagined Eurasian socialist network formed by the Latin alphabet, 183–184, 210–211; Orientalist genealogy of alphabetization in China, 18–19, 86. *See also* Chinese Latin Alphabet (CLA/Sin Wenz); Chinese latinization; Dungans and Dunganese-New Dunganese Alphabet; Gwoyeu Romatzyh (GR); National Phonetic Alphabet (NPA); phoneticization; Pinyin and pinyinization; Roman alphabet; Scientific Research Commission of the Far Eastern Committee of the New Alphabet (DVKNA); Unified New Turkic Alphabet (UNTA)

alphabetic labor time: as the benchmark for efficiency, 12, 87; Chinese script reforms motivated by, 115; grounding in Western historical experience, 14, 25–26; Müller's Physiological Alphabet, 62–63; Sharaf's comparison of Arabic script with the Latin alphabet, 164

Amoy (Xiamen) language: Lu Zhuangzhang's alphabetization of, 24–25, 66; Lu Zhuangzhang's *English and Chinese Dictionary of the Amoy Dialect*, 66; in Wang Bingyao's *A Record of Phonetic Letters*, 41

INDEX

Anatomy, Descriptive and Surgical (Gray), 44–45, 49

Arabic script: compliance with NOT, 163; cyrillization of, 162; and Ibrahimov's promotion of a cultural literary federation of Turkic languages, 165–166; physiological suitability to movements of the hand, 164; typewriter invented in Kazan for, 199–200, 265n33; Xiao'erjin transcribed using, 156, 171

Arbatov, Boris, 177

Ayres, Leonard P.: Basic English vocabulary identified by, 96; handwriting scale invented by, 95–96

baihua, *baihua* movement, 4; rapprochement between spoken and written language advocated by, 119; Xiao San's defense of, 196

Baptist Mission Press, printing in a variety of scripts and languages by, 62

Basic Chinese (Hong Shen): ambiguous reception of, 114; ideological drive behind, 109–110, 112–114; as a manifestation of the modern age of information, 115; regional differences attended to, 112–13; Yen's Thousand-Character Primers contrasted with, 92, 109–111

Basic English (Ogden and Richards): Ayres's Basic English vocabulary, 96; Basic Chinese inspired by, 92; Hong Shen's Basic Chinese compared with, 92–93, 111–114; psychological theory of communication, 112–113; Rockefeller Foundation support for teaching Basic English, 109; as a weapon of empire, 108

Beijing Mandarin: asserted as the national pronunciation of characters, 70–71, 74; designation as the national language by the GMD, 3, 17, 191; education in the frontiers conducted in, 216, 221n22; NPA's representation of, 14; Peill's Mandarin Syllabary, 78, 79, 80–82; Wade's romanization of, 64–65; in Wang Bingyao's *A Record of Phonetic Letters*, 41

Bell, Alexander Melville, 48

Bilokh, Yakob, 181, 182

bopomofo. See National Phonetic Alphabet (NPA)

brain and brain science: brain as the seat of consciousness, 25, 46, 51–52; "Broca's area" identified for speech, 49; the eighth consciousness (*ālaya*) of Buddhism located in, 5; Liang Qichao on cerebral efficiency for children's education, 52–53; Shen Xue's encephalocentric imagination of the body, 25, 27, 44, 51–52, 248n41. *See also* cognition and cognitive management; intelligence tests; neurophysiology

brain-*qi* (*naoqi*): explained in terms of *dianqi* (electricity), 45; galvanist theories of electricity and the body, 44

brain-*qi* tendons (*naoqijin*) (nerves): brain connected to the outside world by, 44; Hobson and Chen's concepts of, 44, 45; Tan Sitong on electrified bodily cognition, 5

Broca, Pierre Paul, 49

Buck, Pearl, 103

Buddhism: Confucian-cum-Buddhist values of benevolence, fairness, and faith associated with three brain parts, 51; Confucian-cum-Buddhist view of existence according to Shen Xue, 51–52; the eighth consciousness (*ālaya*) located in the brain by Tan Sitong, 5; Yogacara thought proposed as an influence on Liang Qichao's thoughts about education, 249n67

Cai Xiyong: background of, 28; Chinese guide to European-style double entry bookkeeping written by,

[296]

29, 246n9; Chinese stenography (*Chuanyin kuaizi*) invented by, 25, 26, 29–30, *31*, 32–33; the value of script redefined in terms of labor efficiency, 27, 41, 43, 46, 55

Cai Yuanpei: handy characters supported by, 146; manifesto promoting Sin Wenz signed by, 205; 1913 conference convened by, 57, 68, 75

Cai Zhang: Cai Xiyong's book on accounting published by, 29; Cai Xiyong's textbook on shorthand published by, 32, 246n13; Chinese shorthand improvements, 32–33; Yuan Shikai's recognition of his contributions, 246n17

Canton and Cantonese languages: London Missionary Society based in, 62; Vasilii Pukhov, 198, 208, 264n26; Roman alphabet used by missionaries for Cantonese, 40; signs needed for a script for, 67–68

Central Propaganda Bureau, Wang Shijie as head of, 215

Chao, Yuen Ren: and the Commission for the Revision of Phonetic Symbols, 220, 267n12; Gwoyeu Romatzyh (GR) invented by, 2, 189, 191–192; Hong's Basic Chinese considered valuable, 114; and IHP, 218; knowledge of "dialects," 192, 198

character frequency analysis, as a manifestation of the modern age of information, 114–115

Chen Guangyao: on the need for simplification of characters to educate frontier populations, 268n23; "President Sun Yat-sen's Will" ("Jianxie zongli yizhu jie"), 122–123, *124*, 257n8

Chen Heqin, revised Binet-Simon intelligence test translated into Chinese with Liao Shicheng, 99–100, 101. *See also* character frequency analysis

Chen Lifu, 215, 219, 220, 222, 267–268n14

Chiang Kai-shek: James Yen's Mass Education Movement supported by, 103; New Life Movement (NLM) initiated by, 143; Wang Shijie ordered to investigate simplified characters, 144, 150

China Continuation Committee (CCC), 80–81

China Inland Mission (CIM), Wade's transcription of Beijing Mandarin challenged by, 65

Chinese Academy of Sciences (CAS), scripts for Turkic nationalities devised by Soviet experts for, 230–231

Chinese Academy of Sciences (CAS)–Institute of Linguistics: minority script reforms, 230; stand-alone letters demanded for spoken sounds, 228

Chinese Latin Alphabet (CLA/Sin Wenz): failure of, 226; GMD's prohibition of, 2, 22, 153, 206–207, 212, 266n61; invention of, 2, 189; promotion in the Far Eastern Soviet Union, 199; regional languages embraced by, 113; Vrubel's criticism of it as "bourgeois," 201–202

Chinese latinization, as a product of transnational Eurasian history, 20–22, 59–60, 86, 91, 142, 156–158, 173–174, 209–212; multilingual coexistence envisioned by, 198

Chinese latinization–Chinese Latinization Conference in Moscow (1936): Chinese latinization criticized at, 202–203; emphasis on linguistic representation, 197–198; Xiao San's speech questioning the regional use of CLA at, 210–11, 226

Chinese Latinization–Chinese Latinization Conference in Vladivostok (1931), Chinese Latin Alphabet (CLA) finalized at, 153–154, 186, 196

[297]

INDEX

Chinese typewriters: Chinese information history encapsulated by, 18–19, 86; Chinese Phonetic Typewriter patented by the Underwood Typewriter Company, 76, 252n48; Ming Kwai Chinese Typewriter, 123; Remington Standard Typewriter using the Mandarin Syllabary, 80

Chinese writing systems: alienation from, 2, 7; eight principles of *yong* (*yongzi ba fa*), 35–36, *37*; linguistic inclusion/exclusion determined by scripts, 14–17, 58–59; Lu Zhuangzhang's alphabetization of Min vernaculars, 24–25, 66; phonetic scripts contrasted with, 11–12; radicals invented by Mei Yingzuo, 38. *See also* Chinese latinization; linguistic representation; National Phonetic Alphabet (NPA); Pinyin and pinyinization; script invention; script reform

Chobanzade, B., *173*, 208

Chou, Siegen K. (Zhou Xiangeng): experiment with the directions of reading Chinese, 136–137, *138*; gestalt of reading Chinese characters, 135–136, *137*

cognition and cognitive management: in early twentieth-century American psychology of education, 91, 94–95; Frank Bunker Gilbreth's efficiency studies, 93–94; the heart (*xin*) viewed as central to, 25; impact on Chinese psychologists, 91–92; the Mass Education Movement's commitment to the principles of, 102–103; Soviet latinists' engagement with Scientific Organization of Labor, 187–188. *See also* brain and brain science; intelligence tests; neurophysiology

Commission for the Revision of Phonetic Symbols for Regional Sounds Across the Nation, 220–222, 267n12

communication: defined as a neurophysiological act of labor by Shen Xue, 1, 46; scripts as critical technologies for constructing a modernizing knowledge economy, 4–9, 11–12, 19; the social and political *context* for communication embedded in Basic Chinese, 114; transcendental thought grounded in material infrastructures of information by Tai Sitong, 5; wartime communication engineering, 214–217. *See also* Basic Chinese; Basic English; global information age; knowledge economy; linguistic representation; Morse code; telegraphy and telegraphic communication; writing systems

Conference for the Unification of Pronunciation (1913): NPA selected at, 43, 57–58, 72, *73*, 76; scholars assembled at, 68; Wang Pu as the last chairman of, 74, 81

Confucianism: birth of Confucian institutes, 267n3; combined with Islamic knowledge in Han Kitab, 170; Confucian-cum-Buddhist values of benevolence, fairness, and faith associated with three brain parts, 51; Confucian-cum-Buddhist view of existence according to Shen Xue, 51–52; NLM's traditional conceptual vocabulary associated with "nativeness," 143

Cooke, William, 35

cuneiform, 16

DeFrancis, John: language politics tied to script reforms, 3; missionary romanization promoted by, 60

Deng Xiaoping, technocratic reforms of, 241

Dewey, John, 99, 107

dianqi (electricity): brain-*qi* (*naoqi*) explained in terms of, 45; invented as a term by Macgowan, 43–44, 248n40

[298]

Du Dingyou: background of, 125, 134; eight ways of "seeing" a character, 139–141, *140*; proposal for simplified characters, 125, *141*, 142

Dudgeon, John, 44–45, 46

Dungans and Dunganese: central place in the history of Chinese latinization, 170–171; language spoken by Dungans as a mixture of vernacular languages, 170. *See also* New Dunganese Alphabet; Xiao'erjin

DVKNA. *See* Scientific Research Commission of the Far Eastern Committee of the New Alphabet (DVKNA)

eight principles of *yong* (*yongzi ba fa*), 35–36, *37*

Elementary Physiology (Porter), 45

Esperanto: Chinese anarchists' support for, 69; handy characters criticized as the path to, 259n43; impact on Chinese script reformers, 20, 60; Japanese anarchists' support for, 20, 69; Zhang Taiyan's Syllabary to Record Sounds as a reaction to, 20, 71–72

First All-Union Turcology Congress (1926): anti-imperial spirit of, 157; latinization of Turkic languages decided at, 154–155, 161, 165–167

Fu Sinian, 218, 219, 221, 268n22

Gastev, Aleksei K.: NOT coined by, 158; poetry, 158, 177; seamless integration of machines and humans envisioned by, 158, 160–161, 177

Gilbreth, Frank Bunker: efficiency studies, 93–94; philosophy of the Mass Education Movement compared with, 103

global information age: emergence from the industrial age of capitalism, 8–9, 26, 239–240; entanglement of missionary romanization, 60–61;

its impact on script, 58–59, 116; latinization as a radical instantiation of, 187; metamorphosis of communication practices during, 8, 10, 22–23, 155; negotiation of demands in separate historical contexts, 158; socio-technical practices of communication in China challenged by, 8–12, 15–17, 23, 89, 114–116; transnational dimensions of revolutionary thought in, 20–23, 155

GMD. *See* Nationalist Party

Gray, Henry, 44–45, 49

Guomindang. *See* Nationalist Party

Gwoyeu Romatzyh (GR): invention by Yuen Ren Chao, 2, 189, 191; reliance of Qu Qiubai's latinized alphabet on, 189, 191–193, 201; as a romanized version of the National Phonetic Alphabet, 189

handy characters: animosity towards their use, 148, 259n43; *shoutouzi* contrasted with *jiantizi* (simplified characters), 146–147; typesets for three hundred simplified characters, 146, *147*

Hobson, Benjamin and Chen Xiutang, 44, 45

Hong Shen, 106. *See also* Basic Chinese

Hu Huaichen, proposal for simplification of characters, 121–122

Huey, Edmund B., 95

Iakovlev, Nikolai: on the latinization of the Dunganese Xiao'erjin, 170, 173, 174; theories about the "economy of signs," 162, 260n13; UNTA promoted by, 162, 168

Ibrahimov, Galimjan, 165, 167

information history: "Chinese" information history encapsulated by the Chinese typewriter, 18–19, 86; Chinese information history as more than technical tinkering, 19–22;

[299]

INDEX

information history (continued)
  close link between mass literacy and the management of Chinese characters, 27, 33, 43, 114–115; different information societies imagined through script reforms, 55–56. See also global information age
Inner Mongolia: the term "cadre" (Ch. ganbu) in, 233; under the influence of Japan, 222
Institute of History and Philology (IHP): dialectological surveys planned by Luo Changpei, 218; establishment of, 215; founding members of, 218; Fu Sinian's advocation of sinicization (hanhua), 219
intelligence tests: Binet-Simon Intelligence Scale, 97, 98, 101; racial bias in, 97–99; revised Binet-Simon intelligence test translated into Chinese, 99–100, 101; soldiers tested as part of the Chinese measurement movement, 101–102

Japan and Japanese: Chinese writing system adopted in, 12; Esperanto embraced by Japanese anarchists, 20, 69; hiragana, 193, 196; Inner Mongolia under the influence of, 222; Japanese kana as inspiration for Wang Zhao's Mandarin Syllabary, 67, 70; participation in the Cold War "code race," 240; script reform discussed in, 10; Sino-Japanese War, 25, 28–29, 48, 67
Jesuits: seventeenth-century romanizations, 60–61; translations of Western anatomical knowledge, 246n4, 248n41
Judd, Charles H., 95

Kangxi Dictionary (Kangxi zidian), 38, 247n30
knowledge economy: mass literacy as the precondition for a modern knowledge economy, 15, 27, 33, 43, 89–90, 114–115; scripts as critical technologies for constructing a modernizing knowledge economy, 4–9, 11–12, 19
Korea and Korean: Chinese writing system adopted in, 12; hangul, 196; Koreans in Far Eastern USSR, 199, 200, 204; latinized Korean, 200; Nazım Hikmet's "Alioğlu Ahmet" imagined about the Korean War, 182, 263n56; participation in the Cold War "code race," 240; pinyinization not carried out for, 235

labor time and efficiency: cerebral energy saved by simplified characters, 54; communication defined as a neurophysiological act of labor by Shen Xue, 1, 46; of entering Chinese characters into Morse code, 1, 10–11, 26, 34, 47, 228; Müller's physiological approach to linguistic transcription, 62–63; of the scientific practice of counting, 104–105; the value of script redefined in terms of labor efficiency by Cai Xiyong, 27–27, 41, 43, 46, 55; the value of script redefined in terms of labor efficiency by Shen Xue, 27–28, 47–49, 55; the value of script redefined in terms of labor efficiency by Wang Bingyao, 26, 27–28, 33–34, 41, 43, 46, 55. See also alphabetic labor time
Laikhter, I., 202, 204
Lao Naixuan, 58, 59, 67–68, 225
latinization: handy characters as the first step toward latinization of Chinese, 148; latinizatsiia not romanization used in Eurasia, 183; Lenin's alleged dictim on latinization as the "revolution in the East," 155, 165, 166, 211, 261n22; movement to latinize Arabic script, 21, 154–155, 157–158, 187; of Turkic, 154–155, 161, 165–167; of Xiao'erjin, 172–174, 184. See also Chinese latinization

[300]

INDEX

Lenin, Vladimir: alleged dictum on latinization as the "revolution in the East," 155, 165, 166, 211, 261n22; Dziga Vertov's, *Three Songs About Lenin,* 166; latinization of Russian not supported by, 162; New Turkic Alphabet supported by, 158

Li Fanggui, 218, 220, 221

Li Jiarui, 122, 123, 132

Li Jiesan, 32, 67

Li Jinxi: *A Brief History of the National Language Movement,* 3, 226; hostile relations with latinists, 226–227; infrastructural and economic reasons for supporting NPA, 75–76; literacy in the frontiers discussed at the Commission for the Revision of Phonetic Symbols, 220–222; as a member of the National Language Commission, 215, 219; plan for textbooks for the ethnic frontiers, 222–223

Liang Qichao: cerebral efficiency for children's education promoted by, 52–53; neurophysiology terminology employed in his theory of the novel, 53, 249n68; preface to Shen Xue's treatise, 27, 48; Yogacara thought proposed as an influence on his thoughts about education, 249n67

Liao Shicheng, 99–100, 101

Lin Yutang: character simplification using *suzi* publicly endorsed by, 119, 123, 125, 145; and the Commission for the Revision of Phonetic Symbols, 220–222, 267n12; Du Dingyou's proposal for simplification endorsed by, 125, 134, 142; handy characters not supported by, 148; as a member of the National Language Commission, 215; Ming Kwai Chinese Typewriter invented by, 123; Xu Zemin's proposal for simplification endorsed by, 125, 142

Lindsley, David P., 30

linguistic representation: linguistic inclusion/exclusion determined by scripts, 14–17, 58–59, 191–192. *See also* Chinese latinization; Chinese writing systems; latinization; phonocentrism; Pinyin; script invention

linotype machines: demand in the Soviet Union for, 187, 199–200; machines using the Mandarin Syllabary, 80

List of Frequently Used Uyghur Words with Phonetic Symbols (Xu), 222

Liu Fu, 122, 123, 132, 198, 220

Liu Shipei, 69

Liu Tingfang (Timothy Tingfang Lew), about, 125–126. *See also Psychology of Learning Chinese, The* (Liu)

London Missionary Society: Benjamin Hobson as a missionary-physician for, 44; Robert Morrison's *A Dictionary of Chinese Language,* 62. *See also* Peill, Sidney G.; Wang Bingyao

Lu Xun, 259n43

Lu Zhiwei, 99–100, 101

Lu Zhuangzhang: alphabetization of Amoy (Xiamen), 24–25, 66; *English and Chinese Dictionary of the Amoy Dialect,* 66

Lufei Kui, 7, 54, 120–122

Lunacharskii, A., 162

Luo Changpei, 218, 220, 225, 230

Ma Xueliang, 223

Macgowan, Daniel Jerome: *dianqi* (electricity) invented as a term, 43–44, 248n40; Lu Zhuangzhang's *English and Chinese Dictionary of the Amoy Dialect* printed by, 66; Manchu/Chinese "electrical communication of signs" (*dianqi tongbiao*), 35, *36*; telegraphic dial plate invented by, 35; translation of galvanism, 248n40. *See also Philosophical Almanac* (Macgowan)

[301]

INDEX

Mandarin language: loan words that projected Han chauvinism, 233; *The Standard System of Mandarin Romanization*, 65–66. *See also* Beijing Mandarin

Mandarin Syllabary (Wang): exclusion of other languages from its composition, 58; initial support by foreign missionaries, 75; Japanese kana as inspiration for, 67, 70; Northern Vernacular Syllabary as its original name, 70. *See also* Wang Zhao

Mao Zedong: CCP's transition to a technocratic party after his death, 241; impact of his Little Red Book, 22; Stalin's advice on Chinese phoneticization, 228; "Talks at the Yan'an Forum on Art and Literature," 209

Marx, Karl: characters Ma-ke-si for his name, 227; on historical presuppositions, 13; Zhou Youguang's Marxist theory of fusing machines, scripts, and labor, 229

Mass Education Movement (MEM): commitment to the principles of cognitive management, 102–103; intelligence tests given to soldiers as part of the Chinese measurement movement in education, 101–102; Rockefeller Foundation support for, 103, 105–106

mass literacy: late-Qing interest in, 11, 27; as the precondition for developing a modern knowledge economy, 15, 27, 33, 43, 89–90, 114–115; question of script linked to, 90; transnational scientific networks supporting it, 91–93

May Fourth intellectuals: Chinese characters blamed for cultural backwardness, 3, 89. *See also* Li Jinxi; Qian Xuantong

Mei Yingzuo, 38

Miao people: Miao Phonetic symbols invented by Maurice Hutton, 268n23; "sour-soup language" (*suantanghua*) of, 235

Min vernaculars: pseudo-Roman signs invented by Lu Zhuangzhang for, 66; shorthand adopted by Li Jiesan for, 32, 67; signs needed for a script for, 67–68. *See also* Amoy (Xiamen) language

Ministry of Education of the Republic of China: Basic English supported by, 109; Commission to Promote Phonetic Symbols, 194, 217; expanded literacy in Mandarin as constant challenge for, 223; National Phonetic Alphabet promulgated by, 75, 80; participation in the Central Phonetic Literacy Movement Commission, 267–268n14; Phonetic Symbols ordered for publications issued by, 220, 267n13; standardized Mandarin education in the frontiers ordered by, 220–221; 324 simplified characters promulgated by, 120, 142–143, 144, 144–145, 145, 149, *149*, 150; Wang Shijie as head of, 144–145, 150

missionaries: Benjamin Hobson, 44, 45; Continuation Committees, 80–81; dictionaries with Chinese characters printed by, 62, 251n11; Henry Porter's *Elementary Physiology*, 45; promotion of the NPA, 20, 60; Protestant romanizations, 60–61; role in the history of Chinese script reforms, 59–60, 66, 75, 78, 80–82, 85–87; Wang Zhao's Mandarin Syllabary initially supported by, 75. *See also* Jesuits; London Missionary Society; Peill, Sidney G.; Wang Bingyao

Mongols and Mongolian: cyrillic writing system for, 232–223; information-processing systems for, 240–241; representation in the "unity of the five races" (*wuzu gonghe*), 217; use of Phonetic Symbols

[302]

ordered by the Ministry of Education, 217
Morrison, Robert A., 62, 63
Morse code: economy of signs in, 40, 247n32; the English alphabet as its base, 37–38; nonalphabetic Chinese characters as incompatible with, 1, 10–11, 26, 34, 47, 228; Viguier's *Dianbao xinshu* (New telegraph codebook), 37–40, *39*, 247n30
Moses, Robert, 58–59
Mott, John R., 80
Müller, F. Max: *Proposals for a Missionary Alphabet*, 62–63; racist attitude toward local languages and scripts in India, 62, 86

National Conference on Language Work (1986), 238
National Conference on Minority Education (1951), 238
Nationalist Party (Guomindang, GMD): Beijing Mandarin designated as the national language by, 3, 22; CLA prohibited by, 2, 22, 153, 206–207, 212, 266n61; Highest Commission of the Ministry of National Defense, 219–20; National Language Commission, 215, 219–220, 223, 268n14; Phonetic Symbols brought to Taiwan, 223; simplification of characters prohibited by, 2, 120, 153, 212, 227, 268n23; Uyghur Phonetic Symbols introduced by, 222–223; Yen's primers backed by, 92. *See also* Chiang Kai-shek; Ministry of Education of the Republic of China
National Phonetic Alphabet (NPA): adaption by missionaries in Wu regions, 82; as *bopomofo* in Taiwan, 2, 71–72; correspondence between Qian Xuantong and Wu Zhihui using NPA, 77–78, 252–253n49; and the dialectics of the global information age, 58–59, 116; efficiency of telegraphic transmissions

associated with, 43, 76; invention by Zhang Taiyan, 20, 59, 71, 72, 75; missionary evangelism facilitated by, 82, *83*; promotion by Western missionaries, 20, 60; promulgation of, 2, 75, 80; selection at the 1913 Conference, 43, 57–58, 72, *73*, 76; *The Truth* published by, *84*; typeface prepared for, 76, 77
Nazım Hikmet (Xikemeite): at the Asia-Pacific Region Peace Conference (1952), 182; biographical details, 175, 178; friendship with Xiao San, 178, 182–183; "Gioconda and Si-Ya-U" ("Jokond ile Si-Ya-U"), 178, *179*, 180–181, 184, 262n53; internationalist vision, 181–182, 262n53; "To Be Mechanized" ("Makinalaşmak"), 175–177, 180, 262n47; translations of his poems into Chinese, 263n56
neurophysiology: analysis of eye movements reading Chinese, 135, *136*; optimum patterns of physical movements studied, 161; Shen Xue's theories of language and writing, 1, 6–7, 46, 49; terminology employed in Liang Qichao's theory of the novel, 53, 249n68; theories about aphasia, 6, 46, 49–50, 249n60
New Alphabet. *See* Scientific Research Commission of the Far Eastern Committee of the New Alphabet (DVKNA); Unified New Turkic Alphabet (UNTA)
New Dunganese Alphabet: based on Arabic script in use, 172; textbooks and literature printed in, 173; Unified New Turkic Alphabet identified with, 21, 172–173, *174*. *See also* Dungans and Dunganese; Xiao'erjin
New Life Movement (NLM), 143–144, 145
New Treatise on Anatomy (Hobson and Chen), 44, 45
Ni Haishu, 225, 227, 237

Nie Gannu, 205, 225, 226
1913 conference. *See* Conference for the Unification of Pronunciation (1913); Shanghai Missionary Conference
NOT. *See* Scientific Organization of Labor

Ogden, C. K., 850 essential words in English identified by, 108. *See also* Basic English (Ogden and Richards)
Ogle, Vanessa, 54–55
Osgood, William Dauphin, 44–45, 46
Ottoman Empire: movement to latinize the Arabic script, 21, 154–155, 157–158, 187; non-Euro-American telegraph line established in, 9; Pan-Islamism, 166

Pan Guangrong, 147–148
Peill, Sidney G.: as chairman of the Phonetic Promotion Committee, 80–82; linguistic problems in disseminating of simple medical information faced by, 85; Mandarin Syllabary of, 78, 79, 80–82
People's Republic of China (PRC): CLA in use until 1958 in, 153, 224–225; Deng Xiaoping's technocratic reforms, 241; minority script reforms, 2, 23, 216, 230–231, 234; script reform as central to revolutionary endeavors, 216, 224, 226–28; transition into a computer age, 239–241; Zhou Enlai, 38, 216, 234, 238
Philosophical Almanac (Macgowan): on the eight principles of *yong* (*yongzi ba fa*), 35–36, 37; on the theory of telegraphy in China, 34–35, 38
phoneticization: Liu Tingfang's critique of, 126; mass literacy in conjunction with reducing labor time associated with, 27, 33, 40, 43; overseas Chinese works on, 245n1; 'Phags-pa Script, 25; Phonetic Symbols for Tibetan and Mongolian languages, 217–218, 223; Stalin's views about Chinese phoneticization, 228; *The Standard System of Mandarin Romanization*, 65–66. *See also* Chinese latinization; Gwoyeu Romatzyh (GR); National Phonetic Alphabet (NPA); Pinyin and pinyinization; Unified New Turkic Alphabet (UNTA)
Phonetic Promotion Committee (PPC), 80, 81–82
Phonetic Symbols: the CCP's adoption of Pinyin compared with, 224; the GMD's appropriation of, 2, 71–72, 86, 185, 186–187, 188, 193–195, 207–208; importation to Taiwan, 86; for regional languages, 206, 217–223; use in James Yen's primers, 113; use in telegraphic communications, 43. *See also* National Phonetic Alphabet (NPA)
phonocentrism: historical emergence of, 12; script reforms associated with, 4, 243n3
Pinyin and pinyinization: CLA and, 22; during the Cultural Revolution, 237; as the international standard for transcribing Chinese characters, 2; invention of, 2, 223; the PRC's pinyinization campaign, 17, 22–23, 216, 237; the PRC's pinyinization campaign's failure in the frontiers, 223, 234–236, 268n23; Xiao'erjin colloquially known as the first Pinyin, 171; Zhou Youguang on the purpose of Pinyin, 227, 234; Zhou Youguang's efforts with telegraphic communications, 43, 224, 228; of the Zhuang writing system, 234, 235
Polivanov, Evgenii, 173, 208, 263n2
Porter, Henry, 45
Pott, Francis L. H., 81
Primordial Sounds for a Prosperous Age (*Shengshi yuanyin*) (Shen), 1, 48
Principles of Scientific Management, The (Taylor), 91, 93
print technologies: iron hand presses, 8, 9, 61–62; material issues troubling revolutionary latinists, 199–203,

211–213; missionaries as leading printers with technical know-how, 61–62; copper molds for places with special dialects, 220. *See also* linotype machines; typewriters

Proposals for a Missionary Alphabet (Müller), 62–63

psychology: Cai and Abernethy's research on learning characters, 129–130; Du Dingyou's eight ways of "seeing" a character, 139–141, *140*; measurement movement spearheaded by American behavioral psychologists, 91, 95, 100–101; NLM's construction of a psychology based on "nativeness," 143; phenomenology of seeing characters, 125. *See also* Ai Wei–psychology of learning characters; cognition and cognitive management; intelligence tests

Psychology of Learning Chinese, The (Liu): Ai Wei's study compared with, 131; distribution of characters according to the number of strokes, 127, *128*, 129

Pukhov, Vasilii S., 198, 208, 264n26

Qian Xuantong, 121; correspondence with Wu Zhihui using NPA, 77–78, 252–253n49; handy characters not supported by, 147–148; on nativeness, 144; NPA advocated by, 118; on "saving brain energy" (*sheng naoli*), 7

Qing dynasty: changing temporal awareness in the late Qing, 55; late-Qing script reforms, 53–55, 66–67; Lifanyuan reorganized as the Mongolian and Tibetan Affairs Department, 267n5; literacy required to support industrial values of efficiency and productivity, 27, 53–55, 87, 239; Manchu as the official language of, 35; phonetic scripts proposed during, 14–15, 24; Self-Strengthening Movement, 5, 26, 28–30; Sino-Japanese War, 25, 28–29, 48, 67; Taiping Rebellion, 26, 28; telegraphic communication during, 10, 27, 38, 40, 43, 46–48, 239; "unity of the five races" (*wuzu gonghe*), 217. *See also* Shen Xue

Qu Qiubai: Chao's GR criticized by, 191–193; Chinese Latin Alphabet attributed to, 188–189, 201; and the Chinese Latinization Movement in Moscow, 154; *Chinese Latinized Alphabet* publication, 154, 174, 189; as a leading member of the CCP, 174, 188

racial bias: embodiment by technologies and infrastructures, 18, 59, 250n3; Max Müller's racist attitude toward local languages and scripts in India, 62, 86; quantification of intelligence, 97–99

Republic of China. *See* Chiang Kai-shek; Ministry of Education of the Republic of China; Nationalist Party (Guomindang, GMD)

Richards, Ivor. *See* Basic English (Ogden and Richards)

Rockefeller Foundation: Gary Plan for education reform supported by, 94, 105; teaching Basic English supported by, 109; Ting Hsien Experiment supported by, 103; Yen's Mass Education Movement supported by, 103, 105–106

Roman alphabet: Jesuit romanization, 60–61; Müller's proposal alphabets for non-Roman scripts in India, 62–63; *The Standard System of Mandarin Romanization,* 65–66; telegraphic Morse code originally designed for, 26, 34; the term "latinization" (*latinizatsiia*) used in Eurasia for, 183; use by missionaries for Cantonese, 40; Wade's transcription of Beijing Mandarin (Pekingese) into, 64–65. *See also* Chinese latinization; Gwoyeu Romatzyh (GR); Pinyin

INDEX

Schjellerup, H. C. F. C., 37
Schumpeter, Joseph, 151
scientific knowledge: mass literacy movement supported by transnational scientific networks, 91–93. *See also* neurophysiology; Western science
Scientific Organization of Labor (NOT), 158–159, 187, 199
Scientific Research Commission of the Far Eastern Committee of the New Alphabet (DVKNA): Chinese latinization as a revolutionary dream of, 212; CLA promoted in the Far Eastern Soviet Union by, 199; founding of, 198–199
script invention: material politics of, 16–17, 59, 153, 231–235; optimum integration between the alphabet and the human, 15. *See also* writing systems
script reforms: debates in the PRC after the Cultural Revolution, 238, 271n1; ending by the State Council (1986), 2, 23; material contradictions generated by modernization exemplified by, 13–15, 58–59, 64–65, 87–88; material issues troubling revolutionary latinists, 199–203, 211–213; role of missionaries in, 59–60, 66, 75, 78, 80–82, 85–87; "spirit of informationalism" creatively embodied by, 151; the value of script redefined in terms of labor efficiency by Cai Xiyong, 27–27, 41, 43, 46, 55; the value of script redefined in terms of labor efficiency by Shen Xue, 27–28, 47–49, 55; the value of script redefined in terms of labor efficiency by Wang Bingyao, 26, 27–28, 33–34, 41, 43, 46, 55. *See also* phoneticization
seal script: "official script" as a simplified form of, 123; in Shen Xue's speed tests for writing Chinese, 47; Zhang Taiyan's Syllabary to Record Sounds based on, 71
Shanghai Document (Bilokh), 181, 182
Shanghai Missionary Conference (1913), China Continuation Committee (CCC) at, 80–81
Shanghainese: CLA/Sin Wenz proposed for, 205, 206; common characters in Shanghai's culinary culture, 112; primer for Shanghainese prepared by Ni Haishu, 225; romanizations of, 46–47, 64
Shanghai Script Reform Society, 225–226
Sharaf, Galimjan: Arabic letters for Turkic supported by, 163–164
Shen Xue: access to English publications on aphasia, 6, 46, 49–50, 249n60; encephalocentric imagination of the body, 25, 44, 51–52, 248n41; on writing as physiological phenomenon, 1, 48; "pearl-bones," 48, 248n55; the value of script redefined in terms of labor efficiency, 47–49, 55
Shen Youqian (Eugene Shen): analysis of eye movements in reading Chinese, 135, *136*; Hong's Basic Chinese dismissed by, 114
simplification and simplified characters: cerebral energy saved by, 54; GMD's prohibition of, 2, 120, 151, 153, 212, 227, 268n23; phenomenology of seeing characters associated with, 125, 132–133, 135, 139–141, 150–151; *suzi* from historical texts, 122, 123, 132. *See also* handy characters
Sin Wenz. *See* Chinese Latin Alphabet (CLA/Sin Wenz)
Song dynasty: civil service exam, 11; simplified characters in materials dating from, 121
Soviet Union: engineering of new machinery for nationalities, 236; reliance of Soviet linguists on publications by Chinese linguists,

198; Russification policy, 162, 187–188, 201–202; Stalin's order to cyrillize all national languages, 187–188, 208, 214, 221, 228, 230. *See also* Dungans and Dunganese; Scientific Research Commission of the Far Eastern Committee of the New Alphabet (DVKNA)

State Council of the PRC: Chinese Script Reform Research Commission established by, 225; First National Conference on Minority Education, 231; script reforms ended in 1986 by, 2, 23

Syllabary to Record Sounds (Zhang Taiyan): nativist politics reflected in its graphic interface, 71–72; selection as the National Phonetic Alphabet, 20, 59, 71, 72, 75

Taiwan: *bopomofo* used as an input method on computers, 2; participation in the Cold War "code race," 240; present-day Taiwanese system of transcription, 71–72; relocation of the GMD to, 223

Tan Sitong, 5–6, 7, 66

Taylor, Frederick Winslow, 91, 93

telegraphy and telegraphic communication: Chinese characters in relation to, 1; Cooke and Wheatstone's telegraphic dial pad, 35; efficient transmission associated with the NPA, 43, 76; electric telegraphy as a metaphor for the nervous system, 5; introduction to China in the 1870s, 26; Macgowan's *Philosophical Almanac* on the theory of telegraphy in China, 34–35, 38; Western endeavors to penetrate non-Western markets associated with, 9–10. *See also* Morse code

Tenishev, Edkhiam, 231–232

Thompson, E. P., 54

Thorndike, Edward Lee: Basic English impacted by his work, 107; handwriting scale invented by, 95–96; statistical word count in English by, 104; "Whatever exists at all, exists in some amount," 100

Thousand-Character Primers (Yen), 130; championing of workers, farmers, and soldiers as its political goal, 105, 109; Chinese knowledge economy fueled by, 103; as the data set for Ai Wei's study of the psychology of learning characters, 130; GMD's backing of, 92; Hong Shen's critique of, 92; linguistic efficiency championed by, 92, 109; and the link between mass literacy and the management of Chinese characters, 114–115; as a manifestation of the modern age of information, 114–115; Mass Education Movement in China founded on, 104

Three Songs About Lenin (Vertov), 166

Tibet and Tibetan: communities in Amdo, 231; numerical method to process Tibetan syllabaries, 240; pinyinization not carried out for, 235; representation in the "unity of the five races" (*wuzu gonghe*), 217; use of Phonetic Symbols for Tibetan ordered by the Ministry of Education, 217–218

time and temporality: changing temporal awareness around the turn of the nineteenth century, 54–55; clockwork schedule of industrial capitalism, 54–55; incense sticks used for timekeeping, 115–116; of Nazım Hikmet's "Gioconda and Si-Ya-U," 181; spatial and temporal order of a reader's eye, 139–140; spatiotemporality of writing, 137–139; temporal flow of information maintained by Arabic letters, 163–165. *See also* alphabetic order–alphabetic labor time; labor time and efficiency

Ting Hsien Experiment, 103

INDEX

transnationalism: Esperanto proposed in response to, 69; imagined Eurasian socialist network formed by the Latin alphabet, 183–184, 210–211; latinized typewriters as expressions of the material limits of internationalism, 199–200; political economic forces of the global information age, 20–23, 155; world missionary movement, 80

transnational scientific networks: mass literacy movement supported by, 91–93; in script invention, 230–235; Shen Xue's access to English publications on aphasia, 6, 46, 49–50, 249n60

Tsai, Loh Seng (Cai Lesheng), and Ethel Abernethy, 129–130

Tuodayewa (Todaeva), Buliash K., 270n51

Turkish Alphabet Revolution, 10, 177. *See also* Ottoman Empire

typewriters: for Arabic script, 199–200, 265n33; latinized typewriters as expressions of the material limits of internationalism, 199–200; the Soviet latinized typewriter, 200; in Thorndike's handwriting scale, 95; UNTA typewriters, 193. *See also* Chinese typewriters

Unified New Turkic Alphabet (UNTA): All-Union Central Committee of the New Alphabet as the name for, 168; creation of, 168, *169*; as the New Alphabet for all, 168, 261n35; New Dunganese Alphabet identified with, 21; New Turkic Alphabet developed in Baku, 155, 158, *159*, 165; typewriters for, 193

Uyghur: information-processing technologies for Uyghur Arabic script, 241; latinization attempt by the PRC, 1; new Cyrillic script composed for, 232–233; and the Soviet latinized typewriter, 200; Uyghur Phonetic Symbols introduced by the GMD, 222–223

Vasil'ev, B. A., 170

vernacular languages: dialectological surveys planned by Luo Changpei of the IHP, 218; fifth tone (*rusheng*) of the southern provinces, 64–65, 67, 192; inclusion in Lao Naixuan's Simple Script, 58, 59, 67–68, 225; regional languages embraced by the Chinese Latin Alphabet, 113. *See also* Amoy (Xiamen) language; *baihua* and the *baihua* movement; Miao people; Min vernaculars; Shanghainese

Vertov, Dziga, 166

Viguier, S. A. (Waijiye), 37–40, *39*, 247n30

Vrubel, Stanislav Antonovich, 201–202

Wade, Thomas Francis, transcription of Beijing Mandarin by, 64–65, 70

Wang Bingyao: Chinese telegraphic code in shorthand invented by, 25, 32, 33–34, *42*, 66–67; as a pastor in the London Missionary Society, 140; the value of script redefined in terms of labor efficiency, 26, 27, 33–34, 41, 43, 46, 55

Wang Li, 198, 220

Wang Qingren, 248n41

Wang Shijie: as head of the Central Propaganda Bureau, 215; as head of the Ministry of Education, 144–145, 150

Wang Zhao: Beijing Mandarin asserted as the national pronunciation of characters, 70–71, 74; biographical details, 70; as vice-chairman of the 1913 conference, 68, 69–70; Wu Zhihui's vision of a national alphabet *and* a national language contrasted with, 68, 70–71. *See also* Mandarin Syllabary

Western science: on aphasic progression, 49–50, 249n60; appropriation of

INDEX

Western medical terminology by missionaries, 247n23; proliferation of Chinese translations of, 9, 27; Taylor's *The Principles of Scientific Management*, 91, 93; "traditional" Chinese sciences challenged by, 11; word-gestalt studies, 135–136
Wheatstone, Charles, 35
Williams, Raymond, 13, 15
writing systems: development in conjunction with bureaucratic and administrative apparatuses, 12; Shen Xue's speed tests for writing Chinese, 47; spatiotemporality of writing, 137–139. *See also* alphabetic order; Chinese writing system; Dungans and Dunganese; script invention; script reform
Wu Rulun, 70
Wu Zhihui: career in script and language reforms, 68; as chairman of the 1913 conference, 68, 69–70; correspondence with Qian Xuantong using NPA, 77–78, 252–253n49; handy characters not supported by, 148; Wang Zhao's vision of a national alphabet *and* a national language contrasted with, 68, 70–71

Xiao'erjin, Arabic script used to transcribe it, 156, 171; Chinese words written in *Tanksukname-i Ilhani*, 171, *171*; latinizing of, 172–174, 184; twentieth-century literacy in, 171, *172*. *See* Dungans and Dunganese; New Dunganese Alphabet
Xiao'erjing. *See* Xiao'erjin
Xiao San (or Emi Siao): biographical details, 178; CLA promoted by, 189; CLA's use for multiple regional languages questioned by, 210–211, 226; cognitive dimensions of the Latin alphabet questioned by, 188, 210–211, 214; and the DVKNA, 198, 264n28; friendship with Nazım Hikmet, 178, 182–183; Nazım Hikmet's "Gioconda and Si-Ya-U" written in honor of, 178, *179*, 180–181, 184; role in the Chinese Latinization Movement, 178
Xikemeite. *See* Nazım Hikmet
Xu Shen: on *huiyi*, 257n8; *Shuowen jiezi* compiled by, 121, 126
Xu Xihua. *See* List of Frequently Used Uyghur Words with Phonetic Symbols (Xu)
Xu Zemin: proposal for simplification of characters, 130, 132, *133*; impact of Ai Wei's psychology of learning characters on, 130–132

Yellow Emperor's Inner Canon, 25, 245–246n3
Yen, James: intelligence tests given to soldiers as part of the Chinese measurement movement, 101–102; resistance to demands of the U.S. State Department, 106; Rockefeller Foundation support for is Mass Education Movement, 105–106; Ting Hsien Experiment, 103. *See also* Thousand-Character Primers (Yen)
Yen, W. W. (Yan Huiqing), 109
Yu Daoquan, 240

Zhang Taiyan. *See* Syllabary to Record Sounds
Zhang Zhidong: Cai Xiyong charged with management of the Guangzhou Foreign Affairs Bureau by, 28, 29; Hubei Railroad Bureau established by, 29
Zheng Guanying, 47–48
Zhirkov, Lev, 162–163, 167, 202
Zhou Bianming, 198, 220
Zhou Enlai, 38, 216, 234, 238
Zhou Youguang: biographical information, 227, 237; efforts with telegraphic communications, 43, 224, 228; invention of Pinyin, 2, 213, 223; on the purpose of Pinyin, 227, 234
Zhang Shuhuang, 148

GPSR Authorized Representative: Easy Access System Europe, Mustamäe tee
50, 10621 Tallinn, Estonia, gpsr.requests@easproject.com